INDUSTRIALIZATION IN INDIA

INDUSTRIALIZATION
IN INDIA

Growth and Conflict in the
Private Corporate Sector
1914-47

RAJAT K. RAY

DELHI
OXFORD UNIVERSITY PRESS
BOMBAY CALCUTTA MADRAS
1979

Oxford University Press

OXFORD LONDON GLASGOW
NEW YORK TORONTO MELBOURNE WELLINGTON
NAIROBI DAR ES SALAAM LUSAKA CAPE TOWN
KUALA LUMPUR SINGAPORE JAKARTA HONG KONG TOKYO
DELHI BOMBAY CALCUTTA MADRAS KARACHI

Printed in India by P. K. Ghosh
at Eastend Printers, 3 Dr Suresh Sarkar Road, Calcutta 700 014
and published by R. Dayal, Oxford University Press,
2/11 Ansari Road, Daryaganj, New Delhi 110 002

For
Sujata

Preface

This book is the outcome of a project undertaken by me in 1974 while at the Indian Institute of Management, Calcutta, for which the IIMC provided generous financial assistance and computer and other facilities. Subsequently a visiting fellowship offered by the Australian National University in 1975 enabled me to expand the report on the project considerably, thus giving it its present shape. This book could not have been written but for the help I received from Professor Kamini Adhikari, Chairman of the Entrepreneurship Research Cell, IIMC, and Professor D. A. Low, Vice-Chancellor, ANU. I am also intellectually indebted to Professor Amiya Kumar Bagchi, Dr A. D. D. Gordon, Dr Clive Dewey, Dr C. J. Baker, Mr David Curley and Shri Dipesh Chakravarti. Finally, I received invaluable help from Shri V. C. Joshi, former Deputy Director of the Nehru Memorial Museum and Library, and from my father, Shri K. K. Ray.

R. K. R.

Presidency College
Calcutta
June 1978

Contents

Tables

Introduction

At the beginning of the First World War, European managing agency houses enjoyed unchallenged supremacy in the private corporate sector of the Indian economy. At the end of the Second World War this supremacy had been been broken and Indian entrepreneurs, advancing by rapid strides in the inter-war period, were now in a position to take over the businesses of departing aliens. On the whole there had been substantial progress in regard to the expansion of the industrial complex as well as the Indianization of corporate enterprise. At the end of British rule, India had a larger industrial sector, with a stronger element of indigenous enterprise, than most underdeveloped countries of the world. Yet she remained one of the poorest countries of the world at the time of independence; and subsequent developments showed the pitiful technological dependence of the newly emerging economies of India and Pakistan on the advanced countries of the West. What historical process had produced this state of things at the end of British rule? No solution to this problem will be possible without taking into account certain developments of long-term significance that took place in the period marked by the two world wars. It is intended in this work to examine some of these developments: the considerable expansion of the private corporate sector; the growing share of Indian businessmen in that sector; and the overall failure of that sector to transform the economy from a predominantly agricultural to a predominantly industrial one.

These economic developments had ramifications in the spheres of politics and administration. As the struggle between imperial interests and national aspirations became increasingly bitter, the private corporate sector was riven by deep tensions. The tensions arising from the private sector affected equations in the political sphere. Conversely, constitutional reforms and civil disobedience campaigns had clear implications for the sphere of commerce and industry. It must be borne in mind, however, that the economics and the politics of the private sector had a complex interrelationship that would not yield to any ready-made formula. It has been assumed too facilely that participation in foreign trade in a dependent capacity would invariably breed political collaboration, whereas production of industrial goods for the domestic market would necessarily dictate political opposition. But as we shall see, the shifting patterns of interests and interconnections in the private sector were too fluid and too complex to permit the use of clear-cut categories like 'comprador' and 'national' bourgeoisie.

In the light of the complex interaction between economics and politics, an answer must be sought to the problem of backwardness. Several hypotheses—limited demand, official indifference or technical deficiency—have been put forward by economic historians of India to explain why no industrial breakthrough had occurred. The relevance of these hypotheses will be tested in this work by means of case studies of the specific conditions of several industries. It is felt that this approach will be a useful corrective to the tendency to emphasize one set of factors at the expense of the rest, which may perhaps be somewhat misleading. It will be the aim of this work to arrive at an explanation that will take into account the diverse circumstances of different industries. If nevertheless we seek to identify any particular set of factors that had a general significance because of its demonstrable relationship to other factors, it may perhaps be found in the problems of backward technology. These problems, as we shall see, were closely connected with several other economic factors, such as the difficulties of export and the problems of marketing at home.

Recent research has identified a long-term constraint on industrial growth in India: the limited size of the market.[1] This problem can be better understood in relation to another long-term constraint, that of backward technology. For this deficiency prevented India's industrialists from capturing external markets on the basis of free competition with the manufacturers of advanced countries. Production for a narrow domestic market prevented economies of scale and attainment of maximum efficiency. That in turn made Indian industries weak and unable to stand in free competition with those of the advanced countries. As a result there was a woeful dependence on a sheltered domestic market—shelter which naturally inhibited the will and ability to attain competitive character in the international market.

[1] Amiya Kumar Bagchi, *Private Investment in India 1900–1939*, Cambridge, 1972.

For the study of these problems the period chosen embraces the years before as well as during the Second World War—a period that offers a perspective different from that of 1900 to 1939, a period surveyed authoritatively by A. K. Bagchi. A contrast of the crucial decade 1937–47 with the period of the First World War and its aftermath brings into greater prominence the problems of technology. Most of the industries which grew during the period studied by A. K. Bagchi did not rely heavily on the most advanced technology, since they were concerned with articles of mass consumption and not heavy capital goods. The long-term constraint imposed by a narrow technological capacity stood out clearly only when Indian entrepreneurs sought to achieve the transition from the manufacture of articles of mass consumption to the production of heavy capital goods.

The problems of producing heavy capital goods on a weak technological base were of a different order from that of cotton, jute and other light manufactures, as we hope to show by means of case studies of consumer goods industries and capital goods industries. The successful manufacture of consumer goods and capital goods depended equally on the attainment of higher quality and lower cost. Such efficiency could only result from substantial economies of scale by production for enlarged markets. The teeming millions of India constituted a fairly large domestic market for many consumer industries. But in an underdeveloped country like India the market for capital goods was necessarily narrow, so that their manufacture obviously depended on expansion of markets at home and, if possible, capture of markets abroad. The attainment of these objectives in turn depended on cost reduction and quality production. Here was a vicious circle in which market problems and technical problems were closely linked to each other by means of a circular relationship. This work will explore these interrelationships in order to pinpoint the difficulties of an industrial breakthrough at the end of a fairly successful period of consumer manufactures starting with the First World War.

The merit of this approach is that it not only reveals the ultimate difficulties of a breakthrough but also the excellent possibilities of progress up to a certain point. For consumer industries based on the mass market at home faced no really difficult technical problems, and it was on this front that, with the aid of discriminating protection, rapid progress was achieved after the First World War. In the next phase, i.e. the production of basic and heavy capital goods during and after the Second World War, Indian industry faced much more formidable technological problems, arising from the absence of essential equipment, machinery, raw materials, technical know-how, trained personnel, etc.

The technical distinction drawn above between different phases of industrialization is important not merely for an explanation of economic backwardness but also for specific analysis of the changing relationship between imperial interests and national enterprise. Three different phases may be identified in the process of Indian industrialization. The first phase, ending with the outbreak of the First World War, was characterized mainly by the production of export goods in areas of natural advantage (jute, tea, etc.), together with a growing tendency to produce goods for the domestic market in those areas where competition with their imported counterparts was not serious (coarse piece-goods etc.). The second phase, commencing with the First World War, saw substantially increasing production of consumer goods for the mass market within India, helped by diminished imports (due to war, tariff and depression) and relatively simple technology (which was acquired within a fairly short gestation period). Finally, the last decade of British rule saw the beginning of another phase—the production of capital goods for a domestic market that was often too narrow for really efficient, low-cost production. Production in this phase was hampered by new difficulties because many basic prerequisites of production were lacking within the country and the import of the necessary technology was very costly.

Each of these different phases of industrialization saw changing relationships between foreign and indigenous capital. In the pre-war phase, European managing agencies found no serious competition from Indian competitors, since the export bias of industry in this period placed Indians at a disadvantage. Indian capital was engaged mainly in so-called comprador activities, such as import and distribution of piece-goods and other manufactures, and supply of various primary produce and raw materials to big European corporations for processing in India or abroad. The sphere of Indian capital was speculation, old-fashioned finance and domestic trade, rather than industry.[2] These activities expressed its subordinate role in the eco-

[2] The exception to this rule was coarse cotton manufactures in Bombay, in which Indian enterprise played an important role.

nomy. The inter-war period, by contrast, saw sharpened conflict between foreign capital and indigenous enterprise. This conflict arose from the resistance of foreign interests to increasing import substitution under predominantly Indian initiative in the domestic market for goods of mass-consumption. From the period that began with the Second World War, the process of import substitution extended from consumer goods to capital goods and a new area of conflict between foreign manufacturers and Indian entrepreneurs was opened up by this process. At the same time, however, a new relationship of collaboration was dictated by the formidable technical problems posed by the production of capital goods. While Indian houses were in a position to mobilize the capital resources, they had to rely on foreign partners for the necessary technology. The advent of independence saw the gradual emergence of an uneasy partnership between foreign expertise and Indian finance on unequal terms.

The formidable problems posed by the transition from consumer goods industries to capital goods industries led to a paradoxical insistence by Indian capital on foreign collaboration and socialist planning at the same time. The changing politics of the private sector, which were so closely connected with the underlying economic processes, form an important theme of this work. The transition to the new phase of production brought about at the same time a profound change in the nature of foreign interests operating in India. The full logic of this change was revealed only after independence. But within the chronological limits of this work we shall try, as far as this is possible, to trace the portents of the change. Its most striking external manifestation during the period under review was the decline of the India-based European managing agencies and the appearance of multi-nationals operating from Europe and America on the Indian industrial scene. The older European agency houses and the intrusive multi-national corporations were set apart from each other by the fundamentally different technological and organizational roles which they were to play within the burgeoning Indian economy.

These were signs of a deeper process of change in the working of foreign interests in India, which must be seen against the background of the changing role of India within the British empire in its geopolitical and economic setting. We shall therefore begin by examining, in the first chapter, the general background to the operation of imperial economic and political interests in India in the light of the world-wide crisis of imperialism in the period encompassing the two world wars. In response to this imperial crisis, the economic policies of the Government of India underwent significant changes. These in turn assisted the development of the Indian houses within the corporate sector, earlier dominated by foreign interests.

The big Indian houses which came to dominate the corporate sector as monopoly concerns after 1947 showed remarkable similarity of development over time. Most of these houses began in a dependent capacity, servicing foreign interests by trade, speculation and agency business of various sorts. At some point they switched over from so-called comprador activities to industrial investment, and finally the most successful among them, having acquired large financial assets in trade and consumer industries, turned their surplus funds to hitherto untried engineering, chemical and metallurgical industries of an advanced type. In historical-chronological terms, therefore, the popular distinction between comprador and national bourgeoisie, as we shall see, was somewhat blurred. Nor is it easy, as we shall see, to relate the political attitude of Indian businessmen to their economic role so precisely.[3] The evidence will rather indicate that political disaffection was characteristic of speculators, traders, brokers—'marketeers' of all sorts—rather than industrialists. But this is to anticipate the evidence. All that we need emphasize is that politics and economics of the private corporate sector in India were tortuously intertwined, and need to be unravelled to the extent possible to provide an insight into the process of industrial development.

[3] The distinction is emphasized in the writings of Soviet scholars. See, for instance, A. I. Levkovsky, *Capitalism in India: Basic Trends in Its Development*, Bombay, 1966, p. 311. For critical discussion, Thomas Arnold Timberg, 'The Rise of Marwari Merchants as Industrial Entrepreneurs to 1930', Harvard Ph.D. thesis, 1972; Sunil Kumar Sen, *The House of Tata*, Calcutta, 1975, pp. 137–41.

CHAPTER 1

The Environment and Logic of Private Investment

The First World War ushered in a new phase of British imperialism in India—a phase which was fundamentally different from the pre-war period in the method of appropriation of India's commodity surplus by Britain. The new mechanism for the transfer of India's commodity surplus to Britain during the inter-war period was the interest charged on India's vastly increased sterling debt, which became a determining element in the relationship between India and Britain. Expressing this change in a somewhat blunt formula, R. P. Dutt used the term financial imperialism to describe Britain's new hold over India.[1] The Second World War, by bringing about the liquidation of India's sterling debt, decisively ended this phase of British domination over India. The British decision to quit India, due no doubt to many complex economic and political reasons, was perhaps facilitated by the liquidation of India's sterling debt, for many years the most important 'vested interest' of Britain in India. In this respect the period from the beginning of the First World War to the end of the Second World War was clearly a distinct one in the evolving relationship between Britain and India.

To see this period in perspective, it is necessary to bear in mind the pre-war basis of Britain's economic domination over India. India had been vitally important to Britain in the pre-war years in three respects—as a vast market for British manufactures, as a guaranteed outlet for profitable investment and as a crucial link in the settlement of Britain's balance of payments. The last aspect of the Indo-British economic relationship was perhaps the most important. It ensured the transfer of resources from India to Britain through a complex series of multilateral trade balances. India's political subordination had resulted in an artificially heavy trade deficit with Britain, which had arisen from the imposition of the home charges (civil and

[1] R. Palme Dutt, *India To-day*, Bombay, 1947.

military charges, guaranteed interest on railway debt, etc.) and the enforced import of invisible services (shipping, insurance, etc.). To meet this deficit India had under pressure developed a large trade in exports to countries with which Britain had a normally adverse commodity balance. India's export surplus with regard to other countries balanced Britain's trade deficits with the rest of the world. As a net earner of non-sterling foreign exchange which went to meet her sterling obligations, India enabled the British to command an increasing volume of imports from countries outside the sterling area. It is likely that if her politically induced trade deficit with Britain had not compelled India to gear her production to the earning of a large export surplus with the rest of the world, Britain would not have been able to increase her foreign trade to the extent that she achieved in the nineteenth century.[2]

In the post-war period there was a clear shift in the relationship between India and Britain in all these respects. Not that the importance of India to the British economy declined; but there was a change in the nature of the benefits flowing from the possession of India. In the triennium before the First World War, the U.K.'s share in India's total imports was 62.8 per cent; on the eve of the Second World War it stood at 30.5 per cent. Britain's diminishing share in the Indian market was connected with a perceptible change in the commodity composition of the foreign trade of India. From 1920–4 to 1935–9, India's imports of manufactures came down from 76.7 to 64.4 per cent, while her exports of manufactures increased from 24.8 to 30 per cent. At the same time her imports of raw materials increased from 7.4 to 19.8 per cent, and exports diminished from 50.2 to 46.7 per cent.[3] At the end of the inter-war period, India was not only consuming less British manufactures, but had also started competing with British products in many external markets. It is true that in a period of diminishing exports British industrialists clung all the more tenaciously to their shrinking empire markets. The system of imperial preference was designed to preserve a market for British manufactures by political means. To Manchester in the thirties, the shrinking Indian market appeared to be more, not less, important in a world of increasing difficulties. Imperial preference did help, for a time, to boost England's exports

[2] S. B. Saul, *Studies in British Overseas Trade 1870–1914*, Liverpool, 1960.
[3] R. L. Varshney, 'Foreign Trade' *in* V. B. Singh (ed.), *Economic History of India: 1857–1956*, Bombay, 1965, pp. 457–9.

to India. The U.K.'s share in India's imports rose from 35.5 per cent in 1931–2 to 40.6 per cent in 1934–5. By 1936–7, however, this share had once again sunk to 38.5 per cent and two years later it had dropped to 30.5 per cent. After the failure of imperial preference, British manufacturers could no longer count on India as a stable market. Nor was India as profitable an outlet of investment as she was before the First World War. The flotation of railway loans in England, which had guaranteed British investors private profit at public risk, became increasingly difficult on account of hostile Indian opinion. During the thirties, new British investments went largely into gold, copper, lead, oil, rubber and tin in other countries.[4] Diminished Indian capital expenditure in England for railway construction had led to an actual reduction of home charges by the late thirties. Finally, there was an increasing shift from multilateral to bilateral settlement of obligations in the trade of India and Britain. The importance of India to Britain as a net earner of non-sterling foreign exchange declined perceptibly in relation to Malaya. With regard to the United States, with which Britain had a huge deficit, Malaya was producing in 1929 an export surplus of £46 million compared to India's £19 million.[5] By 1937 the process had gone even further, so that India was now producing an export surplus with regard to the USA of only £12 million.[6] The decline in India's trade balance with the United States forced the pace of increasing direct transfer to Britain. By 1937 there had been a virtual 'elimination of India's great offsetting triangular trade balances with Britain and the rest of the world, under influence of depression, economic nationalism and secular growth and change'.[7] The process was facilitated by imperial preference which led to a relatively greater rise in India's exports to Britain (especially raw cotton, wheat and leather) than in Britain's exports to India.

Structural changes in the British economy lay behind the changing economic relationship between India and Britain in the inter-war period.[8] Britain's former role as the workshop of the world, the world's banker and the clearing house for the multilateral obligations of international trade visibly declined. Before the First World War,

---

[4] Alfred E. Kahn, *Great Britain in the World Economy*, New York, 1946, p. 187.
[5] Ibid., p. 233.   [6] Ibid., p. 253.   [7] Ibid., p. 250.
[8] *See* Kahn; A. J. Youngson, *Britain's Economic Growth 1920–1966*, London, 1967; R. S. Sayers, *A History of Economic Change in England 1880–1939*, London, 1967.

roughly one-fourth of Britain's total production was geared to export. On the eve of the Second World War she was exporting only one-eighth of her products. The older export-oriented industries of Britain—coal, textile, iron and steel, engineering, etc.—declined in relation to new industries producing mainly for the home market—electrical goods, automobiles, aircraft, rayon, hosiery, chemicals, etc. The decline of the traditional export industries reduced the need to import raw materials of the old types. This reduction was more than counter-balanced by the increased importation of other raw materials and manufactures—such as non-ferrous metals, oil and petroleum, rubber, pulp and timber—for feeding the rising electrical, chemical, paper and building industries. Since these imports were processed mainly for consumption at home, the thirties saw a 'self-sufficiency boom'. Britain increased her consumption by reducing overseas investment, new capital issues falling from £115 million in 1925–9 to £31 million in 1932–6.[9] Net capital outflows from Britain during 1929–33 were virtually nil and after that period new issues were more than counter-balanced by heavy repatriations of foreign debt, resulting in a net import of capital during 1936–8. For the thirties as a whole, Britain's foreign investments seem to have undergone a real decrease.[10]

Not only did Britain turn inwards in an economic sense; politically also she became increasingly tied down after the rise of Germany under Hitler. Under these circumstances Britain was compelled to shift more and more of her political and military commitments throughout the East to the Indian empire. Even if commercially India was of declining value to Britain, she came to occupy a crucial position in Britain's world strategic and political calculations. Heavy reliance on the Indian army to uphold the British position in the East against the rising power of Japan entailed heavy military expenditure, which swelled India's sterling debt, already increased enormously by her military contribution in the First World War. Increased military expenditure and rising indebtedness went together; and the financial aspect of the economic relationship between India and Britain came to overshadow the commercial aspect. This new relationship was predominantly that of debtor and *rentier*, not of supplier of raw materials and manufacturer of goods. In this relationship the transfer of resources from the colony to the metropolitan country was more direct and lacked the compensating ad-

[9] Youngson, op. cit., p. 124.   [10] Kahn, op. cit., pp. 194–5.

vantages of the pre-war relationship which had brought India important benefits in the shape of increased commerce and improved communications and services. The real burden of transfer was now much heavier. For world strategic considerations Britain came to rely, more than ever, on the Indian army. To maintain the army and to pay for the First World War, India became more indebted to Britain; as a result the home charges became much more burdensome after the war.

In the post-war years the home charges pressed down much more heavily on Indian finances not merely because of their greatly increased volume but also due to basic changes in their composition. As Table 1 will show, total expenditure in England by the Government of India was 57 per cent higher in 1924–5 than that in 1913–14.

TABLE 1

STERLING EXPENDITURE OF THE GOVERNMENT OF INDIA IN THE U.K. CHARGEABLE AGAINST THE REVENUE

Item	1913–14 £	1917–18 £	1924–5 £
Civil expenditure	3,539,841	3,752,505	4,811,980
Military expenditure	5,462,817	6,434,649	10,096,267
Interest on ordinary debt	2,087,884	6,161,537	8,116,293
Interest on railway debt	3,530,773	3,571,703	6,514,647
Railway, irrigation & civil works expenditure	5,690,358	6,144,663	2,349,589
TOTAL	20,311,673	26,065,057	31,888,776

SOURCE. *Finance and Revenue Accounts of the Government of India*, 1913–14 to 1924–5, Delhi, 1914–.

NOTE. Civil expenditure comprises civil, post & telegraph, mint charges, famine relief and insurance.

But there was more to it than this. A few years before the war, in response to Indian criticism of the economic burden imposed by the home charges, Sir Theodore Morison had made a distinction between unproductive charges and productive (i.e. those generating more revenue) charges and had pointed out that such unproductive expenditure as civil and military charges and interest on ordinary debt which had arisen from India's political subordination to Britain were only about half of the total charges, the rest being meant for useful expenditure on railways, irrigation, and civil works and stores which contributed to India's economic development.[11] Including interest on the railway debt among the productive charges (a procedure which contemporary Indian nationalist opinion did not favour), we find that on the eve of the First World War, unproductive charges (civil and military expenditure and interest on ordinary debt) were £11.09 million and productive charges (interest on railway debt and railway, irrigation and civil works expenditure) were £9.22 million. Technically, therefore, Theodore Morison was correct in his analysis, though some of the railway debts, which had been contracted long ago by guaranteeing a certain rate of interest to British investors while throwing all risks on the Indian public, were no longer contributing to the productive capacity of India. All this changed rapidly during the war, and while at the conclusion of hostilities the productive expenditure (as defined by Morison) still stood at £9.71 million (practically the same as the pre-war figure), unproductive expenditure had gone up from £11.09 million to £16.34 million. In the post-war years this figure continued to rise, and while productive expenditure actually went down to £8.85 million in 1924–5, unproductive expenditure rose to £23.02 million due to a very steep rise in military expenditure and the interest on the ordinary debt. The entire increase in the home charges during the war and its aftermath was due to unproductive expenditure related to defence requirements, both by way of direct expenditure on the army and indirectly by the floating of war loans which swelled the interest on the ordinary debt.

Subsequently some reduction was achieved in military expenditure in accordance with the recommendations of a committee headed by Lord Inchcape, but the level of the home charges was kept up by the interest on the public debt, which was not amenable to such immediate curtailment. India's steadily increasing sterling debt became the decisive element in the home charges during the twenties and the thirties; unable to meet these heavy charges, the Government of India was compelled every year to transfer unpaid demands to the public debt and to pay a heavier interest on it (Table 2). India's sterling debt before the war had arisen mainly from wars and expeditions, and from the guaranteed railway debt.[12] Besides the public debt chargeable to the revenue, there were other sterling

---

[11] Theodore Morison, *The Economic Transition in India*, London, 1912.

[12] *Congress Select Committee Report on the Financial Obligations between Great Britain and India*, Bombay, 1931.

TABLE 2

HOME CHARGES AND PUBLIC DEBT OF INDIA

Years	Home charges £	Public debt £	Interest paid on debt £
1913–14	20,311,673	177,064,757	5,912,796
1917–18	26,065,057	236,942,654	9,938,905
1924–5	31,888,776	341,040,430	12,556,031
1934–5	28,503,796	383,685,070	14,307,955

SOURCE. *Finance and Revenue Accounts of the Government of India*, relevant years.
NOTE.   Public debt included the ordinary, railway and irrigation debt.

loans as well as the British capital invested in Indian commerce and industry through companies registered in Britain. In 1928 G. D. Birla estimated that an annual export surplus of Rs 110 crores would be needed to meet India's current liabilities. As the export surplus, with the onset of depression and the consequent fall in the value of exports, did not usually exceed Rs 50 crores, her liabilities were annually increasing.[13] According to the estimate of Y. S. Pandit, the servicing of this total sterling debt absorbed 45.16 per cent of the export surplus earned by India during 1898–1914. A. K. Banerjee's subsequent estimate shows that in the post-war period from 1921 to 1938, interest on debt absorbed 60.78 per cent of India's entire merchandise balance.[14] However, the real position of India after the war in respect of debt services was worse.

From 1898 to 1913 the annual average of India's interest payments to Britain was Rs 153 million. This was more than offset, according to Y. S. Pandit's calculations, by an annual inflow of Rs 202 million from Britain, so that there was a net export of new British capital to India to the extent of Rs 50 million a year on the average during the last two decades before the First World War. The war interrupted this inflow of British capital. Between 1923 and 1930, according to calculations made by D. H. N. Gurtoo, the annual average of new issues of British capital amounted to no more than a reinvestment of slightly over half the average annual interest and dividends paid by India. With the onset of the depression, new issues of British

[13] Purshotamdas Thakurdas Papers, file no. 107, pt. 1, 1931. G. D. Birla to Walter Layton, 20 May 1932.

[14] Arun Kumar Banerjee, *India's Balance of Payments Estimates of Current and Capital Accounts from 1921–22 to 1938–39*, Bombay, 1963, p. 89.

capital thinned out and the British financial crisis of 1931 put a stop to the export of capital to India. From 1932 to 1938 India was called on to pay, in addition to the interest and dividends, part of the principal lent to her earlier. There was a 'sudden, massive and persistent withdrawal of capital from India'.[15]

In the thirties the financial aspect of the relationship between India and Britain thus became more and more oppressive for the colony, the metropolitan country being now engaged merely in cashing in on its former financial assets in India in order to uphold its strategic commitments in the East. The strategic, political and financial aspects of the relationship between the two countries gained ground at the expense of the diminishing exchange of goods and services. This was the last, perhaps the most unproductive, phase of British imperialism in India. It was suddenly and drastically brought to an end by the Second World War. Britain's great 'vested interest' in India, the sterling debt, was wiped out by her enormous borrowings from India in order to meet the financial requirements of the Second World War. The net result was that India became a creditor, not a debtor, at the end of the war. Her sterling balances in London amounted to Rs 16,404.7 million in 1946. Her interest earnings on foreign assets exceeded her interest payments on foreign liabilities by Rs 13 million in 1946 and by Rs 54 million in 1947.[16] The Second World War wiped out at one stroke the financial stake of Britain in India, removing thereby a potential impediment to her withdrawal at the end of the war.

Industrial Growth 1880–1947

We have outlined above the changing framework of the economic relationship of India with Britain within which the growth of India's industries took place during and after the First World War. On the one hand the diminishing inflow of British investment enabled Indian merchants and manufacturers to seize the initiative for developing newer industries; on the other hand the repatriation of British capital acted as an adverse factor on general conditions of trade and industry which had been particularly prosperous during 1900–14 on account of an ample inflow of British capital.

[15] Dukh Haran Nath Gurtoo, *India's Balance of Payment (1920–1960)*, Delhi, 1961, p. 96.
[16] Ibid., p. 37.

In 1911, encouraged by these signs of prosperity, Sir Theodore Morison optimistically predicted that India's industrial transformation was near at hand.[17] The prediction remained unfulfilled at the time of independence three decades and a half later. India in 1947 was still a predominantly agricultural country and organized industry accounted for a relatively small share of her total production. Compared to other tropical and underdeveloped countries, however, India's industrial growth and capital formation was quite impressive, both before and after the First World War. A comparative study of tropical development between 1880 and 1913 shows that India had done better in organized industry than most other tropical countries, such as Egypt, Kenya, Uganda, Nigeria, Indonesia, Philippines and Venezuela. Only Colombia and Brazil seem to have done as well as India in this period. Brazil had an average annual growth rate of about 4 per cent in industry between 1880 and 1913. Colombia enjoyed a 5 per cent average annual increase of manufacturing output from 1905 to 1925. India's annual rate of industrial growth from 1880 to 1913 was about 4 to 5 per cent.[18] In the inter-war period, again, India did better than most other tropical countries. During this twenty-year period the yearly growth-rate of manufacturing activities in the Philippines was 4.7 per cent;[19] for India the corresponding rate of growth, as estimated by K. Mukerji, was 6.4 per cent. Brazil did nearly as well as India. Taking 1939 as the base (= 100) for both countries, the index of industrial production grew as follows: 1924—Brazil 42, India 48; 1932—Brazil 61, India 68; 1937—Brazil 89, India 103; 1940—Brazil 105, India 124.[20] Relative rates of growth in manufacturing production as estimated by the League of Nations in 1945 permit a comparison of India with a wider range of countries in the inter-war period. With 1913 as the

[17] Morison, op. cit.

[18] *See* Arthur Lewis (ed.), *Tropical Development 1880–1913: Studies in Economic Progress*, London, 1970.

[19] John H. Power & Gerardo P. Sicat, *Industry and Trade in Some Developing Countries: The Philippines*, London, 1971, p. 12.

[20] For Brazil, Werner Baer, *Industrialization and Economic Development in Brazil*, Homewood, Illinois, 1965, p. 21; for India K. Mukerji, 'A Note on the Long Term Growth of National Income in India 1900–01 to 1952–53', in V. K. R. V. Rao *et al.*, *Papers on National Income and Allied Topics*, Bombay, 1962. Baer's and Mukerji's indices are not comparable in any reliable manner because of different methods of estimation. But then no two sets of indices for different countries are strictly comparable.

base year (= 100), the index of the manufacturing production of the world in 1938 stood at 182.7. The position of the different countries in 1938 in relation to the base year is set out in Table 3.

TABLE 3

INDEX OF MANUFACTURING PRODUCTION

(Base 1913 = 100)

Country	Year 1938	Country	Year 1938	Country	Year 1938
South Africa	1,067.1	India	239.7	Roumania	177.9
U.S.S.R.	857.3	Sweden	232.2	Norway	169.2
Japan	552.0	New Zealand	227.4	Canada	161.8
Greece	537.1	Chile	204.2	Latvia	158.0
Finland	300.1	Netherlands	204.1	Germany	149.3
		Denmark	202.1	Czechoslovakia	145.5
		Italy	195.2	Hungary	143.3
		Australia	192.3	U.S.A.	143.0
		World	182.7	Austria	127.0
				U.K.	117.6
				France	114.6
				Poland	105.2
				Belgium	102.1
				Switzerland	82.4
				Spain	58.0

SOURCE. League of Nations, *Industrialization and Foreign Trade*, USA, 1945, Table III.

From Table 3 it appears that India's rate of industrial growth was well above the world average, though her position would not have been as favourable if per capita manufacturing production were to be considered. So far as the rate of growth of manufactures was concerned, five countries—U.S.S.R., Japan, Finland, South Africa and Greece—advanced faster than India among the 28 countries listed by the League of Nations. India, being like Japan a late starter in industrialization, suffered less from the difficulties of the twenties and the great depression of the thirties than the advanced countries, as will be apparent in Table 4 below. India, like Japan, was able to increase her manufacturing production during the First World War and its aftermath in sharp contrast with Italy, Canada and the United States which attained their pre-war level of production only in 1922. For Chile and Germany the attainment of the pre-war level

TABLE 4
ANNUAL INDICES OF MANUFACTURING PRODUCTION 1913–38

Year	Japan	India	Chile	Italy	Germany	Canada	U.S.A.	World
1913	100	100	100	100	100	100	100	100
1920	176.0	118.4	—	95.2	59.0	99.1	93.2	93.2
1921	167.1	112.6	—	98.4	74.7	89.4	81.1	81.1
1922	197.9	116.3	72.7	108.1	81.8	99.0	99.5	99.5
1923	206.4	116.5	77.9	119.3	55.4	108.3	104.5	104.5
1924	223.3	133.0	77.9	104.7	81.8	106.4	111.0	110.0
1925	221.8	132.0	89.6	156.8	94.9	116.5	120.7	120.7
1926	264.9	144.7	111.0	162.8	90.9	132.2	126.5	126.5
1927	270.0	151.5	115.8	161.2	122.1	141.0	134.5	134.5
1928	300.2	133.0	127.7	175.2	118.3	153.5	141.8	141.8
1929	324.0	157.3	156.3	181.0	117.3	162.7	153.8	153.3
1930	294.9	144.7	156.7	164.0	101.6	147.5	137.5	137.5
1931	288.1	155.3	116.3	145.1	85.1	128.2	122.5	122.5
1932	309.1	155.3	132.4	123.3	70.2	108.5	108.4	108.4
1933	360.7	167.7	146.2	133.2	79.4	108.5	121.7	121.7
1934	413.5	190.2	159.4	134.7	101.8	127.7	136.4	136.4
1935	457.8	205.4	183.6	162.2	116.7	141.0	154.5	154.5
1936	483.9	216.6	188.6	169.2	127.5	154.2	178.1	178.1
1937	551.0	234.9	196.6	194.5	138.1	174.8	195.8	195.8
1938	552.0	239.7	204.2	195.2	149.3	161.8	143.0	182.7

SOURCE. League of Nations, op. cit.

of production was delayed until 1926. On the eve of the Great
Depression, India, Chile, Italy, Canada and the USA were producing
roughly one and a half times more than before the First World War;
only Japan had been able to increase her production by three times
the pre-war level. From 1930 to 1932 both Japan and India experienced a brief interruption of growth, but then both nations forged
ahead of other countries, Japan much faster than India. The advanced countries, Canada, Germany and the United States, were the
slowest to recover from their difficulties, pre-depression production
level being attained by them not before 1935. Italy and Chile, which
like India were somewhat backward countries in terms of industrial
output, made a faster recovery, but in the late thirties Indian industrial development was appreciably faster than any of these
countries except Japan. For a more careful consideration of trends
in Indian industry during the whole period under review, S. Sivasubramanian's calculation of national income from the secondary
sector may be considered. From 1913–14 to 1946–7, large-scale

2

manufacturing grew at a rapid rate of 7.3 per cent. However, since small-scale industries (which until 1940–1 outweighed organized industry) grew only at the rate of 0.6 per cent, the overall income from the secondary sector increased at the slower rate of 2.5 per cent per annum (see Table 5).

TABLE 5

NATIONAL INCOME IN INDIA FROM SECONDARY SECTOR AT 1938–9 PRICES
(in million rupees)

Year	Mining	Manufacturing	Small-scale industries	Total
1	2	3	4	5
1900–1	89	298	1,251	1,638
1901–2	93	459	1,294	1,846
1902–3	94	485	1,349	1,928
1903–4	103	501	1,411	2,015
1904–5	109	521	1,516	2,146
1905–6	115	616	1,394	2,125
1906–7	122	633	1,428	2,183
1907–8	130	555	1,403	2,088
1908–9	131	557	1,301	1,989
1909–10	129	602	1,479	2,210
1910–11	136	570	1,565	2,271
1911–12	137	573	1,724	2,434
1912–13	146	678	1,627	2,451
1913–14	155	635	1,592	2,382
1914–15	152	651	1,645	2,448
1915–16	151	705	1,586	2,442
1916–17	162	690	1,694	2,546
1917–18	165	675	1,704	2,544
1918–19	170	641	1,610	2,421
1919–20	168	681	1,264	2,113
1920–1	155	729	1,337	2,221
1921–2	143	747	1,370	2,260
1922–3	139	740	1,578	2,457
1923–4	151	626	1,798	2,575
1924–5	159	822	1,863	2,844
1925–6	161	845	1,902	2,908
1926–7	166	960	1,818	2,944
1927–8	174	1,083	1,890	3,147
1928–9	174	865	1,940	2,979
1929–30	183	1,080	1,991	3,254

(Continued)

TABLE 5 (Contd.)

1	2	3	4	5
1930–1	173	979	2,233	3,385
1931–2	159	1,026	2,068	3,253
1932–3	146	1,112	2,060	3,318
1933–4	148	1,056	2,123	3,327
1934–5	167	1,191	2,183	3,541
1935–6	182	1,288	2,006	3,476
1936–7	185	1,411	1,877	3,473
1937–8	212	1,504	1,892	3,608
1938–9	205	1,701	3,054	3,960
1939–40	212	1,751	1,982	3,945
1940–1	258	1,779	1,963	4,000
1941–2	289	2,139	1,712	4,140
1942–3	305	2,330	1,402	4,037
1943–4	275	2,599	1,027	3,901
1944–5	208	2,548	1,556	4,312
1945–6	212	2,749	1,840	4,801
1946–7	192	2,173	1,942	4,307

SOURCE. S. Sivasubramanian, 'Income from the Secondary Sector in India, 1900–47', in *Indian Economic and Social History Review*, October-December 1977.

Both in the period preceding the First World War and in the period following it, India's considerable industrial development occurred through import substitution. The pace of import substitution was faster after the war, partly due to the erection of high tariff barriers and partly due to the more effective assemblage of supply factors—such as raw materials, skilled labour, technical expertise and financial resources and business experience. It has been surmised that given effective encouragement and tariff protection by the government, 'India could have completed the stage of industrialization through import substitution by 1913—an accomplishment which was postponed for nearly half a century'.[21] Government assistance, including protection, is not, however, a sufficient condition (though it is a necessary one) for industrial growth, as the differing experiences of Japan and Brazil, both of which enjoyed protection in the pre-war period, might indicate. The argument in the case of India runs as follows:

[21] Arthur Lewis, *Tropical Development*, Ch. 12, 'India', by Russell Lidman and Robert I. Domrese, pp. 327–8.

Just as in agriculture one can put one's finger on the decisive cause of slow growth—inadequate expenditure on irrigation—so also in manufacturing industry one major failure stands out—inadequate development of iron and steel production. In the course of establishing her railway network (the third largest in the world), India generated a very large demand for iron and steel products. Had she developed an iron and steel industry from say 1860 onwards and the industries linked therewith (especially coal mining and engineering) she would by 1914 have been one of the largest industrial producers in the world.[22]

Whether India could have achieved industrial transformation by effectively utilizing the opportunities of railway construction must by the very nature of the question remain for ever in the sphere of scholastic speculation. What can be tested is the proposition that a strong mercantilist policy of protection is important in so far as it can assist the successful assemblage of factors of production for import substitution in a given country; and of course the prevailing conditions in the given country will determine the effectiveness of that policy as a catalyst. From this point of view, it is important to note that the Brazilian cotton-mill industry,[23] which obtained assistance from the government in various forms, did not perform noticeably better in the pre-war period than the Indian cotton-mill industry, which advanced by rapid strides in the face of Lancashire opposition and official indifference. India might or might not have been in a sufficient state of preparedness for successful assemblage of supply factors for import substitution, had she been given protection in the age of railway construction. In the period after the First World War she managed, under the stimulus of protection, to assemble the factors of production needed for substitution of a wide range of imports. This, it must be noted, was not an overnight achievement and took some time. Given the level of India's production capacity, a gestation period, different in length for different industries, was necessary for substitution of each import.

It is also interesting to note the limitations of import substitution spelt out by the authors of the argument about the pre-war possibilities of industrial transformation in India. Lidman and Domrese observe in this connection:

[22] Ibid., pp. 321–2.
[23] For an account, *see* Stanley J. Stein, 'The Brazilian Cotton Textile Industry', *in* Simon Kuznets *et al.*, *Economic Growth: Brazil, India, Japan*, Durham, N.C., 1955.

Of course, one must not exaggerate the extent of the opportunity presented by import substitution. Since the Indian farmers had only a tiny surplus, most of which they exchanged with handicraft workers, India's imports of manufacture per head was very small. It would soon have been exhausted by a large scale industrial growth rate of say 10 per cent per annum. Continuance of this rate would have required either major agricultural change, yielding a larger surplus, or development of a large export of manufactures.[24]

The very process of import substitution on a large scale was, however, bound, in the long run, to create a new demand for basic capital goods.[25] A typical instance was the move for the inception of a cotton-textile machinery industry by the Birlas on the eve of the Second World War. Such a move was possible because by then the cotton-textile industry had established its dominance in the domestic market for piece-goods. Having completed a substantial phase of import substitution, India seemed poised on the threshold of a new stage in industrial growth. The outbreak of the Second World War hastened the transition to the new phase of production. It implied a structural transformation of India's industrial economy, leading to production of heavy chemicals, sophisticated machinery, aircraft, automobiles, locomotives, ships and a variety of other heavy capital goods. The enormous needs of global war considerably shortened the gestation period for this new phase of production. But for the brakes on the private sector's efforts for a technological and manufacturing breakthrough in certain directions which the Government of India, under pressure from Britain, applied during this process of transformation, India might have emerged from the war with an appreciably broader industrial base for launching the five year plans.

The Pursuit of Profit

Since the successive phases of import substitution and capital goods production took place under the initiative of the private (mainly corporate) sector, it is necessary at this stage to formulate some kind

[24] Arthur Lewis, op. cit., pp. 328–9.
[25] For a discussion of the factors which may prevent import substitution from generating new demand, see A. K. Bagchi, *Private Investment*, pp. 13–19. The assumption that these factors limited the growth of demand between 1900–39 does not seem to apply with equal validity to the succeeding—admittedly exceptional—phase of 1939–47.

of hypothesis about the factors governing investment decisions by business groups, both foreign and indigenous. This may be in undue haste. No general statements about factors governing investment in Indian business and industry can have any claim to validity unless they are based on adequate appreciation of the variable sets of factors that might have come into play in different industries at various times over different parts of the country. Appreciation of these differences and of the weight of particular conditions would induce a healthy scepticism about many of the broad generalizations on an inadequate factual basis that have characterized much of the economic history of India. However, a hypothesis may be applied merely as an analytical tool at this stage, if only to throw critical light on important general statements which have previously been made on the subject. Later we shall examine the record of different industries and the distribution of its control among different business groups in order to test the utility of our propositions. For the proper understanding of investment, it will be necessary to examine the circumstances of each industry separately in the light of the attitudes of the different business groups involved in it.

Our starting proposition is a neo-classical one applied in a more forthright manner than has been thought to be applicable to India by precisely those economists who have professed unshakeable faith in the laws of demand and supply in a Western context. This proposition is that private businessmen in India, whether foreign or indigenous, would be guided primarily, if not exclusively, by relative rates of profit. To put it in another way, the clue to the commodity composition and rate of growth of capital would be found, for Western and native businessmen alike, in the structure of profit incentives. This is a proposition which some economists, while professing the universality of the laws of demand and supply, have not believed to be valid for India, where the dominant values have been held to be 'non-economic' in character. Added to this assumption of neo-classical economics about the private businessman's perpetual pursuit of profit is our second proposition: the non-applicability, especially in a colonial country like India, of the neo-classical condition of perfect competition. This implies that if Indians have been found to be lagging behind in their response to profit incentives determined by the supposedly universal laws of demand and supply, this is not because they are exceptions to universal economic laws, but because the operation of such laws has been restricted by conditions of imperfect competition. If profit opportunities have been found to exist in some areas which Indians did not utilize, it is because these opportunities have been restricted by cartels and monopoly groups. To put the two propositions together: variations in the rates of profit and variations in businessmen's access to these rates constitute an adequate (if not complete in all respects) explanation of the record of private investment in India from 1914 to 1947.

Recently A. K. Bagchi has argued in favour of an approach that 'looks at the profitability of investment and ease of entry into different fields by European and Indian industrialists to explain the major changes in the levels and patterns of investment'.[26] There is, however, an important body of literature, the influence of which still continues to be felt, which emphasizes 'demotivating' factors of a cultural and sociological character. Because of the influence of these non-economic motivations, private businessmen's response to profit incentives is held to be sluggish; or according to a variation on this theme, their response is held to be too speculative and irrational, with too great a tendency to make a quick profit by non-productive activities (this tendency is said to arise from a traditionally speculative business ethic). Curiously this theme constituted a common element among two contending schools of thought during India's struggle for independence. L. C. A. Knowles, defending Britain's mission in India, asserted, 'Nor did the English ever have the same sense of values as the Indian peoples, whose outlook in life is essentially non-economic'.[27] A typical statement of the opposite point of view came from B. D. Basu, who commented sharply, '. . . ever since the British acquired power in India, it has been their systematic policy not to develop and encourage the indigenous industries and trades of India and to paint Indians as lacking in energy and business capacity, incapable of organizing industries, hoarding their wealth and not investing the same for the creation and maintenance of new industries'.[28] Thus on the one hand there was the 'incapability thesis', and on the other hand, the 'conspiracy thesis'; common to both was a belief in the private businessman's (Indian in one case, European in the other) inability or unwillingness to

[26] Ibid., p. 24.
[27] L. C. A. Knowles, *Economic Development of the British Overseas Empire*, London, 1924, p. 267, quoted in Bagchi, op. cit., p. 20.
[28] B. D. Basu, *Ruin of Indian Trade and Industries*, Calcutta, 1935, pp. 111–12.

maximize profit by productive investment in the most promising fields of business and industry in India.

Statements about the shyness of Indian capital from risky ventures in modern enterprises often went together with logically inconsistent statements about the speculative tendencies of Indian merchants and traders.[29] European administrative and commercial opinion sought to rationalize the position of foreign capital in India in terms of the lack of Indian enterprise and capital, and was at the same time extremely critical of the highly risky operations of the Bania classes in the stock markets. Indian merchants were held to be too cautious and narrow-minded and too venturesome and speculative at the same time. A typical expression of this low opinion of native business ability came from Lord Curzon at a ceremonious meeting of the Bengal Chamber of Commerce: 'The whole industrial and mercantile world is one great field for the tiller to till, and if the man who lives on the spot will not cultivate it with his own spade, then he has no right to blame the outsider who enters it with his own plough.'[30] Such a simplified view of the question of Indian participation in business and industry failed to take account of three important factors: the availability of surplus liquid assets for investment in new fields by the merchant classes (who might be expected to invest the whole of their normal working capital running existing enterprises), the forward push of opportunities for investment in new industries (which would have to offer similar if not better rates of profit than the existing enterprises and which in addition must not be barred by monopolies to new entrants) and the backward pull of traditional enterprises (which might offer improving prospects of profit as well as safer and more efficient employment of assets). The differential impact of these factors on different regions and different industries determined the rate of participation of particular groups of Indians in modern business and industry.

It is generally agreed that in Bombay the cotton-mill industry, which was given a big boost by the cotton boom of the sixties, did not suffer from lack of initiative or shortage of capital, the early mills being financed by the surplus profits made by Indian merchants in the cotton trade during the American Civil War and the opium

---

[29] For a formidable assault on the theory of lack of Indian enterprise and capital as a limiting factor in development, see A. K. Bagchi, op. cit.

[30] *Report of the Bengal Chamber of Commerce*, vol. 2, 1902. Speech of Lord Curzon at the 50th anniversary of the Chamber.

trade with China. The pioneer companies progressed with fully paid up or sufficient capital in almost every case and the mills were equipped with the best machinery available on cash terms; their success encouraged further projects to which the investing public contributed liberally. The captains of the industry, while ignorant of the machinery and the processes of manufacture, had intimate knowledge of the cotton trade. They not only gave careful and personal attention to the economic working of the different departments, but readily responded to the innovation of the ring-spinning frame (which J. N. Tata substituted for the mule or fly throstle in the Empress Mills at Nagpur for the first time), which revolutionized the industry.[31] The group of ring-spinning factories set up in Bombay in 1884 were enthusiastically backed by investors and during the next ten years cotton mill flotation took place on a massive scale, ensuring the future of the industry in spite of the manipulations of Manchester.

The progressive character of Indian business leadership in Bombay has sometimes been attributed to the special activity of immigrant groups, such as the Parsis and the Jews, whose influence on the introduction of modern business has been said to be great in proportion to their numbers. In this formulation, 'persons from outside the native Indian population and not subject to the pressure of the ancient scheme of things', took the lead in industrial development, though some 'pure' Indians were also admitted to have taken a part.[32] This last admission was more important than the author of the observation, D. H. Buchanan, realized when he made it in 1934, for by then the business initiative in the cotton-mill industry had definitely passed to the traditional bankers and merchants of Ahmedabad, men of Bania extraction who had developed the best labour relations in India in spite of Buchanan's conclusion that Banias, though possessed of capital and eager for profits, were ignorant of the administration of labour.[33] It may also be noted in this connection that in the early development of the cotton-mill industry in Bombay, the Parsis were followed closely by the Bhatias and then by the Khojas, two similarly small but purely native groups who owned a disproportionate share of modern in-

[31] S. M. Rutnagar, *Bombay Industries: The Cotton Mills*, Bombay, 1927, p. 46.
[32] D. H. Buchanan, *The Development of Capitalist Enterprise in India*, London, 1966, pp. 142–5.
[33] Ibid., p. 146.

dustry in relation to their numbers and who were nevertheless conspicuously traditional in their social ethic. The early lead of the Parsis in the cotton-mill industry was apparently due to the successful collaboration by which they had developed, as partners of the British, extensive trade relations (mainly in opium) with China, where much of the yarn of the early Bombay mills found a ready market. The Banias forged ahead when the cotton-mill industry became more oriented to the domestic market, in which the advantages of the British connection were no longer of crucial importance.

The cotton textile industry had not required massive initial investment, so that the pioneer Parsi bankers and merchants had been able to start the mills mainly with their own capital with contributions from friends and relatives. The Bhatia merchants who followed the Parsis also subscribed the bulk of the share capital themselves and allotted the rest of the capital to members of their small and well-knit community. Such methods would have been somewhat inadequate in the case of the iron and steel industry, also financed mainly by Bombay, where the shares of Tata Iron and Steel company were floated in 1907. The estimated initial requirements in this case (to the tune of Rs 24 million) were so vast that the Tatas, knowing that such a sum had never been raised in India before, looked to the London money market at first, and it was only after two years of unsuccessful negotiation in London that Dorabji Tata turned in 1907 to Bombay, at a time when the local capital market was depressed, with a direct appeal to the nation. A new factor, a political factor, gave Tatas the opportunity and the climate to raise the entire capital in India. This was the new wave of enthusiasm for Swadeshi enterprises which swept through India in 1907. However, the importance of this new factor should be estimated cautiously in terms of the actual capital structure of TISCO, which clearly reveals that the part contributed by the ordinary public in a wave of nationalist enthusiasm as such was small compared to the more substantial contributions of hard-headed businessmen. That there was unprecedented patriotic fervour no one will deny. 'From early morning till late at night', remarked the construction engineer for TISCO (Axel Sahlin) later on, 'the Tata offices in Bombay were besieged by an eager crowd of native investors.'[34] Some 8,000 small investors had subscribed within three weeks; but

[34] F. R. Harris, *Jamsetji Nusserwanji Tata: A Chronicle of His Life*, Bombay, 1958, p. 190.

what these patriotically inspired ordinary folk had subscribed for were the fairly safe cumulative 6 per cent preference shares amounting to Rs 6 million out of Rs 24 million raised by TISCO. The bulk of the capital, i.e. Rs 17 million, was subscribed by a small group of very rich men who subscribed to the more risk-bearing ordinary and deferred shares. The remarkable fact in the flotation of TISCO was the willingness of these hard-headed businessmen, at a time of depression in the capital market, to subscribe to such an unprecedented amount of capital. Swadeshi enthusiasm had apparently stirred Indian businessmen in Bombay deeply; but the heavy reliance on friends and relatives for raising TISCO's equity capital, which was also characteristic of early mill agents like Wadias, Petits and Tatas, was a continuing link with past methods of raising capital. All the same Sir Dorabji Tata could be justly proud of the achievement, 'as for the first time in India's financial history I had succeeded in raising for industrial purposes such a vast sum from the hidden wealth of India for the development of our mineral resources'.[35] But a more severe test for his capital raising ability came in 1916 with the initiation of the Greater Extensions programme, which was initially expected to cost Rs 100 million. Due to catastrophic increases in equipment cost abroad in the post-war years the actual cost rose to Rs 180 million. It was expected at first to meet the estimated original cost from profits, 'but this great increase meant that in addition to what could be ploughed back, considerable fresh capital had to be obtained and that at a time when there was little confidence among investors'.[36] In the event, it was found possible to raise only Rs 81 million as share capital—and that only by floating Rs 69 million worth second preference shares—in addition to the Rs 40 million that could be ploughed back from profits. In order to meet the deficit, TISCO had to raise about Rs 70 million by borrowings. These included an issue of £2 million of 7½ per cent debentures in London. Even the debentures did not suffice and a number of loans had to be taken, including Rs 20 million from the Imperial Bank, Rs 5 million from the government, Rs 9 million from F. E. Dinshaw, Rs 10 million from the Maharaja of Gwalior, and Rs 1 million from Sir Sassoon J. David. So serious was the financial situation of the Company that Tata Sons had to give their leading creditor F. E. Dinshaw a permanent share of their managing agency

[35] Verrier Elwin, *The Story of Tata Steel*, 1958, p. 36.
[36] Ibid., p. 56.

commission. Even for a managing agency of the repute of Tata Sons, there were very considerable difficulties in raising the enormous requirements of TISCO in the early 1920s and the resort to the £2 million debenture capital in London proved the limitations of the capital market in Bombay, which was by far the most active in India.

TABLE 6
THE INITIAL CAPITAL STRUCTURE OF TISCO
(lakhs of rupees)

Subscribers	Total Capital	Ordinary Shares	Deferred Shares	Comulative 6% Pref. Shares	Debentures
(a) Issued to Tata Sons as fully paid in part payment for the concession (mining etc.) transferred by them	15.00	15.00	—	—	—
(b) Issued to a syndicate of promoters for services promoting the Company	1.00	1.00	—	—	—
(c) Agreed to be taken up in cash by promoters and friends	155.15	134.00	6.15	15.00	—
(d) Subscribed by 8,000 members of the public	60.60	—	0.60	60.00	—
(e) Subscribed by Maharaja Scindia of Gwalior	6.00	—	—	—	6.00
Total Initial Capital	237.75	150.00	6.75	75.00	6.00

SOURCE. *Tata Steel Diamond Jubilee 1907–1967*, p. 163; Elwin, *The Story of Tata Steel*, 1958, p. 36.

TABLE 7

SHARE CAPITAL STRUCTURE OF TISCO AFTER THE GREATER EXTENSIONS

(lakhs of rupees)

Item	Total Capital	Ordinary Shares	Deferred Shares	First Preference Shares	Second Preference Shares
1. Initial Capital	231.75	150.00	6.75	75.00	—
2. Capital Issue for the Greater Extensions	813.66	112.35	7.67	—	693.64
3. Capital at the end of the Greater Extensions					
TOTAL	1,045.41	262.35	14.42	75.00	693.64

SOURCE. *Tata Steel Diamond Jubilee*, p. 170.

Indian initiative in modern business and industry in other centres tended to lag far behind Bombay. In Calcutta the forward push of opportunities for investment in industry came only with the First World War, which loosened the grip of foreign capital and brought enormous liquid assets into the hands of Indian (especially Marwari) traders and speculators. Later, traditional merchant families in north India enthusiastically put their money into the sugar manufacturing industry when protection made it a profitable field of investment. In south India, where there was no big Indian push in modern industries until the onset of the depression, the backward pull of traditional enterprises along with the lack of power until the development of hydroelectricity might have acted as inhibiting factors. The leading merchant community, the Nattukottai Chettis, were able, simply by traditional banking and commercial operations, to increase their assets from Rs 100 million in 1896 to Rs 800 million in 1930.[37] During the thirties, when depression caused a fall in the profits from trade and money-lending, investment in modern manufactures by South Indians increased perceptibly. The Indian Industrial Commission, in explaining the tendency of the trading classes in India (apart from those in Bombay) generally to stick to their

[37] *Madras Provincial Banking Enquiry Committee Report*, Madras, 1930, pp. 186–7.

hereditary calling, clearly pointed to the greatly increased opportunities in traditional lines of business which the introduction of modern business and industry brought about. After the construction of the railways the trading classes found that large and certain gains were to be made in trade and money-lending, while modern industries 'offered only doubtful and, in most cases, apparently smaller profits'.[38]

The same explanation was extended by the Indian Industrial Commission to cover the apparent shyness of foreign capital from new enterprises. European managing agencies, which prospered only too well along conservative and stereotyped lines to bother about undeveloped industries with uncertain prospects, naturally preferred, like Indian merchant houses, 'a safe profit from trade, or from such established industries as jute and cotton manufacture, to a doubtful return from such ventures as metallurgical and chemical manufactures'.[39] This prosaic reason was something which impatient nationalist critics, who believed in a Machiavellian design on the part of foreign rulers and businessmen to keep India underdeveloped, found difficult to believe. Latterly a more sophisticated variation on the conspiracy theme has been suggested by Amartya Sen. He challenges the thesis that the business and commerce bias of foreign capital was a perfectly natural result of the free play of private profit motives. The argument which he rebuts is that foreign capital, which like all private investment was naturally swayed by the pull of the market, found it profitable to work for export markets (the big markets in the past being the industrial countries), rather than for domestic consumers whose purchasing power was extremely low.[40] Observing that a low level of per capita consumption can very easily go with a very big total market, depending on the size of the population, Amartya Sen points to the vast market for cotton manufactures in India, which was of very obvious concern to Manchester. 'There was no problem of creating a market for cotton goods in India, and the British reluctance to go into this field certainly cannot be explained in terms of "the poverty of the local consumer". In fact the growth

[38] *Indian Industrial Commission 1916–18 Report*, Calcutta, 1918, p. 72.

[39] Ibid., p. 51.

[40] This thesis of market limitation as an explanation of the export bias of foreign capital, put forward by Ragnar Nurkse, is criticized by A. K. Sen ('The Commodity Composition of British Enterprise in Early Indian Industrialization, 1854–1914', in *Deuxième Conférence Internationale L'Histoire Economique, Aix-en-Provence, 1962*, Paris, 1965).

of this industry led to considerable alarm and action in Lancashire, . . . and the explanation for British reluctance must be found in things other than the lack of a domestic market.'[41] This presumed reluctance, Sen suggests, 'might be explainable in terms of socio-logical forces rather than of purely economic ones', for there was no indication of a dearth of profits in cotton textiles. Contrasted with some of the less profitable fields of British investment such as coffee, cotton textiles were clearly more attractive. Even in the profitable British enterprise of tea planting, the well-known Jorehaut Company, which paid on an average the very high dividend of 15 per cent during the first thirty years of its existence, was no more profitable than Empress Mills, which paid on the average 16 per cent during the first twenty years. But in taking to cotton manufacture in India, British civil servants and capitalists, Sen points out, would have been open to the charge of being unpatriotic. They could not be expected to be indifferent to the prevailing atmosphere of strong feeling against cotton manufacturing in India which had been worked up by Lancashire propagandists. Suggesting a 'social ethos' hypothesis as a better substitute for the 'conspiracy' argument, Sen observes that 'since an individual entrepreneur lives in a particular society and belongs to a certain class of it, he might have some strong values that he might adhere to even at the expense of sacrific-ing some personal profit opportunities.' An established industry such as the Manchester textile industry was, meant the existence of strong vested interests and their propaganda against cotton manufacturing in India for individual and unpatriotic profit-seeking might go some way to explaining the supposed reluctance of British entrepreneurs to seek profit at all costs.

The assumption of a homogeneous British national interest against Indian cotton textiles would, however, as Sen explicitly recognizes, be very weak indeed. Lancashire machinery manufacturers and ex-porters were instrumental in furthering the development of the cotton textile industry in India in competition with imports of British-made piece-goods and fabrics. Their heavy involvement in the early development of Indian cotton textiles took the form of direct subscriptions for the share capital of newly floated companies and the deferred payment system for machinery purchases. In order to exclude competitors a British machinery manufacturing firm would often buy up shares of a newly floated company for securing

[41] Ibid.

the contract for machinery, and after the mill started working they would sell the shares at a discount and invest the sum in buying the shares of another newly floated company.[42] No social ethos against 'unpatriotic' conduct was strong enough to deter Lancashire machinery manufacturers from helping the infant Bombay industry to its feet. Nor was that ethos sufficiently powerful to check progressive British involvement in the cotton-mill industry of Bombay. From the beginning the cotton-mill industry had a strong leaven of European influence. The early ventures of C. N. Davar and Ranchhodlal Chhotalal were in association with European partners. The firm of Killick Nixon set up the Kohinoor Mills, quietly ignoring the effect on their Lancastrian principals whose cotton goods trade made up their chief line of business until then. Sassoon, Brady, Killick, Greaves Cotton, and Finlay interests came to dominate the Bombay industry, a fact which was reflected in the common office arrangements of the Bombay Mill-Owners' Association with the Bombay Chamber of Commerce.[43] The number of mills under foreign control increased from 14 in 1895 to 29 in 1915,[44] and although in that year the firm of Greaves, Cotton & Co. had to give up their mills, ten years later foreign firms were in control of 31 per cent of the spindles, 30 per cent of the looms and 48 per cent of the paid-up capital of the cotton-mills in Bombay (see Table 8). The failure of Greaves Cotton & Co. was due to the stoppage of the yarn trade with China and the general trade depression of 1915. This firm was a purely export-oriented one, controlling the largest number of spindles in Bombay for producing yarn for export, but no looms for producing piece-goods for home consumption. After its collapse British cotton manufacturing interests managed to effect a transition from their yarn export bias to piece-goods production for home consumption, the Sassoons (with 13,500 looms), the Finlays (with 2,452 looms) and the Bradys (with 2,351 looms) being in the lead.[45] The upcountry European mills in Kanpur and the Binny group of mills in south

[42] S. M. Rutnagar, op. cit., p. 48.

[43] S. D. Mehta, *The Indian Cotton Textile Industry: An Economic Analysis*, Bombay, 1953, pp. 1–3.

[44] Mills under Indian control meanwhile went down from 56 to 52 (Rutnagar, op. cit., p. 54).

[45] Indian groups with comparable production capacity in 1924–5 were: Currimbhoy Ebrahim (9,774 looms), Wadia (7,806 looms), Petit (7,312 looms), Tata (5,708 looms) and Morarji Goculdas (1,607 looms) (Rutnagar, op. cit., pp. 54–61).

TABLE 8
DISTRIBUTION OF BOMBAY COTTON-MILL AGENCIES, 1924–5

Communities	Mills	Spindles	Looms	Paid-up Capital
1. Indian				
(a) Parsis	22	978,200	25,600	359,92,000
(b) Hindus	19	831,700	15,150	333,45,000
(c) Muslims	15	587,650	10,810	321,53,430
TOTAL	56	2,397,550	51,560	1,014,90,430
2. Foreign				
(a) Jews (Sassoons)	14	652,000	13,500	761,50,000
(b) Europeans	11	421,500	8,160	190,11,200
TOTAL	25	1,073,500	21,660	951,61,200
GRAND TOTAL	81	3,417,100	73,220	1,966,51,600

SOURCE. S. M. Rutnagar, op. cit., p. 55.

India, it may be noted, had been producing cotton goods almost exclusively for the domestic market from their very inception. As a useful corrective to the general impression of the export bias and conservatism of European enterprise, Binnys deserve a special mention. With Buckingham and the Carnatic Mills under their control—two of the most profitable in the whole of India—they at first sold their products locally, but after the *swadeshi* movement they were sold all over India. By using longer staple local cottons of the Cambodia variety, they went over to the production of high quality cotton goods for the domestic market in fierce competition with Manchester.[46]

Nor would Amartya Sen's surmise of a conscious British decision not to invest in Indian iron and steel manufacture stand up to close scrutiny. In a complex and vast project like an iron and steel works, no firms located in Britain could be expected to assume a pioneering role in such a distant and underdeveloped country as India without local collaboration. No wonder Lord Curzon's invitation to British

[46] A. K. Bagchi, *Private Investment*, p. 190.

3

capitalists to start an iron and steel works in India evoked no response, particularly in view of the lower production cost of iron and steel goods in Britain, which could be more profitably marketed in India at that time (even with the added charges of sea freight) than goods produced in India at immense initial cost. Only a British firm located in India could be expected to assume such a role. The European-controlled Bengal Iron and Steel Company, which had been producing pig iron for the domestic market on a small scale since 1889, could not take up such a role on account of its small size and inefficiency, bred by long government refusal to extend any protection. Thus the mantle fell on Tatas, who expected at first to start the new venture with the collaboration of British capital. Too much should not be read into Dorabji Tata's ultimate failure to raise the share capital for TISCO in Britain in 1907. Sen observes, 'The precise factor which allowed the Tatas to make this appeal to *swadeshi* [i.e. in raising the share capital in Bombay], would have acted as a scare to the iron and steel interests in England, from whom Tata was trying to get financial help earlier.' Such a scare, however, was never alleged by any contemporary acquainted with the inside story, least of all by Tatas. Two contemporaries who undertook in-depth research on the subject, Lovatt Fraser and Frank Harris (none of whom showed a tendency to minimize the earlier reluctance of the British government to help Indian iron and steel), emphasized an altogether different set of reasons behind the reluctance of British financial interests to back TISCO. There was no real reluctance, but there was a demand for a disproportionate degree of control over TISCO by British investors. The financiers would have gone ahead if their demand for control had been conceded by Tatas, and at one stage four-fifths of the required capital was actually promised. That they ultimately did not finance the project was principally due to a periodic phase of depression in the money market in London, which had always been ready to put capital into speculative ventures in 'China or Patagonia or Timbuctoo' but had shown a traditional unwillingness to invest in new enterprises in India on account of thorough acquaintance with market, labour and raw material conditions in India. Money being 'tight' at the time, all new projects were looked at askance. The sum asked for was very large and would have met with a doubtful reception if the works had been projected for England. There was, moreover, genuine doubt, especially on the part of railway officers, about India's ability to make good quality steel in spite of the excellence of the iron deposits.[47]

Subsequently, when the First World War put the profitability of the iron and steel industry in India beyond doubt, the Calcutta-based European firm of Burn & Co. floated the Indian Iron and Steel Company in 1919. Due to the collapse of the steel boom in the early twenties the IISCO was forced to confine its production to pig iron and it was not until the steel industry recovered in the late thirties that Burn, now under a joint Indian and European controlling group, commenced production of steel under the newly floated Steel Corporation of Bengal. In addition, the purely European Calcutta firm of Bird & Company, in association with Cammel Laird and Co. of Britain, projected in 1921 (at the height of the steel boom) a United Steel Corporation of Asia (TUSCAL) with an intended capacity of double the steel ingot output of TISCO. But with the collapse of the world steel market in the following year this project had to be shelved; the steadily diminishing consumption of steel in India ruled out the profitability of two big steel firms in India, so that TUSCAL, a latecomer, had to yield place to the already established TISCO.[48]

For both foreign and indigenous firms in India profitability remained throughout the period under review the guiding consideration. That is not to deny the role of cultural attitudes, political motivations and sociological factors altogether, the weight of which we shall consider more carefully later on. But it must be emphasized that the exact significance of non-economic motivations can never be appreciated until the possibility of explanation of investment decisions in terms of the structure of profit incentives has been thoroughly explored. This is something which propagandists and scholars, who emphasized cultural attitudes and political motives, did not always care to explore in the past. In the last analysis an explanation in terms of economic structure is bound to carry more conviction than a superficial appeal to sociological factors. Such an explanation of structure must not be confined merely to questions about what the opportunities were and who were in a position to exploit them. The structure of profit incentives was not something

---

[47] F. R. Harris, *J. N. Tata*, p. 189; Lovatt Fraser, *Iron and Steel in India*, Bombay, 1919, pp. 51–2; Elwin, *Tata Steel*, p. 35.

[48] For an account of this abortive British enterprise in Indian steel, *see* Godfrey Harrison, *Bird and Company of Calcutta: A history produced to mark the firm's centenary, 1864–1964*.

given, but was itself determined by the overall structure of governance and society. For the modest scope of this work, however, it will be considered sufficiently rewarding if the explanation of investment decisions in the period under review can be offered in terms of the given structure of profit incentives (whatever its origin), together with a more exact consideration of the weight of motivations beyond the scope of strict economics.

One important qualification to the profitability thesis must be added here, but this is also an economic, not a sociological, qualification. It is this. The decision for reinvestment of profits is taken by foreign firms on a somewhat different basis from that of native investors. In the case of the latter, provided that there is profitable scope for ploughing back profits in the given industry or for employing those profits in a new enterprise, there is no serious economic check to the normal business motive of profit maximization. In the case of the foreign investor the periodic need for remittance dictates an attempt at striking an optimum balance between remittance and reinvestment, so that there is no question of systematic and consistent attempts at profit maximization. Moreover, there is the possibility of changes in the profitability ratio of remittance and reinvestment so that in particular circumstances remittance may become more *profitable* (apart from the question of political insecurity) in relation to reinvestment. Given that reinvestment opportunities in the national economy are not restricted, the rate of capital formation would be that much lower as the proportion of foreign capital in the private sector is higher and the incentive for remittance in relation to the incentive for reinvestment is stronger. As we shall see, this question became an important factor after the First World War. There was the possibility of earning higher rates on exchange of the rupee for the pound. There was also the possibility of employing more profitably at 'Home' than abroad the profits earned on exported capital, especially during the uncertain thirties. Finally there was the growing uncertainty about the ultimate destiny of British rule in India as the national movement gained momentum.

CHAPTER 2

The Record of Private Investment in India 1914–1947

Aggregate Share Capital Formation 1914–47

Measurement of the rate of capital formation in the private corporate sector as a whole, which would embrace banking, transport, commercial and industrial capital, is a problematic task even at the purely theoretical level, supposing that all kinds of relevant information were available. Were the balance sheets of all companies in existence during the period under review available, then a beginning might have been made by computing the total assets of these companies year by year under categories which are not comparable to each other, such as banks, trading companies and manufacturing, planting, mining and power-producing companies. For each set, a different price index series, based on prices of buildings, machinery (where relevant), raw materials (where relevant), particular commodities (in the case of purely trading concerns), etc. would have to be prepared so that the assets of different years can be truly comparable. The materials for such an ambitious project do not exist in the case of India during 1914–47. The real value of imports of machinery has been computed by A. K. Bagchi for the period 1900–39 as an indication of the rate of capital formation in manufactures. Such a method cannot be applied to plantations, mines, agencies and commercial firms, the weight of which in the overall index of industrial and trading activities must remain a matter of guesswork. This necessary but speculative task is beyond the scope of our study and for a rough guide to overall capital formation, A. K. Bagchi's index of the real value of machinery may be consulted.

The *Investor's India Year Books*, it is true, give the balance sheets of many companies during the whole period, but the assets of all the companies analysed in this annual series could have rarely amounted to more than half of the total assets employed in the private corporate sector in this period. The annual government reports on *Joint Stock Companies in British India and the Indian States* give a more complete (but not always exhaustive) coverage of companies at work, but no balance sheets analysing the real assets sunk in buildings, plant, etc. are given, only the paid-up capital of each company being mentioned. These companies again are classified according to their line of business into banking, transport, trading and manufacturing, planting, mining and other sorts of companies, the total paid-up capital under each heading being cited every year. The paid-up capital of a company is not a reliable guide to its total assets sunk in land and buildings, plant and machinery, and other assets, the real value of which can be computed over a number of years by preparing index numbers of relevant prices. Such a procedure is of course not applicable to share capital. Moreover, from company to company the proportion of share capital to borrowed capital is known to vary radically. Bigger companies, especially European companies, had relatively easy access to banking facilities in the period before independence, so that their share capital might stand at a lower nominal amount than that of Indian companies compelled to rely more on share capital. However, share capital is an important element in industrial finance and its growth in a traditional 'capital market' (if such it could be called) dominated by *sarafs* and *mahajans* was an important indicator of the modernization of business and the expansion of the corporate sector. For what it is worth, the increase of paid-up capital of companies registered in India from 1914–15 to 1946–7 is given in Table 9 as an indicator of the growth of the corporate sector. Due to major changes in price levels during this period, the totals of nominal paid-up capital for different years are not comparable. An index number series of wholesale prices is provided in the table and the nominal paid-up capital series has been adjusted at 1915 wholesale prices in column 3, but it should be borne in mind that the level of wholesale prices is determined mainly by agricultural commodities, and as such changes in wholesale prices do not bear any exact relationship to changes in the prices of the components of industrial capital. Adjustment by wholesale prices is not a satisfactory method of comparing the real value of paid-up capital over a number of years.

It is a remarkable fact that the nominal value of paid-up capital increased by more than six times from 1914 to 1947, the annual rate of increase being 16.85 per cent. The increase in share capital occurred by leaps rather than by a continuous upward spiral. During the First World War the corporate sector did not grow much, but in

TABLE 9

PAID-UP CAPITAL OF COMPANIES REGISTERED IN INDIA
1914–15 TO 1946–7

Years	Index of Paid-up Capital (1)	Index of Wholesale Prices (2)	Paid-up Capital at 1915 Prices (3)
		(1914–15 = 100)	
1914–15	100	100	100
1915–16	106.2	121.05	87.73
1916–17	113.6	128.94	100.65
1917–18	124.5	148.02	108.45
1918–19	117.2	181.57	95.54
1919–20	155.0	184.86	152.24
1920–1	207.8	155.26	247.42
1921–2	278.6	152.63	283.40
1922–3	308.2	141.45	332.56
1923–4	333.2	145.39	324.17
1924–5	342.3	149.34	333.25
1925–6	338.6	142.10	355.85
1926–7	341.7	132.89	365.38
1927–8	336.9	132.23	338.58
1928–9	336.9	133.55	333.57
1929–30	348.1	112.50	413.23
1930–1	342.4	83.55	461.04
1931–2	357.5	82.89	360.35
1932–3	345.7	79.61	359.94
1933–4	369.2	78.28	366.06
1934–5	373.5	83.55	349.94
1935–6	369.9	82.23	375.84
1936–7	383.8	89.47	352.74
1937–8	372.2	86.84	383.47
1938–9	387.1	88.15	381.35
1939–40	404.8	88.14	404.85
1940–1	411.6	96.90	374.39
1941–2	433.6	119.0	353.07
1942–3	448.1	162.80	327.54
1943–4	471.6	180.10	426.30
1944–5	518.5	182.40	511.96
1945–6	578.6	199.10	530.07
1946–7	639.2	221.90	573.52

SOURCE. *Joint Stock Companies in British India and the Indian States*, published annually by the Government of India.

the boom which followed it (1920–2) and even after its collapse (1922–5), the index of paid-up capital went up from 155 to 342. The real value of the increase was probably much less than the figures deflated at constant 1915 prices, because the prices of buildings and machinery as well as raw materials of certain types increased phenomenally. The doldrums of the late twenties and the depression of the thirties put a stop to this growth of the corporate sector. At the outbreak of the Second World War the index number of nominal paid-up capital was 387, the marginal increase having occurred after 1933 when it stood at 345. In the early thirties the nominal value of share capital was more or less constant and did not decline in its total amount; its real value increased due to the decline in the prices of raw materials and the greater decline of the prices of agricultural commodities in relation to the prices of manufactures. The second leap in the nominal value of share capital occurred during the Second World War. There was a phenomenal increase in the index number of paid-up capital from 387 to 639, and even allowing for the wartime rise of prices the increase must have been substantial. However, since there was not much increase in plant due to restricted imports of machinery during wartime, much of the increase must have taken place in liquid assets, more of which was needed in view of the overworking of plant to meet wartime needs.

The increase in the nominal value of the share capital after 1919–20 was probably considerably exaggerated due to the more effective machinery for gathering data about registered companies. Many companies which had not been included in the previous annual lists of joint stock companies in British India were now more methodically listed by Company Registrars. In addition, companies registered in native states were also included for the first time; formerly only Mysore was considered along with British India. From 1920–1 the same methods of calculation were adopted, so that the series became more reliable when the new machinery for registering and listing companies had been perfected in the next few years. Nevertheless another extraneous element continued to swell the nominal value of paid-up capital after 1920–1. This was the incorporation of existing partnerships as public limited companies, as well as the conversion of private limited companies, which were not exhaustively listed by the Registrars, into public limited companies. Another significant factor was the transfer of many companies working in India but registered in Britain to India in the form of 'India Limited' companies. These external factors no doubt accounted for a significant part of the obviously exaggerated increase in nominal share capital from 1920 to 1947.

How did the growth of rupee share capital (the share capital of companies registered in India) compare with the growth of sterling share capital (the share capital of companies at work in India but registered outside)? A comparison throughout the period cannot be easily undertaken, for the exchange rate between the rupee and the pound fluctuated enormously in the early twenties. Moreover, foreign banking, insurance and transport companies at work in India had operations throughout the East and there is no means of knowing the exact amount invested by them in India. Assuming, however, that the proportion of total capital employed by them in India in relation to other countries did not change very much over the years, a comparison of the rate of growth of rupee and sterling capital is possible (Table 10). From this comparison, it appears that sterling capital in India did register increases during the period as a whole, though at a slower average annual rate of 4.9 per cent and at periods which did not coincide with upward movements in rupee capital. In the early twenties, when much of the increases in rupee capital took place, there was not much investment in sterling shares, but by contrast the main increase in sterling capital took place from 1924 to 1934, when rupee capital was not growing much. From 1934 onwards there was a slow decline in sterling share capital employed in India.

The question of the relative weight of rupee and sterling share capital has been complicated by fluctuations in exchange as well as by the operation of sterling companies in other countries. Setting aside banking, insurance and transport companies, however, it may be assumed that the bulk of the capital of other sterling companies was employed in India. A comparison with rupee companies in the sphere of mining, plantations and trade and manufactures in 1924, when the rupee was finally fixed at 1s. 6d., shows that sterling share capital stood at £224 million, while rupee share capital amounted to £161 million. In 1947 the respective figures were £464 million and £289 million. This shows that sterling capital invested in shares remained predominant throughout the period. The share of the Indian corporate sector in Indian business and industry was sub-stantial but definitely less than that of the foreign corporate sector. It must be borne in mind in this connection that the distinction between the foreign and the Indian corporate sector was not economically a very sharp one. Much of the Indian corporate sector was controlled by foreign interests, so that rupee and sterling share capital cannot be equated with native and foreign business interests.

TABLE 10

PAID-UP CAPITAL OF STERLING AND RUPEE COMPANIES
1914–15 TO 1946–7

Years	Rupee Companies	Sterling Companies
	(1914–15 = 100)	
1914–15	100	100
1915–16	106.2	100.4
1916–17	113.6	97.8
1917–18	124.5	144.6
1918–19	117.2	166.5
1919–20	155.0	144.7
1920–1	207.8	140.7
1921–2	278.6	146.7
1922–3	308.2	162.8
1923–4	333.2	180.4
1924–5	342.3	172.5
1925–6	338.6	188.8
1926–7	341.7	207.2
1927–8	336.9	215.3
1928–9	336.9	229.0
1929–30	348.1	253.4
1930–1	342.4	254.9
1931–2	357.5	255.6
1932–3	345.7	362.6
1933–4	369.2	271.5
1934–5	373.5	198.7
1935–6	369.9	251.8
1936–7	383.8	248.0
1937–8	383.8	248.0
1938–9	387.1	265.0
1939–40	404.8	267.6
1940–1	411.6	270.0
1941–2	433.6	262.5
1942–3	448.1	242.0
1943–4	471.6	256.5
1944–5	518.5	250.1
1945–6	578.6	257.9
1946–7	639.2	257.4

SOURCE. *Joint Stock Companies in British India and the Indian States.*

Nor is it useful to separate rupee and sterling shares in terms of the distinction that sterling shares were raised in Britain and rupee shares in India. Foreign interests controlling rupee and sterling capital in India ultimately built up their assets mainly from salaries and ploughed-back profits to India. The net real inflow of sterling capital during this period was not big; India had never in fact been a favourite field of British investment. In economic terms it does not matter much whether assets obtained in India were subscribed to sterling or rupee shares. What all this implies is that down to 1947 foreign interests continued to be preponderant to an extent which the mere comparison of sterling and rupee shares will not reveal.

To go back to the question of rates of real increase in capital invested in Indian business and industry, it is clear now that our statistics of share capital provide no reliable indication of the rate of capital formation during the period under review. It is particularly so because in a period of fluctuating prices, even assuming share capital to be in constant ratio to borrowed capital, there is no means of adjusting share capital at constant price. Wholesale prices in India were determined by prices of agricultural commodities, and these prices do not bear close relationship to the cost of the components of capital employed in business and industry. The object of the present study is not therefore the ambitious one of estimating the real growth of capital in India from 1914 to 1947. What the statistics in this work do provide is a basis for a study of the commodity composition of capital, and its regional and racial distribution.

The Object Use of Share Capital 1914–1947

Some changes took place in the object use of capital (i.e. the share capital analysed in the tables) in India from 1914 to 1947, but these did not amount to a structural breakthrough in a new direction. Even at the beginning of the First World War manufactures accounted for a predominant share of the capital employed in India (both rupee and sterling). The proportion of manufactures went up after the war in the case of rupee capital. In sterling capital the proportion of mining increased in the late twenties and the early thirties due to phenomenal increases in the invested shares of petroleum and manganese. However, in the absence of knowledge of the part of sterling capital (especially in banking which also showed substantial increase in its proportion) employed elsewhere than India, it is on the composition of rupee capital that we must concentrate. There was all-round increase of shares invested in banking,[1]

TABLE 11

OBJECT USE OF RUPEE CAPITAL 1914–15 TO 1946–7

(Percentages)

Period	Banking	Transport	Manufacture	Plantation	Mining	Estate
1914–15	10.37	13.12	55.12	6.11	12.00	2.26
1915–16	10.17	14.85	53.68	6.15	11.21	2.84
1916–17	9.91	16.07	53.29	6.19	10.58	2.82
1917–18	10.66	15.99	52.65	6.26	10.28	3.05
1918–19	9.01	3.62	62.35	7.75	11.92	3.46
1919–20	7.58	13.51	56.20	6.44	10.64	2.69
1920–1	6.51	10.83	58.47	5.61	8.47	2.28
1921–2	6.05	10.76	59.74	4.59	7.16	2.37
1922–3	5.35	7.64	62.10	4.22	9.60	2.37
1923–4	3.47	8.80	64.04	3.90	9.24	2.28
1924–5	3.82	8.52	64.56	4.10	8.85	2.20
1925–6	3.73	8.18	63.52	4.39	9.11	2.60
1926–7	3.89	7.82	63.82	4.54	9.10	2.63
1927–8	3.98	8.00	63.19	4.97	8.95	2.72
1928–9	4.02	8.00	61.88	5.20	8.94	2.64
1929–30	4.27	7.95	61.16	5.18	8.49	3.72
1930–1	4.42	8.19	61.67	5.67	8.53	3.62
1931–2	4.27	7.90	62.77	5.45	8.15	3.53
1932–3	4.57	8.12	60.89	5.59	8.45	3.78
1933–4	4.98	7.80	59.97	5.55	8.55	3.68
1934–5	5.06	7.74	60.23	5.50	8.22	3.85
1935–6	5.44	7.88	59.41	5.56	8.46	3.92
1936–7	5.02	7.64	61.23	5.29	7.69	4.32
1937–8	4.80	7.94	62.47	5.14	7.69	4.32
1938–9	4.25	7.85	63.35	5.14	7.12	4.25
1939–40	4.29	7.74	63.45	5.03	6.84	4.20
1940–1	3.89	8.12	65.27	4.90	6.51	4.21
1941–2	4.07	7.83	66.09	4.63	6.53	4·13
1942–3	4.39	7.25	66.17	4.64	6.35	4.08
1943–4	4.57	7.02	65.09	5.25	6.14	4.04
1944–5	6.14	6.48	64.18	5.25	5.69	3.99
1945–6	6.80	7.20	63.32	5.09	5.51	3.71
1946–7	7.20	8.48	62.96	4.95	5.20	3.64

SOURCE. *Joint Stock Companies in British India and the Indian States.*

[1] Share capital provides no indication of the real size of banks, which rely on deposits. The paid-up capital of banks has been included in the tables because it must be calculated in computing the total amount of share capital in India, which has been accepted here as a guide to the size of the corporate sector.

transport, manufactures, plantations and mines, but the proportion
of manufactures improved to a limited extent in relation to others. A
closer scrutiny reveals that this increase was due to the extraordinary
growth of certain new types of manufactures, and not of established
manufactures like jute which increased at a slower pace than industry
as a whole. The distinction between well-established enterprises and
newer types of ventures gives a better insight into the changes in the
object use of capital than a distinction in terms of banking, transport,
manufactures, plantations, mines and estates. In Table 12 the move-

TABLE 12.1
RUPEE CAPITAL IN OLD AND NEW ENTERPRISES
1920–1 TO 1946–7

Period	Old Enterprises	New Enterprises
1920–1	866,850,107	259,896,047
1921–2	1,130,457,157	329,311,061
1922–3	1,143,314,148	376,508,663
1923–4	1,203,394,734	485,203,168
1924–5	1,213,590,428	475,360,306
1925–6	1,203,562,538	439,227,959
1926–7	1,195,338,126	495,155,067
1927–8	1,180,759,149	425,928,057
1928–9	1,208,630,128	408,035,075
1929–30	1,227,780,128	427,013,079
1930–1	1,199,278,168	427,127,077
1931–2	1,204,731,144	430,930,068
1932–3	1,227,840,160	447,710,053
1933–4	1,266,042,184	508,131,062
1934–5	1,261,716,188	539,650,085
1935–6	1,251,908,164	564,247,088
1936–7	1,274,508,196	618,369,084
1937–8	1,254,505,146	680,475,090
1938–9	1,250,378,098	757,861,086
1939–40	1,273,572,557	821,539,031
1940–1	1,317,494,825	871,753,980
1941–2	1,349,197,075	958,399,359
1942–3	1,395,460,939	985,249,662
1943–4	1,459,718,235	1,006,112,407
1944–5	1,610,777,318	1,080,491,095
1945–6	1,740,146,726	1,251,593,945
1946–7	1,903,428,753	1,299,997,362

SOURCE. *Joint Stock Companies in British India and the Indian States.*

ments of share capital in established and younger enterprises may be studied comparatively from 1920–1 onwards. The established enterprises were joint stock banking, insurance, navigation, tram and railways, agency business (including managing agencies), cotton-mills, cotton gins and presses, jute-mills, jute presses, tea, coffee, coal and gold. The younger enterprises were chemicals, iron and steel, shipbuilding, engineering, tanneries, canvas and rubber, cement, printing, tea-box, tobacco, soap, brass, aluminium, public service companies (electricity, telephone, etc.), paper-mills, flour-mills, saw-

TABLE 12.2
RUPEE CAPITAL IN OLD AND NEW ENTERPRISES
1920–1 TO 1946–7

Years	Old Enterprises		New Enterprises	
	Index (1921–2 = 100)	Percentage	Index (1921–2 = 100)	Percentage
1920–1	100.00	56.27	100.00	16.62
1921–2	130.40	54.09	126.70	15.75
1922–3	131.89	49.44	144.86	16.28
1923–4	138.82	48.14	186.89	19.40
1924–5	140.00	47.26	182.90	18.51
1925–6	138.84	47.37	169.00	17.29
1926–7	137.89	46.63	190.52	16.85
1927–8	136.21	46.72	163.88	16.85
1928–9	139.42	47.81	156.99	16.14
1929–30	141.63	47.01	164.34	16.63
1930–1	138.34	46.69	164.34	16.63
1931–2	138.97	44.91	165.80	16.06
1932–3	141.64	47.35	172.26	17.26
1933–4	146.05	45.71	195.51	18.34
1934–5	145.55	45.03	207.64	19.26
1935–6	144.42	45.11	217.10	20.33
1936–7	147.02	44.26	237.92	21.47
1937–8	144.71	44.93	261.82	24.37
1938–9	144.24	43.05	291.60	26.09
1939–40	149.22	42.59	316.10	27.05
1940–1	151.98	42.67	335.42	28.23
1941–2	155.64	41.48	368.76	29.46
1942–3	160.98	41.58	379.09	29.31
1943–4	168.39	41.26	387.12	28.43
1944–5	185.81	41.41	415.73	27.77
1945–6	200.74	40.09	481.57	28.83
1946–7	219.57	39.69	500.19	27.11

SOURCE. *Joint Stock Companies in British India and the Indian States.*

and timber-mills, oil-mills and sugar-mills. The decline in the proportion of older enterprises, which were mainly under European control, was largely due to the faster growth of fresh enterprises, in which Indians had an equally important if not much greater role to play. The average annual rate of growth of share capital in the new enterprises was 15.4 per cent; in the older enterprises it was 4.6 per cent. The proportion of shares invested in older enterprises came down from 56 per cent in 1920–1 to 40 per cent in 1946–7. The proportion of shares invested in new enterprises went up from 17 per cent to 27 per cent in the same period. This did not account for the whole of the decline of the proportion of shares invested in the older enterprises. Motor transport, rice-mills, rubber plantations, estates and breweries attracted a great deal of new share capital and this also accounted for part of the proportional decline of the investment in the older enterprises. If we consider these developments along with the more than average growth of sterling share capital in motor transport, printing, chemicals, iron and steel goods, engineering, cement, manganese and petroleum, then there is reason to think that the commodity composition of capital underwent a significant though not radical diversification and sophistication during the period under review.

Regional Distribution of Capital

Many of the established industries, such as jute, tea and coal, were concentrated in an industrial complex around Calcutta. Another such centre was Bombay, where cotton-mills were mainly concentrated though Ahmedabad had its own share of the industry. The new industries had a wider regional distribution, especially cement, glass, sugar, paper, chemicals, etc. The statistics provided by the official reports on *Joint Stock Companies in British India and the Indian States* do not adequately reflect this diaspora of industry. This was because the companies listed by these reports were placed under different provinces according to the place of registration and not the location of plant. These statistics can tell us something about the sources of capital and entrepreneurship but nothing about the location of industry.

From these figures it is at once clear that rupee capital operated throughout the period mainly from Calcutta (Bengal) and Bombay, while sterling capital operated mainly from Calcutta. Indeed the share of Calcutta in sterling capital continued to increase in the thirties and the forties. The other great centre of business and industry, Bombay, saw relatively much smaller inflow of sterling capital. So far as rupee capital was concerned, Bengal had a slight

TABLE 13

PERCENTAGE DISTRIBUTION OF CAPITAL 1914–15 TO 1946–7
(according to places of registration)

Years	Rupee Capital				Sterling Capital			
	Bengal	Bombay	Madras	U.P.	Bengal	Bombay	Madras	U.P.
1914–15	41.01	42.01	7.45	5.08	55.96	31.87	2.64	2.48
1915–16	42.82	40.84	7.42	5.79	66.41	22.37	5.10	1.60
1916–17	43.71	39.10	7.01	5.46	63.89	24.08	4.65	2.53
1917–18	45.99	36.81	6.81	5.28	74.70	16.44	3.93	1.71
1918–19	43.44	39.89	6.66	5.04	72.88	19.26	3.55	1.48
1919–20	45.90	37.57	6.09	2.54	65.22	25.02	4.02	1.72
1920–1	46.95	37.89	5.97	1.98	64.01	27.53	3.63	1.44
1921–2	43.62	39.81	4.72	4.91	55.92	36.95	3.64	1.68
1922–3	42.05	41.82	4.64	4.57	50.75	40.98	2.89	1.49
1923–4	41.57	41.97	4.67	4.84	41.60	49.83	2.68	1.22
1924–5	42.61	41.42	4.95	4.99	40.43	53.56	2.52	1.18
1925–6	42.49	40.73	4.92	5.10	45.71	44.70	2.98	1.32
1926–7	41.90	40.24	4.97	5.11	46.47	44.68	3.16	1.26
1927–8	42.56	39.48	4.99	5.04	42.79	49.06	2.90	1.16
1928–9	42.65	39.48	5.27	5.06	53.02	38.93	2.90	1.99
1929–30	41.97	39.43	5.87	4.95	53.52	38.51	2.90	0.98
1930–1	43.56	38.16	5.84	4.48	54.27	38.80	2.85	0.98
1931–2	43.64	38.13	5.72	4.46	55.63	37.81	2.85	0.97
1932–3	44.66	38.55	5.61	2.99	62.51	31.56	2.59	0.90
1933–4	48.24	34.96	5.50	3.06	62.93	31.25	2.65	0.91
1934–5	47.32	34.77	5.62	3.37	47.11	44.13	3.76	1.30
1935–6	48.08	34.98	4.91	3.30	65.54	27.49	3.05	1.03
1936–7	46.27	34.10	5.96	3.86	67.92	20.98	3.09	1.04
1937–8	40.68	37.35	6.72	3.96	73.36	16.53	2.58	0.96
1938–9	40.82	37.20	6.64	3.84	76.01	15.31	2.11	0.98
1939–40	40.42	36.60	7.27	3.69	76.19	14.19	1.89	0.94
1940–1	40.70	37.46	6.06	3.37	65.41	16.74	1.88	0.84
1941–2	40.43	37.67	6.21	3.21	76.85	15.96	2.33	1.03
1942–3	39.27	37.48	6.34	3.04	81.61	12.01	2.33	1.03
1943–4	38.66	35.66	6.32	2.97	80.00	11.40	2.28	1.00
1944–5	37.92	35.13	6.86	2.67	82.51	10.05	1.10	1.04
1945–6	37.34	34.56	6.97	2.43	79.76	12.86	1.02	1.00
1946–7	35.28	30.56	8.44	2.90	32.54	29.12	5.60	2.57

edge over the Bombay Presidency throughout the period, and together the two provinces continued to enjoy as much as 78 per cent of total investment in India up to as late as 1941–2, a figure not much less than that for 1914–15, which stood at 83 per cent. It was only at the very end of the period in 1947 that the combined share of Bengal and Bombay went down to 65 per cent for rupee capital and 61 per cent for sterling capital (which in 1914–15 stood at 87 per cent and in 1942–3 at 93 per cent). The provinces which came up in that year in respect of sterling capital were Madras (5 per cent), Travancore (5 per cent) and Gwalior (21 per cent), and in the case of rupee capital, Madras (8 per cent), Panjab (4 per cent) and Delhi (3 per cent). Until 1946 the preponderance of Bombay and Calcutta was apparently due to the relative ease with which capital could be raised in their organized stock exchanges and the political and administrative convenience of locating head offices in the two great commercial Presidency towns of India. It also reflected the tendency of sterling capital to focus on Calcutta and the concentration of India-based entrepreneurship (both European and Indian) on Calcutta in the east and Bombay in the west. The overall impression of the period as a whole was one of relatively little change in the regional bases of capital and entrepreneurship, and the comparatively much broader capital base of Calcutta in relation to Bombay and other minor centres of business and industry.

Racial Distribution of Capital

No foreign company operating in India during this period had any significant Indian participation and as such the total amount of sterling share capital in India, which was much greater in amount than rupee share capital, may be regarded as wholly foreign. The distribution of rupee share capital between foreign and native controlling interests is more difficult to determine. In the first place, the *Joint Stock Companies in British India and the Indian States* does not give any information about ownership or management of the listed companies. The other available source, the *Investor's India Year Book*, does throw light on the management of companies, but its coverage is by no means complete. It analysed only public (not private) limited companies which offered their shares to the public. The companies which had their shares quoted in the stock exchanges of Calcutta had a fairly thorough coverage, while the coverage of

4

companies operating through the Bombay stock exchange, though in some years less thorough than that of Calcutta, was not unsatisfactory. The other centres of business and industry in India, however, received little attention from the *Investor's India Year Book*, which tended to concentrate on the bigger companies of the Presidency towns. Published annually by Messrs Place, Siddons & Gough, it also showed a tendency to give greater space to European controlled companies.

The second difficulty about determining the racial distribution of capital is a theoretical problem. The companies controlled by European managing agencies had a number of native investors, so that, strictly speaking, ownership was mixed. This technical consideration, however, will give a very misleading impression about the *control* of capital. A few Indian directors appointed for the sake of appearances on the board of a European-managed company did not imply mixed control. The managing agency, therefore, has been taken to be the decisive criterion of the foreign or indigenous nature of a company in this study; where a company was under no managing agency, the board of directors has been scrutinized. This procedure, it may be noted, is in accordance with a ruling given by M. K. Gandhi in a controversy between Scindia Steam Navigation Co. and Bombay Steam Navigation Co. about what 'Swadeshi' was and what 'Videshi'. Gandhi's ruling was the following, 'As regards the definition of a Swadeshi Company, I would say that only those concerns can be regarded as Swadeshi whose control, direction and management either by a Managing Director or by Managing Agents are in Indian hands'. Regarding companies with an Indian directorate but managed by non-Indians (as in the case of the Bombay Steam Navigation Co. managed by Killick Nixon & Co.), Gandhi stated that he had no objection to foreign capital, but management must be in Indian hands for an industrial undertaking to be truly Swadeshi.[2]

A study of the admittedly fragmentary statistics processed from the *Investor's India Year Books* reveals a limited trend towards Indianization. For studying this process of partial Indianization, companies managed by Indian managing agencies may be considered together with companies under the control of mixed Indo-European managing agencies or boards of directors, since at the beginning of the period racial exclusiveness was very strong, so

    [2] Purshotamdas Thakurdas Papers, file on Bombay Steam Navigation Co. Ltd., 1937–40.

that partnership between Europeans and Indians was itself a straw
in the wind. A big jump in the proportion of Indian and Indo-
European share capital took place during the boom of 1920–2.
From 34.64 per cent in 1914 this proportion had risen to 51.49 in
1922, and in the late twenties it rose still further to reach 55.96 per
cent in 1927. In the early thirties there was not much increase in
Indian participation but when in 1937 there was a boom, the Indian
proportion (including mixed companies) rose once again to 60.29 per
cent. However, leaving aside companies with mixed control, the
European share in rupee capital remained greater than the purely
Indian share right until the end of the period, when in 1947 the
latter shot up to 51.61 per cent. If we also keep in mind the amount
of purely foreign sterling investment in India, then the gains of
Indian capitalists would look much smaller. Throughout the period
foreign controlling interests dominated the private corporate sector,
although Indian capitalists made some visible gains at the end of
each world war.

One noteworthy fact was the tendency of European rupee capital,
like sterling capital, to focus on Calcutta. In 1914, 81.26 per cent of
total European rupee investment in India was concentrated in Calcutta and at the end of the period in 1947 this proportion was still
72.28 per cent. Indian capital, by contrast, focused on Bombay,
which accounted for 87.25 per cent of total purely Indian investment
in 1914. This proportion had fallen to 68.59 per cent of the total at
the outbreak of the Second World War as a result of some increase
in the proportion of Indian capital operating from Calcutta, which
had risen from 7.31 per cent in 1914 to 18.03 per cent in 1939.
During the Second World War and its aftermath Indian (mainly
Marwari) capitalists in Calcutta rapidly rose to a position of emi-
nence, which was reflected in the fact that in 1947 Calcutta enjoyed
39.20 per cent of purely Indian capital in the country as a whole
(Bombay's proportion of purely Indian capital having declined to
45.49 per cent).

As a result of the concentration of European and Indian capital
in Calcutta and Bombay respectively, the racial composition of
capital in the two cities was fundamentally different at the beginning
of the period. In 1914, 81.24 per cent of the capital employed in
Calcutta was European and only 2.87 per cent was Indian (15.85 per
cent of the share capital being mixed). In Bombay, the proportion of
Indian capital was 48.63 per cent, and of European capital, 41.53 per

cent (9.83 per cent being mixed). This pattern remained essentially the same until as late as 1944 though Indian capital increased in proportion to European capital in both Calcutta and Bombay. European capital in Calcutta and Bombay in that year was 63.09 per cent and 33.79 per cent of the total respectively. Indian capital was 16.85 per cent of the total in Calcutta and 48.0 per cent of the total in Bombay (the proportion of mixed capital being 20.04 per cent in Calcutta and 18.20 per cent in Bombay).

TABLE 14

RACIAL COMPOSITION OF CAPITAL IN INDIA 1914–47

Years	European (%)	Mixed (%)	Indian (%)
1914	65.35	13.73	20.91
1916	70.80	9.47	19.72
1917	70.18	9.15	20.65
1918	71.99	14.82	13.17
1919	65.58	18.31	16.09
1920	59.18	15.95	24.86
1921	55.23	20.49	24.27
1922	48.49	14.18	37.31
1923	50.13	22.68	27.17
1924	47.69	15.33	36.96
1926	45.14	20.76	34.09
1927	44.03	23.96	32.00
1928	53.57	16.32	30.09
1929	44.17	24.93	30.89
1930	44.11	21.12	34.76
1931	42.72	22.72	34.54
1932	43.29	19.12	37.57
1933	44.95	19.49	35.54
1934	44.27	25.26	30.45
1935	44.93	21.06	33.99
1936	47.42	23.24	29.32
1937	39.69	24.85	35.44
1938	39.16	32.03	28.80
1939	39.72	26.37	33.88
1940	41.05	28.12	30.81
1941	40.06	23.27	36.66
1942	36.31	26.00	37.67
1943	47.98	24.26	27.74
1944	44.25	21.94	33.80
1947	26.31	22.06	51.61

SOURCE. *Investor's India Year Books*, published annually by Messrs Place, Siddons and Gough, Calcutta.

The dominant position of European capital in India as a whole, but especially its exclusive monopoly in Calcutta, was the most striking feature of the period, Bombay being the only big stronghold of native enterprise (though even there European influence was strong). Not until 1947 did a structural breakthrough occur in Calcutta, the most important centre of business and industry in India. In that year the purely Indian share in the rupee capital invested in the city came to outweigh European capital. But the continued dominance of sterling capital in that city still ensured the stronger position of British interests in the eastern part of India and, indeed, over India as a whole.

CHAPTER 3

Private Investment in Specific Industries

CONDITIONS in business and industry were profoundly altered after the First World War. In the twenties and thirties new industries, such as cement, paper and sugar, became very profitable. Much of the new issues of share capital moved into these relatively more profitable industries. The established industries, such as cotton, jute, tea and coal, did not yield similar profits, and investment in these industries showed a tendency towards stagnation from the late twenties onwards. The iron and steel industry was in great difficulty during the twenties and it was not until TISCO became well-organized after the full implementation of the Greater Extensions scheme in 1934 that the industry was profitable. This attracted new investment in iron and steel goods and a boom in the late thirties resulted in a much greater inflow of investment in iron and steel on the eve of the Second World War.

Table 15 compares the rates of profit with the amounts of investment for seven industries during 1928–41. It would be naïve to expect too close a correspondence between the general profitability of an industry (regardless of regional and firm variations) and the share capital invested in that industry (which cannot give a true picture of the total real assets sunk in it). There is no automatic relationship between profitability and investment. If demand goes up, an overcapitalized industry with excess production capacity can earn high dividends without being induced to deploy further real assets. By contrast, even under conditions of declining demand and profitability, an industry with a narrow production base may be driven to large-scale capitalization in order to reduce production costs per unit. All that can be reasonably expected is a broad similarity in the long run in movements in profitability and investment. The figures in Table 15 do not belie this reasonable expectation. They also reveal in some industries huge simultaneous rises in the rates of profitability and investment in the short run. Between 1932 and 1936 sugar was the most profitable industry and it absorbed fantastic increases of paid-up capital at the annual rate of 43.2 per cent during those five years. After this profitability went down and investment began to level off. Profitability rose again with the outbreak of the Second World War, but by then the industry apparently had sufficient reserve production capacity to meet new demand without further heavy inputs of capital. From 1937 onwards iron and steel and paper were two of the most profitable industries and these two industries absorbed nearly half the total increase of paid-up capital in all seven industries between 1937 and 1941. The rest of the increase of paid-up capital occurred mainly in the cotton textile industry, the profitability of which also rose to great heights during the same period. In the tea and jute industries, which relied almost entirely on export markets, the onset of the world economic depression resulted in drastic reduction of profitability, which remained persistently lower than the pre-depression level throughout the 1930s.[1] But both these industries were highly organized monopolistic enterprises which were able to absorb the shock without any large-scale liquidation of companies, and in fact some slight increases of paid-up capital took place due to the forceful entry of new (quite often Indian) competitors.

At this stage we must turn to an examination of the factors governing profitability in different industries. Since new investment depended on the pull of profits, it is essential to analyse these factors in order to have some understanding of the overall rate of growth in business and industry. Here, however, one problem confronts the investigator. While it is possible to find tangible reasons why certain industries made rapid progress or remained stagnant, it is more difficult to explain in such concrete terms the overall failure to achieve like Japan a rate of growth sufficient for a take-off. Many industries, characteristic of a society in which rapid industrialization is taking place, came to India fairly late or not at all. An explanation of why these did not develop at an earlier point must also go into a total explanation of India's performance in industry. In other words, the problem is two-fold: since some definite industrial development did occur, and since this development was not sufficient for a take-off, the problem is to explain the visible growth of some industries and the virtual absence of other enterprises. In order to tackle this problem, we shall select some organized industries of our period in

[1] Except one single year, 1937, for tea.

TABLE 15

Profits and Investment in Selected Industries 1928–41

(Base 1928 = 100; total investment in lakhs of rupees)

Item	1928	1929	1930	1931	1932	1933	1934	1935	1936	1937	1938	1939	1940	1941
Total Investment														
Cotton	4,092	4,039	3,674	3,625	3,747	3,670	3,658	3,452	3,714	3,723	3,755	3,898	4,119	4,205
Jute	1,674	1,707	1,757	1,841	1,853	1,875	1,818	1,848	1,913	2,028	2,038	2,049	2,035	2,089
Tea	1,185	1,236	1,310	1,316	1,316	1,414	1,422	1,419	1,398	1,280	1,302	1,330	1,307	1,294
Coal	1,060	1,009	973	960	998	1,108	1,085	1,106	1,037	961	878	871	875	881
Sugar	194	192	204	203	244	446	666	766	949	978	1,117	1,164	1,213	1,231
Iron & Steel	309	320	319	318	311	369	382	379	379	338	515	815	907	910
Paper	121	130	103	97	102	103	104	104	105	169	243	247	270	308
All Industries	8,635	8,633	8,340	8,360	8,571	8,985	9,135	9,074	9,495	9,477	9,848	10,374	10,726	10,918
Profit Index														
Cotton	100	99.1	37.9	52.5	82.8	33.9	90.1	89.0	98.8	138.2	154.6	220.1	489.1	760.7
Jute	100	85.6	37.9	8.7	12.6	19.8	34.4	39.8	25.9	11.1	13.6	48.8	46.8	49.2
Tea	100	59.8	14.9	−19.8	−1.1	93.9	50.2	63.5	70.8	108.4	96.2	95.4	141.3	219.5
Coal	100	98.4	122.1	91.2	75.0	60.3	59.7	63.8	62.5	71.8	139.1	140.2	114.9	110.3
Sugar	100	79.6	93.6	144.5	253.9	254.2	194.2	157.7	247.0	122.3	179.4	180.0	247.3	219.8
Iron & Steel	100	18.6	70.6	78.0	66.2	90.3	169.2	192.9	179.0	211.6	289.3	300.7	387.3	403.3
Paper	100	93.2	91.3	86.6	92.4	110.8	108.1	136.4	157.4	182.8	151.8	358.7	432.2	488.4
All Industries	100	78.0	47.1	27.8	34.6	44.2	62.6	69.6	63.1	61.1	72.4	99.9	135.4	169.4

(Continued)

TABLE 15 (Continued)

Item	1928	1929	1930	1931	1932	1933	1934	1935	1936	1937	1938	1939	1940	1941
Investment Index														
Cotton	100	98.71	89.79	88.59	91.56	89.69	89.39	84.36	90.76	90.98	91.76	95.26	100.66	102.76
Jute	100	101.97	104.69	109.98	110.69	112.01	108.60	110.39	114.28	121.14	121.74	122.40	121.57	124.79
Tea	100	104.30	110.55	111.06	111.06	119.33	120.00	119.15	117.98	108.02	109.87	112.24	110.30	109.20
Coal	100	95.19	91.79	90.57	94.15	104.53	102.36	104.34	97.83	90.66	82.83	82.17	82.55	83.11
Sugar	100	98.97	105.16	104.64	125.77	229.90	343.30	394.85	489.18	504.12	575.77	600.00	625.26	634.54
Iron & Steel	100	103.56	103.24	102.91	100.65	119.42	123.63	122.65	122.65	109.39	166.67	263.75	293.53	294.50
Paper	100	107.44	85.12	80.17	84.30	85.12	85.95	85.95	86.78	139.67	200.83	204.13	223.14	254.55
All Industries	100	99.98	96.58	96.82	99.26	104.05	105.79	105.08	109.96	109.75	114.01	120.14	124.22	126.44

SOURCE. For profit index, Office of the Economic Adviser, Government of India, *Recent Social and Economic Trends in India*, prepared by S. Subramanian and P. W. R. Homfray, Delhi, 1946, table XVII, Economic Adviser's Index of Industrial Profits.

which the factors favouring growth may be readily observed, as well as some other industries that spring up only at the very end of our period, in which the reasons for slowness or absence of development may be detected in the light of the reasons that led to their emergence during or after the Second World War. A balanced understanding of the process of industrial growth in India must be based on a proper appreciation of why certain industries did not develop until the end of the period under review or even thereafter, whereas some other industries underwent substantial expansion before the close of our era. In the latter category we may mention cotton textiles, steel, shipping, coal, paper, sugar, glass, safety matches, magnesium chloride and sulphuric acid. All these were important industries of the inter-war period. In the former category, we may mention caustic soda, aluminium, automobiles, cotton textile machinery, machine tools and sewing machines. These industries came into their own only during the forties and the fifties, especially after independence.

The above-mentioned industries have been chosen as case studies for the present investigation. They developed in India at different points in time. Cotton textiles, steel and coal were established industries that were already important at the beginning of the First World War. Shipping, paper, sugar, glass, safety matches, magnesium chloride and sulphuric acid were not well-developed industries before the First World War; they attained considerable proportions during the inter-war period. Caustic soda, aluminium, automobiles, cotton textile machinery, machine tools and sewing machines, although their manufacture was begun in the late thirties or during the Second World War, were not industries that had commenced production on a considerable scale at the time of independence.

The specific points of time at which the chosen industries developed historically indicate certain well-marked phases of the process of industrialization in India. In proper order of succession they indicate a long-term direction, a shift in the commodity-pattern of private investment. These changing patterns of industrial growth are in turn connected with political, social and economic changes which closely affected the structure of differential profit incentives.

1. Cotton Textiles

Growth

In spite of the cold indifference of British officialdom and the active hostility of the most organized and politically influential cotton manufacturing interests of the world, the cotton textiles industry had made steady progress in Bombay and Ahmedabad before the First World War. Admittedly that progress had not always been in competition with Manchester, for Bombay devoted a good part of her productive capacity to export of coarse yarn to the Far East and had not yet produced on a big scale the finer varieties of piece-goods that was the special preserve of Manchester in the domestic cloth market of India. Nevertheless competition there had been, and the growing alarm of Manchester was justified by the expansion of the Indian mill output of grey goods by two times and of figured, coloured and miscellaneous goods by five times between 1900 and 1914.[2] This was clearly intrusion into hitherto closed preserves, although much of the earlier progress, achieved without any protection, had been possible only because the expansion of mill output had taken place in coarser varieties in which Manchester had no stake. It would have been a little strange, as Buchanan observed in 1934, if cotton textiles had not developed in India: the country was producing one-fifth on the world's supply of raw cotton, occupying a place next only to the United States; it had an abundant supply of relatively cheap labour (which became cheaper as the mills moved further inland even though Bombay lost this advantage in relation to Japan); and it had, in its vast population, one of the biggest mass markets for low-priced cotton goods in the world. Amidst all difficulties, continued growth of the industry was ensured by these tremendous advantages. The record of this progress by import substitution is contained in Table 16.

The greatest progress, resulting first in drastic reduction and then in virtual disappearance of imports, was obviously registered during the thirties and the forties. Indian mill production of cloth rose from 2,259 million yards to 4,269 million yards between 1926–7 and 1938–9, whereas imports of cloth went down from 1,759 million yards to 631 million yards during the same period. It is noteworthy that the increase of 2,010 million yards in mill production was more

[2] A. K. Bagchi, *Private Investment*, p. 232.

TABLE 16
SHARE OF INDIAN MILLS AND IMPORTS IN TOTAL CLOTH SUPPLY

Item	1906–7 to 1908–9	1916–17 to 1918–19	1926–7 to 1928–9	1936–7 to 1938–9	1948 to 1950
Mills (%)	16	37	41	68	77.7
Imports (%)	57	43	39	13	Less than 1

SOURCE. S. D. Mehta, *The Indian Cotton Textile Industry: An Economic Analysis*, Bombay, 1953.

than the decrease of 1,128 million in imports.[3] At the same time Japan increasingly replaced Britain in cloth imports. It was in the thirties that Manchester finally lost her dominance in the market for cotton piece-goods in India. However, the growing inflow of cheap Japanese goods, which reached its most ample proportions in the thirties, delayed the completion of the processes of import substitution until the Second World War. Certain defects, which Lalubhai Samaldas pointed out at the beginning of our period, were responsible for the gradual, but not perhaps unsatisfactory, progress of the cotton mill industry: 'As long as we have to depend for our plant and machinery on foreign countries, as long as we are behind these countries in our knowledge of technological chemistry, and as long as we are not able to produce cotton equal in quality to American and Egyptian cotton, we shall find it difficult to compete on fair terms with Manchester or other centres of weaving industries.'[4] The heavy reliance on foreign machinery and chemicals meant that while the textiles industry itself continued to grow, it did not stimulate the more basic industries on which it relied for production. There was thus a leakage of gains from increased production which, under more balanced conditions, might have stimulated the iron and steel, engineering and heavy chemical industries.

1. *Raw materials.* The late entry of the Indian cotton-mills in the sphere of production of finer yarn and piece-goods was a natural consequence of the quality of Indian raw cotton, which was short-stapled and unsuitable for spinning yarns above 30 count. Cotton textiles in India developed in that branch for which her

[3] S. D. Mehta, *The Indian Cotton Textile Industry: An Economic Analysis*, p. 143.
[4] *Indian Trade Journal*, January 1914, p. 114, quoted in A. K. Bagchi, op. cit., p. 237.

raw cotton was suitable—coarse yarn and piece-goods—and for which there was, in addition, the mass demand of a poor people whose taste for finer varieties developed only with the slow rise of per capita income. After the development of coarse goods, the next step in production was finer goods. The difficulty was that long-stapled cotton suitable for finer goods developed late and to an inadequate extent. Although cotton-mill owners showed an interest in the procurement of long-stapled cotton for production of finer goods, short-stapled cotton did not yield ground to the long-stapled variety easily. Its continued cultivation was guaranteed by its great demand and consequent profitability. It was the world demand for Indian short-stapled cotton—particularly Japanese demand—that determined the relative profitability of short- and long-stapled cotton in India. Indian mills did not have controlling influence over these relative rates of profitability since they consumed less than half of the cotton produced in India, so that their demand for long-stapled cotton took time to be effective, especially in view of the fact that in England, which mostly relied on American cotton, there was only a fickle demand for the better varieties of Indian cotton.

The obstacle was not, however, insuperable. Japan, which relied mainly on short-stapled Indian cotton, had solved the problem by mixing it with a certain percentage of Egyptian and American cotton. Since Bombay had a natural advantage for importing high grade cotton from Egypt, from where it was but a short haul to the west coast, there was nothing to prevent India from resorting to the same method. In fact, during the First World War, imports of long-stapled cotton, mainly from Egypt and East Africa, had risen to 58,000 tons from a pre-war average of 12,000 tons. Imports of this variety fell to the old level after the renewed invasion of finer cotton goods from Britain at the end of the war. But a breakthrough occurred in the thirties, when imports of long-stapled cotton soared to 77,000 tons in 1935–6 and to 96,000 tons in 1938–9.[5] The number of spindles engaged in spinning finer Egyptian cotton increased from 20,000 in 1912 to 31,000 in 1930, 7,40,000 in 1935, 4,02,000 in 1939 and then by a leap during and after the Second World War, the number increased to 17,45,000 in 1949.[6] It may also be noted that by the early part of the 1930s, some progress towards cultivation of finer cotton had been made in India. In 1932, 18 per cent of the cotton

[5] Vera Anstey, *The Economic Development of India*, London, 1957, p. 518.
[6] S. D. Mehta, op. cit., p. 10.

crop in India was of the long staple variety, though in 1926 this proportion had only been 6 per cent. With the increase in irrigated area, Panjab and Sind began to concentrate on the production of American type cotton in the thirties, and by the end of our period supplied a major part of the needs of the cotton-mill industry in India. This will be clear if we compare the cotton imports of divided India from different countries in 1948–9: Pakistan (which inherited the cotton growing tracts of Panjab and Sind) supplied 61,90,000 bales, Egypt 51,20,000 bales, East Africa (with Sudan) 34,60,000 bales, and the United States 5,10,000 bales out of the total import of 1,61,70,000 bales.[7] It will thus be seen that once imports from Egypt had been organized and high grade cotton cultivation had been successful in Panjab and Sind, the progress of mill production of finer cotton goods was rapid in India.

2. *Machinery and Technology.* Textile machinery, the chemicals and the technology used in mill production of cloth in India were imported from Britain before the First World War and this state of affairs continued until the outbreak of the Second World War. In peace-time the heavy reliance on supplies from Britain presented no difficulty to the Indian cotton textile industry. A sophisticated technology, represented in the beginning by managers and machinery installers from Lancashire and later on by Parsis who learnt their job from the same Manchester school, had been gradually built up in Bombay around plant and equipment imported from Britain. With the gradual replacement of Europeans by Indians in the skilled staff of managers, mechanical engineers and carding, spinning and weaving masters,[8] this technology became cheaper and readily available within the country. The heavy Manchester bias of that technology, however, ensured the continuance of imports of machinery exclusively from Britain, at a time when India could have adopted the more up-to-date equipment of America and Japan. Although the machinery imported from Britain was both good and new—at least half the looms in use in 1927 had been set up only after 1909[9]—it was more suitable for the conditions of production

[7] Tulsi Ram Sharma & S. D. Singh Chauhan, *Indian Industries: Development, Management, Finance and Organisation*, Agra, 1965, pp. 452–3.

[8] Buchanan, *Capitalist Enterprise*, p. 211. The proportion of Europeans in these lines had been reduced from 42.4 per cent to 28.4 per cent between 1895 and 1925.

[9] *Report of the Indian Tariff Board, Cotton Textile Enquiry, 1927*, Calcutta, 1927.

in Manchester than for Bombay and Ahmedabad in the inter-war period. No doubt, as the Indian Tariff Board certified in 1927, the mills in India compared favourably as regards building construction, modern machinery and up-to-date labour-saving devices with the mills in Lancashire, but Lancashire had ceased to set the standard after the First World War. The prejudice in Lancashire against automatic looms—which was based on the unsuitability of automation for the great variety of specialized textiles produced there by skilled weavers—acted against the adoption of automatic looms by mill-owners in India, where a definite advantage could be gained by mass production of standardized textiles by automatic looms on the Japanese pattern. The advantage to be gained from automatic looms was proved by the production record of the Binny mills in south India, which by 1930 had employed 2,300 automatic looms and were producing, with nothing but Indian cottons, 'high class cotton suitings as well made as in any country'.[10] This successful experiment did not lead to the spread of automatic looms in the thirties, the decade during which Japan acquired a decisive edge over India by using Toyoda automatic looms on an extensive scale.

Japan had developed her own textile machinery and technology, in contrast with India's reliance on foreign machinery and expertise. It is, however, difficult to see how India could have developed her own textile machinery in the inter-war period in view of the infancy of the iron and steel industry, and a forced attempt to do so by protection would merely have pushed up production costs at a particularly difficult time for the textile industry. No doubt, as a result of the lack of a textile machinery industry, India was unable to install new plant during the First World War to meet increased demand and had subsequently to pay abnormally inflated prices for imports of machinery. But reliance on foreign machinery did not prevent the textile industry in India in the twenties and the thirties from switching its emphasis first from production of yarn to production of piece-goods and then from production of coarser to production of finer cloth. The Bombay mills, which marketed 72 per cent of their products in the form of yarn in 1907–8, put only 38 per cent of their products to the market in the form of yarn in 1924–5.[11] The dominance of British managing agencies in the cotton textile

[10] The above observation was made by Arno Pearse in 1930. *The House of Binny*, Madras, 1969, p. 211.
[11] Buchanan, op. cit., p. 214.

industry of Bombay proved no hindrance to relatively greater increase of looms than of spindles after the war. In 1924–5 the loom–spindle ratio in the British-managed mills of Bombay was 1 : 49.1, and in the Indian-managed mills it was 1 : 46.5.[12] But while in the inter-war period the well-organized textile machinery export business of Britain adequately met the changing needs of the Indian cotton textile industry, the virtual absence of an Indian textile machinery industry prevented the Indian cotton mills from seizing the great opportunities of the Second World War for increasing and renovating their plant. The increased targets in production were met merely by over-exploitation of existing machinery and additional inputs of labour and not by any genuine expansion of productive capacity.

India was also dependent on foreign countries for dyestuffs and other chemicals needed in cotton textiles, but except in wartime this dependence was no hindrance to expansion of bleaching and dyeing operations. During the First World War the Binny mills in Bangalore had to discontinue the manufacture of dyed twist on account of the difficulty of obtaining dyestuffs, until then largely a German monopoly.[13] After the war, bleaching and dyeing expanded slowly, for each mill tended to erect its own separate bleaching and dyeing works, which naturally prevented economies of scale. In the thirties there was a jump in bleaching and dyeing operations. A fair indication of the growth of dyeing and bleaching facilities in the Bombay mills was their water consumption, which rose from 42.51 million gallons in 1908–9 to 86.10 million gallons in 1938–9 and 313.78 million gallons in 1948–9.[14] The technological backwardness of the cotton textile industry in India was especially apparent in the virtual absence of printing facilities in the twenties, at a time when these had been established even in countries like Brazil and Mexico, not to speak of Japan.[15]

The conclusion is inescapable that in the twenties and the thirties Japan forged far ahead of India technologically. The Japanese had made excellent progress in printing and some of the most modern bleaching, dyeing and printing works in the world were in Japan at the beginning of the thirties. Between 1927 and 1932 Japanese technical efficiency improved considerably owing to general adoption of warp stop motion on looms by the mills under the big combines,

[12] Rutnagar, op. cit., p. 55.　　　[13] *The House of Binny*, p. 177.
[14] S. D. Mehta, op. cit., p. 20.　　[15] *ITB Cotton Textile Report*, 1927.

resulting in large reduction of workers per loom, and more extensive use of automatic looms, leading to mass-production of standardized goods.[16] In spite of India's impressive advance in cotton textiles during the thirties, the technological gap between India and Japan continued to widen.

3. *Power.* The cotton-textile industry in Bombay was dependent, up to the First World War, on regular supplies of coal from Bengal and Bihar, which entailed a long and expensive railway haul across the peninsula. The vast distance separating the coalfields in the east from the cotton tracts in the west led to the formulation of a great hydroelectric scheme by Tatas which became operational during the First World War. Although initiated under Indian enterprise, the scheme also attracted the support of British cotton manufacturing interests in Bombay. The undertaking of the Sassoons to take a substantial amount of electric power from the scheme when it was completed was characteristic of the optimistic and dynamic attitude of the British managing agencies in Bombay and it helped in finding the enormous capital needed for the scheme. Without the assured supply of electric power which the great Tata hydroelectric scheme made possible, the great and rapid expansion of the cotton-textile industry in Bombay after the First World War would have been difficult. Nevertheless it must be noted that although hydroelectricity gave the cotton mills a clean and reliable supply of power in Bombay, it did not cheapen the cost of power. Electric power was more expensive than coal and this was a disadvantage to Bombay in view of the much cheaper rates at which electric power was supplied to Japanese mills. Although inland centres could provide the cotton textile industry with much cheaper labour, this competitive advantage could not be properly exploited without solving the problem of supply of power in the inland tracts where cotton was grown. The extension of hydroelectric schemes in south India, where cotton was grown in considerable quantity but coal was not available, contributed to the expansion of the cotton-mill industry in south India in the thirties. The share of the Madras Presidency in the total production of yarn in India rose from 6.3 per cent in 1921–2 to 13 per cent in 1938–9 as a result of the completion of several large hydroelectric schemes.[17] The unusually rapid expan-

---

[16] *Report of the Indian Tariff Board Regarding the Grant of Protection to the Cotton Textile Industry*, Calcutta, 1932.

[17] T. R. Sharma & S. D. Singh Chauhan, *Indian Industries*, p. 458.

5

sion of the spinning industry in Coimbatore, Madurai and Tirunelveli was a consequence of the completion of the Pykara Hydroelectric scheme and the readiness of local industrialists to take advantage of new sources of power. The construction of the Mettur Dam led to the expansion of the industry in Mettur, Salem and Singharapet.[18]

4. *Labour.* In comparing labour efficiency in Japan, India and Britain, it is interesting to note that in 1927 the average number of looms per worker in these countries stood at 2.5, 2, and 4 to 6 respectively. Japan gained a decisive advantage in respect of labour by 1932, when the average number of looms per worker there increased to 6 while in India and in Britain it stood still at 2 and 4 respectively.[19] The opinion of big Marwari cloth traders, expressed to the Indian Tariff Board in 1932, that the fine dhotis of Indian mills were as good as any imported goods was some indication that the Indian worker's efficiency in fine weaving had improved in relation to Britain. While this explained the rapid inroads of Indian mill-woven finer cloth on imports from Manchester, the Indian cotton-mill industry in its coarser products was at the same time threatened by the much greater relative increase in the efficiency of Japanese labour at the turn of the decade (see Table 17). The predominantly female textile labour in Japan had proved both pliable and skilled. Two shifts, made possible by adequate dormitory housing near the shed, had considerably increased working hours and had proved parti-

TABLE 17

COMPARATIVE LABOUR EFFICIENCY IN JAPAN, INDIA AND BRITAIN
FOR LOW COUNT COTTON MANUFACTURE IN 1932

Source	Looms per Weaver	Average Efficiency per Loom %	Working Hours Index (Britain = 100)	Wages (Rs per worker per day)
Ordinary looms (Japan)	5.5			
Japan Average	6	95–6	250	2–4
Toyoda Looms	50			
Britain	4	85	100	4–8
India	2	80	125	2

SOURCE. *ITB Report*, 1932, p. 112.

[18] M. M. Mehta, *Structure of Indian Industries*, Bombay, 1961, p. 167.
[19] *ITB Reports*, 1927 & 1932.

cularly economical. The use of female labour on such a scale was inconceivable in Bombay, nor did the prevailing labour laws permit such long working hours. The Indian Tariff Board noted in 1932:

The relative cheapness of Indian labour, in spite of its low efficiency, appears to give India a considerable advantage over Lancashire and the United States of America. But in the case of Japan, while the level of wages is perceptibly higher than in India, especially if it is taken to include all expenses incurred by mills for boarding, recruiting, etc. the difference in efficiency far outweighs the higher wages paid in Japan. While it must be admitted that in respect of the labour cost per unit of output the position of the Indian industry is inferior to that of Japan, it must at the same time be recognized that it is not inferior to that of other textile manufacturing countries.[20]

The Japanese worker's efficiency, according to an interesting report by Arno Pearse on the Japanese textile industry, was a product of the general prevalence of a marked group spirit fostered by the social and religious traditions of the country, the compulsory system of education and the provision of extensive facilities for physical and technical training. The difference in the conditions of Indian labour in both these respects was well-marked.[21] The lower efficiency of Indian labour was one reason why the use of automatic looms in India was considerably delayed in relation to Japan. Mill-owners argued that without an increase in the number of looms handled by each worker in India, it was not profitable to use automatic looms.

5. *Capital and enterprise.* Cotton-textile manufacturers in India showed a certain amount of toughness in dealing with the difficulties of the thirties, but there is little doubt that the mill-owning class in Bombay let slip some opportunities in the twenties. The Indian Tariff Board in 1927 concluded that it had not grasped many advantages for the production of higher counts of yarns and the manufacture of bleached, dyed and printed goods. Bombay's moist climate was suitable for production of finer yarns and its position on the coast afforded an opportunity for cheap import of long-staple cottons from Egypt. The full exploitation of these opportunities was delayed until the thirties. The Indian Tariff Board criticized the Bombay mills in 1927 for gross over-investment of paid-up capital in relation to the increase in looms and spindles after the First World War. With overcapitalization went imprudent distribution of high dividends by Bombay mills in the post-war boom, amounting to

[20] *ITB Report on Cotton Textile Industry*, 1932.   [21] Ibid.

47 per cent in 1920, 40.5 per cent in 1921 and 21.5 per cent in 1922 on the pre-existing paid-up capital (excluding the capital of large new flotations).[22] A greater reserve would have enabled the Bombay mills to weather the financial difficulties of the late twenties and the early thirties, which ultimately enforced the recourse to the writing down of the amount of paid-up capital. The Japanese mills had also paid similarly high dividends during the post-war boom, but with greater foresight they had set apart a larger sum for depreciation. The Indian Tariff Board also found lacking in the Bombay managing agencies that personal care in the management of mills which was characteristic of the Ahmedabad mill-owners. However, it must be noted that some of the most successful mills in India were located in inland centres with their managing agencies based in Bombay.[23]

Unlike jute manufacture which was predominantly a Scottish enterprise, cotton manufacture was dominated by a mixed group of British and Indian textile magnates. The European managing agencies which had taken up cotton manufacture were also heavily involved in imports of cloth, but this did not prevent them from exploiting the domestic market and from seeking technological improvements. The house of Binny, which proved to be the most progressive cotton manufacturing agency in India during the inter-war period, had a big import business with R. Barclay & Co. and Reiss Bros. Ltd. for grey, bleached and dyed piece-goods, with John Glen & Sons for prints and saris, and with United Turkey Red Co. for coloured yarn.[24] The same house of Binny pioneered the use of automatic looms in India, effectively used Cambodia cottons for production of finer counts of yarn, set up the largest khaki dyeing plant in the world under one management (together with their own sodium bichromate plant for the khaki dye erected for the first time in India in 1940)[25] and organized the most complete and efficient domestic marketing agency in India for selling their cotton goods throughout the country between 1935 and 1945.[26]

6. *Market*. Because of their strong connection with the home market, the cotton mills had a much greater impact on the national economy of India than the jute mills, which were engaged almost exclusively in export. This difference in markets strongly influenced their respective attitudes to the primary producers of cotton and jute, the peasantry, from whom they obtained their raw materials.

[22] *ITB Report*, 1927.   [23] Ibid.   [24] *House of Binny*, p. 255.
[25] Ibid., p. 91.   [26] Ibid., pp. 228–34.

For the greater part of the period under review, the world market prices for jute were not at a sufficiently high level to give the mills the expected margins of profit unless they could squeeze the profits out of the primary producers by violently forcing down the prices of raw jute. The Indian Jute Mills Association, which regulated the output and raw jute purchase policy of the different mills, was a monopolistic body with great political influence, and its resources and power kept the prices of raw jute at an abnormally low level even during the First World War, when the mills were earning record profits.[27] In the cotton-mill industry there was no direct contradiction, of the kind characteristic of the jute-mill industry, between the profit earning capacity of the mills and the standard of living and purchasing capacity of the primary producers. While it was in the interest of the jute mills to erode the ability of the peasants to hold the crop in expectation of better prices, the cotton mills were interested in raising the consumption of the peasants. The jute mills had no such interest, since their manufactures were sold to foreign customers.

The Modi-Lees Pact of 1933 between Lancashire and Bombay cotton manufacturing interests showed the intelligent appreciation of the mill-owning class of Bombay of the need to expand their domestic market. Under this pact, while agreeing to reserve a certain part of the cloth market in India for Manchester, the Bombay mill-owners negotiated for larger purchases of Indian cottons by Britain, so that the income of the cultivators might be raised. The Modi-Lees Pact was followed by greater consumption of Indian cotton by Britain, though the chairman of the Bombay Mill-Owners' Association argued that this was due not to the pact but to the favourable parity of prices. Whatever the reason, the increased purchase of raw cotton by Britain was undoubtedly beneficial to Indian agriculturists. The Chairman of the Bombay Mill-Owners' Association expressed the hope at the annual general meeting on 10 March 1937 that the rise of raw cotton prices to remunerative levels during that year would increase the purchasing power of the rural population and that, with a moderate increase in the rural market, the cotton mills would be able to sell their manufactures profitably.[28] Next year, when the total quantity of goods produced

[27] *See* Bagchi, op. cit., Ch. 8.
[28] *Bombay Mill-Owners' Association Report for the Year 1936.* Chairman's speech, 10 March 1937.

by the Bombay mills still proved to be somewhat in excess of the demand, the Bombay Mill-Owners' Association urged that in order keep up the present high level of mill production the newly elected provincial governments should try to better the lot of the cultivators in order to improve their purchasing capacity.[29]

Even through the great depression of the thirties, it is surprising to note that the domestic market for cloth in India continued to expand. From 1897–9 to 1937–9, there was a substantial increase of the cloth available for consumption in India from 3,202 million yards to 5,496 million yards (increase = 2,500 million yards), which was accompanied by a substantial increase of *per capita* consumption by 3.4 yards in the following manner:[30]

Item	1896–7 1898–9	1906–7 1908–9	1916–17 1918–19	1926–7 1928–9	1936–7 1938–9	1948–50
Cloth available for *per capita* consumption in yards	11.0	12.6	9.8	13.0	14.4	12.7 to 12.9

It must be noted, however, that the rapid accumulation of stocks by mills from the twenties onwards implied a gap between *per capita* availability of cloth and *per capita* consumption of cloth. In 1926–9 the stocks of cloth with Indian mills were 12.7 per cent of the total production. This figure increased to 16 per cent in 1930–3, 15.3 per cent in 1934–7 and 18.1 per cent in 1938–40. In effect this meant that *per capita* consumption was considerably lower than the 14.4 yards of cloth available *per capita* on the eve of the Second World War. The accumulation of stocks compelled the mills to give very favourable terms to the wholesale dealers.[31] The Second World War solved the crisis of accumulating stocks, and gradually a sellers' market emerged through the diversion of productive capacity to war needs, hoarding and malpractices by traders and mill-owners, and strong general inflationary pressures on the Indian economy, failure of the transport system to meet civilian needs and failings of the government machinery set up to control the cotton-textile industry. Gross profits rose fantastically during the war: Rs 5 crores in 1939, Rs 7

[29] *Bombay Mill-Owners' Association Report 1937.*
[30] S. D. Mehta, *Textile Industry*, p. 126.
[31] *Bombay Mill-Owners' Association Report 1937.*

crores in 1940, Rs 23 crores in 1941, Rs 46 crores in 1942, Rs 109 crores in 1943, Rs 61 crores in 1945 and Rs 41 crores in 1946. The Secretary of the Textile Labour Association, Khandubhai Desai, commented in the *Harijan*:

An industry in which only 50 crores of capital have been primarily invested and whose fixed capital does not exceed 100 crores of rupees and whose pre-war yearly value of product was only 60 crores, has been permitted to earn, in one single year, a profit of 109 crores and the average of the entire period of seven years worked out at 53 crores a year . . . From 1943 to 1945 the industry has made annually, on an average, profits which are nearly equal to their total fixed investments, i.e. in these three years they have taken out from the consumers two and a half times the value of their plants in profits alone.[32]

7. *Foreign monopoly and economic nationalism.* It was not merely an expanding domestic market, but also a growing share of it at the expense of Manchester, that enabled the cotton-mill industry to grow almost continuously through the difficulties of the inter-war period. Initially the established monopoly of Manchester proved difficult to breach; and it was the onset of the world economic depression that led to the accomplishment of this difficult task. The slow progress in the twenties was due partly to the established market channels of Lancashire which fanned out in every direction from Calcutta, the biggest centre for the distribution of piece-goods in India. The import business in Calcutta was largely in the hands of big Marwari cloth merchants who served as agents of British textile interests. However, these Marwari cloth merchants were not uniformly reliable agents of Manchester, for disputes about contracts broke out frequently between the Marwaris and the British exporters and the Marwaris were increasingly influenced by the rising tide of nationalism. During the non-cooperation movement the Marwari Chamber of Commerce, which represented the piece-goods importers in Calcutta, organized a boycott of British cloth from the mixed motive of patriotism and the need to dispose of accumulated stocks.[33] During 1921, a year of depression in trade all over the world and especially in the cotton-mill industry outside India, the Bombay mills were not affected by world conditions, and were able to distribute high dividends due to the boycott movement which kept up the

[32] *Harijan*, 19 January 1947, 'Indian Textile Industry (1940 to 1946)'.
[33] *Marwari Chamber of Commerce Ki Report* (in Hindi), 31 March 1920 to 30 June 1924.

demand for Indian cloth.[34] The non-cooperation movement, however, exhausted itself without producing any permanent impact on Manchester's established channels of trade through Calcutta. The civil disobedience movement of 1930–2, together with trade depression and protective tariff, proved much more decisive in breaking Lancashire's hold over the Indian market. Since all three factors came into play at the same time, it is impossible to determine the relative weightage to be given to each cause. It is interesting to note, however, that during the civil disobedience movement a politically conscious move was made by the Marwari cloth merchants of Calcutta to establish a trade link with the Gujarati mill-owners of Ahmedabad, both groups being strongly affected by the religious–nationalist ethic of Gandhi. At the suggestion of the big Marwari importers of cloth in Calcutta, G. D. Birla wrote to the nationalist mill-owner of Ahmedabad, Ambalal Sarabhai (who urged participation by Indian businessmen in civil disobedience):

You know Marwaris are mainly responsible for the establishment of the Manchester market in Calcutta. If they once decide to wash their hands clean of foreign piece-goods business and devote themselves to the Swadeshi cloth business, they can perform miracles. There are people in this town among the cloth dealers who could purchase the whole production of your mills for 12 months ahead. ... I wish you and Bombay mill-owners could take advantage of this situation.[35]

The fact that the big Marwari importers in eastern India were now ready to help mill-owners in western India no doubt increased the size of the market to which the latter had access. Another very important factor which led to the decline of Manchester in the Indian market was the invasion of cheaper Japanese goods. While in 1915–19 the UK share in India's cloth imports was from 70 to 95 per cent and the Japanese share was between 2 to 28 per cent, in 1926–40 the respective shares were from 32 to 80 per cent and from 14 to 55 per cent.[36]

8. *Government policy.* The increasing threat of Japanese competition worked an important change in British policy towards the cotton-textile industry in India. The Government of India made

[34] Rutnagar, *Bombay Industries*, p. 66.
[35] Purshotamdas Thakurdas Papers, file no. 100/1930, G. D. Birla to Ambalal Sarabhai, 30 April 1930.
[36] S. D. Mehta, op. cit., p. 143.

strenuous efforts in the thirties for preserving a market in India for both British and Indian made cloth. It was apprehended at first that the new policy of imperial preference would benefit Lancashire more than Bombay, but as the operation of the Modi-Lees Pact within the framework of imperial preference ultimately proved, Indian textile interests gained more from imperial preference than did Lancashire. If progress in cotton manufacture in the inter-war period was not entirely satisfactory, it is difficult to see how the blame could be laid at the door of government policy. It is true that the role of the government in helping the industry could have been more active. The Government of India did not implement the Tariff Board's recommendation in 1927 that a combined dyeing and bleaching works for all Bombay mills should be set up with government financial assistance. Nevertheless the expansion of bleaching and dyeing operations in the thirties was quite impressive, and no official assistance was eventually found to be necessary. In the vital matter of giving protection to the Indian textile industry against the threat of cheaper Japanese goods, the coincidence of British and Indian interests enabled the Government of India to follow an adequately protective tariff policy.[37]

Conclusion

It was only during and after the Second World War that the cotton-textile industry in India established an unchallenged monopoly over its vast domestic market and began competing with Lancashire in foreign markets. Given Japan's much greater technological superiority and labour efficiency during the late twenties and the thirties, the textile industry in India could not be expected, even with more active government assistance and private enterprise, to have attained such a commanding position before the Second World War. However, the effects of past government neglect continued to be felt for some time after the First World War, and cotton-textile enterprise in India proved deficient during the twenties in seizing the opportunities for production with finer counts of cotton and manufacture of bleached, dyed and printed goods. Some of the very considerable achievements of Indian textile enterprise during the thirties in substituting imports from Lancashire could no doubt have been possible a decade earlier if that enterprise had been imbued with the characteristic optimism of Japanese mill combines. But such optimism

[37] *ITB Reports*, 1927 & 1932.

could have been generated only by the reservation of the home market for local entrepreneurship before the First World War. During the thirties, as a result of effective government assistance against Japanese competition and greater cultivation of long-stapled cotton at home, textile enterprise in India made as rapid progress in the production of finer cotton goods as could be expected under the circumstances, especially those relating to India's comparative labour advantages and disadvantages in relation to Britain and Japan.

2. Steel

Growth

Since TISCO was the only big company in India to produce steel until 1940 and since IISCO commenced producing a comparatively small quantity of steel thereafter, the growth of the steel industry in India may be analysed with reference to the key indices of the growth of TISCO in Table 18 and the absolute figures of steel ingot (crude steel) production by TISCO in Table 19. TISCO started with an initial rated capacity of 100,000 tons of steel only, which was quickly reached during the First World War. The company came into its own only with completion of the Greater Extensions Programme in the middle of the twenties, when the output of finished steel increased by a leap to 425,000 tons of finished steel. With routine additions and substantial improvements of plant and machinery during the next decade, the output of finished steel rose to 600,000 tons in 1935. The production of steel ingots, which stood at 851,000 tons in 1936–7, reached the one million mark with the outbreak of the Second World War, but it remained stagnant at that level throughout the war years, and finished steel was produced at an average of 764,800 tons from 1940–1 to 1947–8. In fact production of finished steel came down to 750,000 tons by the end of the hostilities as a result of very heavy wear and tear of machinery. There was virtually no expansion and little replacement of plant during the Second World War. The growth of TISCO and of crude steel production in India as a whole during the war was disappointing. From 1943 to 1947 the total output of crude steel in India showed as a matter of fact a slow and almost continuous downward trend.[38] However, the Second World War brought about a great sophistication and diversification of TISCO's steel products.

[38] *Tata Steel Diamond Jubilee*, graph showing crude steel production, p. 164.

TABLE 18

KEY INDICES OF THE GROWTH OF TISCO

(average annual values)

Period	Output of Finished Steel (000 tons)	Gross Block (million rupees)	Daily Employment (No.)	Gross Profit (million rupees)	Output per man (tons)	Gross Block per man (tons)	Profit per ton (rupees)
1912–13 to 1917–18	74.8	30	9,478.5	5.9	7.89	3,165	78.9
1918–19 to 1923–4	125.0	141	22,664.8	7.3	5.52	6,202	58.7
1924–5 to 1934–5	414.5	227	20,178.9	11.9	20.54	11,249	28.7
1935–6 to 1939–40	701.4	302	19,309.2	35.8	36.32	13,468	51.0
1940–1 to 1947–8	767.8	497	21,795.0	69.3	35.23	15,459	90.3

SOURCE. *Tata Steel Diamond Jubilee*, p. 139.

TABLE 19
STEEL INGOT PRODUCTION OF TISCO
(tons per year)

Year	Tons
1911–12	3,000
1912–13	31,000
1915–16	123,000
1920–1	170,000
1923–4	235,000
1924–5	370,000
1925–6	471,000
1927–8	600,000
1930–1	625,000
1936–7	851,000
1937–8	899,000
1939–40	1,018,000
1941–2	1,084,000
1943–4	1,092,000
1946–7	1,029,000

SOURCE. *Tata Steel Diamond Jubilee*, p. 78.

Clearly the growth of TISCO hinged on the Greater Extensions Programme until the Two Million Tonne Programme was finalized in 1956. The Greater Extensions were carried out at a time when owing to the post-war slump the odds were heavily loaded against TISCO. As the official historian of the Company wrote at its 50th anniversary:

This world-wide slump struck TISCO in the middle of the Greater Extensions Programme and brought it to the verge of ruin, from which it was saved only by the courage and patience of its leaders and later by the support extended to it by the Government of India. In 1920 the programme was only half completed and it was too late to go back. Orders for plant could not be cancelled; the plan to establish associated industries on the spot largely failed; there were strikes; costs of production rose; capital expenditure on the town and welfare activities went up—they had to go up—from 25 to 133 lakhs of rupees; the rate of exchange operated against India.[39]

If a very tough, courageous and cautious group of men at the helm of TISCO affairs had not forced the programme through, TISCO would not have been ready to meet the onslaught of the world economic

[39] Elwin, *Tata Steel*, p. 60.

depression. On the eve of the world economic depression the company's production of finished steel, for the year 1927–8, was 429,000 tons and its share of the domestic market for steel was 30 per cent. In 1932–3, at the height of depression, production stood at 427,000 tons and the captured share of the domestic market had gone up to 72 per cent. The whole of the fall in the demand for steel in India was borne by imported steel.[40] Throughout the period the works steadily maintained an output equivalent to 75 per cent of its capacity. Few steel industries in the world were able to maintain such an output. Without raising any fresh capital, TISCO was able to spend a sum of Rs 3 crores on capital improvements and replacements of plant.[41] In view of this performance, it will be useful to look at the exact nature of the impact of the depression on the steel industry in India. Before the depression the Tariff Board had calculated that by 1934 TISCO would be able to earn manufacturer's profit to the extent of 8 per cent (a total of Rs 1 crore) on the capital value of the plant. In the event TISCO did earn a manufacturer's profit of Rs 31 lakhs, but this amounted to 2.5 per cent on the capital. However, in the meanwhile it had met a very expensive strike at the works in 1928, which cost the company Rs 200 lakhs, and but for this loss, manufacturer's profit would have been 5.5 per cent. Again, but for a shortfall arising from a policy of selling its wares in new markets and for encouraging the use of its steel by subsidiary industries (a policy which also included selling of products at lower than commercial prices in order to monopolize the market at the cost of the smaller re-rolling mills), manufacturer's profit would have stood even higher at 6.5 per cent. The loss arising from the fall in market and prices as a result of the depression was only 1 per cent of the shortfall in the estimated profit of 8 per cent.[42] This was because the fall in prices, loss of railway orders, loss on tested steel due to shrinking markets, etc., which caused a total loss of Rs 2.89 crores, was nearly counterbalanced by the steep fall in the cost of raw materials due to the collapse of coal, spelter and stores prices, resulting in a total gain of Rs 2.61 crores (see Table 20). On the whole the depression, by giving TISCO a dominant position in the market for steel in India, proved to be beneficial to the steel industry of the country. It undoubtedly quickened the pace of import substitution, as in the case of cotton textiles. At the end of the depression, when the Tariff Board sat again

[40] *Report of the Indian Tariff Board on the Iron and Steel Industry,* Delhi, 1934.
[41] Ibid.   [42] Ibid.

in 1934 to review the progress of the steel industry and the question of further protection, TISCO was found to be able to dispense with protection in the main areas of its production.

TABLE 20
LOSSES AND GAINS OF TISCO 1927–33

Losses (lakhs of rupees)		Gains (lakhs of rupees)	
1. Fall in prices	73	1. Fall in coal prices	200
2. Loss on tested steel	33	2. Fall in spelter prices	16
3. Additional freight	23	3. Fall in prices of stores	45
4. Loss of railway order	160		
			261
	289	Balance loss	248
5. TISCO strike	220		
	509		

SOURCE. *ITB Report on Iron and Steel*, 1934.

1. *Capital and enterprise*. Setting up a steel industry from scratch, with its vast technological and financial problems, was an altogether different proposition from the unplanned and gradual growth of cotton and jute textiles, and required entrepreneurship of a different order. The story of TISCO cannot be understood in terms of the exceptional personality of J. N. Tata alone (who died in 1904, two decades before the completion of the Greater Extensions, the decisive event of TISCO history), for while Jamsetji undoubtedly supplied the bold and original idea which flowered into TISCO, it was the much broader family of Dorabji, Ratanji, R. D. and J. R. D. Tata who took the real decisions concerning plant location, financing of capital needs and labour relations which made TISCO a success. The younger members of J. N. Tata's family drew upon the resources and experience of a wider group of family friends, plant-level executives and leading figures in Bombay business and industry. This group of men, each of whom made a specific contribution to the overall decision-making, showed a strength in adversity and a boldness at the right hour which sprang from team spirit rather than individual genius. Dorabji Tata, the eldest son, was the man who conceived the Greater Extensions and he physically took part in the

epic search for the site of TISCO through the heart of the wild iron belt of India, besides conceiving the bold idea of appealing to *swadeshi* for initial capital requirements. R. D. Tata, together with his elder brother Dorabji, overcame the much greater difficulty of financing the Greater Extensions by raising loans personally guaranteed by both of them and by attracting further financial support by giving a permanent share of their managing agency commission to the most important financier. And again, R. D. Tata came to the rescue at a directors' meeting when the encompassing difficulties of TISCO in the midst of the Greater Extensions prompted the suggestion that the company be made over to the government. In realizing the vast needs of TISCO, Dorabji and R. D. Tata showed tenacity of purpose, ability to tap potential sources of support and a willingness to take personal risks and sacrifice individual advantages. Later on Ardeshir Dalal and Jehangir Ghandy were instrumental in the nearly complete Indianization of the works; and finally R. D. Tata's son, J. R. D. Tata, implemented decisions on the labour management front which put TISCO in the front rank in the matter of new experiments in labour relations and labour commitment to production tasks.[43] It will thus be seen that TISCO drew on a broader pool of business experience and management resources than was usual for the bigger companies of the day, which tended to be merely family concerns.

Such a broad basis of entrepreneurship was enjoined by the vast tasks of management which were involved in setting up TISCO. These tasks may be outlined as follows: (1) finding the essential raw materials, high grade iron ore and coking coal, and locating the plant near raw materials, markets and water supply; (2) finance for the initiation and extension of the works; (3) construction of the new steel works and an entire township under very troublesome conditions near a jungle village; (4) recruitment of expert personnel and long-term planning to replace foreign skilled personnel with less expensive Indian managers and technicians; (5) management of a vast labour force, improvement of productivity per man and administration of the township on modern, improved lines; and (6) provision of research and development facilities for overcoming technical problems and diversifying products.

The management of TISCO performed all these tasks with sufficient effectiveness to enable TISCO to attain a high level of efficiency

[43] *See* Elwin, op. cit.

and to dispense with protection by 1934. Careful attention to costs, foresight and restraint in financial management, willingness to carry through massive outlay in the midst of staggering difficulties and boldness in implementation of high risk decisions characterized that management. Prudence of management, exhibited particularly by R. D. Tata, was balanced by a broad sweep and originality of vision, which Sir Dorab in particular seemed to have inherited from his father. The first aspect of TISCO management was exhibited in the steady build-up of depreciation and reserve during the years of difficulty from 1920 to 1935, when no dividends were distributed. Addressing the shareholders in 1925, R. D. Tata had this to say: 'We are like men building a wall against the sea. It would be the height of folly on our part to give away any part of the cement that is required to make the wall secure for all time. . . . And we should not think of dividends until we have done that. . . . But make no mistake about this point. We hold this money in trust for you. But you yourselves hold it in trust for the Indian nation.'[44] This attitude was in strong contrast with the attitude of Bombay cotton-mill owners. Through the years of depression to 1933, TISCO set aside Rs 4 crores as depreciation, which went mainly into plant extension and improvement; neither Britain nor America were so fortunate in setting aside sums for depreciation.[45] The same spirit of cautious trusteeship for the nation that was exhibited in R. D. Tata's exhortation to the shareholders communicated itself by an easy transition to Dorabji's ambitious and dynamic plan for the Greater Extensions. Recalling Jamsetji's vision of a strong self-supporting India at a directors' meeting in 1916, Dorabji proposed a vote of absolute confidence in the engineer, Perin, who had drawn up a cautious and rather conservative programme of extension—a realistic engineer's programme. He then turned to Perin, and in the words of Keenan (General Superintendent) who later recorded the scene with feeling in his autobiography,

said gravely that whatever he needed to expand the plant so as eventually to supply India's total steel requirements was his to command. There was a moment of silence as the men around the table realized the sweeping significance of the pledge. Then Perin rolled up his unpretentious proposals. And with them he discarded the conservative Perin. Men of later generations who have never seen

[44] *Tata Steel Diamond Jubilee,* p. 4.
[45] *ITB Report on Iron and Steel,* 1934.

the grand old man, usually refer to him as 'that extravagant Mr Perin'. But he was neither to blame for the prodigal spending that followed nor should he receive all the credits for its benefits. It was typical Tata courage and Tata initiative that now launched the Company on its vast new programme.[46]

TISCO had to buy at inflated prices, and a saving of two and a half crores of rupees might have been effected if the plan had been delayed till 1924.

But had there been delay, the chances are that there might have been no extension at all and TISCO might have gone the way of so many other companies that perished in the depressions of the twenties. As things turned out, it was all to the good that the Company went ahead and, in the dark days that soon came upon the commercial world, had the plant running to full capacity which was raised from the original target of 72,000 tons of finished steel to half a million annually.[47]

The courageous decision for the Greater Extensions, which nearly ran TISCO into the rocks, placed the steel industry in India on a sound foundation. Vision and boldness went into the expansion of the steel industry in India during the post-war slump and the world economic depression, but the same cannot be said of Indian entrepreneurship when the next opportunity came at the end of the depression in 1935–6. Neither Tatas, nor Bird Heilgers, nor Martin & Burn, all three of whom had plans long simmering for a new steel plant, showed sufficient courage for starting a second really big steel works when the steel demand once again showed signs of expansion in the late thirties. The eventual additions carried out by Tatas and Martin & Burn were not on a sufficiently broad basis to meet the full demand during the Second World War. To this point we shall revert later on.

2. *Government policy.* Jamsetji Tata, the pioneer of the steel industry in India, had long concluded, rightly, that an iron and steel industry could not be started without the support of the Government of India. It was not until the end of the nineteenth century that such support was forthcoming. When the scheme for TISCO was finally launched in all earnestness, it was with the active, one might say impatient, backing of Lord Curzon. J. N. Tata also squared the India Office by obtaining the support of the Secretary of State, which undoubtedly counted with officials lower down the scale. What caused this sudden and radical change of official outlook, which had

[46] Quoted by Elwin, op. cit., pp. 53–4.   [47] Ibid., p. 54.

in the past so powerfully discouraged steel enterprise? One answer, suggested by Amartya Sen, is that Continental steel had largely replaced British steel in the Indian market at about this time, and that as a result a powerful social ethos in the business world of Britain, which had so long discouraged the industrial development of India, had ceased to be an insurmountable obstacle. To this it has been rejoined, by A. K. Bagchi, that the replacement of British steel by Continental steel in India had taken place on private account, and not in the vital area of government and railway orders, which were almost exclusively reserved for British steel.[48] Unless TISCO could make an inroad into the deep official prejudice against non-British steel and the unalterable policy of 'buy British' consistently followed by government and railway officials, it could not hope to get a share in the vitally important custom of government, and without that there was obviously no point in starting a works at all. Since the vested interests of British steel manufacturers could not be said to have undergone any radical change, the change must be looked for in the important area of government thinking. There is reason to believe that the change in the climate of official thinking was caused by political and strategic considerations of the British-Indian Empire as a whole, especially as these were conceived by Lord Curzon, whose imperial vision and pursuit of strategic interests from the Persian Gulf to the heart of Tibet dictated the build-up of India as a broader base of power for the effective pursuit of these interests. During and after the First World War, when the menace of German hegemony in Europe threatened to tie Britain down to its Continental commitments, the need for a stronger base of power in India for upholding British strategic and political commitments in the East was realized even more acutely, as the proceedings of the Munitions Board for making India self-reliant showed clearly.

Whatever the reasons for the change in government policy, it was undoubtedly due to the change that J. N. Tata and his successors seized the initiative in the manufacture of steel. Without the railway connections no iron and steel works could be launched, and the Government of India, which had formerly been tardy in meeting such essential requirements of the industry, readily built forty miles of new railway from the iron ore mines to the steel works at a cost of a quarter million sterling. Railway freight concessions were given for carriage of raw materials and dispatch of manufactures. Above

[48] *See* A. K. Sen, 'Commodity Composition...', & A. K. Bagchi, op. cit., pp. 298–303.

all there was the vital undertaking of the government for purchase of 20,000 tons of steel rails annually on certain conditions. TISCO on its part invested heavily in government goodwill during the First World War by concentrating on supplying war requirements to the exclusion of all other profitable activities. Despite the profitability of pig iron, the company turned most of its pig iron into steel in order to relieve the steel shortage. It offered its products to the government at one-third to one-fourth of what could be obtained in the Calcutta market on account of wartime shortages. It stopped its very profitable production and sale of ferro-manganese to the United States in response to a request from the government to devote all its productive capacity to iron and by so doing relinquished profits exceeding Rs 100 lakhs. It also subscribed Rs 57 lakhs to the Indian War loans.[49] When TISCO asked for protection, it was able to point to all these services in war and it got back in the total value of protection much more than the sum it had invested in official goodwill. The managers of TISCO entertained no doubt whatever that the company would never have survived the crisis of the twenties and the thirties without protection. As the Chairman of TISCO, N. B. Saklatvala, told the shareholders in 1931, 'If protection has not paid you dividends, it has at least preserved your property'.[50]

The discriminating protection offered by the government, which just sufficed to ensure the existence of TISCO, compelled the company to be efficient in its operations. A. K. Bagchi, however, has argued that the cautious protection of the Government of India had an inhibiting effect on the growth of the steel industry and the growth of ancillary industries.[51] While government proved willing to protect the existing steel works and some ancillary industries, it was unwilling to meet the demand for ten-year protection by Bird and Martin Burn, both of whom at this time projected new steel works. In 1926, the Indian Iron & Steel Company and the projected TUSCAL (United Steel Corporation of Asia represented by Bird) were ready to go ahead with plant construction providing that government extended protection to steel for ten years. It was explained that the investing public would not put up the money for these new ventures without this guarantee. Soon, however, the market for steel collapsed. Had TUSCAL, with its very large productive capacity, been launched, either TISCO or TUSCAL would have been squeezed out by the

---

[49] *Tata Steel Diamond Jubilee*, p. 18.   [50] Ibid., p. 174.
[51] A. K. Bagchi, op. cit., p. 19.

depression, as will be clear when we look at the subsequent size of the steel market in India. It is difficult to see how government could have ensured the existence of two large steel works in India in the thirties without artificially propping them up with enormous bounties. However, a bolder policy of protection towards ancillary industries might have ensured a more comfortable existence for TISCO by creating a larger market for its products. In 1921, besides TISCO with its subscribed capital of Rs 10 crores, the following companies which depended on its steel supplies were on the verge of collapse on account of the post-war slump:[52]

Name of Companies	Issued Capital (lakhs of rupees)
1. Enamelled Ironware Ltd.	10
2. Tinplate Co. of India Ltd.	75
3. Agricultural Implements Co. Ltd.	25
4. Indian Steel & Wire Products Ltd.	25
5. Calmoni Engineering Co. Ltd.	28
6. Peninsular Locomotive Co. Ltd.	16.5

Many of these companies were resumed at a later date under changed management and more favourable conditions, but had government enabled them to maintain production by effective protection, then TISCO would have found a large and ready market on the spot. However, quite a few ancillaries did get protection and survived to see better days. Instead of taking an integrated approach suited to the interdependence of industries, government examined the case for protection of each industry separately. But in any case it could not, without a severe drain on the public finances, have ensured the survival of two steel works of TISCO size.

It was with the outbreak of the Second World War, when the requirements for steel for defence cried out for expansion of existing plant, that government showed a strange unconcern. The causes of this surprising lack of concern to develop the defence production of the country, which was exhibited in the case of many vital industries, were deeply rooted in the night watchman attitude of the then government and will have to be examined later. With regard to

[52] *Tata Steel Diamond Jubilee*, p. 171.

TISCO, its official historian has commented: 'The Second World War had less impact on TISCO's fortunes than the First. The then Government showed less concern to develop the Indian steel industry than it had a quarter of a century before.'[53] This loss of dynamism of the government in an hour of great opportunity set the steel industry back many years.

3. *Foreign monopoly*. Unlike the cotton-textiles industry, which had to fight a long battle against the monopolistic interests and political pressure of Manchester, the steel industry did not have to struggle against a similar monopoly of Birmingham, for that monopoly had been breached already by Continental steel except in the sphere of railway and government orders. In that important sphere also, TISCO from the very beginning enjoyed substantial patronage from the government, and to ensure its continuance and open lines into the administration, TISCO systematically recruited skilled white personnel as senior executives, including a sprinkling of former ICS officers. Tatas, unlike some big nationalist houses in the private sector, enjoyed excellent race relations; and by the very nature of steel manufacture, the connection between government and TISCO (which could not have existed without it) was bound to be strong. Some opposition from foreign steel interests there was in the beginning. British-dominated import houses in Calcutta, Bombay and Madras launched a propaganda campaign against Tata steel, which was rumoured to be of poor quality: 'as bad as packing-case wood —and would probably last as long'.[54] The exigencies of the First World War soon put a stop to these insidious rumours and a working alliance was 'established unconsciously' between the engineering trade of the country (which was mainly British) and Tata steel.[55]

Later on, with the onset of depression and dumping of Continental steel a close connection was established between TISCO and British steel interests in the early thirties, just as severe Japanese competition brought about a *rapprochement* between Bombay and Manchester. At the same time TISCO reached an agreement with British steel manufacturers to send its sheet bars to Britain for being rolled as galvanized sheets and re-exported to India with lower duty under the scheme of imperial preference. TISCO retained the right to

[53] Elwin, *Tata Steel*, p. 87.

[54] *Tata Steel Diamond Jubilee*, p. 160.

[55] Dorabji Tata commented on this at the annual meeting of the Company on 28 November 1916. Ibid., p. 160.

increase its own production of galvanized sheets. At first it proposed
to do so in financial and technical collaboration with Summers & Co.
in England, the entire technical and works management to be taken
on by Summers & Co. and both sides to put down 50 per cent of
Rs 1 crore of capital needed for a second galvanized sheet mill in
India. Ultimately TISCO gave up the plan for collaboration with
Summers & Co. on the ground that Indian political opinion would
be against it and consequently it might endanger the case for protection in the Tariff Board and the Legislative Assembly.[56] The original
plan for a tie-up agreement with Summers & Co. had been due to
the acute difficulties in raising capital in 1932 (TISCO had plans for
a Rs 1.3 crore Coke Oven and Clearing Blast Furnace Gas plant and
Rs 1 crore galvanized sheet mill which had to be financed at the
same time). There was also some misgiving that sheet mill techniques
had not yet been perfected in the world and consequently it was felt
to be a risky enterprise. Ultimately, however, TISCO went ahead
with its plan for creating a sheet mill in record time single-handed.
Channels of trade and vested interest, as J. R. D. Tata pointed out to
a Director objecting to negotiations with British steel interests, did
not prevent Tatas from expanding their output continuously and
diversifying their products.[57] Tatas had a hard job allaying doubts
about whether the entry of British steel manufacturers under imperial
preference would not result in the loss of the market to TISCO. In
contrast with general Indian business and political opinion, the Tata
group was in favour of imperial preference on account of its tangible
benefits, such as a market for Indian pig iron and sheet bars in
Britain.[58]

But the galvanized sheet agreement with Oriental Steel Co., which
represented the British manufacturers, did not work smoothly, and
there were frequent disputes about the division of the market in
India and breaches of the agreement on both sides.[59] Subsequently,
when TISCO went in for production of specialized high speed steels,
it met considerable opposition during and after the Second World
War. The supply of high silicon steel sheets used in the manufacture of

[56] Purshotamdas Thakurdas Papers, file no. 117, confidential note, 12 February
1932.
[57] Ibid., file no. 117, J. R. D. Tata to R. G. Saraiya, 24 November 1934.
[58] Ibid., file no. 117, Note on Pig Iron and Galvanized Sheets arrangement
with British Iron and Steel Manufacturers, 10 November 1932.
[59] Ibid., file no. 117.

electric motors, dynamos and transformers had so long been a foreign monopoly. A long battle had to be fought with the help of public opinion before TISCO's special steel, TISCROM, was accepted for the Howrah Bridge.[60]

4. *Market.* TISCO started with an original production capacity which was designed to meet only a small part of the total demand for steel in India. But that total demand itself was limited at that stage of the economic development of the country, being confined to the requirements of the railways and the demand for structurals and other steel products for buildings and for the creation of some basic social overheads such as construction of roads, bridges, harbours and expansion of posts and telegraph. Except for some engineering firms like Burn and Jessop in Calcutta, there was hardly any steel-processing industry in India, the production of these firms also being oriented to railway requirements. The steel market suddenly expanded during the First World War, when the government commandeered almost the entire production of TISCO. With the development of many steel consuming industries during the war, the prospect of a growing steel market with the coming of peace seemed to be bright. This expanding prospect provided the push behind the Greater Extensions Programme. IISCO was also floated at this time by Burn for producing iron and steel, and Bird in collaboration with Cammell Laird & Co. of Britain came forward with the TUSCAL plan, designed to produce 450,000 tons of rolled steel, pig iron, ferro-manganese, coke and other products. The difficulties of the twenties, however, compelled IISCO to concentrate on pig iron production only, and TUSCAL, for which there was a prospect as late as 1926 when TISCO had absorbed 37.3 per cent of the total steel market of one million tons by means of the Greater Extensions, had to be shelved when the steel market collapsed with the onset of the depression. Had the Government of India encouraged the initiation of TUSCAL by giving protection for ten years, there would have been no market for it during 1930–5. In 1932–3, when the consumption of saleable steel in India had hit the lowest mark of 725,000 tons, TISCO was already supplying 431,000 tons out of this requirement[61] and it was using less than 75 per cent of its productive capacity, which was steadily expanding with routine plant additions. There was simply no room for a plant with a capacity of over four lakh tons as TUSCAL was projected to be.

[60] Elwin, op. cit., p. 75.   [61] A. K. Bagchi, op. cit., p. 329.

But undoubtedly TUSCAL had been planned on an appropriately large scale, permitting low cost working and latest production techniques. Bird, its representative, had large financial resources and were already in control of necessary raw materials: coal from its Burrakur and Karanpura mines, coke from its Loyabad ovens, iron ore from its Orissa Minerals, limestone and dolomite from its Bisra quarries, electricity from its Sijua Power Station and refractory bricks from its Kumardhubi works.[62] The capital required for financing this ambitious project was so large—Rs 20 crores—that it had not been possible to raise it in the difficult twenties without the assurance of government support for ten years. Though the steel market recovered once again after 1935, it did not reach the pre-depression level until after the outbreak of the Second World War, and TISCO was now supplying 66 per cent of these requirements with an expanding productive capacity. Average consumption of saleable steel in India from 1935-6 to 1938-9 was 1,038,000 tons and average TISCO production during these years was 682,500 tons. This held little cheer for TUSCAL, but the market could be expected to grow in the circumstances and, as subsequent events proved, this was the last (though by no means the most attractive) opportunity for launching TUSCAL. The Government of India was not willing to supply the facilities for a new steel works during the Second World War in view of more urgent needs for munitions, and after the war an independent government appropriated the further expansion of the steel industry for the public sector. Had the representatives of TUSCAL taken the plunge in 1936-7 in expectation of a rapid expansion of the market in the near future—the clouds of war had already appeared on the European horizon—then TUSCAL might have benefited from the extraordinary requirements of the Second World War.[63]

As it was, Martin and Burn, encouraged by the partial recovery of demand, floated the Steel Corporation of Bengal in 1937 with a small projected capacity of 200,000 tons of finished steel. By so doing they kept within the confines of the existing market for steel, which would not have comfortably accommodated a works of TUSCAL scale; but the narrow base of SCOB permanently affected its possibilities of cost reduction and efficiency attainment. A larger productive capacity would have been easily absorbed by the requirements of

[62] Godfrey Harrison, *Bird and Company of Calcutta: A history produced to mark the firm's centenary (1864-1964)*.

[63] The history of this abortive project is briefly traced in the work cited above.

the Second World War. TISCO itself drew up in 1935 a plan for a new works, with a capital of Rs 7 crores and a productive capacity of 400,000 to 600,000 tons of finished steel a year. TISCO did not go ahead with this plan and eventually went in for a less ambitious scheme of extension and modernization, costing Rs 5.5 crores, under which a new blast furnace was erected, an electric power plant was installed and the coke-oven plant was entirely rebuilt. The partial recovery of demand in the late thirties thus led to the expansion of the existing steel works and the initiation of a smaller new steel works, but market trends were not sufficiently encouraging to stimulate a second works of TISCO size.

Given the size of the market, the progress of the steel industry was not at all unsatisfactory and during the years of depression import substitution was quite effective. That the total market itself was inelastic in the twenties and shrinking in the thirties was not due to any lack of effort on the part of TISCO to create effective demand for its products within the country. Along with Greater Extensions, it had been planned by TISCO in collaboration with subsidiary and independent companies to start several steel processing works at Jamshedpur, the idea being that these new concerns would get their steel requirements from TISCO at practically no cost of transport and TISCO would get a large and ready market for its products on the spot. Due to the difficulties and even disasters of the associated companies in the early twenties, the plan did not materialize then and it was only in the thirties and the forties that the projected concerns started working. The Burma Mines Corporation, which started an office in Jamshedpur in 1921 for a smelting and refining plant for zinc ore did not manage to set up the plant at all. The Calcutta Monofieth Works, which produced castings for jute mill machinery, was brought to an end by the slump in the jute trade. The works were taken over by the Jamshedpur Engineering & Manufacturing Co., but it was not until 1939 that it started producing chilled cast-iron rolles and wheels under the Indra Singh group. The Indian Steel & Wire Products Ltd., which also started producing rods, wire nails, barbed wire, etc. in the thirties under Indra Singh, was another company which descended from a collapsed wire and wire-nail producing concern of the early twenties. Peninsular Locomotive Company, which was also started at Jamshedpur in 1921 for producing locomotives, perished in the stresses of the twenties. Its works, taken over by East Indian Railways for producing undercarriage frames for railway rolling-stock, was closed down during the Great Depression. Reopened during the Second World War for producing armoured vehicles from the plates supplied by TISCO, this works was subsequently bought in 1945 by Tatas for the newly floated Tata Locomotive and Engineering Co. (TELCO) which at long last started producing locomotives in 1952. The Agricultural Implements Co., which was another independent company which collapsed in the post-war slump due to stiff foreign competition and technical inability to meet the local preferences for varied designs, was taken over by TISCO in 1925. Under its more efficient management, with the help of new and renovated plant which replaced the old machinery, the concern started turning out agricultural implements from high quality carbon steel in subsequent years. The Indian Hume Pipe Factory, started under the Walchand group in 1926 at Jamshedpur for producing reinforced cement-concrete hume pipes, was one concern which got off to a successful start. Tinplate Company of India, which started production of containers from TISCO tin-bar in 1923, had to wage a long struggle with the help of protection before it got going. More active government backing of all these concerns would have ensured a bigger market for TISCO, though probably not a market large enough to accommodate TUSCAL.

5. *Location and raw materials.* The plant for TISCO was located after long and scientific investigation at a site which was the best possible in India, near the sources of best quality iron ore and passable coal with ready access to the largest market in India—Calcutta. Low cost limestone and dolomite for flux was also available nearby, though the better quality limestone had to be transported from Katni on the western side of India. Long afterwards an American expert, comparing the locational advantages of American and Indian steel plants, worked out the ton–mile requirements of iron ore, coal and flux to make one ton of steel as follows: Jamshedpur 334 ton–miles, Burnpur 441 ton–miles, Pittsburg 604 ton–miles, Gray Works in Indiana 1,037 ton–miles and Kaiser Steel Mill in Fontana 1,502 ton–miles.[64] India was the cheapest producer of pig iron in the world, and dolomite and limestone for flux were cheap and of good quality. So, although coal was both expensive and of high ash content, the Indian steel industry enjoyed definite cost advantages

---

[64] Cited in T. R. Sharma & S. D. Singh Chauhan, *Indian Industries*, p. 436.

in the supply of raw materials in relation to the major steel producing countries.[65]

6. *Skilled personnel and labour.* If nevertheless the cost of production per unit of steel in India was higher than imported steel initially, this was due to the higher cost of labour per ton of steel than in advanced countries. Buchanan concluded that on the average the ratio of Indian and American labour for producing the same quantity of steel was nearly three to one.[66] Of course wages at Jamshedpur for ordinary labour were lower than in American steel centres (though wages of unskilled labour were substantially higher in relation to other industries in India). But the covenanted staff, who had to be imported for filling the supervisory positions initially, swelled the wage bill of TISCO. Yet this initial investment was absolutely necessary for starting the works and for training Indians, and a substantial sum had also to be invested in technological institutes for training of Indians who were eventually to replace foreigners. At the same time a huge outlay in building the township of Jamshedpur was necessitated by the plan of getting a stable and permanent labour force on the spot. All these initial investments pushed up the labour costs of production per unit, but in the long run these investments resulted in substantial reduction of cost of labour per ton of steel. Output per man rose from 5.52 tons during 1918–23 to 20.54 tons during 1924–34 and to 36.32 tons during 1935–9 (*see* Table 18).

The Jamshedpur Technical Institute, opened in 1921, proved to be very useful in training suitable Indian personnel for managerial and technical positions. The gradual elimination of covenanted staff which was made possible by training Indians at the Institute resulted in substantial reduction of labour costs. The process of Indianization of the works was rapidly achieved under the stewardship of Ardeshir Dalal from 1931 to 1944.[67] The first Indian General Manager for the works, Jehangir Ghandy, was appointed in 1938. At the same time attention was paid to the training of skilled operatives and artisans at an Apprentice School which was started in 1927 for turning out fitters, welders, machinists, blacksmiths, moulders, pattern-makers, etc. The technical training programme in Jamshedpur freed TISCO from dependence on foreign technical personnel within two decades and after independence provided technicians for India's new public sector steel works.[68]

[65] Vera Anstey, *Economic Development*, p. 250.

[66] Buchanan, *Capitalist Enterprise*, 290.

[67] *Tata Steel Diamond Jubilee*, pp. 23–4.   [68] Elwin, op. cit., pp. 68–70.

Equally impressive were the achievements of TISCO in the task of building up a suitable labour force for the steel industry. The planned township of Jamshedpur, the annual cost of maintaining which was borne entirely by TISCO, provided a very high level of services and amenities. From 1928 onwards TISCO also made systematic use of bonus incentive for winning labour's co-operation in increasing production. These bonuses for higher production culminated in the Profit-Sharing Bonus of 1937, unique in India at that time, and in 1951 J. R. D. Tata declared his firm belief that the profit-sharing scheme had been a powerful factor in the good relations which the company and its employees had enjoyed since its introduction.[69] Another factor which promoted better industrial relations was the formation of a single Tata Workers' Union under Congress leadership in 1937, which ended the long-standing rivalries which had plagued TISCO's trade union politics before and since the costly strike of 1928.[70] Undoubtedly the systematic effort for improving industrial relations since the strike of 1928, which cost the company Rs 220 lakhs as against the loss of only Rs 28 lakhs due to collapse of prices and markets in the Great Depression, considerably strengthened the foundations of TISCO and resulted in higher productivity per man.

7. *Research and technology.* The progress of know-how for high quality steel was slow for TISCO until the opening of a full-fledged Research and Control Laboratory in 1937. Demands for special steels during the Second World War brought forth a wide range of innovative responses from this laboratory, which speeded up the diversification of TISCO products. The production of armour plates for building 'Tatanagars' (armoured cars used on the North African front), alloy, tool and special steels, and stainless steels in bar form was made possible by the research of the laboratory. The construction of the Howrah Bridge provided the incentive for the production of alloy high tensile structural steel for the first time in India. After a long struggle with foreign vested interests TISCO ultimately succeeded in preventing the use of imported high tensile steel for the bridge and supplied the TISCROM steel with which the bridge was almost entirely constructed.[71] Subsequently TISCO went in for production of specialized acid steels for turning out wheels, tyres and axles to meet the requirements of the Indian railways during the

---

[69] Ibid., p. 112.   [70] Ibid., p. 109.
[71] *Tata Steel Diamond Jubilee*, pp. 82–3.

Second World War. One remarkable achievement of the Research and Control Laboratory during this war was the reduction of high grade ferro-tungsten, a principal ferro-alloy for the manufacture of high speed steels, from wolfram ore obtained from Jodhpur and elsewhere.[72]

Conclusion

The establishment of the steel industry in India on a sound basis was made possible by natural advantages, government backing and high enterprise. It was the size of the market which, until 1935 at any rate, prevented a higher rate of growth in this industry. From 1935 to 1945, however, a cautious attitude on the part of Tatas, Bird, and Martin Burn and a strange indifference of the Government of India to building India up as a broader base of power resulted in the loss of opportunities for rapid and vast expansion of the steel industry. In the event, due to wear and tear of machinery, the industry emerged from the war with a lower productive capacity.

3. Shipping and Shipbuilding

Growth

The Indian shipping and shipbuilding industry, which was considerable at the beginning of the nineteenth century, was virtually extinguished in the latter part of the century by the tightening monopoly of British trading and shipping interests. The advent of steamships delivered the final blow to the craft of wood-built sea-going vessels which had flourished in Bombay under the Wadia master-builders for a time in the early decades of the nineteenth century. The subsequent ventures of Indian merchants and entrepreneurs to run steamships, either on the coast or over the seas, were destroyed by monopolistic combinations led by the P & O (in the sphere of overseas shipping) and the BISN (in the sphere of coastal shipping). Almost all of the several shipping companies which were formed from time to time by Indians up to the First World War were compelled to go into liquidation by the use of monopolistic devices, such as rate-cutting and deferred rebates.[73]

One prominent instance of this was the abortive attempt of J. N.

[72] Ibid., pp. 87–8.
[73] *Report of the Marwari Association 1923*. Written statement of the Marwari Association to the Indian Mercantile Marine Committee.

Tata in association with the Japanese line, Nippon Yusen Kaisha, to break the monopoly of the P & O and its associates in the shipping business between Bombay and the Far Eastern ports. Exorbitant rates were being charged against Indian shippers of yarn, opium and cotton to China and Japan by a ring of foreign companies led by the P & O, which had at the same time granted large rebates on freight to foreign shipping interests based on Bombay. The combined attempt of the Tatas and the NYK to break this monopoly in 1893–4 met a hostile reception from the British government, which took the view that the Tata–NYK agreement was a combination to prevent non-Japanese vessels from obtaining any part in the carrying trade in cotton and opium between India and Japan. The Indian cotton manufacturers, on whom J. N. Tata had relied heavily, one by one withdrew their contracts from the Tata Line, deserting a national enterprise which had been launched in their own interests. The P & O had meanwhile cut the rates from Rs 19 to Re 1–8, and had even offered to carry cotton free to Japan. Cautious by nature, J. N. Tata refused to face a severe and certain loss. The Tata Line was wound up within a year but the NYK obtained a foothold in the profitable carrying trade between Japan and India through this venture.[74]

Swadeshi Steamship Co. met a similar fate. Started in 1906 by Chidambaram Pillai, a leader of the extremist Congressmen of south India, for the carriage trade between Tuticorin and Ceylon (Sri Lanka), this new Swadeshi venture, unlike the Tata Line, obtained feverish patriotic support as a result of the Swadeshi movement. BI, which had monopolized the trade so long, cut the rates in vain, for Indian traders began to boycott BI and entrust all their cargo to the Swadeshi line. Finally BI and British officials, including port authorities acting in BI interests, deliberately sabotaged the Swadeshi line. Several 'accidents' were engineered in which its ships were rammed both in port and at sea, and the port authorities in Tuticorin and Ceylon held up the clearance of its ships. Official influence was used to deter customers and the Swadeshi line's office was harassed by minute checking and rechecking of its accounts by local officials, who acted at the instigation of the sub-collector of Tuticorin, Walter, who had once shared a house with a manager of BISN.[75]

[74] F. R. Harris, *J. N. Tata*, pp. 93–8.
[75] D. A. Washbrook, 'Political change in the Madras Presidency 1880–1921', fellowship dissertation, Trinity College, Cambrige 1971.

The final blow was the arrest and transportation of Chidambaram Pillai, in whose absence the Swadeshi line disintegrated.

The only Indian shipping company that got away was a small concern called Indian Cooperative Steam Navigation Co., formed in 1905 for carrying passengers along the Coromandel coast. Up to the end of the First World War, Indian interests were never able to secure more than 5 per cent of the vast coastal and overseas shipping business of India. The first successful big Indian shipping company was Scindia Steam Navigation Co., formed in 1919, with which the subsequent history of Indian shipping and shipbuilding was closely bound up. Upon the establishment of this small Indian toe-hold in the navigation business, it was estimated that approximately 90 per cent of the coastal trade and 98 per cent of the import–export trade was still served by foreign shipping companies.[76] The subsequent progress of Scindia Steam Navigation Co. and the smaller Indian concerns which that company took under its shelter was slow, being determined not so much by economic as by political factors. On the eve of the Second World War, the share of Indian shipping in the coastal trade was 21 per cent, while the share of British shipping in that sector was still 79 per cent.[77] Indian shipping had virtually no place in overseas trade, the small beginning in that direction by Scindia having been speedily brought to an end by the P & O–BISN combine in the early twenties. In coastal shipping, the only sphere in which Indian interests had broken through, the British lines—the British Indian Steam Navigation Co. Ltd., the Asiatic Steam Navigation Co. Ltd., etc.—still held the lion's share, but eight Indian concerns were also operating in 1939: the Scindia Steam Navigation Co. Ltd. (1919), the Bengal–Burma Steam Navigation Co. Ltd. (1928), the Indian Cooperative Navigation & Trading Co. Ltd. (1905), the Ratnagar Steam Navigation Co. Ltd, the Malabar Steam Navigation Co. Ltd. (1928), the Merchant Steam Navigation Co. Ltd. (1921), the Eastern Steam Navigation Co. Ltd. (1919) and the Haj Line Ltd. (1937). Of these, Scindia, Bengal–Burma, Indian Cooperative, Ratnagar and Haj Line were already in the Scindia group, and in 1939 a British concern, the Bombay Steam Navigation Co. Ltd., was taken over by Scindias. This premier Indian shipping company further acquired control of the Eastern Steam Navigation Co. Ltd. in 1941, though by then its Haj Line was

[76] *Report of the Marwari Association 1923.*
[77] Walchand Hirachand Papers, file no. 590, Development of Indian Shipping.

extinct. The overall share of Indian shipping in the coastal trade contracted during the Second World War due to the discriminatory working of official controls. It was not until the end of our period, in 1947, that Scindias established the first regular overseas services between India and America. Scindias had also launched a ship-building venture before the outbreak of the war, but due to official obstruction the shipbuilding yard at Visakhapatnam was not completed until 1947 and the building of the first Indian steamship was delayed until 1948.

The growth of Indian shipping and shipbuilding enterprise practically meant the growth of Scindia Steam, for even smaller Indian companies which were outside its direct control survived only because of its help. When that company was formed in 1919 by Walchand Hirachand with the help of Narottam Morarji, the possibility of its survival was not great. Walchand thought at first of both a passenger service between India and Britain and coastal services along the Indian peninsula to Burma. He had to give up the first project speedily when the Inchcape interests made it virtually impossible to run a service to Britain. Walchand managed to have the newly purchased ship of the company, the *Loyalty*, repaired in Britain only after great difficulties. One after another reputable firm in London refused to undertake the repair of the *Loyalty* out of fear of Britain's premier shipping magnate, Lord Inchcape, until the firm of Gellatley, Hankey & Co., where the young James Mackay (the future Lord Inchcape) had once served as a clerk, took up the repair job at the instance of a partner of the firm who was annoyed by Lord Inchcape's arrogant treatment of his former colleagues. Once the ship was repaired, Walchand found it difficult to get passengers through regular clearing agents, who had been threatened with dire consequences by Lord Inchcape, and was thus reduced to advertising for passengers himself and enrolling them in his own office in a separate room in his hotel. Once the passengers had been secured in this manner, Walchand failed to get heavy cargo for 1,500 tons of ballast needed by the *Loyalty* to sail with the passengers. Several firms which sent machinery and implements to Bombay, including the Tata branch in London, refused to send their goods by the *Loyalty* upon direct overtures by Walchand, and the engineering firm of Richardson & Cruddas, which at one stage agreed to send 1,500 tons of cargo to their Bombay agents through Scindias, withdrew the offer when pressure was exerted by Inchcape interests. Ultimately

Walchand had to secure the ballast by buying on his own 1,000 tons of cement and 500 tons of pig iron for shipment to Bombay, where he proposed to sell these goods on his own account as a general merchant. After this maiden venture,[78] it was decided that it would be more profitable for Scindia Steam for the moment to concentrate on the coastal trade to Burma, in which Indian trading interests were firmly established, and to postpone plans for a regular service to Britain, where the necessary contacts were lacking.

Once the six Scindia steamers, bought from Palace Shipping Line for one million pounds after much obstruction by official authorities in London, started plying on the Bombay–Rangoon line, BI reduced rates from Rs 18 to Rs 6 per ton and the new company lost lakhs of rupees. Lord Inchcape then proposed to buy up Scindia Steam by offering terms to the Scindia directors, most of whom, including Narottam Morarji, had been unnerved by the ferocity of BI's rate war. But the courage and far-sighted patriotism of Walchand Hirachand, aided by the strenuous efforts of Scindia's able and devoted manager, M. A. Master, were responsible for the rejection of the attractive offer of Lord Inchcape for Scindia Steam. Instead a ten-year agreement was reached with BI in 1923, by which Scindia Steam acquired recognition of the right to carry cargo along the coasts of India, Burma and Ceylon. Scindias had to give up the plan for a service to Britain and a clause in the agreement prohibited the Indian company from carrying passengers on the coastal routes. At that time Scindia Steam owned seven steamers with a total tonnage of 29,126 tons. It was provided in the agreement that the Company could acquire only seven more steamers with an addition of 35,000 tons until 1927, and that the gross tonnage of Scindias was not to exceed 75,000 tons until the expiry of the agreement in 1932.

This agreement put a long-term political check to the normal growth of Scindias under the logic of economics, and Walchand, who had formulated elaborate plans for passenger traffic on the Indian coast which he had to give up, regarded the agreement as a 'slavery bond'. Under this agreement Scindia Steam found itself restricted, in 1928, to 14 steamers with a gross tonnage of about 64,000 tons, though it was able to finance an additional growth of 80,000 tons of shipping and thus raise its gross tonnage to 150,000 tons. Nevertheless, the agreement was an important landmark in the history of

---

[78] For a more detailed account of this venture, see G. D. Khanolkar, *Walchand Hirachand: Man, His Times & Achievements*, Bombay, 1969.

7

Indian shipping, for this was the first time that British navigation interests recognized the right to existence of an Indian concern and clearly Scindias, which had sustained heavy losses, could not have continued as an economic concern without the agreement, which firmly established *swadeshi* shipping on the coastal trade for the first time within living memory.[79]

Upon the expiry of the BI–Scindia agreement, a new seven-year tripartite agreement between BISN, Asiatic and Scindia was concluded in 1933 under the auspices of the Commerce Member of the Government of India, Sir Joseph Bhore. Under this agreement Scindias were allowed to increase their tonnage to 100,000 tons, and to carry passengers on two out of four lines between India and Burma. But Scindia Steam's sphere of operations was confined to the coastal trade under the agreement. Walchand sought to get round this contractual obstacle to Scindias' entry in overseas shipping by trying to form a new passenger line between India and Europe named the Hind Lines, but he could not obtain government help for this ambitious project, which in consequence he gave up. Walchand's dream of Indian overseas shipping enterprise and passenger traffic under Scindias did not come to fruition until after independence.

In coastal shipping, however, although Scindia Steam was confined by agreements to 64,000 tons until 1927 and to 100,000 tons until 1939, expansion of Indian enterprise took place through smaller companies not bound by these agreements, and Scindias indirectly increased their share in coastal shipping by acquiring control over many of these companies in the process of saving them from destruction by BISN and allied foreign concerns. In 1932 Scindias gave a loan of Rs 3,50,000 to the Bengal–Burma Steam Navigation Co., which had been plying two steamers since 1928 between Burma and Chittagong, to help out this small and financially unsound Muslim enterprise in a rate war launched upon it by BISN, and as a result Scindias obtained the managing agency of Bengal–Burma. Thereupon BISN ended the rate war and a compromise was reached between BISN and Bengal–Burma under which the latter's two steamers were allowed to carry passengers and mail between Chittagong and

[79] For an account of the agreement and the subsequent growth of Scindia, see *Walchand Hirachand*, and N. G. Jog, *Saga of Scindia: Golden Jubilee Souvenir —Struggle for the Revival of Indian Shipping and Ship Building*, Bombay, 1969.

Rangoon on a profitable basis.[80] Subsequently in 1933–5 foreign shipping companies launched another rate war on four small Indian companies formed between 1919 and 1928 for plying steamers on the west coast between Cochin and Karachi: Merchant Steam Navigation Co., Malabar Steamship Co., National Steamship Co. and Eastern Steam Navigation Co. As member of the Tripartite Conference which had allocated definite shares in the coastal trade between BISN, Asiatic and Scindias, the latter's narrow self-interest would have been served by forcing the smaller Indian companies off the west coast, but Scindia Steam rejected the invitation of the foreign companies to join the rate war and came to the aid of the Indian concerns. Ultimately the rate war was brought to an end in 1935 by the Bhore award, which allocated 85 per cent of certain trades on the west coast to small Indian companies outside the Tripartite Conference. In 1937 Scindias obtained control of two small shipping companies plying three passenger steamers on the Konkan coast—Indian Cooperative (formed in the Swadeshi era) and Ratnagar (formed by Mafatlal Gagalbhai)—which offered their managing agency to Scindias in a fierce rate war launched upon them by Bombay Steam Navigation Co., which, although mainly financed by Indian investors, was managed by the European firm of Killick Nixon in Bombay. For the first time Walchand carried the war into the enemy lines by deciding to acquire controlling interest in Bombay Steam and in response to his appeal Indian shareholders of Bombay Steam sold a controlling block of shares to Scindia Steam. As a result Killick Nixon & Co. were compelled to transfer the managing agency of Bombay Steam to Scindias, which got valuable aid in this war of attrition from G. D. Birla who persuaded the Indian directors of Bombay Steam not to stand against national interests.[81] Scindias also sought in 1937 to break the monopoly of the Haj traffic to Jedda by Mogul Line, managed by Turner Morrison and controlled by the Asiatic, by opening Haj Line. Immediately Mogul Line launched a rate war, which the government resolved in favour of Turner Morrison in 1939 by awarding 75 per cent of the Haj traffic to Mogul Line and only 25 per cent to Haj Line. In protest Scindias withdrew from the Haj traffic in the current Haj season. Upon the outbreak of the Second World War the government re-

---

[80] Walchand Hirachand Papers, file no. 328, speech of Walchand Hirachand as Chairman of Scindia, 1933.
[81] Walchand Hirachand Papers, file no. 602.

quisitioned Scindias' most popular steamer for the Haj traffic for war needs and took over complete control of that traffic—a control that worked in such a way that Mogul Line obtained complete monopoly and Scindias were driven out.[82]

In 1940 the total tonnage of Indian steamships in the coastal trade was 131,748 gross tons, which was well below the total tonnage of 150,000 gross tons demanded by Scindias alone in 1928. At the same time the total tonnage of British steamships exclusively engaged in overseas freight from India was 2,756,400 gross tons.[83] Although the Tripartite Agreement confining Scindia Steam's share in coastal shipping to 100,000 gross tons had expired in 1939, on pretext of war the British authorities and the BI put off the framing of a fresh agreement. All Walchand's efforts with the government to get the agreement amended or cancelled and to win liberty for Scindias to increase their tonnage and to participate in overseas traffic were in vain. Not only was Scindia Steam unable to increase its freight business during the Second World War, but on the contrary, since 16 out of its 19 steamers were requisitioned by the government for carrying munitions and troops, the business left to it was purely nominal, and British companies enjoyed a practical monopoly not only of overseas, but also of coastal, shipping.[84] At the end of the war Scindias' gross tonnage had come down to 72,000 tons, eight of its steamers having been sunk in the war and those returned by the government having badly deteriorated.[85]

1. *Equipment.* The most vital equipment of the shipping industry was of course the ships, and in the absence of a shipbuilding industry, the shipping companies in India had to rely for the supply of ships on British sources. The weakness of a shipping industry without a supporting shipbuilding industry was amply demonstrated by the early difficulties of Walchand in repairing the *Loyalty* and purchasing the six steamers of Palace Shipping Line in England in 1920. The Government of Britain was at first reluctant to sanction the purchase of the steamers and finally gave their consent to the transaction only with the proviso that no more ships were to be purchased by Scindias for the moment. Walchand's purchase of six steamers with a gross tonnage of 26,734, against the reluctance of other Scindia directors to take such a bold step at one throw, paid dividends in the long run. But initial difficulties were encountered in obtaining assistance from

[82] Ibid., file no. 326.   [83] *Walchand Hirachand*, p. 388.
[84] Ibid., p. 550.   [85] Ibid., p. 560.

stevedoring and bunkering firms, which had been threatened by BISN. Walchand solved the problem by setting up a subsidiary concern called Eastern Bunkerers' Ltd. (initially a private firm called Nanavati & Verina which had been running a stevedoring and bunkering business with success). The difficulties and expenses of repairing the *Loyalty* in England also persuaded Narottam Morarji and Walchand Hirachand to bring the celebrated shipping engineer Knudsen from England to Bombay with the idea of starting at first a plant for repairing ships and then a yard for building ships. But the untimely death of Knudsen led to the postponement of these projects.[86] In 1935 Walchand renewed the attempt to start a plant for repair of steamers and requested the Chairman of the Calcutta Port Commissioners for a site. But the Port Commissioners' Chairman was not helpful in this matter and Walchand's attempt at getting a site in Calcutta was frustrated.[87] Finally, upon the outbreak of the Second World War, Walchand obtained a suitable site in Visakhapatnam for a shipbuilding yard. The policy was now to take advantage of the war requirements for launching a shipbuilding enterprise at one throw instead of a step by step programme of expanding the mercantile marine, building a plant for repair of vessels and setting up a yard for building ships. Walchand's idea was that once the shipbuilding yard had been set up to supply war requirements, the industry would continue to grow after the cessation of hostilities by supplying the needs of India's growing marine transport. He reckoned that building ships would not be technologically difficult, since all raw materials were available in India except engines, propellers and some other machinery, which would have to be imported initially. But he entertained no illusions about the attitude of the government. Sivaswami Iyer wrote in a letter that government would not dare to impose restrictions on the new enterprise (though no help could be expected from the government in view of the key importance of the shipbuilding industry in Britain). He replied: 'As regards the Shipbuilding industry, I fully agree with you that we cannot expect any encouragement and help from the British Government in the development of the Shipbuilding Industry in this country, but I wonder if they would not impose any restrictions in connection therewith.'[88] The initiation of the shipbuilding industry was thus purely a result of patriotic private

[86] Ibid., pp. 176–7.   [87] Ibid., pp. 308–9.
[88] Ibid., pp. 380–1.

initiative and events fully bore out Walchand's misgivings about official obstruction.

The problem of the Indian shipping industry was that it could not become strong and self-sufficient without a shipbuilding industry, but on the other hand the shipbuilding industry had to await the expansion of the mercantile marine. In Japan NYK had acquired 140 steamers before government stepped in to assist the shipbuilding industry; but the growth of NYK itself was the result of government contribution of a quarter of its capital and official guarantee of 8 per cent interest on the balance of the share capital. The result of government assistance was the rapid growth of the shipbuilding industry in Japan and consequent attainment of self-sufficiency by the Japanese shipping industry between the 1890s and the 1920s.[89] The Indian mercantile marine, which until the outbreak of the Second World War had succeeded in obtaining only 21 per cent of coastal shipping and had been excluded from overseas shipping, had been stunted by government indifference, and yet without its growth a steamship-building industry could not hope to find a market at home. It was not until the extraordinary demand for vessels upon the outbreak of the Second World War provided a special incentive that a shipbuilding industry could be started in India under purely private initiative. Had government assistance been forthcoming, a start could have been made as early as the twenties. The Indian Mercantile Marine Committee in 1924 had in fact recommended that government should help setting up a steamship-building company by providing one-third of its capital and placing all government and port trust orders with it. But these recommendations received no consideration from the government until the outbreak of the Second World War.

It might have been expected that the special requirements of war would bring about a change in government policy, but Scindias' request for government assistance for a shipbuilding yard during the Second World War met with the cold and extraordinary response that the Government of India had decided 'not to encourage actively the merchant shipbuilding industry in India as a part of their war effort'. This was at a time when the Government of India was desperately placing orders for ships in America, Australia and Canada, and was even proposing to construct a ship-yard in Turkey by giving a £2 million loan to the Turkish government.[90] But Walchand had been expecting this and had started construction of a shipbuilding

[89] Ibid., pp. 307–8.   [90] *Saga of Scindia*, pp. 128–30.

yard at Visakhapatnam with no expectation of government aid. Even such a courageous and self-reliant enterprise proved helpless in the face of restrictions imposed by the government. Government's sanction for essential imports from Britain during the war was not forthcoming, and when in spite of that some progress in construction of a ship-yard had been achieved, the government ordered the removal of all equipment at Visakhapatnam to Bombay for urgent repairing of vessels damaged in the war. Not until March 1946 did Walchand succeed in shifting back the equipment from Bombay to Visakhapatnam. By getting the construction done piecemeal, he had a yard with two berths completed in 1947. Next year Scindias built their first two steamers.

2. *Capital and enterprise.* Scindia Steam Navigation Co. was a co-operative venture launched with great resources of enterprise, managerial talent and capital; it could not have survived and grown without these resources. Unlike other enterprises in India such as steel, this was not a family concern and from the beginning its management was highly professionalized and its control was vested in a broad group of big and courageous capitalists with a patriotic outlook. The company was floated by Walchand Hirachand,[91] who supplied the initial drive and subsequent energy behind this patriotic enterprise; Narottam Morarji brought to it the reputation and large resources of the great cotton textile house of Morarji Goculdas; and Lalubhai Samaldas's and Kilachand Devchand's vast trading connections ensured it a market. It was managed with great ability by outstanding executives, such as M. A. Master, Sarabhai Haji and G. L. Mehta, whose professional skills and experience went with partriotic commitment and political imagination. But above all it was the dogged determination of Walchand Hirachand, who unlike J. N. Tata showed himself ready to bear certain and enormous losses, and to reject attractive offers from BI for purchase of Scindia Steam, that the company turned the corner between 1919 and 1923. Narottam Morarji, Lalubhai Samaldas and other directors of Scindias were at one stage ready to sell the whole concern to BI, but Walchand averted this calamity to national enterprise by skilful manoeuvres.[92]

Because of the large and prestigious group which stood behind this co-operative venture, there was no difficulty in raising the initial

[91] *Walchand Hirachand*, pp. 397–403.
[92] Ibid., pp. 171–209.

share capital of Rs 4.5 crores, a large chunk of which apparently came from Maharajas, princes, zamindars, sardars and other feudal elements, about whose hoarded wealth and unwillingness to invest much had been heard from interested British quarters.[93] So far as coastal shipping was concerned, Scindias were in fact able to finance more than double the tonnage allowed by the agreement with BISN. In 1928 Scindia Steam, applying to the government for revision of this agreement, stated that it could provide the necessary finance for an additional 80,000 tons of shipping costing Rs 1.6 crores, in the following manner: (1) Rs 50 lakhs in cash, (2) Rs 60 lakhs by allotment of 4,00,000 shares of Rs 15 each not yet allotted (capital already paid up being Rs 90 lakhs, namely, 6,00,000 shares of Rs 15 each quoted at the time at about Rs 20), and (3) Rs 50 lakhs to be borrowed from the builders of the new ships.[94] Clearly this showed the reputation for financial soundness which Scindias had acquired by 1928. Overseas shipping, however, required additional financial resources which Scindias were not in a position to raise at that time without government assistance. It was estimated that to enter the foreign trade Scindias required 10 ships with 7,000 tons gross tonnage costing about Rs 150 lakhs. For raising this sum Scindias asked the Government of India in vain for a loan at $\frac{1}{2}$ per cent above the government rate of borrowing, navigation bounties, and preference in carriage of government stores from Britain to India. There is also some evidence that the existing Indian shipping enterprise (there were few Indian entrepreneurs willing to face the enormous risks taken by Walchand) was stretched to the limit in fighting for its share of coastal shipping and that a broader supply of reckless private initiative was needed for venturing into overseas shipping without government aid. When the Government of India refused aid to the proposed Hind Lines in 1936, Walchand Hirachand, who was already interested in transport of Haj pilgrims and manufacture of automobiles, aeroplanes and ships, was compelled to bring the scheme for the Hind Lines to a full stop. It is interesting to note that G.D. Birla, whom also Walchand Hirachand had associated with the scheme, was similarly committed to a great variety of new enterprises.[95] The number of pioneers in Indian industry being limited, the existing ones were fully engaged in taking advantage of the new lines of enterprise which were opening up in the late thirties.

As it was, Scindias ran into financial trouble by venturing into the

[93] Ibid., p. 63.   [94] Ibid., p. 224.   [95] Ibid., pp. 267, 271.

steamship-building enterprise without government aid. Scindias diverted their war profits and fresh capital to the extent of Rs 5 crores to the Visakhapatnam shipyard. As a result of the establishment of this key national industry and in the absence of timely government help, Scindias had to mortgage all their assets and raise debentures of Rs 5 crores in 1948 for running its legitimate shipping business. This came at a time when Scindias had spent Rs 2 crores in repairing old ships worn out in the war and was proposing to spend a further Rs 5 crores for a passenger service between India and the U.K.[96] As a result the shipbuilding yard at Visakhapatnam had to be nationalized and a new management was appointed for the Scindias under government auspices in 1949, Walchand having voluntarily retired. Thirty years had elapsed since 1919 when he first purchased the *Loyalty* with 5,934 gross tons; he left the company in 1949 with 54 steamers totalling 2,23,384 gross tons.[97]

3. *Technical training.* Scindias followed a systematic policy of training Indians for the navigation, marine engineering and wireless branches. Though initially there were great difficulties in finding technically qualified Indians, an energetic policy with regard to technical training ultimately enabled Scindias to employ Indians exclusively as deck and engine officers, and wireless operators. Of considerable help in this matter was the nautical training for Indians on the *Dufferin* arranged by the Government of India in accordance with the recommendations of the Indian Mercantile Marine Committee. Initially the *Dufferin* trained only navigation officers, but in 1935, under the pressure of Indian lines which were compelled to employ only foreigners as marine engineers, arrangements were made by the government in Bombay and Calcutta for higher training in marine engineering. One initial difficulty was finding employment for trained Indians, since the British lines plying on the coast were unwilling to employ Indians. The *Dufferin* in its first ten years turned out 132 nautical trainees, of whom Scindias could absorb no more than 32 while British ships took on only 10. The flow of young Indians for nautical training would have dried up under these conditions of unemployment but for the action of the Indian National Steamship Owners Association (INSOA) which pressed the matter on the government and moved the authorities to compel the British liners on the coast to give more employment to Indians.[98]

[96] Ibid., pp. 580–1.   [97] Ibid., pp. 585–6.
[98] Ibid., pp. 244–5.

4. *Foreign monopoly.* Ultimately it was not supply factors like capital, enterprise or technical skill which inhibited the growth of Indian shipping in the inter-war period, but the strength of British monopoly. Since 1914 P&O and BI had been brought together under the Inchcape empire, which thus acquired complete interlocking control of India's overseas and coastal shipping. The enormous financial resources and political influence of the Inchcape concerns were used for upholding that monopoly. Before the First World War P&O and BI had succeeded in liquidating all Indian rivals by cutting rates, sometimes even below the working cost, and had usually managed to prevent Indian shippers from patronizing Indian liners by giving deferred rebates, a system that practically turned the latter into permanently attached tenants of British navigation concerns. After the First World War these monopolistic devices were no longer effective in excluding Indian competitors from the coastal carriage trade, but the monopoly power of British shipping was able to restrict the growth of Scindias and lesser concerns on the coast and to deny them a place in overseas carriage trade. Even after the agreement ending the rate war between BI and Scindia Steam, BI succeeded in maintaining its dominant position and keeping Scindias in place by obtaining special concessions from the port and railway authorities for disembarkation and despatch of goods, keeping rates down to a level which were adequate for a big company with large resources but not for a smaller competitor like Scindias, and sailing BI ships even with empty space when in normal circumstances they would have been berthed.[99]

The BI–Scindia agreement itself proved an efficient instrument for maintaining the former's monopoly position. In the first place, Scindias' sphere was restricted to the coastal carriage trade of India, Ceylon and Burma. Although Scindias were not yet in a position to run a regular overseas service, they had definite possibilities in the direction of the carriage trade along many routes east of Suez, including the Persian Gulf, East Africa, Java and Singapore. Scindias were prepared to ply steamers on these routes by 1928, but the agreement with BI prevented them from participating in the carriage trade to these regions, with which Indian traders had large dealings. Secondly, Scindias were restricted in their tonnage to the extent of half their real potential of expansion in 1928, and were denied many profitable routes along the coast under the working of the agreement. Thirdly,

[99] Ibid., pp. 206, 237.

Scindias were prohibited under the agreement from carrying passengers on the coastal routes. This also prevented them from carrying mail, which could not be sent on slower cargo ships. As a result the company could not profit by the postal subsidies of the Government of India, which were being paid to non-Indian liners.[100]

5. *Market*. Lack of overseas contacts compelled Scindias to abandon overseas shipping and to concentrate on coastal carriage business, but even in this more assured field there were initial difficulties in finding custom. Since the rice export business from Burma to India was almost entirely in the hands of Indian traders, Walchand started the coastal carriage trade on the Rangoon–Bombay line. Due to a financial crisis in 1921 in Burma, the only custom secured by Scindias was from some timber merchants of Moulmein and some small shippers of rice, who could not fill Scindia ships. Consequently a subsidiary concern called Narottam Ltd. for buying and selling rice had to be formed in order to fill Scindia ships. This subsidiary concern concentrated on importing rice, sugar and coal not only in Bombay, but in smaller ports like Bhavnagar, Marmagoa and Porbandar which had hitherto been neglected by British liners.[101] But it was not until 1924 that Burma-domiciled Indian traders gave wholehearted support to Scindias. In that year the company consolidated its position in the rice traffic from Rangoon and Moulmein.[102]

Scindia Steam's position considerably improved in 1926 with the opening of the Okha port, in the construction of which Walchand and Scindias actively assisted the Baroda State. The cargo unloaded at this port quickly increased from 14,000 tons in 1926–7 to 68,000 tons in 1931–2. Cargo loaded at Okha in 1926–7 for foreign ports was 2,000 tons; in 1931–2 Okha sent out a total cargo of 711,168 tons to other ports. Scindia largely benefited from this increase in carriage trade as the first big concern to enter the field. Walchand was the director of some cement and salt works around the Okha port and had close relations with the ruler, his ministers, and the traders and industrialists of Baroda State. Foreign shipping lines, which initially ignored the Okha port, began to send in their ships when trade increased. Scindias were largely instrumental in increasing the total carriage trade on the west coast by serving new and

---

[100] Ibid., pp. 223–4, 234.

[101] Ibid, p. 175.

[102] Walchand Hirachand Papers, file no. 326. Speech of Narottam Morarji as Scindia Chairman, 1924.

neglected ports.[103] Their entry into coastal carriage trade also compelled BI to lower the rates and this also led to the expansion of the
total market for navigation concerns. For example, Tatas were at
first unable to supply rails to Burma Railway on account of the high
rate of Rs 40 per ton demanded by BI for shipping the rails from
Calcutta to Rangoon, at a time when freight charges for shipping
exactly the same type of rails from Belgium to Rangoon were no
more than Rs 14 per ton. Afterwards Scindias carried Tata rails to
Burma at the same rate enjoyed by Belgian exporters. Again, BI used
to charge Rs 24 per ton for shipping cotton from Tuticorin to
Bombay, but upon the entry of Scindia the rate came down to Rs 12
per ton. The reduced coastal freight rates enabled Indian merchants
to send goods to distant markets, sell them at competitive rates and
expand their trade. BI monopoly, which had exercised for a long
time a pernicious effect on India's coastal trade, was put in check by
the entry of Scindia.[104]

6. *Government policy.* Throughout the period under review, the
Government of India was indifferent to the shipping and shipbuilding industry in India which, unlike the iron and steel industry, was
not considered vital to British strategic considerations in the East.
Moreover, throughout the period British monopoly remained much
more firmly entrenched in this sphere than in cotton textiles and
steel, in which Japanese and Continental competition considerably
undermined British monopoly in India. Not surprisingly, the Government of India took no action to implement the recommendations of
the Indian Mercantile Marine Committee about reservation of the
coast for shipping companies registered in India, Indianization of
the coastal marine in twenty-five years and financing the shipbuilding
industry in India. To force the hand of the government, Walchand
Hirachand had his officer, Sarabhai Haji, elected to the Legislative
Assembly in order to pilot a Reservation of Coastal Traffic Bill. The
Bill was disapproved by the Secretary of State, Lord Birkenhead,
by senior officials of the India Office in London, as well as by the
Viceroy of India, Lord Irwin, and his officials. Representatives of
the Government of India gave tacit support to British Commerce
members in the Indian Legislative Assembly in their opposition to
the Bill. Sarabhai Haji obtained important support for the Bill from
Motilal Nehru, Lajpat Rai, Shanmukham Chetty and G. D. Birla in

[103] *Walchand Hirachand*, pp. 215–17.
[104] Ibid., pp. 260–1.

the Assembly, and a resolution approving the Bill in principle was passed by a majority of 71 votes to 46 in 1928. But on one pretext or another, government deferred action on coastal reservation. Next year, when Sarabhai Haji resigned from the Assembly in deference to the Complete Independence resolution of the Congress directing its followers to resign from the legislative assemblies, the matter of coastal reservation went into cold storage.[105] Coastal reservation was finally disposed of in the Government of India Act which ruled that there was to be no discrimination against British ships in the Indian coastal trade.

The distribution of patronage by the government assumed an almost automatically discriminatory character on account of the monopoly position of British lines. Scindias were not permitted to carry passengers (and therefore not mail either) under their agreement with BI. Thus a virtual monopoly of government postal subsidies was enjoyed by the BI – P&O combine. When Lord Inchcape came to India in 1922–3 as head of the Retrenchment Committee, he accepted no remuneration for his services to the Government of India, but during his stay he succeeded in securing for BI the mail contract of the government worth five lakhs of rupees a year.[106] P&O also enjoyed the special privilege of carrying mail between Britain and India, for which it received from the Indian treasury Rs 6.86 lakhs a year.[107] In 1928 Scindia Steam requested that it should be given the right to carry mail and government stores on a par with BISN and P&O.[108] No official action could be taken on this request, since government refused to assist Scindias in getting their one-sided agreement with BI, about not carrying passengers, revised. It may be noted in this connection that the postal subsidies had in the past proved vitally important in fostering British shipping and were no small matter for the infant Indian shipping industry. The *Economist* observed on 21 November 1934:

The lions of our liner trades were nurtured throughout their formative years by Government postal subsidies. The money was paid out in the form of contracts between the Government and the shipowners for the carriage of mail on what subsequently became the main trade routes of Britain to the rest of the world. British merchant shipping policy administered through the mail contracts clearly set the precedent which American and other nations are now following.[109]

[105] Ibid., pp. 240–1.   [106] Ibid., p. 262.   [107] Ibid., p. 179.
[108] Ibid., p. 223.   [109] Ibid., p. 262.

If in peace-time the monopoly position of the British-registered shipping companies enabled them also to monopolize the patronage of the government, in wartime the differential controls on shipping imposed by the authorities in Britain and in India served to widen the disparity in the position of British and Indian ships. Walchand Hirachand complained in the *Free Press Journal* on 17 September 1943 that during the Second World War licensing of ships, restrictions on their movements and restrictions on the nature of the cargo to be carried applied only to ships on the Indian register and not on British ships plying on the Indian coastal trade.[110] The Government of India, moreover, requisitioned Scindia's ships in particularly busy seasons, when large profits were to be earned by carriage of Burma rice.[111]

But above all, it was the shipbuilding industry on which restrictions applied by the Government of India had the most crippling effect during the Second World War. In his speech at the first meeting of the Policy Committee on shipping appointed by the Government of India in 1944, Walchand pointed out:

A full-fledged shipbuilding yard owned, controlled and managed by Indians already exists in the country today. India, however, is not allowed to build ocean-going ships. Both His Majesy's Government and the Government of India consider that the building of such ships in India will not be war effort. And yet the cry went forth everywhere 'Let us have ships, more ships and still more ships' during the period of war. Nothing has shown up more glaringly the subservience of the Government of India to vested interests, at the cost of Indian interests, than their indifference—I shall not use a stronger word—to allow the Indians to build ocean-going ships in their own land.

In view of this Walchand concluded bitterly: 'we have a Government which take their instructions from Whitehall, not for the benefit of India, but for furthering the interests of England.'[112]

7. *Economic nationalism*. It was the rise of economic nationalism during and after the First World War that undermined the power of British shipping companies to exclude Indian competitors from

[110] Walchand Hirachand Papers, file no. 616, Discrimination against Indian Shipping.
[111] Ibid., file no. 326, Walchand Hirachand's speech as Scindia Chairman, 1941.
[112] Ibid., file no. 590, Development of Indian Shipping, speech of Walchand Hirachand, 7 December 1944.

coastal traffic altogether. Since British monopoly of shipping was powerfully upheld by the policies of the Government of India, Walchand realized quite early in the battle for *swadeshi* navigation that the war must be waged on a political as well as an economic front. By skilful political moves he built up an agitation in favour of *swadeshi* navigation that ultimately forced Lord Inchcape to come to a compromise. The first move of Walchand was to lobby the Fiscal Commission which, on the basis of a memorandum on the existing state of Indian sea transport submitted by him, recommended that an Indian Mercantile Marine should be brought into being since the resultant lowering of freight rates along the coast would stimulate Indian industries. A direct consequence of the Fiscal Committee recommendation was the appointment of the Indian Mercantile Marine Committee, which gave Walchand and his assistants another opportunity to press the case for Indian shipping. These changes in the political climate of the country, especially the anti-British feeling generated by the non-cooperation movement, brought about a change of BI policy towards Scindias. BI was capable of indefinitely prolonging the rate war against Scindias, whose reserves were fast running out. But Lord Inchcape, who sensed the change in the political climate of India during his Retrenchment Committee work, came to the conclusion that such a course would be inadvisable in view of its incalculable repercussions on public opinion.

Changing his strategy, Lord Inchcape at first made a very attractive offer for purchase of Scindia ships, which Scindia shareholders rejected following an appeal from Narottam Morarji: 'It lies not in my mouth to tell you that, should you regard these matters from the angle of temporary and personal gain, and sell the company, it will be a blow to our country's prestige, with a probability of unwelcome repercussions in India's industrial life, and that our first duty is to adopt the national viewpoint and prevent these things.'[113] In spite of the rejection of the offer by Scindia shareholders, Narottam Morarji continued negotiations with Lord Inchcape under pressure from Lalubhai Samaldas and other directors. At one stage, when it seemed as though the deal would be completed in spite of Walchand's strenuous opposition, Walchand inspired a leading article in the *Bombay Chronicle* of 14 February 1923 strongly criticizing the negotiations:

[113] *Walchand Hirachand*, p. 187.

Mr Narottam Morarji has been an heir to a noble fortune and a nobler name. The Scindia concern, however, he has not inherited, but originated. It is his own contribution to the industrial commercial progress of his country. Let him see to it that he proves himself worthy of his name and fortune, by refusing to betray his own unique enterprise. By his deeds let him be judged, and we tremble at the mere thought of the judgement the country and posterity will pass on him, if in this instance he allows the Scindia concern to be sold to one formidable rival in the seas.[114]

Negotiations for the purchase of Scindia property by the BI broke down in these circumstances, Lord Inchcape characterizing Scindias' trespass into BI's maritime field as piracy and Walchand flinging back with passionate conviction: 'Who are the pirates? We or you?'[115] Once the take-over bid by Lord Inchcape had failed, BI recognized the right of Scindias to exist in the agreement of 1923. It was thus the political climate of the country, surcharged with nationalism, that ensured the survival of Scindias at immense odds.

The subsequent growth of shipping in India was also largely due to the steady build-up of political pressure in the country and the combination of Indian shipping interests under a nationalist banner. Walchand's object in pressing the coastal reservation bill through the Indian Legislative Assembly was not really its enactment, which he knew was beyond reach, but the building-up of public opinion in favour of Indian shipping by focusing on this issue. As he wrote to his office from Britain in 1925, 'This Bill is the salvation of the Scindia company from every point of view. If anything is going to frighten, or rather straighten, Inchcape, it is the passage or at least the agitation for this bill. All possible "noise" should be made, and I would consider money spent on this "propaganda" as money well spent.'[116] The immediate object of pressing the bill, the revision of the existing one-sided agreement between BISN and Scindias before its expiry, was not achieved. However, the next agreement hammered out at the Tripartite Conference under the auspices of Sir Joseph Bhore definitely allowed Scindias more scope to expand. Scindias also benefited substantially from the civil disobedience movement in the early thirties. One reason for BI's refusal to revise its one-sided agreement with Scindias before its expiry was stated by a representative of Lord Inchcape to the Commerce Member, Sir George Rennie, as follows: 'Looking to the good of the B.I., we cannot concur in Mr Walchand's proposals and policies, nor associate ourselves with them.

[114] Ibid., p. 189.   [115] Ibid., p. 191.   [116] Ibid., p. 215.

In view of the way in which his company is taking advantage of the current boycott agitation in India, it is utterly out of the question for us to modify our policy and come to an understanding with him.'[117] During the civil disobedience movement, many Indian merchants boycotted foreign ships and in particular Bombay rice traders brought their rice from Rangoon only on Scindia ships.[118]

The refusal of many Indian merchants to benefit by the private concessions and cut in rates offered by BI was matched by the willingness of Scindias to come to the aid of smaller Indian shipping companies even when they could benefit by combining with foreign lines. In 1930 Walchand had established the INSOA which served as an instrument of unity for Indian lines and as a forum through which Scindias could exercise leadership of Indian shipping interests on a nationalist plank. Scindias came to the aid of four Indian lines operating on the coast which were threatened with extinction by a rate war in which the former had been invited to participate by the foreign lines; the company also helped out the Bengal–Burma, Indian Cooperative and Ratnagar companies by accepting their managing agency. Finally, by an appeal to the nationalist sentiment of Indian shareholders of Bombay Steam Navigation Company, Scindias were also able to take over this powerful foreign rival.

This spirit of nationalism, transcending immediate profit considerations and temporary expedients, which guided the actions of Walchand Hirachand, was strikingly demonstrated by his extraordinary step of refusing to invite any government officials to the foundation-stone ceremony of the first Indian shipyard at Visakhapatnam. In spite of his strict instructions, an invitation went out by mistake to the European Collector of Visakhapatnam. But the foundation was laid not by the Viceroy or the Governor, as might have been considered proper usage, but—at Walchand's invitation —by the President of the Indian National Congress, Babu Rajendra Prasad. The ultimate vision which lay behind this unprecedented step in Indian business annals was voiced by the invitee in no uncertain terms. Rajendra Prasad said in his speech:

Today we may not be able to give you anything more than our sympathy and moral support and even consolation in your disappointment, but there is always a tomorrow, and a brighter tomorrow, for a nation can never fail to rise. . . . If the Government, constituted as they are, are unwilling or unable to lend you active support in this

[117] Ibid., p. 257.   [118] Ibid., p. 258.

most praiseworthy and nation-building enterprise, that constitutes still further condemnation of the political system obtaining in this country, which is devoid of a national outlook or policy and which in vital matters subordinates the interests of India to the economic interests of Britain. Let me repeat that such a system cannot last because it is fundamentally against the spirit of the times and offends the deeper consciousness of the nation. When such a system is replaced by one that is representative of and responsible to the people of this country the serious grievances which you have ventilated and the injustices from which you suffer cannot but be removed and remedied.[119]

Conclusion

The exceptionally powerful British monopoly of the overseas and coastal carriage business of India, which unlike steel or textiles was not threatened by foreign competition, and the consequent unwillingness of the government to foster Indian enterprise in shipping, prevented an Indian breakthrough in this sphere until the end of the First World War. Obviously, exceptional entrepreneurship was necessary for a successful venture in this monopolized business, and the management of Scindia Steam proved to be unusually aggressive and long-sighted, with a broad and professionalized basis. That Walchand and his associates succeeded where a quarter of a century before Jamsetji Tata—with an equally large vision and equally large resources—had failed must be attributed to the changed political circumstances and the powerful current of nationalism after the war. Scindia Steam survived because, unlike Tata Line which was deserted by the Indian merchants, public opinion in India would not have allowed its destruction by foreign interests. However, the dominant P & O – BI combine, with tacit support from the authorities both in India and Britain, was able substantially to restrict the growth of Indian shipping by political agreements. Had the British government, in accordance with the will of the majority in the Indian legislature, decided to reserve the coastal traffic for Indian shipping companies, then under the provisions of the Coastal Reservation Bill *swadeshi* companies would have obtained more than half of the coastal carriage business before the Second World War, whereas less than a quarter of that business was actually secured by native interests before the outbreak of war. With such an expanded share in coastal shipping and with a willingness on the part of the govern-

[119] Ibid., pp. 394–5.

ment to help rather than hinder steamship-building in India, the shipbuilding enterprise envisaged by Walchand from the very start of Scindias might have been launched before the Second World War, the outbreak of which in turn would have stimulated the new industry. As it was, Walchand had to wait until the war broke out to launch his long-awaited shipbuilding enterprise and then the obstructive attitude of the authorities delayed the building of ships, which might have rapidly grown under the war incentive, until after independence. Because the recommendations of the Indian Mercantile Marine Committee and the Indian Legislative Assembly were quietly set aside by the Government of India in the interests of British shipping monopoly, the advancement of Indian shipping and shipbuilding reached a stage by the time of Walchand's retirement in 1949 that could have been comfortably attained on the eve of the outbreak of the Second World War in 1939.

4. Coal

Growth

The growth of the coal industry in India from 1913 to 1944 took place by fits and starts, not by any planned policy for the industry as a whole or by any conscious choice of investment over a long period under the individual initiative of firms. The low quality of Indian coal, transport deficiency, inscrutable cycles, fluctuating prices, erratic and inelastic demand, low return on investment and refusal of government to intervene ruled out any long-term investment policy. Until the statutory fixation of prices of coal in 1944 and the production target fixed in 1956 under the five year plans, the prevailing conditions in the coal industry made it impossible for colliery owners to look forward with an intelligent appreciation of what would happen a year or two afterwards. As the chronicle of the Indian Mining Federation has stated,

The result has been that in periodic moments of tension caused either by outstripping demand or by transport shortage, the industry has been spurred on to achieve higher production but, as it happened on more than one historical occasion, having done so the industry has subsequently been overwhelmed in disappointment and frustration. When the prices have been low and the demand has been weak, the coal industry has unconsciously taken to an output increase programme in a bid to bring about a reduction of raising cost. It is by sheer coincidence of facts that disaster was averted by growth of new demand synchronizing with the period of increased production in a weak market.[120]

By an almost continuous increase of production during the First World War, coal output reached a peak of 22.6 million tons in 1919 from the pre-war production of 14.7 million tons. The depletion of wagon supply during the war led to a fall in production in the next few years, but by 1924, when the wagon supply situation had eased, production had recovered to 21.1 million tons. In 1925 there was a sharp fall in prices, which again reduced production to 20.9 million tons. From 1927 again, under a continuous cost reduction drive, production was pushed up to 23.8 million tons in 1930. Compared to 1920, prices were approximately 40 per cent lower and output approximately 40 per cent higher in 1930. The coming of the Great Depression in this state of overproduction struck the coal industry extremely hard and reduced its output by over four million tons in three years, so that in 1933 output stood at the 1921–2 level of 19 million tons. In the midst of these overwhelming difficulties, the industry once again embarked on a cost reduction drive, gearing up output to 22.6 million tons in 1936 by three annual stages. At this point a substantial increase in demand helped the recovery of the industry, though by 1938 the output was abnormally inflated in a basically weak market. The intervention of the Second World War saved the industry from this implicit state of overproduction. However, wagon shortage and labour difficulties in 1942–3 brought production down from 29.3 million tons in 1940 to 25.8 million tons in 1944. In that year government stepped in to fix prices. The conditions in the coal industry were fundamentally altered and from now on there was never a break in the continuous expansion of output (see Table 21).

1. *Raw materials.* India enjoyed large coal deposits which were far in excess of the needs of her adolescent industries, but the possibilities of export to distant countries on a large scale were restricted by the low quality of much of her coal. Good quality coking coal was scarce and only 7 per cent of the total deposits was coking coal. The ash content was high, even first class coal in Bengal rarely containing less than 12 per cent ash and that in use at the TISCO works containing 17 per cent ash. However, though not of good

[120] *Indian Mining Federation, Golden Jubilee Souvenir 1913–1963: Fifty Years of the Indian Coal Industry and the Story of the Indian Mining Federation,* Calcutta, 1963, p. 15. Henceforth referred to as *Fifty Years of Coal.*

TABLE 21
COAL PRODUCTION IN INDIA 1905–52

Year	Tons (million)	Factors Governing Output from year to year
1905	8.4	Stock exchange boom in coal shares.
1908	12.4	High coal prices.
1912	14.7	Market expansion due to TISCO; wagon shortage.
1914	16.4	Wartime demand.
1917	18.2	Do.
1918	20.7	Do.
1919	22.6	Increasing demand.
1920	17.9	Wagon shortage; high prices.
1921	19.0	New demand due to IISCO; high prices.
1922	19.0	Market expansion; high prices.
1924	21.1	Increase of wagon supply.
1925	20.9	Fall in prices.
1930	23.8	Cost reduction by output increase.
1932	20.1	Slump.
1933	19.7	Do.
1936	22.6	Cost reduction by output increase.
1937	25.0	Do.; recovery of prices; wagon shortage.
1938	28.2	Market expansion; cost reduction by output increase.
1940	29.3	War demand.
1942	29.4	Do.
1943	25.3	Acute wagon shortage; labour difficulties.
1944	25.8	Continuing labour shortage; wagon crisis; fixation of coal prices.
1952	36.8	Development under fixed prices.

SOURCE. *Fifty Years of Coal.*

quality, Indian coal was certainly the cheapest in the world at pit-head prices. The cost of working the mines, most of which were shallow or outcropping mines, was very low.[121]

2. *Labour.*[122] The low wages of labour also helped to keep down the pit-head prices of coal. Per man productivity was not unsatisfactory in comparison with advanced countries in 1921 (see Table

[121] Buchanan, *Capitalist Enterprise*, pp. 258–9.

[122] For the role of land control in ensuring labour supply and the heavy reliance on labour contractors who often discharged entrepreneurial functions, see C. P. Simmons, 'Recruiting and Organizing an Industrial Labour Force in India: The case of the Coal Mining Industry, *c.* 1880–1939', in *Indian Economic and Social History Review*, October–December 1976.

TABLE 22
COAL OUTPUT (tons per head)

Country	1921	1932	1938
England	178	323	369
France	203 (1919)	255	282
Belgium	193	229	317
Japan	136	421	281 (1936)
India	162	170	205

SOURCE. Vera Anstey, *Economic Development*, p. 240.

22). However, in subsequent years, India progressively fell behind these countries in per man coal output. Labour was drawn mainly from the lower strata of tribal agriculturists in the districts around the coalfields of Raniganj and Jharia, and though this labour supply was unstable on account of the strong links of the miners with the land, no absolute shortage of labour was experienced until 1942–3, when high wages prevailing in other industries began to draw labour away from the coalfields, where food and cloth prices had become prohibitive. Energetic government action to ensure labour supply to the coalfields as a means of safeguarding essential war supplies of coal helped mitigate this crisis.[123] In normal circumstances the exceptionally poor agricultural belt around the coalfields and the high proportion of landless tribal population ensured supply of cheap labour to the mines. The irregular hours and work of the miners was a target of criticism. Not only would the miners flee whenever the crops were good, but they had also no fixed hours of work.[124] They entered and left the mines when they felt so inclined. While the quality of labour kept the technological level of mining low, it cannot be said that Indian mining was at a disadvantage compared to other countries in terms of cost of labour per ton of coal. Even when wages rose substantially after the war, pit-head prices of coal in India remained lower than in any other country except South Africa.[125] Colliery owners in Raniganj and Jharia enjoyed the advantage of large numbers of female workers, who were not only less costly but also more tractable than male workers. In 1927 over 28 per

[123] *Fifty Years of Coal*, pp. 139–44.
[124] Buchanan, op. cit., pp. 272.
[125] Vera Anstey, op. cit., p. 235.

cent of the miners in the coalfields were women, employed both in the mines and overground.[126]

3. *Equipment.* One reason why the Indian coal-mines fell behind in per man productivity in the inter-war period was the primitive mining equipment used. Vera Anstey observed:

The root trouble in the industry is that, while coal-mining has now become a scientific, and in some ways a chemical industry, India still attempts to carry it on by means of hand-shovelling and loading. What is needed is the introduction of up-to-date mechanical appliances and methods, worked by a stable body of trained and well-fed workers. Under such conditions the industry would undoubtedly be able to supply neighbouring internal markets with industrial power at reasonable and profitable price for many years to come, even if all efforts at supplying foreign and far distant internal markets were abandoned.[127]

Some of the big European mining companies had already adopted the solution suggested by Vera Anstey, and Buchanan noted that the output per person in one of the mines with up-to-date mechanical hauling apparatus and first class equipment was double the average for Bengal and Bihar.[128]

4. *Capital and enterprise.* The adoption of up-to-date equipment implied heavier investment by colliery owners. Throughout the period, however, coal-mining in India was characterized by low capital intensity compared to jute or cotton textiles. Pointing out the reason for this, the chronicle of the Indian Mining Federation states that 'the return on the investment in the coal industry as a whole has been low notwithstanding the ups and downs of the market over the last four or five decades and most assuredly in the earlier period.'[129] (See Table 23.) Since for the majority of the companies in the inter-war period there were very low profits and sometimes none at all, the total operating surplus being ploughed back in the coal industry as a whole was low compared to cotton textiles, iron and steel, cement and sugar.

Some companies, as Buchanan noted, did pay large dividends in spite of the difficulties of the coal industry.[130] The profitable companies were usually large companies with up-to-date mechanical devices, managed by big European managing agencies based on Calcutta. In 1924 big European companies producing above 50,000

---

[126] Buchanan, op. cit., p. 273.

[128] Buchanan, op. cit., p. 260.

[130] Buchanan, op. cit., pp. 266–7.

[127] Vera Anstey, op. cit., p. 241.

[129] *Fifty Years of Coal*, p. 12.

TABLE 23
PROFIT OF THREE COAL COMPANIES 1925–54
(Gross Block in Lakhs Rs and profit in percentages to Gross Block)

Unit	1925	1935	1943	1954
'A' Company:				
Gross Block	197	211	268	355
Profit	4.5	1.6	6.4	7.8
'B' Company:				
Gross Block	74	118	179	366
Profit	2.6	2.4	1.3	2.0
'C' Company:				
Gross Block	229	250	269	410
Profit	6.4	1.3	1.6	2.4

SOURCE. *Fifty Years of Coal*, Table no. 2, pp. 13–14.

tons of coal produced 12.4 million tons out of the total output of 21.1 million tons in India. Big European coal companies, such as Bengal Coal Company, Equitable Coal Company, New Beerbhoom Coal Company and Burrakur Coal Company, took the lead in developing the coal industry as a large-scale industry on a commercial basis in the late nineteenth century. Their ability to earn large profits and thus to expand their capital base and to apply mechanical devices was connected with their practical monopoly of the largest internal markets (railways and organized big industries) for good quality coal.

There was a large number of Indian-owned collieries of small size producing second class coal mainly for domestic consumption and brick manufacture.[131] Their opportunities for employing greater capital and mechanical devices were limited by the very nature of the coal which they produced and the market for it. One other problem connected with collieries of this type was subleasing on the lines of the *patni* system in agricultural land. The Indian Coal Fields Committee of 1946 concluded that the system of 'salami', by which sub-lessees could immediately get back a part of their capital outlay from under-lessees, had led to the fragmentation and subdivision of coal-mines into a large number of small and often uneconomic

[131] *Indian Mining Federation Report of the Committee 1913–1915.*

units.[132] But in so far as market opportunities permitted employment of greater capital and superior technology in India, there was no lack of capital and enterprise, which was supplied mainly by the large European managing agency houses of Calcutta.

5. *Foreign domination and racial discrimination.* The European managing agencies engaged in coal-mining also controlled jute mills, shipping companies, inland steamers, etc. and had political influence with the railway authorities. They were thus in a position to ensure a large market for their coal, bought mainly by the railways and the organized industries controlled by themselves. The horizontal concentration of jute, navigation and coal interests and the liaison between railway authorities and big Calcutta houses had the effect of denying small Indian colliery owners the largest and most profitable markets. They were also handicapped by the discrimination of the railway authorities in the distribution of wagons for coal dispatch, which involved them in heavy losses from time to time.[133] While these factors restricted the sphere of Indian enterprise in coal-mining, it is by no means clear that such racial discrimination had a restrictive effect on the growth of the coal industry as a whole. It was the European companies which had taken the lead in large-scale production and technological improvements. The financial and commercial monopoly advantages enjoyed by them in the industries of Eastern India as a whole were of definite assistance to the expansion of the coal industry amidst the uncertainties of the trade cycles.

6. *Economic nationalism.* In order to fight racial discrimination and foreign monopoly, Indian colliery owners set up in 1913 the Indian Mining Federation, a rival body to the European-dominated Indian Mining Association. The principal object of the Federation was to ensure a fair distribution of wagons between European and Indian companies, and incidentally to obtain a greater share of the railway custom for Indian companies and to create a wider market for second class coal by encouraging its use for domestic purposes in place of wood.[134] During the civil disobedience movement the Indian Mining Federation circularized an appeal to all Indian commercial

---

[132] M. M. Mehta, *Indian Industries*, p. 73.

[133] For a fuller account of racial discrimination, *see* Ratna and Rajat Ray, 'European Monopoly Corporations and Indian Entrepreneurship, 1913–1922: Early Politics of Coal in Eastern India', in *Economic and Political Weekly*, 25 May 1974.

[134] *IMF Report 1913–1915.*

associations to extend special support to collieries under Indian ownership and this appeal was strongly supported by the national-istic Federation of Indian Chambers of Commerce. A special deputa-tion of the Indian Mining Federation even proceeded to Ahmedabad to wait on the Working Committee of the Congress, but subsequently the plan for a press advertisement campaign was given up and the practical outcome seemed to have been negligible.[135] Just as racial discrimination does not appear to have been a restrictive factor in the coal industry, economic nationalism does not seem to have been a significant factor in favour of its growth either. Undoubtedly the Federation was of some assistance in securing railway custom for second class coal, though its campaign for popularization of second class coal for domestic use did not make any great headway. However, without its active role the development of second class coal in India would have been slower. The growth of second class coal under its fostering care was not a particularly significant factor in industrial growth as a whole, since organized industries like iron and steel relied mainly on first class coal.

7. *Government policy.* Government controls imposed on the colli-eries during the two world wars were designed for the benefit not so much of the coal industry itself as of the railways and other essential industries which consumed coal. Again during the inter-war period government followed a policy of non-intervention regarding the trade cycles which affected the coal industry, and this refusal to intervene in favour of the coal industry also helped other industries, especially the steel industry which, as we have seen, was saved from a difficult situation during the Great Depression by the steep fall in coal prices. The chronicler of the Indian Mining Federation has complained:

Actually, the industry has throughout its long history been made to play a subservient role in the economic mechanism of the country. The Railways, the consuming industries and the Government had each their reasons to find their interest staked in the coal industry. . . . Historically speaking, it is correct to say that the policy regard-ing coal in India has been purely instrumental, i.e. the industry has never been conceded the right to live and thrive for itself but only to eke out a career as an instrument for furtherance of interests other than its own.[136]

While, however, the chronic state of overproduction and recurrent

[135] *Fifty Years of Coal*, pp. 71–2.   [136] Ibid., p. 3.

price falls in the coal industry placed it in an unsound position, it cannot be said that government refusal to intervene in these circumstances was harmful to the growth of the major industries which relied on supply of coal.

During the Great Depression, the Indian Mining Association and the Indian Mining Federation jointly put forward to the government a coal output restriction scheme but the Government of India felt that restriction would do nothing to assist a real rise in demand, without which the existing disequilibrium between the market and the productive capacity could never be set right on a permanent basis. On the other hand, restriction of output might possibly delay the recovery of the market, since an artificial boosting of coal prices under the scheme might tend to retard the general economic recovery. As it turned out subsequently, the refusal of the government to intervene enabled the industry, with its excess production capacity acquired under the cost reduction drive from 1934 onwards, to meet the exceptional requirements for coal upon the outbreak of the Second World War.

The statutory fixation of prices by the government in 1944 proved extremely beneficial to the coal industry, because by then conditions had altered fundamentally and the level of demand was at a much higher plane. The new price structure was not of course the only factor which explained the continuous growth of the coal industry from 1944. There were other stimulating factors, such as a growing export market. Nevertheless fixed prices made long-term planning possible for the first time for coal companies. In eight years from 1944 to 1952, the coal output rose by 11 million tons under these favourable conditions.

8. *Trade cycles.* Until the assumption of entire price control by the government in 1944, the coal industry suffered heavily from the trade cycles of the world capitalist system as it operated from the outbreak of the First World War. Export industries like tea and jute also proved vulnerable to these price-fluctuations, but the range of variation in the case of the coal industry, in spite of the fact that it was oriented mainly to the domestic market, seems to have been even wider. The average price of Bengal and Bihar coal, which stood at Rs 3–12 per ton in 1911, rose to Rs 14–10 in 1922 and fell to Rs 6–5 in 1926, thus fluctuating widely in the twenties. When the Great Depression struck the industry, prices tumbled down below the pre-war level, being only Rs 3–5 in 1935 and Rs 3–4 in 1936. Coal

prices began slowly to move upwards after this, rising to Rs 4–15 in 1937 and Rs 5–3 in 1938. At that level prices stabilized for the subsequent years right up to 1942, when the price of Bengal coal stood at Rs 4–14 per ton. In 1943 the prices of Bengal coal rose to Rs 7–8 per ton and next year government stepped in to fix prices.[137] However, the rise and fall of prices in the coal industry followed a periodical pattern of behaviour and were never as sharp and swift as in the case of jute and tea.

9. *Market.* The pace of industrialization in India during the period under review was not such as to ensure a rapidly growing market for coal. That market was characterized by lack of steadiness and inelasticity of demand, the single most important factor in determining the pattern of development in the coal industry.[138] Throughout the period the railways remained a most important customer for coal. After the First World War the railway consumption of coal ranged from 6 million to 6.5 million tons a year. By 1930 the railway off-take had crossed the 7 million ton mark, but from 1931 to 1933 it relapsed to the level of the early twenties. In the late thirties it again began to rise, reaching 8 million tons in 1937. From 1941 onwards, due to war conditions, the railway demand began to mount rapidly, until in 1944 the annual consumption stood at 10 million tons. Next year it dropped suddenly to 9 million tons.[139] The export market was naturally much more fluctuating. In 1920 exports reached the record level of 1.22 million tons. Then for a couple of years the coal industry made no exports worth mentioning. In 1926 exports revived to 0.6 million tons and rose further to 0.7 million tons in 1929. With the onset of the Depression, exports became negligible, standing below 0.2 million tons in 1936. From 1937 exports revived again and in 1940, as much as 2.1 million tons were exported. In 1944 exports suddenly went down to 0.1 million tons. Fortunately for the coal industry, imports of coal were negligible from the middle of the twenties. In the early twenties there were large imports, especially from South Africa: 1 million tons in 1921, 1.2 million tons in 1922, 0.6 million tons in 1923, and 0.4 million tons in 1924. During the remaining years of the twenties imports fell to 0.2 million tons and in the thirties to 0.1 million tons. During the Second World War there were practically no imports. The coal industry was therefore in a position to supply most of the requirements of organized industries in India. But these requirements again varied .periodically.

[137] Ibid., pp. 3, 26–7.   [138] Ibid., p. 8.   [139] Ibid., p. 9.

The demand from the jute mills and steamships naturally varied a great deal with world trade cycles. However, the consumption of coal by the cotton-textile industry showed gradual increase over a long period of time, which was uninterrupted even in the early thirties. The demand of the iron and steel industry varied a good deal. From 4.6 million tons in 1924 it rose to 5.1 million tons in 1925, fell to 4.7 million tons in 1931, descended to 3.2 million tons in 1942 and rose again to 5.5 million tons in 1945.[140] Bricks and tiles and domestic consumption also absorbed a highly fluctuating quantity of coal.[141]

10. *Transport.* Another factor which recurrently affected the coal industry was shortage of wagons, which ruled out any significant policy-making in advance. The demand–supply situation was determined not so much by the actual tonnage raised by the collieries, but by the tonnage finding effective facilities for dispatch. The Fiscal Commission noted in 1922: 'It is notorious that the railway facility for handling coal has become entirely inadequate. This serves to restrict the market and also to depress the price for that portion of the market, viz. railway companies, to which there is a certainty of being able to make delivery. We have no doubt that these conditions have reacted unfavourably on the coal industry . . .'[142] Another crucial problem connected with rail transport was the high freight on long haul, which tended to push up the price of Bengal Coal at Bombay and Karachi. In an address to the Viceroy in 1922, the Indian Mining Federation commented that incredible as it might appear, it was a fact that freight on one ton of coal from Natal to Bombay, or, with a little favourable exchange, even from Cardiff to Bombay, was lower than the freight on one ton of coal from Jharia to Bombay.[143] Much of the advantage of the low pit-head price of Bengal and Bihar coal was lost owing to heavy freight on the long haul to the large markets in western India, where South African coal often competed with Raniganj and Jharia.

Conclusion

The political factors associated with colonial rule did not have an adverse impact on the coal industry. But its growth was affected adversely by trade cycles, fluctuating markets and transport costs and shortages. Nevertheless the existence of this industry on a large

[140] Ibid., pp. 8–11.   [141] Ibid., pp. 91, 114.
[142] Ibid., p. 63.   [143] Ibid., p. 50.

scale amidst the exceptional difficulties of the period under review was ensured by the comparative price advantages of Raniganj and Jharia coal in relation to imported coal, which derived from cheap labour and shallow mining. Though the coal industry earned comparatively lower profits than many other organized industries, it thereby served the needs of organized industries better. Its growth was indeed faster than that which strict market considerations would have allowed.

5. Paper

Growth

The paper industry in its early stages was a nineteenth century European enterprise located in Bengal and dominated by Heilgers (who managed Titagarh Paper Mills Co.) and Balmer Lawrie (who managed Bengal Paper Mill Co.), two big managing agencies of Calcutta which had run the industry up to the First World War, in spite of stiff competition from European paper manufactured from cheap wood pulp, with the help of government purchase of Indian paper under the revised stores purchase policy from the 1880s and by coordinating production and pricing policies under the aegis of the Indian Paper Makers' Association. There were also a couple of Indian-managed paper manufacturing companies, Upper India Couper Mill and Deccan Paper Mill, which were on too small a scale to have any future. During the First World War the paper mills in India declared high dividends, but unlike jute or cotton-textiles the paper industry did not acquire much additional productive capacity on account of natural limitations. Only one new mill, India Paper Pulp Co. (1918), was set up by Andrew Yule after the war. From 1922 increased foreign competition brought about a crisis in the industry, which persuaded the Government of India to extend protection for seven years to certain branches of paper manufacture in 1925. As a result Indian production of the protected varieties of paper went up from 23,331 tons in 1924–5 to 34,867 tons in 1930–1, but due to increase of consumption in unprotected varieties of paper the proportion of imports to total consumption was virtually unchanged (see Table 24). In 1931–2 the protective duties on paper manufacture of certain kinds were raised still further, but the response of the industry to this incentive was sluggish and a real breakthrough was achieved only in the late thirties. Total

TABLE 24

PRODUCTION, IMPORTS AND COMSUMPTION OF PAPER 1924-5 TO 1930-1 (tons)

Period	Protected Varieties				All Varieties			
	(1) Production	(2) Imports	(3) Consumption	% of (1) to (3)	(4) Production	(5) Imports	(6) Consumption	% of (4) to (6)
1924–5	23,331	20,000	43,331	53.84	27,020	84,943	111,963	24.13
1925–6	24,689	17,000	41,689	59.22	28,221	87,414	115,635	24.40
1926–7	27,741	16,826	44,567	62.23	31,672	100,419	132,091	23.98
1927–8	30,491	18,090	48,581	62.76	34,678	104,450	139,128	24.92
1928–9	33,599	19,065	52,664	63.79	38,222	115,629	153,851	24.83
1929–30	33,491	20,093	53,584	62.52	38,609	137,018	175,627	21.98
1930–1	34,867	14,179	49,046	71.09	39,587	114,690	154,277	25.66

SOURCE. *Report of the Indian Tariff Board on the Grant of Protection to the Paper and Paper Pulp Industries*, Calcutta, 1931.

production of paper increased gradually from 40,558 tons in 1931–2 to 48,531 tons in 1936–7. Throughout this period, Indian paper mills supplied less than half of the total demand for paper (excluding newsprint, etc.) in India (see Table 25). During the next two years,

TABLE 25

PRODUCTION, IMPORTS AND CONSUMPTION OF PAPER (INCLUDING BOARDS, BUT EXCLUDING NEWSPRINT, OLD NEWSPAPERS, ETC., 1931–2 TO 1945–6)

(in tons)

Period	Production			Imports			Grand Total
	Pro-tected	Unpro-tected	Total	Pro-tected	Unpro-tected	Total	
1931–2	35,738	4,820	40,558	12,393	53,284	42,177	82,735
1932–3	35,370	4,847	40,217	11,490	71,886	57,082	97,299
1933–4	38,151	5,507	43,658	13,005	57,312	50,383	94,041
1934–5	40,084	4,517	44,601	11,163	45,542	55,952	100,553
1935–6	42,839	5,260	48,099	12,096	27,746	71,192	119,291
1936–7	43,364	5,167	48,531	11,840	10,438	65,128	113,654
1937–8	97,798	6,013	53,811	14,780	2,722	86,666	140,477
1938–9	51,938	7,265	59,198	13,471	5,745	70,783	149,981
1939–40	59,574	11,239	70,813	17,518	6,656	63,061	133,874
1940–1	65,608	22,054	87,662	9,787	12,188	27,534	115,196
1941–2	63,623	29,924	93,574	1,296	29,784	11,724	105,298
1942–3	65,350	28,210	93,560	860	45,592	3,582	97,412
1943–4	63,743	23,865	87,608	1,725	37,378	7,470	95,078
1944–5	63,120	36,932	100,052	2,346	44,789	9,002	109,054
1945–6	58,851	28,551	97,412	14,311	59,096	26,499	123,911

SOURCE. *Report of the Indian Tariff Board on the Grant of Protection to the Paper and Paper Pulp Industries,* Delhi, 1938; *Report of the Indian Tariff Board on the Continuance of Protection to the Paper and Paper Pulp Industries,* Bombay, 1947.

owing to massive investment by new Indian groups like Birla, Thapar, Dalmia and Bajoria, production jumped by 22 per cent to 59,198 tons. The Second World War further stimulated the industry, so that at the end of the war production had increased by 100.7 per cent in a decade to 97,412 tons. The most significant factor in this development was the rapid rise in the production of unprotected varieties of paper from 5,176 tons in 1936–7 to 58,851 tons in 1945–6 (at a time when production of protected varieties of paper maintained a steady annual average of 64,000 tons). Apparently the unprotected varieties of paper were getting sufficient coverage from the existing revenue duties. During this period Indian pulp proved suitable for a wide variety of papers, in which manufacture was successfully begun for the first time without protective duties. However, in some vital branches of paper manufacture, including newsprint, no beginning could be made on account of natural disadvantages, and India therefore continued to rely heavily on imports.

1. *Raw materials*. The primary reason why in spite of protection as early as 1925 a breakthrough in the paper industry occurred only in the late thirties was the lack of adequate supplies of paper pulp in India. Until the thirties, when bamboo pulp was developed on a commercial basis, the paper industry in India, in the absence of soft wood for making pulp, had to rely on sabai grass, supplies of which had to be brought from as far afield as Nepal, Panjab and UP to Bengal after paying heavy railway freight on a long haul (sometimes 900 miles) of bulky material. The Tariff Board in 1924 concluded that there was 'a natural limit to the quantity of paper which, under existing conditions, can profitably be made from this material, and that this limit has already been approached, if not exceeded'.[144] The possibility of replacing imports of wood pulp by indigenous bamboo pulp on a commercial basis was being explored since 1919, but when the Tariff Board went into the question of paper pulp supply once again in 1931, it was found that the development of bamboo pulp manufacture had been delayed so far because of inherent difficulties of mechanical treatment and digestion of bamboo and the refusal of the government, in accordance with the Tariff Board recommendations of 1924, to give financial assistance to the India Paper Pulp Co. under Andrew Yule.[145] However, progress achieved in the technology of bamboo pulp manufacture and extension of protection to indigenous pulp induced the paper mills under Heilgers, Balmer Lawrie and Andrew Yule to make arrangements for raising their paper pulp making capacity. Between the Tariff Board sessions of 1932 and 1938 these three groups spent in all Rs 47 lakhs on technical improvements in manufacture of bamboo pulp. Partly owing to improvements in the process of manufacture but mainly as a result of protection bamboo pulp replaced imported wood pulp as the main

[144] *Report of the Indian Tariff Board Regarding Grant of Protection to the Paper and Paper Pulp Industries*, Calcutta, 1924.
[145] Ibid., Calcutta, 1931.

9

element in the pulp admixture for paper manufacture during this period. Although with protective duties against imported wood pulp and reduction in the price of bamboo pulp, it became more economical to use indigenous pulp, the pulp making capacity of the mills in 1938 was still not adequate for their paper making capacity, so that they had to incur extra expenses on imports of wood pulp.[146] This problem was solved during the Second World War, when most mills increased their paper pulp making capacity. The decline in wood imports due to the exigencies of war was more than made up by the rise in the consumption of bamboo, sabai grass, waste paper and old rags by the mills (see Table 26). However, the breakthrough in bamboo pulp manufacture did not solve the problem

TABLE 26

PRODUCTION AND IMPORTS OF PAPER PULP IN INDIA

(in tons)

Category of Pulp	1931–2	1936–7	1944–5
1 Bamboo pulp	5,228	19,281	62,300
2 Sabai grass pulp	9,049	11,510	20,000
3 Pulp of other indigenous materials	5,992	7,919	23,000 (estimate)
4 Imported wood pulp	20,081	10,976	7,200

SOURCE. *Report of the Indian Tariff Board on the Grant of Protection to the Paper and Paper Pulp Industry*, Calcutta, 1938; *Report of the Indian Tariff Board on the Continuance of Protection to the Paper and Paper Pulp Industries*, Bombay, 1947.

NOTE. The quantity of pulp made in 1944–5 from other indigenous materials is estimated from the tonnage of waste paper (17,400 tons) and rags, cloth cuttings and hemp ropes (27,328 tons) used for making pulp on the assumption that slightly over half of the tonnage was turned into pulp (as was the case in 1936–7) when 7,919 tons of pulp was made from 14,776 tons of waste paper, rags, cloth cuttings and hemp ropes.

of pulp material for newsprint. The Indian Tariff Board in 1924 had concluded that by using bamboo or grass pulp, Indian mills could never produce newsprint (which required more than 75 per cent mechanical wood pulp) at a cost which would enable them to compete with imported newsprint.[147] Newspapers being

[146] Ibid., Calcutta, 1938.
[147] *ITB Report on Paper*, 1924.

ephemeral things, the overriding consideration in manufacture of newsprint was cheapness of pulp, and in this respect natural factors were against Indian manufacture. Till the end of the period under review, newsprint was wholly imported.

2. *Labour*. In 1938, when the paper industry was poised for a big leap in productivity, the Indian Tariff Board stated confidently that there was no difficulty in obtaining labour for the paper mills. In the established mills in Bengal the labour force appeared to have reached the maximum and it was thought that with technical improvements the number employed might decrease. From 1931-2 to 1936-7 the labour force had increased in the three European-managed mill companies of Bengal in the following manner: (1) India Paper Pulp Co., 710 to 800; (2) Bengal Paper Mill Co., 1,420 to 1,601; (3) Tita-garh Paper Mills Co., 2,670 to 3,277 (increase largely due to renovation and reconstruction work). Most of the labour employed in these mills was permanent and was not seasonal. The new mills which sprang up in Orissa under the Birlas, in Panjab under the Thapars and in UP under the Bajorias enjoyed substantial labour cost advantages in relation to the Bengal mills (see Table 27).

TABLE 27

PERCENTAGE OF LABOUR COSTS IN TOTAL COSTS OF PAPER MILLS IN DIFFERENT REGIONS IN 1948

Mill	Location	Group	Labour Costs (%)
1 Orient Paper Mills Co.	Sambalpur, Orissa	Birla	16.2
2 Bengal Paper Mill Co.	Raniganj, Bengal	Balmer Lawrie	21.1
3 Titagarh Paper Mills Co.	Titagarh, Bengal	Heilgers	21.8
4 India Paper Pulp Co.	Naihati, Bengal	Andrew Yule	27.2
5 Shree Gopal Paper Mill Co.	Jagadhri, Panjab	Thapar	16.1
6 Star Paper Mill Co.	Saharanpur, UP	Bajoria	17.4

SOURCE. M. M. Mehta, *Indian Industries*, p. 247.

3. *Power*. So far as supplies of coal for producing power was concerned, the mills in Bombay and UP were at a definite disadvantage in relation to the Bengal mills, but in the case of the Orient Mills in Orissa under Birla management supply of coal from the nearby Rampur colliery was combined with cheapness of bamboo pulp and labour. The development of paper manufacture in south India,

where there were large bamboo forests, was made possible by the simultaneous growth of bamboo pulp technology and hydroelectric works, from which Mysore and Punalur Paper Mills, both located in the heart of the bamboo growing tracts of Bangalore and Travancore and near the sources of cheap hydroelectric power supply,[148] benefited. Shree Gopal Paper Mills in Panjab under Thapar management, though it had to bring supplies of sabai grass from far afield at high cost, flourished on account of cheap hydroelectric power and other favourable factors.[149]

4. *Equipment.* Throughout the period under review, the paper-mill industry relied on imports for its machinery. This proved a disadvantage when the industry began to expand fast from 1937, especially after the outbreak of the Second World War. The market for paper expanded rapidly and vastly during and after the war, but production lagged behind on account of difficulties in importing machinery. At the end of the war it was found that the paper mills were not in a position to install new plant and increase production before 1950 since the foreign countries from which machinery had been so long imported had been devastated by the war. In chemicals the position was somewhat easier. By the end of our period, some mills were manufacturing their own requirements of caustic soda and chlorine.[150] Mettur Chemical and Industrial Corporation, which was meant to produce caustic soda by the electrolytic process, was in production by 1941 under the Sheshashayi group, followed quickly by ICI, Tatas and Dalmias. All these groups were commercially producing caustic soda in increasing quantities at the end of the war.[151]

5. *Technology.* The Indian achievement in the technology of paper manufacture, especially in respect of bamboo pulp manufacture, was impressive. The Indian Tariff Board observed in 1938:

As regards the question of general efficiency, it may be said on behalf of the mills that India has been the pioneer in the manufacture of bamboo pulp and has not had the advantage of experience of other countries. The properties of bamboo as a raw material for the manufacture of pulp are not precisely the same as those of wood extracted from trees of the coniferous variety since bamboo is a

---

[148] M. M. Mehta, op. cit., p. 190.

[149] Ibid., p. 189; A. K. Bagchi, *Private Investment*, p. 407.

[150] *Report of the Indian Tariff Board on the Continuance of Protection to the Paper and Paper Pulp Industries*, Bombay, 1947.

[151] *Report of the Indian Tariff Board on the Caustic Soda and Bleaching Powder Industry*, Bombay, 1947.

species of grass and not a species of wood. Though the manufacture of bamboo pulp has emerged from the experimental stage, it has not yet reached the level of mechanical and chemical efficiency attained in the manufacture of wood pulp based on the experience of many countries over a long period of time. From this point of view it may be said that the room for improvement in the manufacture of bamboo pulp of different qualities suitable for different kinds of paper is still considerable.[152]

The desired improvement in bamboo pulp of different qualities for various types of paper was rapidly achieved by the mills in the next few years. Special types of paper to which no protection had been given on account of their requirements of imported wood pulp—such as blotting paper, bank paper and kraft paper—were produced during the Second World War in spite of reduced imports of wood pulp. Indian paper mills proved by research that bamboo pulp properly prepared was suitable for manufacture of a large variety of papers.[153]

6. *Capital and enterprise.* During the thirties, when opportunities for large-scale profitable investment in the paper industry were created for the first time, the established European mills in Bengal, Titagarh and Bengal Paper, were never lacking in funds. From 1929 to 1934, Bengal Paper Mill Co. declared dividends at 20 per cent, which rose to 25 per cent in 1935–6 and 29 per cent in 1937–8. Titagarh Paper Mills Co. declared still higher dividends: 35 per cent in 1930–2, 45 per cent in 1932–4, 50 per cent in the half year ending March 1935, 55 per cent in 1935–6, 60 per cent in the half year ending March 1937 and 32 per cent in 1937–8.[154] The India Paper Pulp Company, a private company set up by Andrew Yule in 1919, sustained uninterrupted losses in the first nine years of its existence, until in 1933 it was sufficiently established to be turned into a public company and for its shares to be placed on the market. The large house of Andrew Yule had sufficient resources to finance its growth until 1933 even without any investment by the public.[155] The large new Indian houses which entered the field in 1936–7, Birlas, Thapars, Bajorias and Dalmias, were similarly in command of very large resources. The paper mills in south India which sprang up in the thirties were also well endowed with resources, Mysore Paper Mill Co. being partly financed by the State government of Mysore,

---

[152] *ITB Report on Paper*, 1938.   [153] Ibid., 1947.
[154] A. K. Bagchi, op. cit., p. 404.
[155] *Andrew Yule & Co. Ltd. 1863–1963*, printed for private circulation, 1963.

Punalur Paper Mill Co. being under the management of the large European house of A. & F. Harvey, and Sirpur Paper Mill Co. being a government-owned company of Hyderabad State.

TABLE 28

CAPITAL AND PRODUCTIVE CAPACITY OF PAPER MILLS, 1946

Mill	Management	Registration Year	Paid-up Capital (Rs)	Annual Productive Capacity (tons)
1 Titagarh	Heilgers	1882	65,89,000	31,012
2 Bengal	Balmer Lawrie	1889	15,00,000	11,000
3 India Paper Pulp	Andrew Yule	1918	30,00,000	8,403
4 Shree Gopal	Thapar	1936	29,78,750	8,548
5 Star	Bajoria	1936	29,99,750	3,493
6 Upper India Couper	Indian Company	1879	8,00,000	3,329
7 Mysore	Indian Company with Govt. participation	1936	25,00,000	2,470
8 Deccan	Indian Company	1885	—	2,850
9 Gujarat	Indian Company	—	—	1,254
10 Andhra	Indian Company	—	—	1,556
11 Sirpur	Govt. Company of Hyderabad	1939	41,17,040	4,471
12 Punalur	A. & F. Harvey	1931	5,01,880	3,524
13 Pudunijee	Indian Company	1944	—	153
14 Orient	Birla	1936	41,03,400	10,983
15 Rohtas Industries	Dalmia	1933	50,00,000	9,772

SOURCE. *Report of the Indian Tariff Board on the Continuance of Protection to the Paper and Paper Pulp Industries*, Bombay, 1947.

European entrepreneurship played a crucial part in the development of the technology of bamboo pulp manufacture, to which they committed substantial sums in the thirties. Until then India Paper Pulp Co. under Andrew Yule was the only company engaged in commercial production of bamboo pulp and the financial contribution of Andrew Yule, which ran the company without any profit and without any public investment for nine years, helped the infant bamboo pulp industry on its feet. Heilgers and Balmer Lawrie followed the lead set by Andrew Yule. From 1932 to 1938, India

Paper Pulp spent Rs 10 lakhs, Bengal Paper Rs 11 lakhs and Tita-garh Rs 26 lakhs on technical improvements for bamboo pulp manu-facture. India Paper Pulp spent mainly on installation of new strainers, new digesters, a complete new acid plant, and important alterations to power and water supply plants. Bengal Paper spent mainly on development of the sulphate process of manufacture, installation of a huge crusher, new digesters, up-to-date strainers, bleaching towers and a sulphate recovery plant in addition to improvements in power and water supply plants. Titagarh expended large sums on installation of a bamboo pulp plant, bamboo crushing and chipping machines, new digesters, strainers and bleaching towers, on extension of electrolytic bleach-making plant and on important extensions and improvements of the power plant.[156]

From 1936–7 Indian entrepreneurship seized the initiative in the paper-mill industry. It may be asked why the big Indian houses did not enter this field earlier in view of the large profits which were being earned by the European paper mills in Bengal in the late twenties and the early thirties. The answer might partly lie in the fact that until bamboo pulp manufacture could be definitely estab-lished on a large-scale commercial basis, the scope for new competi-tors was limited in view of the narrow possibilities of sabai grass. The explanation might also be partly found in differing rates of profit in the various industries in which the big Indian houses were interested. Sugar, in which the Birla, Thapar, Bajoria and Dalmia groups invested heavy sums, was definitely more profitable in the early thirties. As soon as paper became more profitable from 1936–7, these groups switched their expanding resources to manufacture paper. They were encouraged by the favourable economic and poli-tical climate created by the let up in the Great Depression and the installation of provincial Congress ministries. Birlas took the lead in the manufacture of kraft paper, which was an unprotected item.[157] Under the stimulus of the new entrepreneurial groups, the manufac-ture of the unprotected varieties of paper, some of which required sophisticated technology, expanded rapidly during the Second World War. From this point onwards European enterprise definitely began to lag behind the new Indian houses. The total productive capacity of paper mills managed by European houses increased by 16,500 tons between 1931 and 1944; at the same time the total productive

[156] *ITB Report on Paper*, 1938.
[157] Ibid.

capacity of Indian-managed paper mills increased by 41,700 tons.[158]
The investment of Andrew Yule, Balmer Lawrie and Heilgers in
bamboo pulp technology seems to have been primarily guided by a
determination to retain and expand their share in the existing
varieties of protected paper. Birlas and other Indian houses on the
other hand appear to have invested also in the manufacture of new
types of unprotected paper, such as kraft paper, to which they
successfully adapted bamboo pulp technology.

7. *Government policy.* The extension of protection to the paper
industry in 1925 extricated the existing mills from a difficult situation, but did not generate any new investment. The impact of protection might have been somewhat limited on account of the wide
range of paper manufactures to which no protection was given on
the ground that they required more than 75 per cent imported wood
pulp in the pulp admixture. But on the other hand the undeveloped
state of bamboo pulp technology at that stage in any case ruled out
any rapid expansion in the production of these unprotected varieties.
In 1932 government refused to grant the application for protection
by the Birla group and others with regard to kraft paper, cartridge
paper, blotting paper, etc. But by then the bamboo pulp technology
was reaching adolescence and in the next decade there was a breakthrough in the production of these papers with the assistance of the
high revenue duties which had already been imposed on imports of
these varieties.

It may be noted that the government contribution to the development of the bamboo pulp technology was quite crucial. Experiments under the auspices of the Government of India established
the technical possibility of pulping bamboo at the beginning of the
twentieth century, and though at that time the process was not
commercially successful, subsequent laboratory experiments at the
government Forest Research Institute in Dehra Dun attained enough
success by the end of the First World War to induce the Government of India to set up a pilot plant, which came into operation in
1924 and helped to solve many technical problems that could be
tackled only at plant level. However, the government did not follow
up the initial success of the pilot plant either by taking up commercial production of bamboo pulp or by extending financial assistance to private entrepreneurs in this enterprise. The Indian Tariff
Board in 1938 found in this inactive policy of the government one of

[158] M. M. Mehta, op. cit., Table XXIII, pp. 62–3.

the reasons why the commercial development of bamboo pulp was delayed until the mid-thirties.

8. *Market*. On the eve of the Great Depression consumption of all kinds of paper had increased from an index of 100 in 1924–5 to 156.86 in 1929–30. Lack of raw materials prevented the paper mills from taking advantage of the expanding market of the twenties. In the triennium before the war consumption of paper (excluding newsprint, etc.) rose again to the annual average of 134,704 tons from the low annual average of 91,358 tons in 1931–4. By then supply factors had been sufficiently well assembled for the industry to take advantage of this moderate increase in demand, the technique of bamboo pulp manufacture having been improved and Indian entrepreneurship being now ready to take the plunge from sugar to paper. The recovery of economic activity after the Great Depression and the rapid expansion of education under the provincial Congress governments from 1937 induced new investment in paper by Indian houses.[159] During the Second World War, again, government commandeered 70 to 90 per cent of the total product of the paper mills and only a small portion was made available for civilian use. The paper shortage in the country was a sign that demand was outstripping productive capacity on account of the inability of the industry to import much new machinery during wartime. If in the coal industry there was a consistent tendency for production to break out of the limitations of the market in order to achieve cost reduction, in the paper industry on the other hand shortages on the supply side reduced the impact of market expansion.

Conclusion

Both demand and supply factors—low consumption in the early thirties and slow development of bamboo pulp manufacture—delayed the development of the paper industry in relation to the sugar and cement industries. Given these factors the paper industry could not have developed simultaneously with the sugar industry in the early thirties. It is possible, however, that if government had undertaken the development of bamboo pulp manufacture on a commercial basis after the success of the pilot plant set up in 1924, then some substantial progress might have been made towards meeting the expanding demand in the late twenties. Even then, it should be noted, some newly-developing industries like cement and sugar

[159] A. K. Bagchi, op. cit., pp. 406, 418.

would have definitely been relatively more profitable at that point in time, and it was natural for Indian entrepreneurship to be drawn to paper only after profits from cement and sugar declined.

6. *Sugar*

Growth

A comparison of the growth of the paper industry with that of the sugar industry, which developed more rapidly than the former, is instructive.[160] The breakthrough in the sugar industry occurred by import substitution within six years from 1931–2 to 1936–7 under the shelter of high protective duties imposed in 1931 (see Table 29).

TABLE 29

PRODUCTION, IMPORTS AND CONSUMPTION OF SUGAR 1926–7 TO 1939–40

(in thousand tons)

Period	Factory Sugar	Khandsari Sugar	Net imports	Consumption
1926–7	121	n.a.	815	936
1927–8	120	n.a.	706	826
1928–9	99	n.a.	859	958
1929–30	113	200	933	1,046
1930–1	150	200	898	1,048
1931–2	221	250	510	731
1932–3	368	275	366	734
1933–4	519	200	249	768
1934–5	622	150	220	842
1935–6	980	125	198	1,178
1936–7	1,137	100	−17	1,120
1937–8	948	125	−35	9,133
1938–9	666	100	− 4	662
1939–40	1,269	125	198	1,467

SOURCE. A. K. Bagchi, op. cit., Table 12.3, p. 372.

Therefore, although imports ceased altogether from 1943–4 onwards, production did not increase on account of inelastic consumption in India and inability to develop exports. What were the factors which favoured such rapid growth and then imposed a ceiling to further development? On the eve of the breakthrough in the sugar

[160] For a more detailed study of the sugar industry, *see* A. K. Bagchi, op. cit.

TABLE 30

PRODUCTION AND IMPORTS OF SUGAR 1936–7 TO 1945–6

(in thousand tons)

Period	Total Production	Total Imports
1936–7	1,237	13
1937–8	1,072	12
1938–9	765	32
1939–40	1,393	227
1940–1	1,340	13
1941–2	898	21
1942–3	1,292	21
1943–4	1,374	—
1944–5	1,034	—
1945–6	1,025	—

SOURCE. *Report of the Indian Tariff Board on the Continuance of Protection to the Sugar Industry*, Bombay, 1947.

industry, the Tariff Board examined in detail how far the industry fulfilled the Fiscal Commission's condition for protection that there should be natural advantages such as abundant supply of raw material, cheap power, sufficient supply of labour, and a large home market.[161]

1. *Raw materials.* On account of heavy transport costs, cane growing areas had to be sufficiently concentrated in order to permit economic manufacture of sugar. Cane growing areas were sufficiently concentrated in 1931 for production of white sugar in UP and Bihar, but not in Bombay and Madras except in certain pockets. The main sugar-cane belt lay almost entirely outside the tropics and the growth and yield of sugar-canes had so far been much below those of tropical countries like Java, the main exporter of sugar to India. Cane was cultivated in small and scattered peasant holdings, rendering improvement in yield and regular supply to central factories extremely difficult.[162] In peninsular India (Bombay and Madras Presidencies), which lay in the tropical belt, per acre yield was higher, but cost of cultivation on account of greater irrigation and manure costs was even higher, so that average cost of sugar-cane per maund in UP and Bihar was estimated by the Tariff Board of

[161] *Report of Indian Tariff Board on the Sugar Industry*, Calcutta, 1931.
[162] Ibid.

1938 to be Rs 0–3–4, whereas in Bombay and Madras it was Rs 0–5–10 and Rs 0–5–0 respectively.[163] An explanation of this differential may be found in the cost items given by the Tariff Board of 1931 for cultivation of sugar-cane in Gorakhpur and Ahmednagar. In Gorakhpur the sugar-cane yield per acre was only 811 maunds as against 1,225 maunds per acre in Ahmednagar, yet the cost of cane per maund was Rs 0–3–6 and Rs 0–5–4 respectively. There were no irrigation costs in Gorakhpur, whereas in Ahmednagar irrigation cost Rs 84–0–0; manure cost Rs 29–5–3 in Gorakhpur and Rs 174–0–0 in Ahmednagar; rent was Rs 12–0–0 in Gorakhpur and Rs 30–0–0 in Ahmednagar.[164] It may also be noted that Madras did not benefit from the excellent research of the Coimbatore Agricultural Station which investigated sub-tropical conditions only and contributed substantially to the spread of improved varieties of sugar-cane in UP and Bihar. Nor had a suitable high-yielding variety of cane been discovered for Bombay by 1931.[165] Madras had a tendency to concentrate paddy on irrigated fields, which was very profitable, and also produced a variety of other profitable crops—such as groundnuts, cotton, plantains, chillies and tobacoo—which limited the acreage of suitable irrigated land for sugar cultivation. The great cash crop of Bombay was cotton, and suitable irrigated blocks for sugar cultivation were created only when the provincial government took the matter in hand in the thirties.

One consequence of the concentration of sugar-cane cultivation in India in the sub-tropical region was a natural disadvantage in relation to Java, which was favourably situated for exporting refined white sugar to India, produced by scientific methods on large farms. A Sugar Committee appointed by the government reported in 1920 that the small size and inefficiency of the factories in India were mainly due to the difficulty in obtaining adequate supplies of cane.[166] The attainment of higher efficiency had to await the substantial extension of the acreage under improved varieties from 817,000 acres in 1930–1 to 3,341,000 acres in 1936–7, which raised the average yield per acre from 12.3 tons to 15.6 tons. This improvement in sugar-cane cultivation has been seen as a beneficial effect of the protection granted in 1931,[167] but it should also be borne in mind that protection was so effective in improving sugar-cane culti-

[163] *Report of the Indian Tariff Board on the Sugar Industry*, Delhi, 1938.
[164] Ibid., 1931.   [165] Ibid.   [166] A. K. Bagchi, op. cit., p. 366.
[167] Ibid., p. 369.

vation only because other crops became less profitable during the Great Depression. At a time when the price of other crops was falling steeply, sugar-cane became relatively more profitable because of the protection the sugar industry received. Walchand Hirachand's Ravalgaon farm was a clear case in point. The chief products of this farm—jaggery and cotton—showed a fall in 1931 from Rs 38 per *palla* to Rs 12 and from Rs 300 per *candy* to Rs 200 respectively. Walchand therefore switched to cultivation of sugar-cane in 1933, being encouraged by the protection afforded to the industry. Walchand's Ravalgaon sugar farm became in time technologically one of the best equipped and most efficient sugar farms in India.[168] It is doubtful if protection would have made such an immediate impact on sugar-cane cultivation if it had been granted earlier, in view of the earlier profitability of other crops. It may also be noted that the discovery of newer and more suitable varieties by agricultural research was bound to take some time. In the twenties the spread of improved varieties was rather slow, since the existing supply of water from rainfall and irrigation could not support some of the high-yielding but less hardy varieties of cane under peasant methods of cultivation. The development of the Sarda Canal and the discovery of more suitable improved varieties for peasant cultivation at the Coimbatore station were factors which contributed to the spread of improved varieties in the thirties.[169]

After the great improvement in supplies of sugar-cane from 1931 to 1937, no striking improvement in the quality of sugar-cane with regard to its sucrose content and yield per acre took place. The Indian Tariff Board reported in 1947 that Java sugar-cane was as yet far superior in these respects. Further improvement would require intensive research at cane-breeding stations and such research would need considerable public expenditure and agricultural extension services by the government.[170]

2. *Power*. The question of cheap power was not material in the case of the sugar industry, for all the fuel required for generating power was provided by the bagasse. Factories could be located near the sources of cane supply anywhere, and in this manner the growth of the sugar industry was unhindered by the considerations of

---

[168] *Walchand Hirachand*, pp. 137–52.

[169] A. K. Bagchi, op. cit., p. 368.

[170] *Report of the Indian Tariff Board on the Continuance of Protection to the Sugar Industry*, Bombay, 1947.

availability of coal and hydroelectricity which restricted other industries.

3. *Labour.* India probably had the lowest labour costs among sugar-producing countries, but her edge in this respect over Java, the nearest sugar-producing neighbour, was by no means considerable. The average wage of 9d. per day in India (1913) was much lower than the average wage of 1s. 6d. in the Philippines, 2s. 8d. in Natal, 3s. 6d. in Mauritius, 5s. in Cuba, 6s. in Hawaii and 17s. in Queensland, but was only a little lower than the Java worker's average wage of 10d. per day.[171] Factories being located near the rural sources of cane supply, it was possible to draw cheap labour from the surrounding villages. Since the season for sugar manufacture in north India extended from the time when the kharif crop was reaped to the beginning of the rabi harvest, months during which agricultural employment was normally low, there was little difficulty in obtaining adequate supply of labour.

4. *Market.* The one great initial advantage which India enjoyed over other sugar-producing countries, including Java, was an exceptionally large home market. Java, Cuba, West Indies, Mauritius and Hawaii had practically no home market for their large product, while India was consuming sugar and *gur* to the value of Rs 60 crores annually.[172] Under such conditions tariff protection of sugar could generate rapid growth up to a point.

On the other hand, the sugar industry has been quoted as the classic instance of the limitation on growth imposed by an inelastic market. It has been shown by A. K. Bagchi that investment rose rapidly in the sugar industry during the phase of import substitution, but fell steeply, as soon as imports had been substituted. Since total consumption within the country was not increasing, there was no further scope for expansion.[173] It is necessary, in this context, to point out another aspect of the problem. While the home market was not expanding in the thirties, it was one of the largest in the world. Sustained growth of the sugar industry at the rate achieved during import substitution was not possible for long. Further growth could be achieved only by raising technical efficiency and exporting sugar. But such a course was not open to India on account of her technological backwardness compared to Java, Mauritius, Hawaii, etc. The per acre yield of sugar-cane and the methods of

---

[171] *ITB Report on Sugar*, 1931.   [172] Ibid.

[173] A. K. Bagchi, op. cit., p. 15.

manufacture prevented India up to 1947 from capturing export markets on any large scale.

5. *Machinery*. For sugar manufacturing machinery India relied completely on imports, but this proved no hindrance at all since the real growth of the industry took place during the years of the Great Depression when prices of machinery were low and there were no hindrances to imports. The largest import of machinery for installation of new plant took place from 1932–3 to 1937–8. During these years prices of machinery were half of those prevalent in 1920. The real value of the machinery imported was much greater than the prices which the importers paid for them. The installation of the plant for the sugar industry was achieved at little cost.[174]

6. *Government policy*. In the twenties, government took no positive action in encouraging the growth of the sugar industry. The revenue duties imposed on imported sugar, however, were quite high. When protective duties were finally imposed in the thirties, the effective rates were around 185 per cent *ad valorem*.[175] Such high rates of duty encouraged many firms to enter the industry at once and the resulting increase in production quickly brought down prices. Government encouragement of the sugar industry thus proved extremely effective in the thirties.

7. *Capital and enterprise*. European enterprise played an important role in the sugar industry in the initial stages, but when the large Indian houses entered the industry under the shelter of protection, the initiative quickly passed to Indian hands. The sugar industry in the twenties was not very profitable and it was reported that factories used inefficient methods of handling cane, used too much fuel and had very old equipment.[176] These bottlenecks in capital and enterprise were removed as soon as the industry became extremely profitable. From its planting origins, the European managing agency of Begg, Sutherland & Co. had grown to be the biggest sugar producing concern in India by the early thirties. By the end of the thirties the Indian house of Narang had outstripped Begg Sutherland in daily crushing capacity. On the eve of the Second World War there were two European houses and three Indian houses with a daily crushing capacity in excess of 2,000 tons: Begg Sutherland (9 factories with a crushing capacity of 6,251 tons), Octavius Steel (2 factories with a crushing capacity of 2,700 tons), Narang (8 factories with a crushing

[174] Ibid., Table 12.2, p. 367.   [175] Ibid., pp. 367–71.
[176] Ibid., p. 366.

capacity of 6,900 tons), Birla (5 factories with a crushing capacity of 5,400 tons) and Dalmia Jain (2 factories with a crushing capacity of 3,300 tons). Some other large houses which played an important role in the spurt of growth in the sugar industry in the thirties were Soorajmull Nagarmull (2 factories with a crushing capacity of 1,550 tons), Govan Bros. (2 factories with a crushing capacity of 2,000 tons), James Finlay (2 factories with a crushing capacity of 1,775 tons), Lyall Marshall (2 factories with a crushing capacity of 1,700 tons), Walchand (2 factories with a crushing capacity of 1,500 tons) and Thapar (3 factories with a crushing capacity of 1,780 tons).[177] The sugar industry thus attracted a number of large Indian and European houses with adequate financial resources, and was never in lack of capital after 1931.

Conclusion

The rapid breakthrough in the sugar industry in 1931–7 was the result of a conjunction of favourable circumstances, of which the most important was the spread of improved varieties of cane, the imposition of very high rates of protective duty, the rapid fall in the profitability of alternative crops and manufactures and the simultaneous entry of a number of large houses into the industry. Even if research in improved varieties had progressed further at an earlier stage and the government had played a more active role in encouraging the industry after the First World War, it is difficult to see how such rapid progress could have been achieved before 1931. Subsequent progress was held up by India's inability to develop exports by improving the yield of sugar-cane per acre and the inelasticity of consumption of sugar within the country. It is interesting to note that though the paper industry obtained protection at least six years earlier than the sugar industry, the breakthrough in the paper industry occurred only after the sugar industry had virtually exhausted its growth potential based on the home market. The differential impact of protection in this instance was due to the differing position regarding the availability of raw material and the state of research on bamboo pulp and sugar-cane.

[177] *Indian Sugar Mills Association: Report of the Committee for the Year 1938–39*, Calcutta, 1940.

7. *Glass*

Growth

The glass industry was practically established in India during the First World War. At the end of the war, in 1918, 20 factories were at work in India, 7 among these being glass bangle-making works located at Firozabad in UP. The period after the First World War was a difficult one for the glass industry. Several glass factories set up during the war suffered from increased foreign competition when peace was concluded. The struggle for existence continued until the decrease in the volume of imports with the onset of the Great Depression. The imposition of higher revenue duties in 1931 gave the industry limited protection. Even during this depression period the glass industry made considerable progress in one direction, i.e. bangle-making, which accounted for a substantial part of imports. Between 1925 and 1931, 15 factories were set up at the glass manufacturing centre of Firozabad. Largely as a result of this the value of imports of glassware decreased even before the imposition of higher revenue duties from Rs 252.89 lakhs in 1926–7 to Rs 248.40 lakhs in 1927–8, Rs 237.49 lakhs in 1928–9, Rs 251.93 lakhs in 1929–30 and to Rs 164.78 lakhs in 1930–1. Alfred Chatterton in 1919 estimated the value of glassware made in India at roughly one-fourth of imports, which stood at the close of the war at about Rs 162 lakhs. The value of glassware made in India at that time was about Rs 40 lakhs, out of which the value of the glass bangle trade of Firozabad was Rs 20 lakhs. In 1932 the Tariff Board estimated the value of Indian glass manufacture at Rs 140 lakhs, whereas imports during the quinquennium ending 1929–30 were worth on the average Rs 250 lakhs annually.[178] Out of the total value of glassware made in India, Rs 115 lakhs came from the glass bangle trade of Firozabad. Imports of bangles at that time were to the extent of Rs 85 lakhs in value. Some progress had also been made in the manufacture of lampware in India, indigenous product accounting for Rs 16 lakhs and imports amounting to Rs 21 lakhs. Imported goods practically monopolized the market for beads and false pearls, bottles, tableware and sheet glass. India was producing Rs 2 lakhs worth of sheet glass and Rs 6 lakhs worth of bottles, as against imports of Rs 30 lakhs and Rs 39 lakhs of sheet glass and

---

[178] *Report of the Indian Tariff Board on the Glass Industry*, Calcutta, 1932.

10

bottles respectively.[179] Till now progress had been achieved almost entirely in the light and relatively simple manufacture of bangles and lampware. Only small beginnings had been made in the manufacture of blown glassware and sheet glass.

TABLE 31
NUMBER OF GLASS FACTORIES IN INDIA 1914–45

Item	1914	1919	1930	1939	1945
No. of factories	3	20	59	80	174

SOURCE. *Report of the Indian Tariff Board on the Glass Industry*, Calcutta, 1932; *Report of the Indian Tariff Board on the Continuance of Protection to the Glass Industry*, Delhi, 1950; *The Calcutta Stock Exchange Official Year Book*, 1967, p. 275.

During the years of the Great Depression there was no progress in glass manufacture in spite of fairly stiff revenue duties. A survey of the glass industry by E. Dixon in 1936 showed that only in lampware and glass bangles was the Indian glass industry competing with imports. However, the depression had hit the bangle trade hard. There was as yet no substitution of imports of sheet glass, from Belgium and Japan, which were rising in value. As for blown glassware, the value of imports in 1935 was Rs 98.68 lakhs and the value of indigenous product was Rs 36.57 lakhs.[180] In the late thirties, however, the glass industry apparently made good progress. The amount of sheet glass produced in India rose from 3 million square feet in 1930 to 6 million square feet in 1939.[181]

It was during the Second World War that the glass industry in India reached some degree of maturity. The industry developed on fairly systematic lines and articles of better quality were produced. Some factories installed automatic or semi-automatic machines for manufacture of sheet glass and bottles, and put in improved furnaces. Although the productive capacity for manufacture of sheet glass doubled during the war, imports (mainly from Belgium) rose still further, being three times the pre-war amount during the trien-

[179] Ibid.
[180] *Bulletins of the Indian Industrial Research Bureau, no. 2: A Survey of the Indian Glass Industry* by E. Dixon, Delhi, 1936.
[181] *Report of the Indian Tariff Board on the Continuance of Protection to the Glass Industry*, Delhi, 1950.

TABLE 32
PROGRESS OF THE GLASS INDUSTRY 1939–45

Item	1939	1945
No. of factories	80	174
Sheet glass (m. sq. ft.)	6	13
Other glass (tons)	43,000	110,000

SOURCE. *ITB Report on Glass*, 1950.

nium beginning from 1946–7. Imports of glass bangles, on the other hand, became negligible during the war. At the end of the war, the country's productive capacity in this direction was in excess of total domestic demand. On the whole, it may be said that although the glass industry came into existence as early as the First World War, it was only during the Second World War that the industry underwent rapid expansion. Even at the end of the Second World War the total market, except in bangles, was dominated by imports.

1. *Raw materials*. The essential raw materials for glass manufacture were silica sand, sodium carbonate (converted into soda ash) and lime. Of these essential raw materials, sand and lime were available in abundant quantities within the country, but until the outbreak of the Second World War soda ash had to be almost entirely imported from Britain. E. Dixon reported in 1936 that India's plentiful supplies of sand had not yet been tested and exploited properly. The majority of the factories derived their supply from the Naini deposits of friable sandstone. The Firozabad bangle factories derived a major part of their supply from the deposit at Sawai Madhopur which had a good reputation. Jewel Glass Works was set up to exploit the sand quarry at Jabalpur, but this quarry had greater impurity.

Next to silica sand, soda ash was the most important raw material and accounted for a major part of the cost of glass manufacture. It was the most expensive bulk raw material used in manufacturing glass, and had to be entirely imported till the late thirties. In UP the imported soda ash formed 26.61 per cent of the total manufacturing cost in 1936, whereas in Bombay and Calcutta the proportion was only about 10 per cent.[182] The glass industry, being mainly located in UP, was at a definite disadvantage in respect of supplies

[182] *Survey of Glass Industry*, 1936.

of soda ash, the cost of which was pushed up by the heavy railway freight from the ports to upper India. In 1936 the glass industry needed about 5,000 tons of soda ash annually and further expansion clearly hinged on its production within the country. Fortunately, this problem was solved by production of soda ash within the country in large quantities during the Second World War. The need for soda ash by the glass industry had risen from 5,000 tons in 1936 to 30,000 tons in 1947 and the expansion of the glass industry implied in these figures would have been inhibited during wartime but for the fact that in 1947 India was producing 21,689 tons of soda ash. The additional demand for soda ash by the glass industry which the infant industry was not yet in a position to meet was being met by imports of chemically produced soda ash from Britain and magdi soda ash of natural origin from East Africa.[183]

2. *Labour and technology.* For successful manufacture of glass, it was essential to know the exact properties of each of the raw materials, to mix them in suitable proportions and to mix them thoroughly. The melting of the resulting batch in furnace was a complex, sophisticated process and afterwards manipulation by hand or machinery to make bangles, lampware, bottles, tubes and sheet glass also needed considerable skill. Not surprisingly, the glass industry in India made its early progress mainly in the manufacture of bangles at Firozabad, where bangle-making had long been established as a cottage industry. The glass industry was an industry in which the availability of skilled labour determined the location of factories. The availability of a large number of cottage workers who at one time had made bangles from the local 'Reh' deposits made Firozabad the biggest centre of bangle-glass and the bangle industry. Here the industry was so concentrated that there was no other centre of bangle-glass manufacture in India.[184]

During the early stages of the glass industry many foreign— especially Japanese—experts were employed and the technology and machinery of the industry bore a strong Japanese stamp.[185] At the end of the First World War there was no Indian skilled labour, the technically qualified personnel being mainly Japanese and Austrian. However, this problem of shortage of technically qualified personnel was quickly solved in the glass industry. The Indian Tariff Board reported in 1932 that the foreign personnel, having taught

[183] *ITB Report of Glass*, 1950.
[184] *Survey of Glass Industry*, 1936.   [185] Ibid.

Indian workmen to the level of requisite skill, had disappeared from the glass factories. There was at this point no shortage of skill and no lack of labour. The expansion of the glass industry in spite of stiff foreign competition after the First World War was made possible by definite cost advantages resulting from availability of abundant cheap labour in UP, which was at the same time a main market for glass products. Here labour was available at rates far cheaper than in Bombay and Calcutta, which compensated for the heavy freight on soda ash.

3. *Economic nationalism*. That the problem of technology and skilled labour could be solved in India within the space of a decade was mainly due to the pioneering role of Paisa Fund Glass Works started at Telegaon near Poona in 1905 by A. D. Kale for the re-generation of Indian industry. The underlying idea of the fund was that a large number of subscribers should contribute small sums for the development of Indian industry and the technical training of Indians. When a total sum of Rs 10,000 had been collected in this way it was decided to start Paisa Fund Glass Works which, being free from the necessity of meeting high interest charges, was able to weather the difficult conditions before and after the First World War. The managers devoted a certain amount of time and attention to the training of employees. The proprietors of the biggest commercial glass works in India in 1936—United Provinces Glass Works at Bajhoi (UP), Ogale Glass Works at Karad (Bombay Presidency) and Bombay Glass Works—all gained training and experience at Paisa Fund Glass Works.[186]

4. *Capital and enterprise*. There were definite initial shortages of capital and entrepreneurship. Only three glass works (including that of Paisa Fund), started in the *swadeshi* era, survived till 1914, when the outbreak of war secured the existence of the industry. After the end of the war the glass industry was once again put in jeopardy by foreign competition, and during the thirties the industry was refused protection. In these circumstances the big European and Indian houses which poured their massive resources into the cement, sugar and paper industries stayed out of glass manufacture. Glass manufacture remained an entirely Indian, mostly small-scale, industry which was *swadeshi* in inspiration. This will be obvious from the fact that the largest units in 1936 were guided by men trained in Paisa Fund Glass Works. The glass industry was not sufficiently

[186] Ibid.

profitable to attract the bigger managing agencies, whether European or Indian. That it attracted some capital and enterprise was initially due to the *swadeshi* spirit.

5. *Government policy.* This *swadeshi* spirit was all the more crucial to the growth of glass manufacture in view of the nature of government support to the industry, which was intermittent. The foundation of the glass industry during the First World War was entirely due to the energetic action of the Munitions Board, which stimulated the large number of factories which sprang up during the war by giving all kinds of assistance. The work of the Munitions Board was not followed up by the government during the post-war period. Protection for the industry was recommended by the Tariff Board in 1932, but the government refused to grant protection on the ground that soda ash was not available in the country. Instead the Government of India granted a refund of duty on all imported British soda ash which was expensive on account of high import duties. Some degree of protection was also afforded to the glass industry by the raising of the revenue duties on imported glassware from 15 per cent to 25 per cent *ad valorem* in 1931.

6. *Market.* In view of absence of protection, the glass industry in India developed in two spurts of growth during the two world wars, when the domestic market was to some extent naturally protected by the exigencies of war. By reducing imports of glass and glassware the two world wars gave a strong fillip to the glass industry. During the inter-war period, stiff foreign competition in the twenties and reduction of consumption in the thirties proved to be the big obstacles to the growth of the glass industry. Foreign competition was especially obstructive to the growth of manufacture of sheet glass and blown glassware, whereas in bangle-glass and bangle manufacture a fall in consumption inhibited growth in the thirties. In 1929–30 India was consuming Rs 200 lakhs worth of bangles (imports Rs 85 lakhs and indigenous product Rs 115 lakhs). In 1936 the total value of factory-produced bangles available in India (excluding the product of cottage industry) was estimated at Rs 61 lakhs (imports Rs 31 lakhs and Indian factory product Rs 30 lakhs). The conclusion seems to be inescapable that in the main branch of Indian glass manufacture, i.e. bangle-glass and bangles, the market was contracting during the Great Depression.

Conclusion

The glass industry was a clear instance in which lack of adequate encouragement by the government prevented peace-time growth on the lines of the cement, sugar and paper industries. The policy of discriminating protection, which resulted in refusal of protection to the glass industry on account of lack of soda ash within the country, definitely set the industry back many years. If the government had followed up the excellent work of the Munitions Board during the First World War and had followed a well-integrated, overall approach to the encouragement of industry by simultaneous assistance to the glass and soda ash industries, instead of examining each case for protection separately and ultimately giving protection to none, then the shortages of raw material, capital and enterprise, and the uncertainties of the market could have been removed. The substantial growth which government policy could have induced in the favourable economic circumstances of the twenties and the late thirties had to await the special stimulus of the Second World War in the absence of protection of the domestic market in peace-time.

8. Match

Growth

From time to time small factories for manufacture of safety-matches had been established in India before 1922, when the imposition of high revenue duties on imported matches led to the real beginnings of the match industry in India. Before this the factories which had been established were with one or two exceptions closed down either on account of insufficient capital or faulty management, or because of unsuitable location.[187] Of the pioneer factories, Amrit Match Factory in Kotah, Bilaspur and Central Provinces and Gujerat Islam Match Factory, both established in 1894–5, managed to survive against severe odds. They had a capacity of about 500–600 gross and 600–800 gross per day respectively. From 1894 to 1910 many factories were set up in Bombay, Berar, Jammu, Belgaum, Satara, etc. and two factories—Oriental Match Manufacturing Co. and Bande Match Factory—were established in Calcutta during the *swadeshi* agitation of 1905–6. The output of these factories varied

[187] *Report of the Indian Tariff Board Regarding the Grant of Protection to the Match Industry*, Calcutta, 1928.

between 300 and 500 gross per day.[188] By 1915 almost all these small factories were closed down except Amrit Match Factory and Gujerat Islam Match Factory, which survived apparently because of their bigger and therefore more viable size.

In 1922 revenue duties were imposed at a sufficiently high level to give protection and the response of Indian entrepreneurship was immediate. Machinery for manufacture of splints, veneers and boxes was obtained from abroad and new plant was set up to manufacture splints with aspen wood imported from Japan and Sweden. In 1923 Esavi Indian Match Manufacturing Co. was set up in Calcutta with a productive capacity of 3,000 gross per day. Next year Adamjee Hajee Dawood & Co. was set up in Rangoon by an Indian Muslim entrepreneur with a productive capacity of 6,000 gross per day. In 1925–6 Mahalakshmi Match Factory at Lahore and Bareilly Match Works in UP, with up-to-date machinery, started functioning. The rapid increase of domestic production led to corresponding decrease of imports from 13.68 million gross in 1921–2 to 6.13 million gross in 1926–7. The largest importer of matches, Swedish Match Company, was threatened with the loss of the whole Indian market. This multinational company countered swiftly by locating factories behind the tariff wall in India, at Ambernath (near Bombay) and Calcutta, in 1924. The subsidiary Indian branch (known as Wimco) set up two more factories in Burma in 1925, and the following year it set up factories in Assam and Parel. The Swedish company in India as a whole began to produce 20,500 gross *per diem*, with an approximate production capacity of 6 million gross per annum.[189]

In Calcutta match manufacture expanded rapidly as a cottage industry with a large number of small concerns in this period. It was estimated by the Tariff Board in 1928 that there were 27 factories in Calcutta.[190] But on account of drastic cost reduction in the larger factories, the cottage industry in Calcutta came under severe pressure and in 1938 there were only 12 smaller concerns in Calcutta. It was claimed that many small Indian factories had been crushed by Wimco, but the cottage industry in any case had no future except in small local markets, such as *mofussil* centres in Bengal like Sainthia, Chittagong, Dacca, Jalpaiguri and Agartala (Tripura), which were near sources of wood supply and were thus supporting

---

[188] K. C. Dasgupta, *Safety Matches and their Manufacture*, Calcutta, no date, (1937?).

[189] *ITB Report on Match*, 1928.   [190] Ibid.

six small concerns in 1938.[191] In view of the advantages of scale enjoyed by the large factories, the Tariff Board was not able to recommend special measures for supporting the cottage industry. Costs had fallen by 50 per cent to 75 per cent in many of the larger factories owing to expansion of output and fall in the prices of chemicals by 1928. Expansion of output had led to cost reduction under the items of wood and labour.[192]

By 1938 the expansion of the match industry had resulted in the opening up of allied business to the value of Rs 65,00,000 per annum in the following manner: wood business Rs 24,00,000; chemicals Rs 16,00,000; paper and labels Rs 14,00,000; packing and sundry materials Rs 11,00,000. Unfortunately, since most of the chemicals and paper and a substantial part of wood, labels and other materials had to be imported, many of the benefits of the growth of the match industry leaked outside. The total value of the trade in finished matches was estimated at this time at Rs 1,20,00,000, and the industry employed 8,000 to 12,000 men per day.[193]

1. *Raw materials*. The raw materials for match manufacture were wood of suitable quality, paper, paste or glue and chemicals of various sorts. The crucial differential between competing countries in match manufacture was in respect of wood. The best wood for manufacture, aspen wood, was not available in India. Grown in Siberia, Manchuria and Scandinavia, it was becoming scarce even in these countries and in consequence it was three times more expensive in 1930 compared to pre-war prices. There was, moreover, 15 per cent *ad valorem* revenue duties on aspen wood after the First World War, which pushed up its price in India. Nevertheless it was still found that, in spite of genwa wood from the Sunderbans being much cheaper, manufacturing costs with indigenous wood were so much higher on account of greater wastage that ultimately the use of aspen wood was cheaper.[194] Forty varieties of wood in India had been found suitable by trials, but these wild grown woods did not permit a very nice finish.[195] Consequently, although indigenous wood largely replaced aspen wood in the manufacture of veneers for

---

[191] *Match Industry, Issued by Commercial Museum, Corporation of Calcutta*, Calcutta, 1938.
[192] *ITB Report on Match*, 1928.
[193] *Match Industry*; K. C. Dasgupta, op. cit.
[194] P. C. Roy, *The Exposition of the Match Industry*, Dacca, no date, (1930?).
[195] *Match Industry*.

boxes, aspen wood continued to be imported for producing splints. The Indian Tariff Board estimated in 1928 that there was an assured supply of timber in Burma, Bengal, Assam, UP and Panjab for nearly half of the total demand in India. India practically supplied all the wood needed for boxes and nearly a third of the wood for splints. The available supply, which was clearly inadequate in quantity and could never compete with aspen wood in quality, could be raised only by massive plantation and patient forest research.[196] Even with further progress in plantation by research and experiment, it was expected that India would not be in a position to supply more than half of the growing demand for suitable wood, mainly from eastern India. But on the western side no suitable wood was available, so that reliance on imported aspen wood was obligatory in Bombay, where the largest factory, that at Ambernath, was situated.

Of the chemicals needed for manufacture of safety-matches, the most important ones—amorphous phosphorus and chlorate of potash—were not produced in India. With the exception of paraffin wax and red oxide, both of which were produced in India, all chemicals had to be imported in 1928.[197] Ten years later it was mentioned in a booklet in connection with the Indian Match Exhibition in Calcutta in May 1938 that certain match chemicals, such as paraffin wax, red oxide, manganese dioxide and glass powder, were being produced in India and that it was possible to produce a few other chemicals in India. No country, it may be noted, had a command of all chemicals needed for match manufacture, but the Indian match industry was at a special disadvantage in view of the undeveloped nature of her chemical industries. Moreover, since the growth of her paper industry was slow, the blue and deep violet papers known as match paper had to be entirely imported as late as 1938, mostly from Sweden, Germany and Norway.[198]

2. *Labour*. The largest single factor in the reduction of the cost of match manufacture was improved efficiency of labour. Both in factories where processes were carried out by hand and in those equipped with modern machinery, the improvement in efficiency was stated by the Tariff Board in 1928 to be remarkable. The labour was said to be capable at this point of a much larger output in the given time and it was also praised for having displayed a greater skill in the various processes, which had greatly reduced wastage of wood.[199]

[196] *ITB Report on Match*, 1928.   [197] Ibid.
[198] K. C. Dasgupta, op. cit.   [199] *ITB Report on Match*, 1928.

Ten years later, at the Indian Match Exhibition of 1938, Indian labour was stated to be efficient, and per man productivity was estimated to be 4 to 7 gross per head per day.[200] As for supply of an adequate number of labourers, there was no problem within a few years of the inception of the match industry. Processes of manufacture were simple and were readily learnt by Indians. The General Manager at the Bareilly works testified that the number of employees in an average Indian factory did not exceed the standard prevailing in Europe, whereas wages were much lower in India.[201]

3. *Machinery.* The initial spread of the cottage industry in Calcutta was largely due to the invention by M. C. Nandi of Comilla, in 1921, of a simple guillotine machine for manufacture of splints and skillets within the fold of the cottage industry. But the process proved to be absolutely unsuitable for bulk manufacture and efficient production. Thus it went out of use, being replaced by German and Japanese machines for the same purpose (Germany and Japan also had cottage industries). After the arrival of these machines, some Calcutta engineering firms commenced manufacture of machines of the same model, adapting them somewhat to indigenous needs. Except the frame-filling machine, which had to be imported, other machines could be had of Calcutta make, which compared quite favourably with foreign machines in output and efficiency.[202] Of this there was clear proof in the fact that many factories in India, Burma, Ceylon, South Africa and Baghdad were running machines of the Calcutta model satisfactorily in 1938. However, German, Japanese and Swedish machines specially adapted to Indian conditions were also being imported.[203]

4. *Government policy.* Lack of support by the government had exposed the smaller Indian match factories to destructive foreign competition and had prevented the growth of the industry in spite of a large domestic market. Government's policy towards the industry did not change to active encouragement after the war, but the need for more revenues led the government to raise the duties on imported matches progressively. The revenue duties on matches were 5 per cent *ad valorem* up to 1916. From 1916 to 1921 the rate of duty was 7.5 per cent *ad valorem*. In March 1921 it was raised to 12 annas per gross, and in March 1922 to Re 1–8–0 per gross. The imposition of duties on imports varying from 100 to 200 per cent

[200] *Match Industry.*   [201] *ITB Report on Match*, 1928.
[202] K. C. Dasgupta, op. cit.   [203] *Match Industry.*

ad valorem gave the industry adequate protection. On the recommendation of the Tariff Board the Rs 1–8 per gross revenue duty was converted into a protective duty by the government in 1928. This was the crucial factor in the rapid growth of the match industry in the inter-war period. Government, however, refused to intervene in favour of Indian match companies against the monopolistic policies of Wimco, although the Tariff Board in 1928 warned the government of the necessity of putting some restraint on possible monopoly bids by Wimco.[204] This policy of non-intervention implicitly favoured Wimco. In 1938 Wimco sold half its shares to Indians. This was considered by the government a sufficient concession to critics.[205]

5. *Market.* The most crucial natural advantage which India did possess in relation to Sweden was a large home market. The demand for matches in India was large and continuous. Between 1900 and 1910 the value of imports rose from Rs 40 lakhs to Rs 81 lakhs, and on the eve of the war it was Rs 90 lakhs. In 1921–2 total consumption at home was roughly 14.5 million gross, and consumption went on increasing in the twenties because of lower prices and improved standard of life. In 1926–7 the total consumption was about 17 million gross, of which 10.5 million gross was supplied by factories in India and 6.13 million gross was imported. Since the total world consumption of matches at this time was 150 million gross, the Indian market was one ninth of the entire world market for matches. In her vast market India had a distinct advantage over Sweden, whose home market was very small, a negligible factor in her world-wide operations.[206]

6. *Capital and enterprise.* The dominant unit in the Indian match industry was Wimco, a subsidiary of a great multinational which dominated the entire world production of matches. Japan, which had dominated the market in India during the First World War, was eliminated from it by 1926–7. This was the consequence of the combination of several Swedish companies in Swedish Match Company, which was formed in 1917 with a capital of £2.5 million. Its capital expanded rapidly to £5 million in 1922, £10 million in 1924

[204] *ITB Report on Match*, 1928.
[205] Klaus Markenstein, *Foreign Investment and Development: Swedish Companies in India*, Scandinavian Institute of Asian Studies Monograph Series, Lund, 1975, p. 65.
[206] Ibid.

and £15 million in 1927. Subsequently it formed a new subsidiary company in the U.S., International Match Corporation, with a capital of $77.28 million. The total capital of these companies gave only a partial glimpse of the extent of their financial resources, the scale of their enterprise and the degree of their political influence throughout the world. The two companies had acquired dominant control over capital vested in match manufacture in 30 countries of the world. The most influential banks in London and New York had a financial stake in these two companies. Huge sums at low interest had been granted by the two companies to several foreign countries in return for concessions. The Swedish Match Company thus came to control 65 to 70 per cent of the world's total demand. It had built factories in practically every important country and to the rest of the world it was supplying matches made in Sweden. No important country in Europe was outside the direct control of the Swedish Match Company except Finland and parts of Central Europe. In Germany, formerly a serious rival, it had acquired 65 per cent controlling interest of the match industry. In the East its most serious competitor, Japan, had succumbed in the export markets and the Swedish company had won complete and crushing victory by acquiring 85 per cent controlling interest of the Japanese industry. 'The object of the Company', observed the Indian Tariff Board in 1928, 'is to secure a position in every possible market in the world, which would enable it eventually to regulate prices.' For this a complete monopoly or a major interest in every important unit of the match industry throughout the world was essential and the 65 to 70 per cent control it had already acquired was not sufficient for price regulation.[207]

Swedish Match Co. made no secret of its intention to capture at least half of the Indian market and exclude all competitors. With this aim of dominating the production in India went a determination to keep up the flow of imports, since it had 20 factories in Sweden manufacturing 30 million gross a year, 95 per cent of which was exported. The company persisted in its opinion before the Indian Tariff Board that the industry had a much higher cost of production in India than in Sweden (including freight) which could never be eliminated. If as a condition of protection it was held that the industry should ultimately be able to dispense with protection, that condition could never be fulfilled in India. This opposition to protection for the industry in India was combined with a persistent

[207] Ibid.

propaganda in favour of imported matches from Sweden even after
Wimco had set up its Ambernath factory with 10,000 gross daily
capacity, though its manager admitted to the Tariff Board that the
aspen matches manufactured there were as good as those from
Sweden. Indian manufacturers complained before the Board (cor-
rectly as the ITB found on investigation) that having large financial
resources at its disposal the Swedish company had tried to squeeze
out local competitors by systematic cutting of prices and propaganda
of an objectionable type. It had cast insinuations against the quality
of Indian products and after setting up the Ambernath factory it
had made several unsuccessful take-over bids against its main
rivals.[208]

The Indian Tariff Board went into the question of the effect of the
domination of Swedish Match Co. in the Indian market on the
growth of the match industry at some length. To the consumers, it
was stated by the Board, the entry of Wimco could bring no harm,
since Wimco would be bound to keep prices down to a level which
would deter others from entering the industry (which did not
require large capital and organization, and was relatively easy to
start). The establishment of a monopoly, it was also predicted, would
reduce the profits of middlemen and dealers. In the case of a company managed by foreign interests this would result in transfer of
additional profits which would otherwise remain in the country.
Further, an important sphere of enterprise would be closed to nascent
Indian capitalism. So the ITB recommended that government should
take measures to protect Indian manufacturers should Wimco make
a bid for complete monopoly. But the Tariff Board also stated definitely that competition by Swedish factories within the country had
not been unfair in terms of prices (though imported matches had
been dumped on the country) and that elimination of Swedish
interests would be undesirable. Further progress of the infant match
industry depended on research and experiment, especially in the
choice of woods, and the co-operation of a firm of world standing
like Swedish Match Co. would be of great value in this matter.[209]
The ITB recommended only that the government should keep an
eye on the activities of the Swedish company, so that it did not
expand its sphere of operations by crushing out Indian enterprise.
At the time Wimco was manufacturing 5 million gross in India and
was importing 3 million gross. Its total share of the market was thus

[208] Ibid.   [209] Ibid.

8 million gross. Indian companies were manufacturing 7 million gross and were importing 1 million gross, and thus they also had an equal share of 8 million gross in the market. Subsequently Wimco's share in the total manufacture of matches went up and during the Second World War Wimco was able to establish a practical monopoly of the Indian market. Wimco's contribution to the government's excise revenue from the match industry was as high as 78 per cent in 1945 (see Table 33). A better idea of the monopoly established by Wimco since the Second World War is provided by the fact that in 1953 Wimco's 5 factories in India were producing 23.3 million gross (73 per cent of the market), leaving 154 smaller Indian factories to produce 8.8 million gross.[210] Only one large Indian company, Esavi in Calcutta, survived Wimco's cut-throat competition.[211]

TABLE 33
WIMCO'S CONTRIBUTION TO THE MATCH EXCISE REVENUE

Year	Wimco's share (%)
1936	49
1937	57
1938	58
1939	59
1940	51
1941	80
1942	70
1943	85
1944	82
1945	78

SOURCE. *The Story of Matches and the Match Industry of India: A Plea for Parliamentary Enquiry into the Practices of Wimco*, p. 37.

Because of the domination of the Indian market by Wimco the match industry did not attract the large Indian houses. There was no room in India for another large combine in view of the unlimited resources and power of Swedish Match Co., which had brooked no

[210] *The Story of Matches and the Match Industry of India: A Plea for Parliamentary Enquiry into the Practices of Wimco* (confidential printed blooklet circulated by an unnamed author, no date, no place), p. 35.
[211] Markenstein, op. cit., p. 65.

rival in any of the advanced countries. There was, however, a limited scope for cottage industries producing for local markets, and a much larger scope for factories of medium size which, being located near the sources of wood supply, were in a position to keep costs down below the level of costs at Ambernath. Thus Indian entrepreneurship in the match industry was on a small or medium scale and the bigger managing agencies which straddled many different industries stayed out of this highly specialized field. The medium Indian factories which survived in competition with Wimco were naturally quite efficient. The ITB found that the costs of several Indian factories were below those of the Ambernath factory. In the matter of wood supply, Indian factories of medium size enjoyed an advantage since their requirements, being moderate, could be obtained cheaply from Indian forests nearby. The ITB noted that many Indian factories besides that at Ambernath were producing matches as good as their imported Swedish counterparts. The entry of Wimco had resulted in reduction of prices and hence Indian factories were no longer enjoying the abnormal profits which they had reaped formerly. But the profits at Ambernath were still lower than those of many of its Indian competitors.[212]

Conclusion

Non-intervention by the government enabled Swedish Match Co. to increase its share of production in India to an extent which the ITB would have found undesirable. So far as the growth of the match industry is concerned, however, it is doubtful if official restrictions on Wimco would have had the desired effects. No doubt Wimco had a stake in importing matches from Sweden which was bound to affect its decisions regarding output in India, but to have restricted its sphere of operations in India would have still further enhanced its import orientation. Since Wimco's aim was to dominate the Indian market by keeping prices down, it did not lag behind in expanding production in response to any increase in demand. Restriction of its sphere would have militated against the technical efficiency of the match industry and might merely have encouraged imports by pushing up the total cost of production in India. So far as the broader interests of Indian industry as a whole were concerned, however, the domination of Wimco in match manufacture was clearly not so beneficial as in the limited sphere of the match in-

[212] *ITB Report on Match*, 1928.

dustry. The vast profits and reserves which Wimco acquired in India obviously could not be reinvested entirely in the match industry in view of market limitations on production. But a home-based managing agency would have tended to reinvest these profits and reserves in other industries in which there was scope for profitable employment of accumulated capital. It may be noted in this connection that Wimco ultimately set up units in other industries in independent India, by employing the assets built up by match manufacture. Before the Five Year Plans, however, it followed no such policy of horizontal expansion and its profits were repatriated, apart from that portion needed to maintain its dominance in the Indian market for matches. It is also possible to imagine that if a big nationalistic house like Birla or Walchand had dominated the market instead of Wimco, that house would have followed a more active policy of substituting imported raw materials by indigenous raw materials. Such an active policy would have stimulated the manufacture of match papers and chemicals. As it was, it was only during the Second World War that Wimco was forced by import difficulties to produce glue for match-boxes and labels, and potassium chlorate, the main chemical for match-heads.[213]

9. *Magnesium Chloride*

Growth

Before the First World War, magnesium chloride—a chemical used in India for sizing yarn—was a monopoly of Germany. Germany had large deposits of carnallite at Stassurt, a mineral containing magnesium and potassium. German supplies were cut off in 1914 and there was a serious shortage and rise in the prices of magnesium chloride. The textile mills used other materials such as calcium chloride for sizing but these were found to be inferior. In 1915 attention was drawn to the almost unlimited supply of bitterns (residual mother liquor left in the salt pans after the sodium chloride or common salt is removed) at Kharaghoda, where the salt works of the Government of Bombay were situated. Government called for tenders for the right to remove the bitterns from the Kharaghoda Salt Works and in 1916 Pioneer Magnesia Works, a newly established private company, obtained the contract. Next year it established a factory in Kharaghoda and commenced wartime produc-

[213] Markenstein, op. cit., p. 65.

11

tion in earnest. After the war the Germans once again invaded the market, with the deliberate aim of destroying this infant rival. Dumping of imports from Germany caused prices to crash from the highest peak of Rs 19 per cwt in 1920 to Rs 2–2–6 in June 1923. With the sterling exchange rate raised to 1s. 6d. there was an extra fall in prices in addition to that caused by dumping, which brought down the general level of prices to Rs 5–6–6 in 1922–3. At this crisis the industry's application for protection was rejected by the Indian Tariff Board, which was extremely pessimistic of its ability ever to survive without protection on account of the high manufacturing costs at Kharaghoda. But subsequently reduction in costs below a level predicted by the Tariff Board and imposition of a 15 per cent *ad valorem* revenue duty enabled Pioneer Magnesia Works to compete successfully with German imports and to double its output from 1,300 tons in 1922 to 2,700 tons in 1927.

The removal of the revenue duty in 1927, however, once again jeopardized the industry. The industry applied for protection and obtained in 1929 a protective duty of 15 per cent *ad valorem*. Thereafter the expansion of production was rapid and exports were undertaken. The highest level of production—9,000 tons—was reached in 1935. During the Second World War there was still further expansion of productive capacity, but production remained much below capacity on account of market restrictions. At the end of the war Pioneer Magnesia Works had a productive capacity of 10,000 tons. The two smaller units—Okha Salt Works and Kuda Salt Works—had a capacity of 3,000 tons and 2,000 tons respectively. The total productive capacity was 15,000 tons a year.[214]

1. *Raw materials.* That this branch of the chemical industry grew so quickly in spite of fierce German competition and was able to export quantities of the Indian product to Europe as early as the twenties was due to very great natural advantages. It was estimated by the Tariff Board in 1925 that 10,000 to 12,000 tons of magnesium chloride of the best quality could be manufactured annually from the bitterns at Kharaghoda alone on the Rann of Kutch. An equal

[214] This account of the industry and the analysis of factors of growth which follows are based on: *Report of the Indian Tariff Board Regarding the Grant of Protection to the Magnesium Chloride Industry*, Calcutta, 1925; *Report of the Indian Tariff Board on the Magnesium Chloride Industry*, Calcutta, 1929; *Report of the Indian Tariff Board Regarding the Grant of Protection to the Magnesium Chloride Industry*, Delhi, 1938; *Report of the Indian Tariff Board Regarding the Continuance of Protection to the Magnesium Chloride Industry*, Bombay, 1947.

TABLE 34

PRODUCTION OF MAGNESIUM CHLORIDE IN INDIA

(in tons)

Year	Pioneer Magnesia Works	Okha Salt Works	Kuda Salt Works	Total
1916	966	—	—	966
1917	1,145	—	—	1,145
1918	1,845	—	—	1,845
1919	1,822	—	—	1,822
1920	1,477	—	—	1,477
1921	851	—	—	851
1922	1,353	—	—	1,353
1923	Nil	—	—	Nil
1924	244	—	—	244
1925	1,411	—	—	1,411
1926	1,965	—	—	1,965
1927	2,713	—	—	2,713
1928	2,804	—	—	2,804
1929	3,273	—	—	3,273
1930	4,402	—	—	4,402
1931	5,192	—	—	5,192
1932	6,755	121	697	7,573
1933	5,626	962	1,474	8,062
1934	5,838	1,483	1,005	8,326
1935	5,365	2,025	1,639	9,029
1936	5,536	37	1,009	6,582
1937	6,972	—	—	6,972
1938	5,074	—	—	5,074
1939	6,998	—	—	6,998
1940	5,863	—	—	5,863
1941	5,833	3,008	—	8,841
1942	7,109	522	1,620	9,251
1943	4,517	485	1,665	6,667
1944	408	477	91	976
1945	1,386	1,981	Nil	3,367
1946	4,506	1,400	192	6,098
1947	5,319	708	240	6,267

SOURCE. *Report of the Indian Tariff Board Regarding the Continuance of Protection to the Magnesium Chloride Industry*, Bombay, 1947.

NOTE. Reduction in output of Okha Salt Works from 1936 was due to dismantling and reorganization of plant. Reduction in total output from 1943 was due to the promulgation of the Cotton Textiles Sizing and Filling Control Order of 1942 which reduced the demand.

quantity could be produced in the Dhrangadhra State ten miles away and later on the bitterns at Kuda Works on the Gulf of Kutch were also tapped. At Kharaghoda bitterns could be brought economically to the factory as the salt pans were served by a network of 40 miles of railway which Pioneer Magnesia Works were in a position to use.

2. *Labour.* Labour was cheap and plentiful in Kharaghoda. The Agarias who worked in the salt pans in this marshy area on the great Rann of Kutch were a hardy and industrious people. They proved well suited to the task of manufacturing magnesium chloride which called for no special skill.

3. *Capital.* The required initial capital outlay was extraordinarily small in proportion to the total value of the product. Capitalization per ton of output at Kharaghoda was only Rs 37, and the sum required to give a 10 per cent return on capital invested was less than Rs 4 per ton. Pioneer Magnesia Works was a private limited company which had no need of investment by the public. The capital invested in the industry was no more than Rs 1.5 lakhs. Since prices were extremely high during the First World War and its aftermath, Pioneer Magnesia Works were so prosperous from 1917 to 1921 that royalties amounting to Rs 2.5 lakhs were paid to the government and the block account was written down to 15 per cent of its original value. Surplus profits during the first six years exceeded Rs 3.8 lakhs—more than two and a half times the fixed capital expenditure of the company. The company was thus in a sound position to withstand German competition after 1922.

4. *Machinery and technology.* The process of manufacture was a simple one and did not involve the employment of skilled personnel and the use of elaborate and extensive machinery. In 1929 the Tariff Board reported that the Indian product was greyish in colour and was therefore regarded as inferior to the whiter imported article. A decade later in 1938 the Tariff Board found that improvements in the processes of manufacture had resulted in a product equal in all respects, including colour, to the imported article. The Indian article was competing on equal terms with the German and French products in Holland and Czechoslovakia.

5. *Size.* The industry permitted quick economies of scale and at Kharaghoda there were no natural difficulties of expansion to the extent of supplying the entire Indian market. Cost of production on 3,000 tons in 1929, which stood at Rs 2–5–4 per cwt, was reduced to Rs 1–12–4 on the basis of 7,000 tons in 1937. With reduction in cost,

the Pioneer Magnesia Works were able to engage in exports.

6. *Enterprise.* Since little initial capital outlay was necessary, the industry did not have to await the entry of the big Indian houses. The pioneering company at Kharaghoda was a concern of medium size which acquired specialized knowledge and experience of the manufacture over an extensive period. It also showed a certain strength in adversity, when prices dropped in 1922 and the factory had to be closed down at the end of the year. During the next two years production ceased and the company had to confine itself to gradual disposal of accumulated stocks. It received no support from the government in this crisis. The industry might have collapsed in spite of strong natural advantages in respect of raw materials and cheap and plentiful supply of labour at Kharaghoda. This, however, did not happen. Without government assistance the company reduced cost of production subsequently with the help of 15 per cent duty (at first for revenue purposes and then for protection). The industry was established on a firm basis by the managers of the company, who also initiated the works at Okha in 1932. In the same year, a smaller concern named Mayurdhwaj Swadeshi Magnesia Works commenced production at the Kuda Salt Works in Dhrangadhra State. Later a big house, Tatas, entered the industry. Okha Salt Works were taken over by Tata Chemicals. To the end of the period, however, Pioneer Magnesia Works continued to dominate the industry.

7. *Government policy.* Government proved tardy in extending help to the magnesium chloride industry, but this did no irreparable damage and in fact contributed to the technical efficiency of Pioneer Magnesia Works, which survived without protection by reducing cost of production. The revenue duties on imports gave a welcome breathing space to the industry. With the grant of protection in 1929, imports came down from 1,778 tons in 1930 to 899 tons in 1939. The government thus found it possible to reduce the rate of the protective duty, which was fairly low to begin with. In 1947 all the companies engaged in producing magnesium chloride agreed that since imports had ceased altogether, protective duties might be removed. Protection, as the Tariff Board stated on the strength of the self-confidence of the industry, had fully achieved its purpose.

8. *Market.* Magnesium chloride could be used for a variety of industrial purposes: (1) for sizing of yarn in textile mills, (2) for manufacture of oxichloride cement for laying jointless composition

floors in buildings and railway wagons, and as stucco in building works, (3) for grinding machinery parts in rice mills, (4) for manufacture of beer, paper and ceramics, (5) for manufacture of tiles, (6) for manufacture of drugs such as epsom salts, (7) as a calatyst for various oxidation processes, (8) for fire-proofing of wood. These various uses of magnesium chloride had not yet developed in India at the time the Tariff Board rejected the industry's application for protection in 1925, the only major use of the chemical at that time being as a sizing material for cotton mills. Later a foreign demand developed in the thirties for the Indian product for the manufacture of oxichloride cement, and exports developed on that basis. To a small extent magnesium chloride was also used in the thirties for grinding machinery parts of rice mills.

One initial advantage of the industry was that an important market—the cotton-mill industry of Ahmedabad—with a total consumption of 1,200 tons, was only sixty miles away from Kharaghoda. But the domestic market proved to be rather inelastic in the long run, and at a time when due to the opening of new units the productive capacity of the industry expanded rapidly, net domestic consumption was estimated to have risen from 6,180 tons in 1930 to 7,032 tons only in 1935. In 1937 consumption rose to the high point of 9,657 tons, but thereafter consumption remained considerably below this high point except in 1942. The industry would not have been able to expand production and reduce costs in the thirties in view of the inelastic nature of the domestic market but for the development of exports. The bulk of exports went to Britain, where these were duty-free, and some also went to Holland, Denmark, Czechoslovakia, Australia, Canada and South Africa. The realized prices of exports gave little margin of profit, but they helped reduce the incidence of overhead charges. From 1943 exports declined due to strict wartime control in Britain, lack of shipping space and stoppage of exports to the Continent. At the same time control orders imposed on the cotton-mill industry virtually eliminated the domestic market. At the very end of the period the industry started functioning regularly again on the basis of pent-up foreign demand, the domestic market still being restricted by the continuance of the control orders of 1942.

9. *Foreign monopoly.* Since the German product had dominated the market, the very question of a magnesium chloride industry had not arisen in India before the First World War. During the war its

TABLE 35
EXPORTS OF PIONEER MAGNESIA WORKS

Year	Tons	Drums
1927–8	247	707
1928–9	517	1,544
1929–30	505	3,122
1930–1	893	3,034
1931–2	2,264	8,039
1932–3	1,857	6,069
1933–4	2,206	7,286
1934–5	2,333	7,348
1935–6	1,869	5,630
1936–7	2,164	6,712
1937–8	1,130	4,167
1938–9	1,639	5,585
1939–40	1,540	5,675
1940–1	824	2,777
1941–2	39	3,282
1942–3	486	1,774
1943–4	177	577
1944–5	150	556
1945–6	2,066	7,655
1946–7	4,715	15,531

SOURCE. *ITB Report on Magnesium Chloride*, 1947.

development was forced by the cutting-off of supplies from Germany. Had Germany not been an enemy country, the grip of foreign monopoly could not have been loosened so early. After the war there was a systematic attempt by Deutsche Chlor Magnesium Syndikat, which controlled the industry in Germany, to undersell Pioneer Magnesia Works. As the whole export trade was in the hands of the Syndikat's distributors, Chemikalien Aktiengesellschaft, prices could be systematically manipulated. The Germans established very low ruling prices in India compared to other countries: £3–19 in India, £7 in Australia and £5–10 to £6 in Britain. The Syndikat negotiated for 70 per cent control of the market, so that Indian manufacture would be confined to about 1,200 tons at high overhead costs. Pioneer Magnesia Works rejected the offer and a price war followed, from which the industry was ultimately rescued by protection. Had this product been a British, not German, monopoly, government might not have been so forthcoming.

Conclusion

The relatively early development of magnesium chloride in relation to some other chemicals was due to the fact that the product was the monopoly of an enemy country during the First World War. Thereafter the survival and growth of the industry was ensured by tremendous natural advantages which overcame the early lack of official patronage—abundant raw materials which could be brought very cheaply by an existing railway network to the factory, and cheap and plentiful supply of labour. Technological problems were few in this industry and financial requirements were low, so that with some improvement in processes of manufacture, export quality was achieved and overhead costs were reduced by expanding production on the basis of exports in an inelastic domestic market.

10. *Sulphuric Acid, Caustic Soda and Other Chemicals*

Growth

Of the two main groups of heavy chemicals—sulphuric acid and the chemicals based on it, and the alkali group of various forms of soda and compounds based on them (such as soda ash and caustic soda) —the first group developed before the First World War, while the second came up during the Second World War. In the field of acids, small factories sprang up at the beginning of the twentieth century. The pioneering concerns were Bengal Chemical & Pharmaceutical Works (1901), Eastern Chemical Works in Bombay (1913) and Messrs D. Waldie & Co. in Bengal (1850s). The Dharamsi Chemical Works, the largest in the field of sulphuric acid, came up as a result of the First World War. Before the Second World War there were 23 factories manufacturing sulphuric acid, most of which had sprung up during and after the First World War. Of these numerous concerns, the following were operating on a fairly substantial scale in the twenties: Dharamsi Morarji Chemical Co., Ambernath; Eastern Chemical Co., Bombay; Parry & Co.'s works at Ranipet in south India; Messrs. D. Waldie & Co., Calcutta; Bengal Chemical & Pharmaceutical Works Ltd., Calcutta; TISCO's unit at Jamshedpur; and IISCO's unit in the Raniganj–Asansol area of West Bengal.[215] Declining imports and increasing requirements during the Second

[215] *Report of the Indian Tariff Board on the Heavy Chemical Industry*, Calcutta, 1929.

World War once again pushed up the production of sulphuric acid, the number of concerns engaged in manufacturing it rising to 36 in 1946.

The development of the alkalis was considerably delayed in relation to the acids, so that when the Tariff Board took up the question of protecting the chemical industries in 1929 there were no alkalis to protect, the only existing chemical industry being based on sulphuric acid which did not need much protection anyway. The first concern to venture in the field of caustic soda, one of the most important alkalis, was Mettur Chemical & Industrial Corporation, which was registered in 1936 but commenced production only in 1941. The ICI subsidiary, Alkali & Chemical Corporation of India, was set up in 1938 but commenced production in 1940. By 1947 Tata Chemicals and Rohtas Industries (Dalmia group) had also entered the field. In 1946–7 these groups together produced 5,730 tons of caustic soda, distribution being as follows: Mettur Chemicals 1,600 tons, Tata Chemicals 2,000 tons, ICI 1,600 tons and Rohtas Industries 530 tons.[216] The market was still dominated by imports, which totalled 21,000 tons in 1947–8. The factors behind the differential growth of the sulphuric acid and the alkali industries are worth exploring for an overall view of the factors which promoted and retarded growth in the chemical industry as a whole.

1. *Raw materials, power and transport.* The basic raw material for producing sulphuric acid, sulphur, was not available in India and the chemical was manufactured by burning sulphur imported from Sicily or Japan. This remained an expensive proposition even after the abolition of the 15 per cent *ad valorem* revenue duty in 1924 on the recommendation of the Tariff Board. The industry nevertheless developed quite early on account of heavy overseas freight due to the weight, corrosive quality and difficulty of handling sulphuric acid. Moreover, a given quantity of sulphur, weight for weight, can produce three times the quantity of sulphuric acid, so that there was a definite advantage in locating factories near the market in spite of the non-availability of sulphur within the country. On the other hand, the lack of sulphur ruled out the development of sulphuric acid as a great industry on the lines of the United States, which had abundant quantities of sulphur and exported some of these to India.

By contrast the basic raw materials for producing caustic soda

[216] *Report of the Indian Tariff Board on the Caustic Soda and Bleaching Powder Industry,* Bombay, 1947.

were available in the country. These were common salt in the electrolytic process and soda ash and lime in the causticizing process. For
the former process cheap electrical power and cheap salt were
essential, while for the latter process good quality lime and a functioning soda ash industry were prerequisites. Since electrical power
production (for industries other than cotton mills) and soda ash
manufacture developed in India only in the late thirties, neither the
electrolytic nor the causticizing process could have been adopted for
manufacture of caustic soda before that time. As for the former
process, salt is produced more cheaply from rock salt deposits by
solution in water, but the only known deposit of rock salt was in the
far north and consequently the chemical industry in India had to
rely on expensive salt produced by solar evaporation. The ICI stated
in a memorandum to the Government of India that the present state
of the salt industry rendered cost of manufacturing all kinds of
chemicals extremely high. Limestone, like salt, was also of great
importance to the chemical industry, especially to caustic soda
manufactured under the causticizing process. But the ICI stated that
the limestone obtainable in India was poor in quality for chemical
manufacture, for which a higher degree of purity was essential.[217]
As for manufacture of caustic soda by the electrolytic process, it was
estimated that at the end of the Second World War only 3 per cent
of India's enormous hydroelectric power resources had been developed. The natural advantages of the caustic soda and other alkali
industries should not therefore be overestimated for the period
under review. The big disadvantage of alkali manufacture in relation
to manufacture of sulphuric acid, however, lay in the relative ease
with which soda ash, caustic soda and other heavy chemicals of the
alkali group could be transported. The small local markets for
sulphuric acid in India were naturally protected by the corrosive
quality of the acid, but the same could not be said of soda ash or
caustic soda, heavy enough as these chemicals were. Heavy raw
materials like common salt, limestone and coal were used for the
manufacture of alkali and the comparative weight of the final
product was much less than that of the raw materials used.

2. *Technology.* One advantage in the manufacture of sulphuric
acid and the chemicals based on it was that the processes of produc-

[217] *The Indian Chemical Industry: A Memorandum Prepared for Submission to
the Government of India by Imperial Chemical Industries Limited,* no place, 1950,
pp. 19–20.

tion were simple. The machinery used in such chemical works was of an automatic type and required little labour and supervision.[218] The alkali industry presented more serious technological problems regarding choice of process and location of plant. For manufacture of soda ash it was desirable to locate the plant in some degree of proximity to salt, limestone and coal, and places with such locational advantages were difficult to find in India. Caustic soda, when produced with the help of soda ash and lime, had similar problems of plant location. On the other hand, when caustic soda was produced by the electrolytic process, two important by-products—hydrogen and chlorine—were obtained and the cost of the main product, caustic soda, could only be reduced to a figure comparable with the landing prices of imported caustic soda by solving the technological problems in making use of the by-products.[219]

3. *Capital, enterprise and organization.* The sulphuric acid industry, which did not require much investment and in which small factories upcountry could earn a profit on account of the heavy cost of transport from larger factories at the ports, was characterized by a large number of small, uneconomic units and the organization of the industry was inefficient. In the Bombay area, an agreement in the twenties between two medium concerns—Dharamsi Morarji Chemical Co. and Eastern Chemical Co.—to divide the available market between themselves at a time when either concern was in a position to supply the whole market had led to uneconomic manufacture, each unit producing a fraction of its possible output at considerably enhanced cost. Even with the existing revenue duties the industry was running at a heavy loss since its cost, including normal profit, was considerably higher than the ruling prices in India (dictated by imports) in the case of salts prepared from sulphuric acid, which were much easier to import (being lighter in weight).[220] Government sought in the thirties, by giving protection, to reorganize the industry on a more efficient basis, but to no effect. The industry continued to be characterized by high cost of production entailed by the cropping up of small plants and the division of existing markets between the bigger concerns. In the Bombay area more efficiency could have been attained if the Dharamsi Morarji Chemical Co. had been the only plant. This concern had the most

[218] *ITB Report on the Heavy Chemical Industry,* 1929.
[219] Vera Anstey, *Economic Development,* p. 247.
[220] *ITB Report on the Heavy Chemical Industry,* 1929.

modern plant and it had the highest productive capacity among the factories exclusively engaged in the production of chemicals, being able to produce 8,000 tons of 100 per cent acid. It was also equipped for manufacture of fertilizers on a large scale.[221]

The alkalis, which needed much greater outlay of capital, came to be dominated by big concerns. The first company for manufacturing caustic soda, Mettur Chemicals, was opened by Dayaram & Sons, a relatively small concern. It immediately ran into financial difficulties, from which it was finally rescued under the more competent management of Sheshashayi Bros. By then the multinational corporation—Imperial Chemicals—had entered the alkali industry in India. The other concerns which entered the alkali industry were without exception big houses—Tatas, Govan Bros, and Dalmia Sahu Jain. Imperial Chemicals located their soda ash plant at Khewra, the only spot in India (subsequently Pakistan) which commanded the necessary locational advantages in relation to supply of raw materials. The Tata plant at Mithapur and the Govan (subsequently Dalmia) plant at Dhrangadhra both suffered from disadvantages of long and costly transport of limestone and coal.[222]

4. *Government policy*. At the time the government went into the issue of protection for heavy chemicals, there was no question of protection for alkalis, which did not exist. Protection for alkalis was not extended until the end of the period. However, in 1947 the caustic soda and chlorine industries were already operating under 36 per cent *ad valorem* revenue duty, with a preferential duty of 24 per cent *ad valorem* on imports from Britain. Since the whole import business in alkalis was given over to Imperial Chemicals during the Second World War, government's policy could be pronounced to be somewhat biased in favour of British chemical interests.[223] In the case of sulphuric acid, nitric acid, hydrochloric acid, magnesium sulphate, ferrous sulphate, potash aluminium, aluminium sulphate, sodium sulphate, zinc chloride, copper sulphate and Glaubers salts, protective duties were briefly imposed in 1931, but they were removed in 1933 as no reorganization of the industry had taken place in that brief span of time.[224] The chemicals industry was one industry in which, due to the interdependence of chemicals

[221] Ibid.
[222] T. R. Sharma & S. D. Singh Chauhan, *Indian Industries*, p. 572.
[223] *ITB Report on Caustic Soda*, 1947.
[224] Vera Anstey, op. cit., p. 354.

as raw material and market for one another, planned development and rationalization under active government supervision would have been very fruitful, as was proved during the First and Second Five Year Plans. The policy of discriminating protection, while suitable for industries like steel and cotton, proved to be entirely unsuitable in the chemical industries.

5. *Market.* The total market for sulphuric acid and salts produced from it in India was estimated in 1929, when numerous small concerns were already functioning, at about 12,000 tons. The two main markets were Calcutta (4,500 tons) and Bombay (6,000 tons). The market had considerably expanded since the First World War, but since most of the chemicals were used by the cotton mills, which were plagued by post-war difficulties, the market remained somewhat limited. These chemical industries depended for success on large-scale production and had to be so organized as to produce sulphuric acid at an economic cost. On this count, there was no market barrier to the establishment of the sulphuric acid on a sound economic basis in Bombay and Calcutta, where the markets were sufficiently large to support one economic plant in each area. The weakness of the industry was not due to the lack of an adequate market for economic production, but to defects of organization. It is possible to surmise, however, that some of these defects could have been removed if a rapid expansion of the market had attracted bigger combines. But until fertilizers, dye-stuffs and rayon industries were established on a large scale, no great expansion of demand for sulphuric acid could be expected. If we compare the demand for sulphuric acid during the Five Year Plans (5,98,000 tons), the demand of 12,000 tons during the early days of the industry appears ridiculously low.

For caustic soda, bleaching powder and chlorine, the market was much larger at the time when manufacture was undertaken in 1940, and in consequence the industry had superior organization. Soap, textiles, paper and vegetable ghee industries, which consumed the above-mentioned chemicals, had already been established on a fairly broad basis. An idea of the size of the market may be formed from the total annual value of the imports in the years before manufacture was undertaken: Rs 34.64 lakhs in 1936–7, Rs 42.81 lakhs in 1937–8, Rs 45.45 lakhs in 1938–9 and Rs 72.31 lakhs in 1939–40. At the end of the Second World War the demand for caustic soda in the country ranged from 67,500 tons to 72,500 tons, the main requirements being 30,000–35,000 tons for soap, 20,000 for textiles, 10,000 for paper and 7,500 for miscellaneous uses.[225]

6. *Foreign Monopoly.* Caustic soda was practically a monopoly of ICI (India) Limited. The monopolistic position of this giant multinational was further buttressed by the Government of India during the Second World War when it was informally given the right to control imports from all other sources. Had this product been a German monopoly like magnesium chloride, it is possible to speculate that the two world wars would have been instrumental in earlier and faster growth of the industry. Because it was a British monopoly, the natural difficulties of starting the industry were further enhanced by political factors.

Sulphuric acid did not encounter such powerful monopolistic interest. A difficult period of severe foreign competition was experienced after the First World War, but this was due to overproduction in Europe as a result of overexpansion of capacity to meet the requirements of war. In Europe the industry was dominated by two giant concerns—I. G. Farben in Germany and Imperial Chemical Industries in Britain.[226] But due to the difficulties of transport, these two concerns had never taken an active part in the trade with India in chemicals based on sulphuric acid.

Conclusion

The very interconnected nature of the chemical industries which retarded their growth under a policy of discriminating protection, could generate sustained and simultaneous development in many directions under a policy of overall planning. Without massive government action there could be no effective solution to the problems of developing the hydroelectric power resources of the country and at the same time encouraging the mutually sustaining growth of heavy chemicals as raw materials and finished chemicals as markets. Naturally those finished chemicals for which there was a ready market in the country and for which the raw materials were available, attracted private investment first, but even in such cases the technological problems quite often retarded development. Dyestuffs, for instance, were much in demand from the cotton mills in the thirties. Private investment was drawn to the sodium bichromate industry for the khaki dye immediately before the outbreak of the

[225] *ITB Report on Caustic Soda*, 1947.
[226] *ITB Report on the Heavy Chemical Industry*, 1929.

Second World War, when there was already a large demand from the khaki cloth manufacturing concern under Binnys. The basic heavy chemicals needed for manufacturing the khaki dye—soda ash and sulphuric acid—as well as the required raw materials of chrome ore, limestone and coal and oil fuel were already being produced within the country. Nevertheless the bichromates industry encountered considerable technological problems in the disposal of the large by-product of sodium sulphate, for which also there was a large demand in India from the textile, paper, glass and tanning industries (fed purely by imports). Initially it was found that the high chrome content left in sodium sulphate after the production of bichromates made it difficult to sell it to the consumer.[227]

As ICI stated in its 1950 memorandum to the Government of India, chemicals like dye-stuffs, plastics and pharmaceuticals had certain features which made rapid development of large-scale manufacture impossible.

The basic organic raw materials are mostly available in India, but the resources of mature chemical industry are required to work these up into the intermediates on which the successful manufacture of the finished product depends. The technical problems are extremely intricate, and the industry requires great flexibility in both the technical and commercial approach to the problem of production; to set up the manufacture on a small scale of an isolated product or intermediate offers no solution.[228]

No country in the world was wholly self-sufficient in respect of finished dye-stuffs and intermediates. Even the most advanced countries in this field—USA, Britain, Germany, Switzerland, etc. —exchanged intermediates and specialities. ICI's four-stage plan for the development of the dye-stuffs industry offered an insight into the technological problems of manufacture in India: first stage, production of finished dye-stuffs from imported intermediates; second stage, building of plants for manufacture of simpler intermediates and sulphuric and nitric acids; third stage, erection of plants for manufacture of further intermediates and for manufacture of more important and yet not too complicated dye-stuffs in addition to those under stage one; fourth stage, manufacture of more complicated colour not produced under stage three.[229] As ICI noted, dye-

[227] *Report of the Indian Tariff Board on the Bichromates Industry*, Bombay, 1946.
[228] *Indian Chemical Industry*, pp. 15–16.   [229] Ibid.

stuff was one industry which required protection from the beginning in order to be economic with a complete range of products in use.[230] Such protection had not been forthcoming under the policy of discriminating protection in the past.

11. Automobiles

Growth

In 1935 selected leaders of Indian business and industry met under the guidance of Sir M. Visveswaraiya, who had taken up the task of lobbying India's capitalist circles for starting an automobile industry, at Tata House in Bombay to consider the question of starting a car factory in the Bombay area. The meeting responded favourably to Visveswaraiya's urgings that with the development of Tata's steel works at Jamshedpur and Bombay's metallurgical workshops, India had now technologically reached the stage for car manufacture. In accordance with the resolution of the meeting, M. Visveswaraiya visited the leading car manufacturing countries in Europe and America for on-the-spot investigation and on his return a meeting of industrialists interested in the car manufacturing business was held on 17 April 1936 at the Indian Merchants' Chamber in Bombay, where an Automobile Factory Committee was appointed to prepare a scheme for car manufacture. Although the committee in its report on 20 May 1936 approved Visveswaraiya's scheme in its broad outlines, doubts about the feasibility of the scheme were expressed at this stage among Bombay's industrial circles, which had been so enthusiastic a year earlier. The scheme made no headway for a time in these circumstances, until it received a powerful push from the setting up of the Congress ministries in the provinces in 1937. Characteristically, it was Walchand Hirachand who first took up the scheme in earnest and he received assurance of patronage from the Kher ministry in Bombay. The Government of India, however, was not forthcoming in the matter of necessary aid for initiating the industry and the resignation of the Kher ministry in 1939 set Walchand's project back many years.[231] Meanwhile in Eastern India the Birla group had also taken up the project of a car manufacturing plant in India, and though neither group received any assistance from the Government of India during the Second World War,

[230] Ibid.
[231] *Walchand Hirachand*, pp. 311–31, 431–56.

Walchand Hirachand and Ghanshyamdas Birla began to push their respective plans in rivalry with each other in spite of numerous obstacles. It was felt by some leading businessmen like Sir Purshotamdas Thakurdas that in a limited market it would not be advantageous for two Indian groups to start car manufacture in mutual competition, and with a view to merging the two schemes negotiations were held in 1942. But no agreement could be reached and in the same year the Birla group formed the Hindustan Motors Ltd. in Calcutta with a paid-up capital of Rs 4.96 crores. Walchand, whose previous attempt to form an automobile company had been foiled by the refusal of official permission for registration, countered by forming in 1944 the Premier Automobiles Ltd. in Bombay with a paid-up capital of Rs 2.2 crores.[232]

In the absence of the necessary import permits from the Government of India there was no question of starting production during the Second World War, but both groups prepared to meet the predictable increase in the post-war demand for cars. Premier Automobiles completed their works and commenced operations for the assembly of cars in March 1947. Due to the threat of partition in eastern India, Hindustan Motors could not decide on the location of their factory until 1947. Both companies installed plant on a scale which was much in excess of potential demand in the immediate future, in the hope that demand would expand considerably in the coming years. In the beginning both companies merely assembled parts of Studebaker (in the case of the Birla group) and Dodge (in the case of the Walchand group) imported from abroad. Hindustan Motors had a comprehensive programme and by 1953 had made substantial progress in the manufacture of parts, unlike Premier Automobiles.[233]

1. *Capital.* The automobile industry required a large initial outlay, but this proved no hindrance because the industry by definition could only be undertaken by those who possessed the necessary capital and Birla and Walchand were big groups with large financial resources. Walchand initially relied on the support of the Congress ministry in Bombay for raising the capital and later on looked to the Mysore State for financial support. These hopes did not materialize, but the sum of Rs 2.5 crores which he had set as the target was ulti-

---

[232] Ibid., p. 480; *Tariff Commission, Government of India: Report on the Automobile Industry*, Bombay, 1953.

[233] Ibid.

mately raised without any political support. The Tariff Commission stated later on that in the case of Premier Automobiles, the financial outlay was adequate. Premier Automobiles had no difficulty in incurring the necessary expenditure of Rs 17 lakhs for machinery under order.[234] Still less was this a problem with the Birla group, which possessed a much broader capital base than Walchand and invested a much bigger sum in their plant under a more comprehensive programme of assemblage as well as manufacture of parts.

2. *Technology and foreign collaboration.* The weakness of these two bigger houses of India lay not in their financial resources, but in their lack of technical know-how. It was this crucial technological weakness that dictated in the case of two most aggressively nationalistic business houses of India the resort to collaboration with foreign manufacturing interests. Precisely those nationalist groups which fought most strenuously against foreign interests for India's transition to a technologically more sophisticated manufacturing stage found it necessary to make large concessions to their opponents in order to obtain access to extremely complex technology. The course of action for making India self-reliant in car manufacture pointed towards technological agreements with foreign car manufacturers which put the Indian capitalist groups in a dependent position. Hindustan Motors entered into technical collaboration with Morris Motors in UK and Studebaker Corporation in USA. Premier Automobiles entered into technical collaboration with the Chrysler Corporation of USA for manufacture of Chrysler products (Dodges) and with Fiat of Italy for Fiat cars.[235] Walchand was quite firm in rejecting the demand of foreign automobile interests for financial control over the projected car industry and it was on this issue that his earlier negotiations with Ford got stuck. But he could not avoid technological dependence and had to turn from Ford to Chrysler, who agreed to sell the technology without demanding financial participation.[236] Both the Walchand and Birla groups were compelled to borrow machinery and equipment as well as technical know-how and skilled personnel from their foreign associates. Both had to rely on foreign associates for the design of their cars. Hindustan Motors had not agreed to have all indigenous car parts checked by the Nuffield group (though in practice they did so) while Premier

---

[234] Ibid.   [235] Ibid.
[236] *Walchand Hirachand*, pp. 431–56.

Automobiles were under an obligation to the Chrysler group to do so.[237]

3. *Components.* The basic raw material for automobile manufacture, steel, had acquired some degree of maturity by the latter part of the twenties. Before this point in time there could be no question of car manufacture in India. Nevertheless, there were still very large gaps in the supply of materials which could not be filled overnight. Some of these materials came to be manufactured in India during the Second World War as a result of further expansion of the industrial base. Had car manufacture been undertaken before the war, it would have been still more dependent on foreign supplies and the cost of production would have left incommensurate margins of profit for some time to come. In advanced countries car manufacturers produced only major components and bought the remaining materials—roller bearings, starting motors, generators, carburetters, air cleaners, oil filters, lamps, bulbs, tyres, fan belts, batteries, wheels, nuts and bolts—from developed ancillary industries. In the United States and Australia the development of the ancillary industries had made considerable progress before the manufacture of complete vehicles was taken up. In India only a nucleus of ancillary industries existed at the beginning of the fifties. Premier Automobiles had to set up their own ancillary industries unit, a costly proposition. The following ancillary industries had developed by the early fifties: pistons (India Pistons started production in 1952), cylinder liners (started by India Pistons in 1952), leaf springs (started by Metropolitan Springs in 1951), electric bulbs (started by Pradip Lamp Works in 1951), fuel pump diaphragms (undertaken by United Trading Co. in 1944 for the Defence Department), etc.[238] Thus the ancillaries developed as a response to the main industry in India, not the other way round.

4. *Market.* The demand for motor vehicles did not expand significantly after the twenties. According to an estimate by General Motors of USA, the minimum volume of demand needed for break-even point was 25,000 vehicles, and it would not be worthwhile manufacturing cars without a demand of 30,000 vehicles. This estimate was for large-scale production without protective duties. From 1922–3 to 1946–7, only in four years (1929–30, 1930–1, 1937–8 and 1941–2) was the desired target of 30,000 vehicles reached. Obviously there was no question of large-scale production, and no scope for

[237] *Report on Automobile Industry.*   [238] Ibid.

drastic economies of scale in India. However, Hindustan Motors and Premier Automobiles calculated that with a protective duty of 33.33 per cent, break-even point could be reached at a much lower figure for small-scale manufacture. The break-even point was estimated by Hindustan Motors at 13,000 and by Premier Automobiles at 7,500. With a small volume of demand, it was therefore held to be possible, with protection, to manufacture vehicles, providing the resources of ancillary industries were properly mobilized and management was efficient.

5. *Enterprise.* Since protection to the extent of 33.33 per cent was out of the question under British administration, it seems that the Walchand and Birla ventures in the automobile industry were a gamble on the future and reflected an aggressive, pent-up desire on the part of sections of Indian capitalists to be independent, to acquire power in relation to foreign interests, to expand the technological and industrial base of Indian society in a dedicated spirit. It must not be thought that such an aggressive sense of mission and a financially questionable willingness to gamble on a still unforeseeable future was characteristic of all sections of Indian business and industrial circles. The initial enthusiasm of Bombay's industrial circles for M. Visveswaraiya's scheme in 1935 waned quickly within the course of a year. Visveswaraiya seems to have banked heavily on the only steel-producing group in India—Tatas—and in fact the Tata group did initially show some interest in the scheme. The head of the Tata group, Sir Nowrojee Saklatvala, presided over the first meeting of Indian capitalists on the car industry arranged by Visveswaraiya, significantly, at Tata House in 1935. Subsequently, however, Tatas did not come forward to initiate the car industry, and it fell to Walchand to venture out in this new field with the encouragement of the short-lived Congress ministry. Visveswaraiya complained at one stage of lack of initiative on the part of Indian capitalists:

There are few undertakings open to us today which promise such good results financially, or for which the time and conditions are more favourable . . . Here, in spite of our many resources and our proved success in some of the industries recently tried, like pig-iron, steel, cement and sugar, we are afraid of making a beginning. If this project is proceeded with, with the necessary unanimity and courage, success is well within our reach.[239]

Many hard-headed businessmen of Bombay did not agree with M.

[239] *Walchand Hirachand*, p. 317.

Visveswaraiya's optimistic view of the situation. The opinion was expressed that under prevailing conditions it was more profitable to import cars rather than manufacture them in India. There was much to justify this proposition from the financial results of General Motors' business of assembling and selling American cars in India, which proved a real 'money-spinner' even judged by American standards. Describing this imported car business as 'a singular goldmine', the *Bombay Sentinel* of 18 April 1941 noted that General Motors had started in India eleven years ago with a capital of Rs 1 crore and within a space of eleven years had reaped a net profit of Rs 1.50 crores.[240] General Motors and other foreign automobile interests systematically opposed the initiation of a car plant in India by insidious propaganda and covert lobbying. Understandably, the response of Indian industrial circles to Visveswaraiya's appeal was somewhat slow in these circumstances. There was no question of initiation of this industry by European houses operating in India, which were guided purely by considerations of profitability and soundness. The conclusion is inescapable that the Indian houses which ultimately took up the Visveswaraiya scheme were motivated by a vision beyond these considerations.

TABLE 36
IMPORTS OF VEHICLES INTO INDIA

Year	No. Imported
1927–8	23,804
1930–1	21,514
1933–4	15,255
1936–7	22,099
1938–9	18,848

SOURCE. *Report on the Automobile Industry.*

6. *Government policy.* The hesitation which M. Visveswaraiya encountered in Indian business circles could have been easily overcome if the Government of India could have been counted upon to support the projected industry. The policy of discriminating protection, under which protection was only given to industries which had existed for some time and which promised to be able to dispense with protection within a foreseeable time, left no scope for extension

[240] Ibid., pp. 440–1.

of protection to a newly born and untried industry like car manufacture, which did not qualify for protection under the conditions
laid down by the Fiscal Commission. Even so, it is significant that
the project was taken up in earnest as soon as a nationalist Congress
ministry came into power in 1937. The resignation of that ministry
had the effect of considerably delaying the initiation of car manufacture. From indifference during the Congress tenure in the provinces
the attitude of the Government of India turned to one of obstructive-
ness during the Second World War. The financial assistance which
the Congress ministry had promised was now refused on the ground
that the car industry did not fall in the category of war effort, the
only category entitled to such aid in wartime.[241] Walchand then
turned to the Mysore State for the necessary help, and the Government of Mysore took up the project with enthusiasm. This support
was subsequently withdrawn when the Mysore Government were
advised, on the Maharaja's inquiry, by the Government of India that
the initiation of the automobile industry during the war would
impede war effort as it would mean release of dollars for machinery,
tools, etc.[242] To start the industry in India during the Second World
War, its inclusion in the list of war efforts was essential, because
without this no permission could be obtained from the Government
of India for the necessary foreign exchange of four million dollars
and for bringing to India at least twelve American technicians.[243]
The unborn industry was thus deprived of the stimulus of the
massive car orders placed by the defence authorities in India with
Ford and General Motors for war requirements.[244]

Conclusion

The technological base of Indian industry probably would not have
been able to support the development of automobile manufacture
before 1935, nor apparently were the Indian industrial circles
materially ready to take up the task before that. Even thereafter, the
technological problems, especially the absence of ancillary industries,
would have meant that the industry would have had to run for
some time without expectations of profit, though no doubt the
increased military demand after the outbreak of the Second World

[241] Ibid., pp. 434–5.
[242] Walchand's letter to Sir Joseph Bhore, the Dewan of Bhopal, 21 May 1941,
quoted in *Walchand Hirachand*, p. 446.
[243] Ibid., p. 446.   [244] Ibid., pp. 447–55.

War might have quickly put an existing car industry on its feet. Under such hypothetical logic of developments, the car industry would have become a substantial industry by 1947, when operations for manufacture were first commenced. The single most important factor which precluded this hypothetical development was the conservative tariff policy of the Government of India before the war and its deliberate discouragement of automobile manufacture during wartime. The British outlook on planning for war production proved to be as conservative as their attitude to tariff protection in peace-time. In response to a question in Parliament about the refusal of aid to automobile manufacture in India by a Labour M.P., the Secretary of State replied uncompromisingly that the resources which the establishment of an automobile industry would draw upon were fully required for the development of war production. Aid could be given to the industry after the war providing it 'did not at this moment draw upon labour and material urgently required for the war production'.[245] Amery, the Secretary of State, also wrote privately to Winterton on 1 May 1941 in a letter forwarded by the latter to Walchand:

You will, of course, agree that we cannot in present circumstances be expected to assist this development unless it is justified on account of war. There are cases in which the supply, for example, of machinery and skilled personnel would be detrimental to war production elsewhere, and things that are in short supply can only be sent to India, if, on balance, that is going to help us to win. I think that the criticism of people like Mr Walchand probably arises from failure or unwillingness to recognize this.[246]

It would appear that in the overall British scheme of production for global war, India was to occupy the position of a supplier of raw materials rather than a manufacturer of finished instruments for waging war, a position strictly analogous to her nineteenth century role in the international economy. The economic rationale was at any rate the same: the most efficient distribution of productive resources from a world-view of things.

12. Aluminium

Growth

Alumina, the intermediate material needed for manufacturing aluminium, is produced from bauxite. Aluminium ingots, manufactured

[245] Ibid., p. 453.   [246] Ibid.

from alumina, are sent to rolling mills for producing sheets and circles, and these are again sent to utensil-making plants for producing hollow-ware and, where more sophisticated industrial uses of aluminium have been developed, to other manufacturing industries. In India the utensil-making plants came first, then the rolling mills and finally the smelter plants for manufacturing aluminium ingots from alumina during the Second World War. At the same time arrangements were also made during the war for production of alumina by exploiting India's bauxite deposits. Aluminium manufactures in India thus developed in four distinct stages.

In the inter-war period the aluminium hollow-ware industry was so well established that it did not face any competition from imported household utensils, the prices of which were at a higher level on account of sea freight. Aluminium Manufacturing Co. catered to the expanding market for aluminium utensils in India. In every bazar aluminium-ware was pushing out brassware and enormous quantities of aluminium were being handled in every town and village. The company's business rapidly expanded with the growing popularity of aluminium for every kind of household use. The factory, situated in Dum Dum, gave employment to 600 men under supervision of European experts and was equipped with a plant embracing the most modern machinery. There had been no attempt on the part of the company to produce the metal itself in India. It was solely engaged in manufacturing finished articles from sheets, ingots, circles and other semi-finished forms of aluminium imported from Britain. The company also specialized in production of modern light alloy sand and die castings which had made rapid progress in motor, electrical and other industries, but in the existing state of industrial development in India, it was for the bazars that the company principally catered and its trade in this direction ran into many hundreds of tons of utensils annually.[247]

Foreign interests had made various investigations into the possibility of producing alumina from India's bauxite deposits in conjunction with hydroelectric schemes, but no concrete plan emerged from these investigations. In 1936 a paper read by an industrial chemist of the Bombay Government, Dr M. S. Patel, on the possibility of producing aluminium in Bombay, which pointed to India's large bauxite deposits and spelt out how these could be exploited for large-

[247] Allister Macmillan, *Seaports of India and Ceylon*, London, 1928, pp. 131–2.

scale manufacture of aluminium, drew the attention of industrial circles, especially that of Walchand Hirachand and Juggilal Singhania. Even before this Walchand had tried in 1935 to obtain the support of the Tata group for a plan for an aluminium plant at Radhanagari in Kolhapur State drawn up by a British engineer named Harry Gibbs, but though the Tata and Walchand groups both showed an initial interest in the scheme it fell through when Tatas lost interest. Later in 1939, when plans for exploiting the Tungar Hill bauxite deposits (to which Dr Patel had drawn attention) near Bombay were pushed by a merchant group either for export to Japan in the form of ore or for manufacture at an aluminium plant in Bombay, Walchand sought to prevent export of ore by trying to obtain the Bombay Congress ministry's support for an aluminium plant under his management. Nothing came of the plan since the Congress resigned from office. During the Second World War, due to urgent war needs the Government of India once again sought to revive Walchand's plan for an aluminium plant at Bombay, but Walchand refused to take up the project as he was already fully committed to pushing his wartime plans for aeroplane, car and ship production, and as the J. K. (Singhania) group had already set up a plant in the eastern region.[248]

The J. K. group, which was coming up fast on India's business horizon and was not as fully tied up as the Walchand group, had pursued the plan for an aluminium plant more vigorously since the publication of Dr Patel's report in 1936. The Aluminium Corporation of India was set up in 1937 by Juggilal Kamlapat in Calcutta. The following year Indian Aluminium Company was set up in Calcutta by a foreign controlling group, the capital being provided by British and Canadian interests in equal amount and the management being assumed by Aluminium Company of Canada which appointed a Managing Director for the Indian subsidiary. Neither the J. K. group nor the foreign company succeeded in commencing production until the later stages of war, the former commencing production in 1944 and the latter in 1943. In 1947–8 the combined production of these two groups came to exceed the total pre-war demand for aluminium in India, but by then demand had increased by about six to seven times and the Indian concerns could meet only 22.5 per cent of the total demand, the rest being met by rising imports.

[248] *Walchand Hirachand*, pp. 517–20.

1. *Raw materials and power*. India possessed abundant quantities of bauxite of better than average quality. The Tungar Hill deposits which were not used for manufacture in this period were estimated by Dr Patel to be good for half a century of production. The Radhanagari deposits in Kolhapur State which also remained unexploited during this period, were reported by engineer Gibbs to be 55 to 60 per cent purer than the bauxite deposits in England, which contained a greater amount of unwanted elements—iron oxide, titanium oxide and silica.[249] However, the production of aluminium on a commercial scale required cheap electricity for the decomposition of the bauxite ore. India possessed abundant water power resources with extensive bauxite deposits from which aluminium could be produced.[250] But hydroelectricity as a considerable source of power was not developed until the end of the period under review, and this was the single most important factor which deterred foreign entrepreneurs who from time to time investigated the possibility of aluminium manufacture in India. At the end of the Second World War the J. K. group and the British–Canadian group both applied for protection on the grounds that Indian bauxite was abundant and of above average quality, that the demand for the metal, though at present limited, was rising and that the only limiting factor was cheap power, a problem that could be taken care of by the development of the post-war hydroelectric schemes.[251] It was the underdeveloped state of India's hydroelectric power resources that dictated the pattern of development of aluminium manufacture.

Indian Aluminium Co., the first to commence production, at first merely imported alumina from abroad and used the imported material for producing aluminium ingots and rolling the latter into sheets and circles. In order to help aluminium production during the war the Government of India allowed the company to import alumina free of duty in 1940. Later the Aluminium Corporation (J. K. group) began to exploit the indigenous bauxite for producing alumina at their plant, and in the absence of cheap hydroelectric power in eastern India the J. K. Group had to obtain more expensive electric power from coal. Once the J. K. group began to produce alumina within the country, duty was reimposed by the government in 1944 on the ground that the indigenous product was

[249] Ibid., pp. 517–18.
[250] Allister Macmillan, op. cit., pp. 131–2.
[251] *ITB Report on Aluminium*.

now available to the British–Canadian controlled company if only they would use it. The latter had located their smelter at Alwaye in Travancore State where cheap hydroelectric power was to be obtained from the Pallisaval hydroelectric scheme.[252]

2. *Capital, technology and machinery.* Adequate financial resources were commanded by both the indigenous group and the foreign group which initiated the new industry, but the technological problems, especially the problem of location, were extremely complex in India. For the J. K. group which had no foreign collaborators the techno- logical problems were rendered additionally complex by the turn of events. Its initial plant was supplied by the firm of Skoda in Czecho- slovakia, which soon came under German occupation. The war interrupted the import of machinery and the J. K. group had to approach the government for facilities and priorities for importing the remaining machinery. As a result production could not com- mence until 1944, and then it was hindered by the ill-assorted nature of the plant and machinery, obtained from different sources and therefore lacking integral design. The plant and equipment of Indian Aluminium Co. was of British and Canadian manufacture, and was better designed on account of its access to foreign technology.[253] But neither group could satisfactorily solve the problem of location, which had peculiar problems in India on account of the undeveloped state of her water-power resources.

Singhanias decided to locate their works at Jaykaynagar near Asansol in the coalfields. A power plant of their own generated elec- tricity from coal at the site of the works, while their bauxite deposits lay 170 miles away from the site of the works. While Singhanias thus decided to set up their alumina plant, smelter and rolling mill at one locale, the Canadians set up the three main units of their works at places at long distances from each other. The rolling mill was located in Calcutta, the main centre of the hollow-ware industry and the largest consumer of sheets and circles. The smelter, which had to be located at a place where cheap and ample electrical power was available, was set up at Alwaye in Travancore State to benefit from the Pallisaval hydroelectric scheme. The alumina works were finally set up at Muri in eastern India, on account of the availability of the two principal raw materials—bauxite and coal. In so far as Singha- nias had every unit of the works at one site and were able to produce their own alumina from indigenous bauxite from the start, they

[252] Ibid.   [253] Ibid.

enjoyed some cost advantages in relation to the Canadians, who had dispersed their works in eastern and southern India, and were moreover using expensive imported alumina initially. In spite of proximity to the coalfields, however, J. K. works had a higher cost of energy in relation to the works of Indian Aluminium Co., which enjoyed much cheaper hydroelectricity. Once Indian Aluminium Co. began to exploit the indigenous bauxite ore, the resulting benefit from cost reduction was limited by the location of the works at three different places. The railway freights on raw materials and semi-manufactured goods for the production of alumina and aluminium were found to be considerably higher than in Canada. In the opinion of the Tariff Board, these mutual advantages and disadvantages of the two concerns cancelled each other out. But the Indian company was found to have unbalanced plant and lack of technical direction whereas the British–Canadian company was found to be enjoying both on account of its association with some of the leading aluminium producers of the world.[254]

3. *Enterprise and foreign monopoly.* At the end of the Second World War the aluminium concerns in India applied for protection on account of severe foreign competition from powerful cartels, which had long been a special feature of the industry in the Western world. It may be interesting to consider how far vested foreign monopoly interests delayed the development of aluminium enterprise in India. It should be noted in the first place that some foreign interests investigated the possibility of producing the metal in India from indigenous ore, but were put off by the problem of undeveloped hydroelectric power resources. While some foreign interests were thus not unwilling to investigate the possibility of reaping higher profits by locating an aluminium plant in India, other vested foreign interests were at work to frustrate such competitive foreign enterprise in India. Harry Gibbs, the British engineer who prepared the plan for an aluminium plant to exploit the bauxite deposits in Radhanagari, originally intended to raise sterling capital in Britain to form a British company with Sir Basil Blackett as Chairman. His plan for raising the necessary capital in Britain was apparently frustrated by the opposition of the British Aluminium Co. and other interested parties.[255] He therefore turned to the Walchand group for raising the capital and forming the company in India. The Walchand

---

[254] Ibid.
[255] *Walchand Hirachand*, p. 517.

group in turn felt unable to proceed without the backing of the Tata group, the largest commercial producers of hydroelectric power in western India. When the Tatas, after showing some initial interest, refused to commit themselves, the entire project fell through in 1935.[256]

It may be asked why initially it proved difficult to raise capital and attract enterprise even in India. The reasons are not entirely clear and can only be guessed. In the first place, there might have been conflicting objectives as to the control of the projected aluminium company, which might have progressed further if a single group had taken the entire responsibility for the works instead of the intended association of a few collaborating groups. Secondly, calculations by Tatas might have shown that cheap electric supply could only be obtained by planning a hydroelectric scheme on a much bigger scale than a single aluminium plant could support by its limited custom. It may be noted in this connection that the cost of hydroelectricity for Bombay cotton-mills was higher than the cost of Bengal coal transported over a vast distance.Thirdly, in the Bombay area at any rate the resources of the really aggressive Indian entrepreneurs seem to have been over-stretched by the simultaneous pushing of many entirely new schemes. This was especially the problem with the Walchand group, which had a smaller capital and organization base than Tata and Birla, and which therefore wanted Tatas to be associated with the new project. Later on during the Second World War Walchand had to deliberately set aside an attractive scheme for aluminium manufacture with government support on account of the numerous new projects over which his resources were thinly spread. In the thirties and the forties, as opportunities for investment in many new industries opened up within a short space of time, pioneering groups with adequate resources were revealed to be somewhat in short supply.

On the eastern side of India, where foreign enterprise had a strong base and new Indian business groups were coming up fast, the availability of a large market for aluminium in Calcutta succeeded in attracting the necessary capital and enterprise from the J. K. group and the British and Canadian aluminium interests. It was under foreign enterprise that the largest quantity of aluminium was ultimately produced during this period, with the help of cheap hydroelectricity from Travancore. Once the possibility of large

[256] Ibid., pp. 518–19.

profits in aluminium manufacture within India had sprung up, foreign enterprise did not lag behind indigenous enterprise. Foreign enterprise moreover had the specialization and technical experience which Indian enterprise lacked in this technologically complex field. The J. K. group was in origin a purely commercial and speculative group with no technical experience of industry and its lack of expertise was severely criticized by the Tariff Board. During the war Aluminium Corporation of India was not able to expand production even up to 2,000 tons, since it required at least one more boiler to step up production to 2,000 tons. Its plant was unbalanced since it had been ordered from two or three different fabricators without proper planning and coordination. It was producing 6,000 tons of alumina, though the rated capacity of the reduction works was only 2,000 tons. On a small output the cost of production of aluminium per unit was high and at the same time there was no market for the surplus alumina. A third boiler, though long needed, had not yet been ordered. The existing management did not supply the missing links with the least possible delay, and the Tariff Board noted 'lack of proper technical direction in the management of the Corporation'.[257]

4. *Market*. Production of aluminium was so far below demand during as well as after the Second World War that market restrictions never operated as a limiting factor since 1939. During the war the civil market was starved for many years, creating extraordinary demand. The Tariff Board reported in 1947 that the Indian public would be likely to use more aluminium in the future and that the establishment of the aircraft industry during the war would expand the market for the metal. Besides utensils, aluminium was also likely to come increasingly in use for cables, packaging, containers, processing and other industrial equipment.[258] One might ask, however, whether there was a sufficiently large market for economic production of aluminium in India before the war. It was estimated that production of 5,000 tons in the case of both J. K. and the British–Canadian works, each of which was producing less than 2,000 tons during the war, would have led to a fall in costs (including profit) from Rs 1,900 per ton to Rs 1,577 per ton. Taking a works of 5,000 ton capacity as the standard economic unit, it is interesting to note that the pre-war market in India would not have supported one such works, let alone two. Average annual import during the three years

[257] *ITB Report on Aluminium.*   [258] Ibid.

before the war was only 3,020 tons. But as the Tariff Board pointed out, the imports in the pre-war years gave no indication of India's real requirements, even for cooking utensils. Before the Great Depression consumption had been at a far higher level, the imports in 1929–30 and 1928–9 having amounted to 8,551 tons and 6,329 tons respectively (which would have comfortably accommodated an optimum plant).

TABLE 37

IMPORTS, PRODUCTION AND CONSUMPTION OF ALUMINIUM

(tons)

| Year | Imports | Production | | Consumption |
		Indian Aluminium Co.	Aluminium Corporation of India (J. K.)	
1935	2,600	—	—	2,600
1936	3,200	—	—	3,200
1937	3,200	—	—	3,200
1938	3,300	—	—	3,300
1939	2,900	—	—	2,900
1940	—	—	—	—
1941	—	—	—	—
1942	20	—	—	20
1943	16	1,272	—	1,288
1944	1,360	1,609	200	3,169
1945	4,572	1,344	900	6,816
1946	10,300	1,800	1,200	13,330
1947–8	15,500	2,500	2,000	20,000

SOURCE. *Report of the Indian Tariff Board on the Aluminium Industry*, 1947, app. 5.

5. *Government policy*. Given the problems of the limited size of the market in the thirties, the need to produce on a large scale in order to effect economies, the complex technology of the industry and the stiff competition from foreign cartels, it is surprising that Indian and foreign enterprise was willing to initiate the new industry without any expectation of government help which could not be given within the framework of discriminating protection. Had government help been forthcoming, a third plant might have been set up in the Bombay area. While the Congress ministry was in office,

Walchand once again revived his plan of an aluminium works near Bombay and in May 1939 asked the Government of Bombay to help him raise the capital by guaranteeing 3.5 per cent interest for ten years. As the Congress ministry resigned soon afterwards, the plan was dropped.[259] During the Second World War the Government of India, under the pressure of immediate requirements, declared aluminium manufacture to be a part of the war effort and helped the infant industry to its feet. The government provided the J. K. group with expert Canadian assistance and provided facilities for import of machinery and other priority materials to both concerns. The Indian industry grew up under the shelter of wartime pooling arrangements and import control.[260]

Conclusion

Market conditions were not particularly favourable for aluminium manufacture during the thirties, but nevertheless it was during this decade, when cheap hydroelectric power became available and Indian enterprise became ready to take up the challenge, that two works were set up simultaneously in 1937–8. Before this decade the technological possibilities of the industry had not been explored properly enough to attract Indian enterprise, and foreign enterprise had been deterred by lack of cheap power. In spite of favourable market conditions in the twenties, one could not reasonably expect either foreign or indigenous enterprise to take the plunge in those circumstances. Once the industry was taken up in the late thirties, its existence and future expansion were guaranteed by the intervention of the Second World War. Everything that could be done to stimulate an industry for war needs was done in the case of aluminium by the government. That production remained below 2,000 tons in both plants was due to technological problems that could not be solved overnight.

13. Cotton-Textile Machinery

Growth

Since the late nineteenth century British textile machinery manufacturers had done a flourishing business by supplying the entire (or nearly so) requirement of the growing cotton-textile industry of India

---

[259] *Walchand Hirachand*, p. 519.
[260] *ITB Report on Aluminium.*

for plant and machinery. It was only on the eve of the Second World War that steps were taken to reduce the heavy reliance of cotton mills in India on textile machinery supplies from Britain, a channel through which a substantial portion of the gains from the burgeoning cotton-textile industry had leaked annually to Britain for more than half a century. It was the house of Ghanshyamdas Birla, the leading representative of Indian national capitalism, that took steps to remedy this state of dependence by forming the Textile Machinery Corporation Ltd. (Texmaco).[261] Shortly after the completion of the factory building and erection of machines, Texmaco's plant in Calcutta was taken over by the government for war purposes. Production, which had begun in the previous year, was interrupted. In 1943 some machines were allowed to be transferred to the Gwalior branch of Texmaco, where some looms were manufactured during the war.[262] A small dividend of 6 per cent was declared in 1943 and 1944 but none subsequently.[263] The main Calcutta works was returned by the government not before 1945, by which time the machinery had undergone heavy wear and tear on account of war work. There was need for extensive re-equipment of the industry, which took a year to design and perfect. Only in 1946 did Texmaco produce one complete ring frame.[264]

Two other textile machinery concerns were set up during the war, one under Acme Manufacturing Co. in Bombay and the other by Textools Ltd. in Coimbatore. In 1946, Texmaco and Textools Ltd. produced 10 and 8 ring frames respectively. The Walchand group also started textile machinery manufacture under Acme Manufacturing Co. registered in 1919. Manufacture of ring frames was commenced by this company in 1947–8, when 16 frames were turned out. By then Texmaco was producing 160 frames. The capacity of Texmaco was 300 ring frames per year and that of Acme Manufacturing Co. was 72.

1. *Components.* Iron and steel, the basic raw material for textile machinery, had become firmly established industries with the Greater Extensions of TISCO in the twenties. The ITB reported in 1947 that

---

[261] *Interim Report of the Indian Tariff Board on the Cotton Textile Machinery Industry,* Bombay, 1947.

[262] *Report of the Indian Tariff Board on the Cotton Textile Machinery Industry,* Bombay, 1949.

[263] *Investor's Encyclopedia 1947; Investor's India Year Book 1957.*

[264] *ITB Report on Cotton Textile Machinery,* 1949.

13

the principal raw materials for manufacture of ring frames, spindles and rings were pig iron, steel bars, tin sheets, steel tubes, wood and certain non-ferrous metals such as brass, aluminium and nickel. Most of these were reported to be already available within the country or could be made available in the near future. In 1947 steel tubes and steel bars for spindle blades and tin sheets of proper quality were not available in the country, but in view of the high efficiency of the steel industry in India the ITB predicted that there would be no difficulty in producing them all in India.[265] In 1951 it was again reported to the Tariff Board that certain raw materials such as steel rods of certain required sizes were not produced by TISCO because the total requirements of such sizes were too small to make their production economical. For this reason the newly opened Star Textile Engineering Works were relying on imports though Texmaco was managing with smaller rods.

The main initial difficulty of the textile machinery industry was that whereas manufacturers in advanced countries could purchase many parts ready-made for production, the Indian manufacturers had to manufacture on their own as many as 17,944 parts falling into 422 groups or varieties. In 1949 Texmaco was manufacturing all parts of the spinning frame except such minor items as bolts, nuts, washers, lappets, springs, ball-bearing chains, cotton tape, felt and leather. The difficulties of initiating such complex industries on a narrow technological base naturally called for exceptional stamina and considerable financial resources.

2. *Capital and enterprise.* Texmaco's paid-up capital in 1947 was Rs 1 crore. As in the case of Hindustan Motors, the Birla group did not hesitate in providing massive capital outlay for the initiation of Texmaco. New Birla enterprises were invariably launched with adequate funds for outlay and great financial reserves. Texmaco had a well-equipped factory planned on modern lines and run by competent supervisory staff.[266] The financial policy of the company was conducted with prudence and restraint. During 1946–8 no dividends were paid except to preference shareholders, and the managing agents received no commission.[267]

3. *Technology and skilled labour.* The technology of textile machinery manufacture had to be imported initially. Fourteen British

[265] *ITB Report on Cotton Textile Machinery*, 1947.
[266] Ibid.; *ITB Report on Cotton Textile Machinery Industry*, 1949.
[267] Ibid.

experts were employed by Texmaco.[268] The quality of the machinery produced by Texmaco was very satisfactory, in spite of the fact that labour could not be trained to British standards in such a short time.[269] The management of the Victoria Mills Ltd. stated to the Tariff Board in 1949 that Texmaco ring frames were as good as any of foreign make. Indigenous looms were also said by representatives of the cotton-mill industry to compare favourably with imported looms at that time.[270] Later in 1951 cotton-textile representatives expressed dissatisfaction with the quality of indigenous fluted rollers.[271]

4. *Market.* The cotton-textile industry in India being one of the large-sized textile industries of the world, there was a very large market for cotton-textile machinery in India. However, as Texmaco pointed out to the Tariff Board in 1949, except for the boom period during 1921–4, the growth of the cotton-textile industry from 1921 to 1947 had been rather slow.[272] During the cotton boom in 1921–2, 1922–3 and 1923–4, the annual value of imports of cotton-textile machinery into Bombay had been Rs 60.8, 65.9 and 44.7 million respectively. Thereafter imports of cotton-textile machinery into Bombay continued up to the outbreak of the Second World War at a more or less steady level of Rs 10.5 thousand.[273]

5. *Government policy.* There being no provision for protection of an entirely new industry in the conditions laid down by the Fiscal Commission, the Texmaco venture was launched before the Second World War without any expectation of aid from the government. Had the protection policies of the government in the inter-war period not been so discriminating, Indian enterprise might have been drawn earlier to textile machinery manufacture in the hope of official support. Without that the houses venturing into the field had to be very sure of themselves before they could take the initiative. Once the initiative had been taken, further progress during the Second World War was obstructed by the government's requisition of the plant for other war purposes. Texmaco stated to the Tariff Board in 1949 that if the main Calcutta works had not been taken over and if the company had been allowed to undertake manufacture of spinning machinery during wartime, it could have acquired considerable technical experience by the end of the war and could have built up strong reserves out of war profits.

---

[268] *ITB Report*, 1947.   [269] Ibid.   [270] *ITB Report*, 1949.
[271] *ITB Report*, 1951.   [272] *ITB Report*, 1949.
[273] A. K. Bagchi, *Private Investment*, Table 7.10, p. 258.

Conclusion

It may be asked why, in spite of the existence of a large market for cotton-textile machinery and the availability of the principal raw materials in the inter-war period, the cotton-textile machinery enterprise came at the very end of that period. Partly the answer may lie in the need for a period of gestation. Indian entrepreneurship needed some time to prepare themselves morally and materially to venture out in this new field, especially since no government aid could be expected. The steel industry also had to acquire some degree of stability and diversification before it could properly feed the textile machinery industries. These initial bottlenecks were not problems which could not have been solved by energetic government action in the early twenties, when with the Greater Extensions of TISCO and the boom in the cotton industry the basic conditions for initiation of the cotton-textile machinery industry came into existence. Again, during the Second World War, when the industry might have rapidly built up a technological and financial base under its own initiative, requisition of the Texmaco plant by the government resulted in the loss of a splendid opportunity which set the industry back many years. But for a narrow war production policy which took no account of the long-term needs of defence production, the textile machinery industry might even have seized the Second World War as the opportunity for supplying the greater part of India's domestic requirements.

14. Machine Tools

Growth

Before the First World War some factory and shop-owners produced machine tools on a small scale for their own use and not for sale in the market. During and after the First World War small manufacturers in Panjab began to sell machine tools in the market. Some engineering concerns undertook manufacture of girder milling and drilling machines, but the general quality being low few of these sold in the market. The earliest quality manufacturer in this line was P. N. Dutta & Co. of Calcutta which commenced production of reasonably good machine tools in 1930. Production of quality machine tools was also undertaken by Cooper Engineering Works (Satara) in 1935 and by Indian Machinery Co. in 1937. The total number of machine tools produced in India before the outbreak of the Second World War was estimated to be no more than about 100 per year. The country's requirements were almost wholly met by imports. With the outbreak of the war imports fell, but not drastically at first. With the entry of Japan in the war in 1943 imports were largely cut off and India's reliance on imports proved a serious bottleneck in equipping her industrial plants for war production. The machine tools industry was called on to make great efforts and it rose splendidly to the occasion with government assistance. From 316 tools in 1942 (of which 273 were graded to be of a certain quality by the authorities) production rose to 8,810 in 1945 (of which 4,121 were of graded quality). The average annual value of machine tools produced in India from 1942 to 1946 was Rs 1.05 crores (of which the value of graded tools was Rs 75 lakhs and of ungraded tools Rs 30 lakhs) at controlled prices. In 1946, when production reached a peak, the value of machine tools produced in India was Rs 1.74 crores and was about 23.5 per cent of the total value of machine tools imported and produced in India during that year.[274]

1. *Raw materials.* In 1947 the ITB reported that the raw materials of heavy character needed for the machine tools industry were practically all available in the country, e.g. pig iron, steel and scrap, limestone, aluminium, lead, antimony, coal and coke, timber and foundry sand; the only heavy raw materials not produced in India were tin and copper. The semi-fabricated stores which had to be imported for producing machine tools were special types of steel sections, ball and roller bearings, special lubricating accessories, plastic, specialized electric gear, 'V' belts, roller and tooth chains and sprockets, and bright machined nuts, bolts, crashers, studs and set screws. The quantities of semi-fabricated stores such as ball and roller bearings needed for manufacture of machine tools were small.[275] On the whole it may be said that with the development of iron and steel in the twenties, the level of sophistication of industries needed for manufacture of machine tools had been reached in India during the postwar boom following the Peace of Versailles. The development of the machine tools industry was not seriously impeded by shortages of essential supplies before the Second World War.

2. *Labour.* During the Second World War, however, the machine tools industry could not fully utilize the opportunities of rapid growth on account of shortages on the supply side. Not only were

[274] *Report of the Indian Tariff Board on the Machine Tools Industry*, Bombay, 1947.   [275] Ibid.

the necessary raw materials in short supply, but there were labour troubles which affected the growth of the industry.[276]

3. *Technology.* A more serious difficulty in the growth of the machine tools industry was the lack of technology and specialization in India. The machine tools industries in advanced countries owed their pre-eminence to specialization and rationalization. The number of firms manufacturing machine tools in 1945 was 186, of which only 9 concerns were stated to have good or fair plant and technical supervision.

4. *Enterprise.* The sudden growth of the industry in response to the needs of war prevented the firms engaged in production from acquiring a specialized character. General engineering firms took up manufacture of machine tools while retaining their other activities. Some of the well-known manufacturers—such as Kirloskars—did switch to exclusive manufacture of machine tools or were planning to do so in the near future.[277] There were many small firms producing sub-standard machine tools. The bigger firms attained a higher level of technological sophistication even without specialized knowledge on the part of the controlling groups. One successful concern which was set up even before the Second World War—Cooper Engineering Works—owed its success largely to the take-over of the firm by Walchand Hirachand in 1940. It was a general engineering workshop at Satara opened in 1922 by Dhanishah Cooper for making agricultural implements. The firm subsequently diversified its operations, taking up manufacture of diesel engines in 1933 and of machine tools (lathes, shaping machines, pillar drills) in 1937. Lack of funds, however, put the concern in an unsound position, until it was rescued in 1940 by Walchand, who went into partnership with Sir Dhanishah. At that time the capital of the company was Rs 2 lakhs; Walchand raised a further Rs 17 lakhs by floating shares worth Rs 7 lakhs and 6 per cent fifteen-year debentures worth Rs 10 lakhs.[278] With this broader financial base the company expanded its production in several directions, but it did not specialize in manufacture of machine tools. There were too many specialized engineering lines and too few capitalists with the right mentality and resources to permit much specialization. Men like Walchand were compelled to devote their entrepreneurial talents and financial resources to as many specialized lines as were in need of these.

[276] Ibid.   [277] Ibid.
[278] *Walchand Hirachand*, pp. 488–92.

5. *Market*. Machine tools were needed in peace-time for maintaining and expanding such industries as manufacture of locomotives, textile machinery, motor-cars, electrical equipment, radio and television sets, mining machinery, etc. in advanced industrialized countries. In wartime machine tools were indispensable for manufacture of armaments, ships, aeroplanes, etc. India had not reached the level of industrial sophistication that goes with the existence of these complex industries. But the market for machine tools in even a relatively backward country like India was not small before the Second World War. Before the war imports of machine tools practically represented the total demand in the country. The value of imports before the war was about Rs 2 crores a year. The market expanded considerably during the war and licences issued for imports were worth Rs 3.04 crores in 1945, Rs 5.64 crores in 1946 and Rs 8 crores in 1947.[279] The increased use of machine tools during and after the war was an index of the expansion of the industrial base of production in India.

6. *Government policy*. The assistance given to the machine tools industry during the war by the Government of India was crucial to its growth. Government appointed a Machine Tool Controller to secure good quality tools for the war industries, the armed forces and the ordnance factories, and to control imports. British technical help and expertise was provided by the authorities and necessary supplies were made available. As a result the industry made rapid progress during the war.[280] Before the Second World War no such assistance was given to the machine tools industry.

Conclusion

For the growth of heavy, technologically complex industries, a large machine tools industry was a prerequisite. But in a technologically backward economy, neither the supply of raw materials nor the total domestic demand was such as to give a natural push to the growth of the industry, and it was only the outbreak of the war and the aid given by the government that drew the engineering firms and large business groups in the country to the machine tool industry. Had government effectively assisted the industry after the First World War, the industry might have come into its own on the basis of the demand for machine tools and the supply of iron and steel

[279] *ITB Report on the Machine Tools Industry*, 1947.
[280] Ibid.

during the inter-war period, but even in those circumstances the big push to the industry would have had to await the development of technologically complex industries, such as automobiles and aeroplanes, during and after the Second World War.

15. Sewing-Machines

Growth

Manufacture of sewing-machines was attempted in India from 1935 onwards, but this was one industry which could not find its feet during the period under review and was only organized properly after independence. An examination of the question why it could not develop before 1947 in spite of the best efforts is therefore likely to give us important insights into the constraints on industrial growth in India. The history of this industry is closely tied up with the history of Jay Engineering Works, begun in 1935 by an enthusiastic Panjabi engineer of Calcutta in a small way and taken over in 1938 by the Shri Ram group. Experiments in the production of Usha, the brand name of the sewing-machine produced by JEW, were interrupted by the outbreak of the Second World War, which necessitated the diversion of its productive capacity to munitions. Towards the end of the war the manufacture of Usha was taken up again. By the beginning of the fifties JEW had captured roughly two-fifths of the domestic market and was also exporting machines at a loss in order to earn foreign exchange for the import of essential raw materials. The following was the number of machines produced in the post-war years:[281]

1945–6	1946–7	1947–8	1948–9	1949–50	1950–1
5,061	6,490	11,763	20,937	27,000	30,000

By 1953 the industry was sufficiently well-established to be able to dispense with protection. The fair price of Usha was already considerably lower than the landing price of the imported Singer

[281] *Report of the Indian Tariff Board on the Sewing Machine Industry*, Bombay, 1947; *Report of the Indian Tariff Board on the Continuance of Protection to the Sewing Machine Industry*, Bombay, 1949. The figures for 1949–50 and 1950–1 are estimates of future production.

machine, but the quality of Usha was lower than that of Singer.[282]

1. *Raw materials.* Considering the level of India's industrial development, JEW was a premature venture. The manufacture of sewing-machines depended on special high quality steels, a field in which the steel plants of India did not venture forth before the Second World War. Some of the re-rolling mills were producing steel castings before the war and theoretically it was possible for JEW to have sewing-machine beds and arms cast at these re-rolling mills.

2. *Equipment.* Apart from special steels, the manufacture of sewing-machines was dependent also on machine tools of good quality. When JEW was taken over by Shri Ram, the machine tool industry had not yet developed sufficiently to supply the requirements. For tool-room equipment, JEW was entirely dependent on imports and these were cut off with the outbreak of war in 1939. It was not until 1945 that the essential tooling could be completed. A German engineer with work experience in Singer reported during the war that the plant and machinery of JEW was old and unsuitable.[283] It had been assembled sporadically and haphazardly by the Panjabi engineer who initiated the enterprise; he imported machine tools and small tools on an *ad hoc* basis and not according to a long-term plan. As a result cost of production was high and production could not be expanded without better tooling. In 1947 the Tariff Board reported that the two most serious bottlenecks in the expansion of output, which would take years to overcome, were in respect of tool-room equipment and technical personnel.[284]

3. *Technology.* Manufacture of sewing-machines was one industry which depended for its growth on extremely complex and sophisticated technology. India had just not attained the level of technological proficiency that was required for successful manufacture during the period under review. At the time when JEW was initiated, not more than a dozen factories located in the most advanced countries of the world were successfully manufacturing sewing-machines.[285] The technological complexity of the process of manufacture will be apparent from the following description by the Indian Tariff Board:

[282] Ibid.

[283] Arun Joshi, *Lala Shri Ram: A Study in Entrepreneurship and Industrial Management*, New Delhi, 1973, p. 360.

[284] *ITB Report on Sewing Machines,* 1947.

[285] Joshi, op. cit., p. 292.

Sewing-machine is an assembly of parts machined out of iron castings, steel forgings and steel sections. A very high degree of precision is required in the finishing of all internal and external dimensions in order to ensure light running and interchangeability of parts. Such of the parts as have to withstand maximum wear and tear have to be subjected to proper heat treatment for hardening. Several machining operations which cannot be accomplished efficiently on ordinary machines require special-purpose machines. All gauges, tools, jigs and fixtures are made by precision machines in the tool room where extra care is required to check their dimensions and ensure hardness of the parts which have to withstand great wear and tear caused by constant use.[286]

The progress of JEW in the face of these technical difficulties was slow and fumbling in the post-war years. Considering these difficulties, it was no mean achievement that by 1949 the fair price of Usha machines was lower than the landing price of imported Singer machines. Nevertheless, consumers held the view—not without reason—that the quality of Singer was appreciably higher than that of Usha.[287]

4. *Labour.* Until 1943 recruitment of labour in JEW was done through contractors, a system which proved a hindrance to the building up of a trained, disciplined and highly productive work force. The contractors, as middlemen, had the management at their mercy. Periodically they resorted to go-slow tactics, made it impossible to impose discipline among the workers and prevented the introduction of an incentive scheme through reward for high quality work. In 1943 Lala Shri Ram deliberately broke the ring of contractors and this was soon followed by a rapid improvement in the quality of work.[288] Nevertheless, the supply of skilled mechanics and machinists remained a major problem. As Lala Shri Ram defined the problem in a letter to the Works Manager in 1944, expansion depended on higher quality and lower cost, which in turn depended on good tools and good workers. To ensure the supply of trained personnel, a training scheme and a reward scheme were introduced in 1944, and the workers were classified into different grades to provide incentive through promotion.[289] In 1947 JEW also introduced a scheme of profit-sharing to the extent of 25 per cent by the staff and workers. Shri Ram's enlightened labour policy solved the

[286] *ITB Report on Sewing Machines*, 1949.

[287] Ibid., 1949.

[288] Joshi, op. cit., pp. 362–3.   [289] Ibid., pp. 363–4.

problem of skilled personnel in this technologically complex industry in the long run.

5. *Capital*. JEW was initiated by B. D. Basil, a Panjabi engineer of small means, with little capital. In the initial stages he received some financial support from two trading groups in Calcutta, Rohatgi and Poddar, but they were not prepared to spend the huge sums that were required to make it a success. Success depended on better designs, new plant and improved tooling, and all this could be financed only by a big group. A fundamental financial reorganization took place with the take-over by Shri Ram in 1938, which solved the problem of capital shortage. Together the Basil, Rohatgi and Poddar groups had contributed share capital to the extent of Rs 50,000. The participation of the Shri Ram group raised the sum of share capital to Rs 4,00,000. In the post-war years, it was the expenditure of huge sums by the Shri Ram group that finally enabled JEW to stand on its feet. From 1946–7 to 1951–2, JEW expenditure amounted to Rs 56,11,000 in the following manner: Rs 1.34 lakhs on land, Rs 16.88 lakhs on buildings and Rs 37.89 lakhs on machinery. In the crucial period of growth of JEW, there was no problem of inadequate finance.

6. *Enterprise*. The ultimate ability of Usha to stand the destructive competition of Singer can be explained only in terms of the nationalist motivations of Lala Shri Ram, who was not deterred by the formidable technical difficulties of JEW, and its dark prospects of future success, from pressing ahead. When Shri Ram took over JEW, he took care to form a national board of directors for JEW, consisting of himself, Padampat Singhania of JK, and Karam Chand Thapar, to emphasize the national status of JEW. Money-making was the least of his motives when he took over this tottering concern. The guiding motive, as he made it clear, was 'to serve the country by producing things which have not yet been produced'.[290] It was this which inspired the will to struggle on through the dark war and post-war years, when the prospects of successful manufacture appeared truly bleak.

If it was the will of Shri Ram which sustained JEW through these years; the original founder of the concern, B. D. Basil, faded gradually from the scene and resigned in 1943. JEW provides a classic instance of the transfer of a technically complex engineering concern from a small entrepreneur to a big capitalist. B. D. Basil, a graduate

[290] Ibid., p. 359.

of Roorkee Engineering College, invented the original design for Usha by experiments at home. But he lacked the resources to carry these experiments on further. He had to hand over JEW to a leading textile magnate of the country because a small entrepreneur could not supply the capital and organization needed for the manufacture of such a sophisticated product. The Shri Ram group was able to provide JEW with two essential conditions of success: huge sums of capital and an all-India marketing organization with four principal sales agencies in Bombay, Delhi, Lucknow and Calcutta, supported by their own sub-agents in small towns of western, northern and eastern India.[291]

On the other hand, the technological contribution of the Shri Ram group to the success of JEW was negligible. Production management was initially left to B. D. Basil alone, Shri Ram taking care of marketing and financing problems. After easing out B. D. Basil, Lala Shri Ram also introduced an effective system of cost control. Significantly, the contribution of the Shri Ram group to the success of JEW lay on the side of organization, not in personal attention to the solution of technological problems. There was a prolonged uncertainty during the war and post-war years as to which product JEW would concentrate upon. This arose from the difficulties of manufacture of sewing-machines, the extent of which was realized only when Shri Ram came face to face with the problems. There was a crisis of faith, which was reflected in experiments with various other products during the war and post-war years: pressure gauges, railway signalling apparatus, water meters, cooking ranges, hurricane lanterns, typewriters, casablanca, textile machinery and electric fans. It was only at the end of the forties that JEW finally came to concentrate on its two main products: sewing-machines and electric fans.[292] This sort of basic uncertainty about the product of the firm was characteristic of a large managing agency house which played a predominantly organizational role in the management of several unconnected enterprises. It would have been inconceivable in the case of a specialized engineering firm with the requisite technological know-how and experience. It was not until the beginning of the fifties that these production problems were solved. But solved they were, in spite of initial fumbling and muddling. In 1950, one of the largest manufacturing concerns of the USA expressed the opinion that JEW was being run on really efficient lines, so that, if

[291] Ibid., p. 298.   [292] Ibid., pp. 353–8.

it was bodily transferred to the U.S.A., the Americans would find very few changes to be made in it, even according to modern U.S. standards.[293]

7. *Market.* When JEW was started, India was a large and attractive market, dominated by Singer products from Britain. It was estimated by the Indian Tariff Board that in the existing conditions of demand for the machine and supply of skilled labour, a firm with a productive capacity of 50,000 machines per annum would be an economic unit. Since the average annual demand from 1937–8 to 1939–40 was about 75,000, there was adequate scope for JEW within the domestic market.[294] This made it possible to build a large and modernized plant designed for mass production with the latest and most expensive technology. But the difficulties of importing raw materials, plant and machinery prevented JEW from taking advantage of the starved domestic market in wartime and the pent-up demand in the post-war years. By 1950 JEW was also exporting sewing machines to Australia, South-East Asia, the Middle East and Africa.[295] Exports were not, however, a profit-making proposition. Usha machines were sold at lower than domestic prices in these foreign markets, mainly in order to earn foreign exchange for the import of essential raw materials without which the quality of Usha could not be improved.

8. *Government policy.* There was no scope, under discriminating protection, for official aid to an entirely new industry like sewing-machines, which in consequence was conceived and initiated entirely outside the framework of tariff policies. This was a measure of the risks which Indian entrepreneurship stood ready to incur in the late 1930s. The policies of the Government of India were negative with regard to sewing-machines. When the Second World War broke out, JEW was required by the government to switch over a major portion of its capacity to production of munitions. Consequently the development of sewing-machine manufacture was held up for years. Not until 1943 was JEW given import licences for importing plant and machine tools from Britain and America, and then its production was confined to the sale of sewing-machines to the Supply Department of the Central Government.[296] Only at the end of the war was

---

[293] Ibid., p. 425.
[294] *ITB Report on Sewing Machines,* 1949.
[295] Joshi, op. cit., p. 428.
[296] *ITB Report on Sewing Machines,* 1949.

it possible to reorganize the factory on mass production lines. In this respect the advent of independence was crucial. The year 1947 brought protection to the sewing-machine industry for the first time, to be continued until 1954. At the same time, JEW received large loans from the Industrial Finance Corporation of India, with which it proved possible to expand the machinery and building considerably. Government aid was thus crucial to the expansion of JEW in the late forties. It is possible that if this form of aid had been forthcoming in the mid-thirties, the progress of JEW would have been speeded up to some extent. On the other hand, it must be stressed that the complex technology of the sewing-machine industry in any case made a relatively long gestation period inevitable. Earlier protection could not have compressed that period radically.

Conclusion

Given the technological backwardness of India and the absence of supporting industries, it is difficult to see how the sewing-machine industry could have developed in India much earlier than it did. It was not until the period of the Second World War that India began to produce some of the essentials for the sewing-machine industry, such as specialized steels and machine tools. It was possible in peacetime to import these essentials, but the finer points of technology could only be learnt through trial and error. Consequently Indian entrepreneurship could not be charged with pusillanimity in this respect, even though a large market for sewing-machines existed within the country. Rather, the venture in this field is to be regarded as a risky step which was based on inadequate appreciation of the difficulties involved. As a biographer of Lala Shri Ram has observed, it is impossible to avoid the conclusion that, 'strategically speaking, the founding of Jay Engineering Works in 1935 was badly timed, its chances of survival wrongly interpreted and plans for overcoming the difficulties only vaguely conceived'.[297] In view of the general level of technological know-how in India, JEW was a premature venture rather than a late starter. This explains why the industry took so long a period of gestation (1935–50) to develop into a going concern. In addition, the indigenous product remained inferior to the imported machine in wearing quality, finish and appearance till the end. The technological gap between Singer and Usha was a symptom of the growing and virtually unbridgeable technological gap between

[297] Joshi, op. cit., p. 292.

advanced countries and underdeveloped nations in the post-war world.

Summing Up

The point which stands out most prominently from our studies of particular industries is how variable was the combination of factors responsible for the growth and stagnation of different industries at different times. If nothing else, the variability of these causal factors reveals the somewhat shaky foundations on which generalizations on industrial processes of growth and stagnation must necessarily rest. It is a useful warning which should guide any attempt at a generalized explanation of India's industrial performance. Nevertheless, this does not mean that the inquiries have to be limited to particular industries and particular years. What is obviously necessary is to single out the many different factors which had a causative role in the growth or stagnation of several industries and to try to consider their influence in the overall context of industrial growth. The task is to weigh the impact of 'economic' factors like supply of raw materials, efficiency of labour, availability of technology, cost of power and level of demand, and to explore the political and sociological setting in which government and private businessmen operated historically.

The interaction of strictly economic factors and socio-political influences brought about major changes in the structure of differential profit incentives during the period under review. These changes in the structure of differential profit incentives led to significant diversification and sophistication of India's industrial products, but were apparently not sufficient to induce the manufacture of the more advanced variety of heavy engineering and chemical goods on a substantial scale before the advent of independence. But the extent of diversification and sophistication, if somewhat limited, was significant enough to indicate that by the time of independence, India had already passed through several distinct phases of industrial development. This will be apparent if we consider the industries chosen by us for case study in their proper order of historical succession. For each of these industries belonged to one or the other of several technologically well-marked and distinctive phases of industrial growth.

These technological distinctions stand out with particular sharpness if we consider associated branches of the same industry. Glass bangles, which were simple to manufacture, were the earliest branch of the glass industry to develop in India. The bangles of Firozabad came to capture a substantial section of the domestic market in India in the favourable conditions of the inter-war period. These same conditions generated the simultaneous growth of several new industries and business oriented to the domestic market, such as coastal shipping, safety-matches, magnesium chloride, sugar and paper. Of these industries only paper presented certain unsolved technological problems, and not surprisingly it took the longest time to achieve a breakthrough. During this same inter-war period sulphuric acid and other chemicals based on it, being easy to manufacture, achieved some progress in spite of the absence of natural advantages. By contrast the alkalis branch of the chemical industry, and the manufacture of sheet glass, had to await the coming of the Second World War. Not that the natural conditions of production were lacking. But the technological problems were of an altogether different magnitude. Indian industry was not equipped to face the technological problems of these and other heavy engineering (automobiles, textile machinery, machine tools, sewing-machines, etc.) and metallurgical (special steels, aluminium, etc.) industries before the Second World War. Industrial growth during the inter-war period had slowly created a market for these basic engineering, metallurgical and chemical goods within India. For instance, the growth of shipping and cotton textiles in the inter-war period had made it possible on commercial grounds to initiate shipbuilding and textile machinery manufacture by the late thirties. But it was the technological 'leap' of the Second World War that finally enabled Indian entrepreneurs, at the end of the war, to branch out on these new lines of manufacture.

The case studies of particular industries thus reveal a specific pattern of industrial growth in India. As mentioned above, this pattern of growth was determined to a large extent by the structure of differential profit incentives, as influenced by changing economic factors and social and political circumstances. The impact of these factors has been studied in relation to specific industries. It is now time to consider them in an overall context, keeping in view the technologically distinctive phases of industrial growth in India.

To sum up the evidence so far, there were three such well-marked phases: the pre-1914 stage, which saw the development of light manufacturing, plantation and mining, and metallurgical industries, which relied heavily on exports and were based on well-established nineteenth century technology easily imported from the West;[298] the inter-war period, which saw the development of a new range of light manufactures of consumption goods for the domestic market, now protected by war, tariff and depression; and finally, a new phase commencing imperceptibly in the late thirties and becoming well-marked only during and after the Second World War, which saw initial efforts in the direction of production of capital goods, the technological problems of which had not yet been solved but for which a domestic market had been created by the previous growth of consumer goods industries in the inter-war period.

[298] Tea and jute were primarily export products. Cotton-textiles, coal and pig iron (but not steel) relied heavily on exports. The technical problems of manufacture in the case of textiles and steel had long been solved as a result of the Industrial Revolution in Britain.

CHAPTER 4

Demand Limitations and Supply Constraints on Private Investment in India 1914–47

In an underdeveloped country, where constraints imposed by the low level of demand for consumer and capital goods, and the initially restricted supply of production factors like capital, technology and skilled labour tend to create vicious circles in the path of industrial development, massive government intervention and aggressive private entrepreneurship are the most obvious ways in which the vicious circles can be broken. That is because among the variables determining the nature and rate of economic growth, government policies and capitalist initiatives are the most elastic factors, other variables on the demand and supply sides being fairly inelastic in the short run, being pre-conditioned by the overall level of the economy.

A. K. Bagchi's voluminous study of private investment in India from 1900 to 1939 points to the inadequate economic policies and racial discrimination of the Government of India as the single most important factor in retarding India's economic growth.[1] S. K. Sen contests the view that government policy stunted industrialization and advances as an explanation of unsatisfactory growth the behaviour pattern of the Indian bourgeoisie who did not seize all the opportunities that were available and who were very unlike the Japanese Zaibatsu and the Chinese comprador bourgeoisie represented by the four families.[2] A. K. Bagchi emphasizes the constraints imposed on the economy by the low level of demand (due to government policies which constrained domestic demand and

[1] Bagchi, *Private Investment in India*, pp. 35–67, 165–74.
[2] Sunil Kumar Sen, *Studies in Economic Policy and Development of India (1848–1939)*, pp. 236–42.

international depression in the 1930s reducing export markets) and does not regard factors on the supply side as crucial constraints. S. K. Sen, while emphasizing the limitations of the domestic market on account of peasant poverty, also gives considerable weight to lack of enterprise on the side of supply factors.

We shall reserve government policies and private enterprise for detailed examination later. If public and private initiatives on a massive scale were essential in order to break the demand and supply constraints on the economy, then it will be useful at this stage to give somewhat closer attention to these economic constraints. The proper appreciation of these constraints—in so far as they proved to be constraints either in the short run or in the long run—must be within a framework of explanation for the limited but appreciable growth of manufacturing output that did take place in the period under review without leading to a take-off for the Indian economy.

1. Demand Limitations

The argument that demand limitations were the crucial constraint on Indian industrial growth is two-fold. In the first place the international markets for India's export products were hard hit by the doldrums of the twenties and the depression of the thirties. This not only affected export-oriented industries adversely, but also reduced the income peasants derived from cash crops sold in international markets. Secondly, since national income on a *per capita* basis was not appreciably rising during this period, industries in India which grew by managing to substitute imports quickly hit the ceiling in a restricted domestic market. Even this limited achievement was not possible in other industries for which there existed a considerable domestic market, since inadequate protection, government discrimination and foreign monopoly practices made import-substitution difficult. Developing this argument, A. K. Bagchi points out that in macro-economic terms India had unutilized supplies of raw materials, labour and capital, which could have been harnessed by a larger demand for industrial goods within India.[3]

The structure of the market for Indian industrial goods was strongly influenced by the changing position of India in the British imperial system during the inter-war period which we have described in Chapter 1. That position, as we have seen, was characterized by

[3] Bagchi, op. cit., p. 24.

cessation of the inflow of British capital, decline of multilateral exchanges in India's international trade, increasing financial burdens imposed by inflated debt and military expenditure, and massive bilateral outflow of resources from India to Britain. These were conditions fundamentally different from the steady inflow of foreign investment and the growing volume of exports which had induced some degree of prosperity in the decade before the First World War. The Great Depression, which severely strained the imperial system, increased the burden on India by curtailing her international trade in merchandise and inducing repatriation of foreign investments. At the same time this turning back of the Indian economy upon itself proved to be of considerable help to native business groups, which gained strength *vis-à-vis* foreign economic interests in proportion to the rising importance of the domestic market in relation to the export markets. The crisis of the imperial system assisted the rapid growth of Indian enterprise and the substitution of imports by indigenous manufactures. The advance of Indian capitalism took place during the inter-war period on a rather narrow front of import-substitution within a relatively inelastic domestic market. In the prevailing conditions that market could not grow rapidly, while the export markets became much less dependable in a world of contracting trade. However, although these were not conditions for generating the easy prosperity that would ensure the rapid rise of consumption at home, they were certainly ideal for the mopping up of the existing demand by Indian manufactures at the cost of imported goods.

The consequences of the fact that *per capita* income and consumption remained low throughout the period are of course incalculable. Low *per capita* income and consumption were a measure of the low effective demand and the small surplus that could be generated within the economy. Studies of national income during the period under review, if they do not indicate any decline in real *per capita* incomes, give no indication of a substantial increase either.[4] Agricultural trends, as reported by George Blyn, were mostly adverse so far as per acre productivity in food crops after 1920 was concerned.[5] From 1921, moreover, the rate of growth of population increased and the ratio of the non-working population in relation to actual workers rose substantially. Under the circumstances, it is surprising

[4] The most recent study is that of S. Sivasubramonian, *National Income of India 1900–01 to 1946–47*, Delhi School of Economics, 1965.

[5] George Blyn, *Agricultural Trends in India: Output, Availability and Productivity*, Philadelphia, 1966.

that domestic consumption showed no definite downward trends, even in the bad years of the Great Depression. G. D. Birla quoted some figures in a pamphlet[6] to argue that the domestic market for goods and services had contracted during the thirties but as will be seen below, the figures quoted by him gave no uniform support to his argument:

Item	1930–1	1939–40
1 Kerosene oil	227,852,059 gallons	222,000,000 gallons
2 Sugar (refined)	1,121,000 tons	1,074,311 tons
3 Cotton piece-goods	601 crore yards	616 crore yards
4 Matches	18,489 gross boxes	21,969 gross boxes
5 Postcards sent	540,779,698	371,895,000
6 Number of third class passengers	550,879,000	513,533,000

Consumption of cloth *per capita* went on expanding steadily from the turn of the century to the outbreak of the Second World War, even through the depression years when cloth available *per capita* increased from 13 yards in the triennium ending 1929 to 14.4 yards in the triennium ending 1939. Consumption of paper and matches also showed increases during the period, while that of steel and aluminium was drastically diminished by the depression. On the whole, allowing for differences from industry to industry, it seems that total domestic consumption remained steady even in the worst years of the depression. The contemporary explanation for this was that the consumption of the population at large was maintained in the early thirties by the utilization of savings in the form of gold and gold ornaments. Between 1922 and 1931 India's net imports of gold amounted to 43 million ounces, of which two-thirds went out of the country during the depression.[7] The large gold exports during the depression years were converted into the mobile purchasing power of the people, shoring up the country's purchasing power at a time when exports had diminished. Later on the situation was somewhat eased when the Ottawa Agreement and the Modi-Lees Pact led to an increase of India's agricultural exports, especially raw cotton, to Britain.

[6] G. D. Birla, *India's War Prosperity: The Myth Exploded*, no date, no place.
[7] P. J. Thomas, *The Growth of Federal Finance in India, Being a Survey of India's Public Finances from 1833 to 1939*, Oxford, 1939, p. 365.

The effects of the depression, it would appear, were less severe on the industries producing mass consumption goods for the domestic market than on engineering and other industries which relied on government purchase of stores. Capital expenditure on the railways nearly disappeared for some time and provincial expenditure on civil works came down by half. The reduction of public works expenditure from Rs 50 crores to Rs 12 crores by the Government of India, which followed deflationary monetary and fiscal policies in order to balance its budgets, contrasted strongly with the increase of public expenditure by the British, American and European governments in order to combat the depression.[8] The *Investor's India Year Book* for the year 1931-2 reported that the engineering, electric power supply and development companies were suffering particularly badly, for owing to the trade depression, the government departments, local authorities and the general public had very little money to spend on development, or even on ordinary repairs and renewals of plant.[9] The other sector of industries which suffered severely from the depression was of course that which catered to external markets, since the elasticity of demand for exported goods was much greater than that for articles of mass domestic use. The organized European-dominated industries of eastern India were badly hit: jute fabric manufacture by the general shrinkage of world trade; tea by the reduction of world purchasing power; coal by the slowing down of demand and transport.[10]

In an absolutely poor country with a narrow consumption pattern, initial small increases in the real incomes of the peasantry are not necessarily the essential prerequisites of industrial growth. Initially such increases are likely to increase *per capita* rural consumption of foodgrains, thus reducing the surplus that could be drawn into the urban sector for building up the industries, as indeed happened during the NEP period in the Soviet Union. Indeed, initial development strategies in such conditions tend to concentrate on how to squeeze a surplus out of the countryside by depressing the total consumption of the rural population, as Russian economic policies under Witte and Stalin have demonstrated.[11] The Government of

[8] Ibid.   [9] *Investor's India Year Book 1931–32.*

[10] See description of conditions in detail in *Investor's India Year Book 1932–33.*

[11] *See* Alexander Gerschenkron, 'Problems and Patterns of Russian Economic Development', and Theodore H. Von Laue, 'The State and the Economy', *in*

India followed no such integrated overall strategies of development, but nevertheless the extraction of a sizeable surplus from the countryside through the operation of impersonal economic forces and wartime government policies proved to be an important factor in the substantial increase of manufacturing output which occurred in India during the period.

The importance of this squeeze on the subsistence economy of the countryside was two-fold. In the first place, this was the obvious process by which capital formation occurred in India during the two world wars. The massive speculation, profiteering and price rises which characterized the two world wars, while causing tremendous social distress to the poor in India, brought into the hands of the business communities large liquid resources which were utilized for the financing of new enterprises. Secondly, this siphoning-off of incomes from large sections of the population into new sectors created a demand for more sophisticated products and capital goods for which the vast body of the poor would have had little use. Any marginal increases in their real incomes and purchasing capacity would not have generated demand for these goods, the increasing use of which depended largely on concentration of incomes in strategic sectors. This necessary process of concentration at the expense of the population at large was assisted by the two world wars.

The two world wars, through increased munitions production at the cost of the current consumption of the population, brought about a redistribution of incomes. This created a demand for heavy capital goods which had previously had very restricted markets. Heavy contributions were laid on the population, both by way of direct war expenditure and by way of indirect contribution of exports. During the Second World War total defence expenditure in India was to the extent of £2053.6 million and the value of contracts placed by the Supply Department in India to meet Allied military requirements was £408 million.[12] Since the national income of India in 1941 was estimated to be about £1,500 million,[13] the war

C. E. Black (ed.), *The Transformation of Russian Society: Aspects of Social Change since 1861*, Cambridge, Mass., 1960; also, Naum Jasny, *Soviet Industrialization 1928–1952*, Chicago, 1961.

[12] A. R. Prest, *War Economics of Primary Producing Countries*, Cambridge, 1948, pp. 31–2.

[13] *The Times*, 6 August 1941 (cited in ibid.), p. 32.

contributions obviously changed the distribution of incomes drastically. The demand for machine tools, aluminium, chemicals, automobiles, rubber goods, etc. rose phenomenally. For the first time it appeared to be possible in these industries to build large plants of the optimum size which could achieve economies of scale by mass-production for an enlarged domestic market. This induced industrialists and businessmen in India to invest large sums in a number of technologically sophisticated new industries.

It would thus appear that the industrial diversification and increase of manufacturing output that occurred between 1914 and 1945 were made possible largely by changes in the structure of the domestic market brought about during the two world wars. The First World War, by its extraordinary programme of munitions production, set the iron and steel industry on its feet. The Second World War, besides giving a boost to the heavy chemicals (alkalis) industry, initiated a number of engineering industries based on the previous achievement in iron and steel, e.g. textile machinery, automobiles, bicycles, sewing machines, machine tools, etc. It brought about a revolution in transport industries, leading to shipbuilding and aircraft manufacture, the latter in turn boosting the infant aluminium industry.

What made these developments possible during the two world wars was not a rise in *per capita* consumption of the rural population, but rather a depression of it. In this respect it is necessary to keep in mind clearly the distinction between the large mass-market for essential consumption goods and the small specialized markets for capital and sophisticated goods. In the long run substantial rises in the standard of living of the population at large could of course popularize the market for the latter kind of goods, but initially the position would be quite different. In the initial stages at any rate a diversion of resources from the population at large was necessary to generate effective demand and capital supply for the basic and heavy industries.

So far as mass-produced essential consumption goods were concerned, such a diversion of resources from the population at large was not likely for a time to produce serious consequences for the industries producing those goods. India enjoyed an advantage compared to smaller underdeveloped countries on account of the size of its population. Though *per capita* consumption was low, the domestic market for such products as piece-goods, sugar and matches was in consequence large. Since the demand for these products was in the beginning met largely by imports from abroad, there were excellent prospects for expansion of these industries during the inter-war period simply by import-substitution. It was true that without an increase in *per capita* consumption the industries advancing by import-substitution were likely to hit a ceiling at some point. This point was in fact reached for the sugar industry in 1937. The cotton textiles industry, in spite of the rise in *per capita* consumption of cloth, might have encountered the same fate but for the intervention of the Second World War. In general, it is not altogether improbable that the outbreak of the Second World War averted the threat of industrial stagnation on several fronts implicit in the low *per capita* income of the population. It is also possible to speculate that if the process of import-substitution had started in earnest before the First World War, and if the rate of substitution had been faster in the post-war period (both ifs might have been realized with a more effective policy of protection), then many consumer industries might have hit the ceiling of the domestic market long before the outbreak of the Second World War.[14]

In fact, those industries with a mass-market which did not have to compete with imports had to encounter this ceiling repeatedly during the inter-war period. The most striking instance was coal which, owing to ridiculously low and inelastic *per capita* consumption, was engulfed by rapid cycles of over-production. Throughout the inter-war period the rate of return on investment in coal was low for most companies which did not enjoy the advantage of specially reserved markets.

However, one possibility should not be overlooked. With an earlier process, and faster rate, of import substitution in the existing mass-consumer industries, a greater demand might have been generated for new capital goods industries. Certainly the impressive expansion of the cotton-textiles industry in the twenties and the thirties was one factor which induced the Birla group to launch their project for a cotton-textile machinery plant (Texmaco) on the eve of the Second World War. It is possible to speculate that if with more active government assistance the cotton-mill industry had achieved full import substitution at the beginning rather than the end of the inter-war period, then it would have been possible to

[14] Such a possibility is implicit in A. K. Bagchi's analysis of the problem for the inter-war period. Lidman and Domrese have specifically suggested the possibility for the pre-war period.

initiate Texmaco or a similar plant simultaneously with the Greater Extensions of TISCO in the early twenties (when for the first time the necessary steel supplies could have been obtained from Tatas). One must not underestimate the difficulties of reserving the domestic market in capital goods for indigenous manufacturers by means of protection. If the government had extended protection to the textile machinery industry before the cotton-textile industry had achieved full import-substitution, then the prices of machinery would have been driven up and the progress of textiles would have been slowed down. Only with some assured and substantial progress in the mass-consumer industries was it possible to initiate capital goods industries without high costs to the former.

As in so many other aspects, the fate of industries was here inter-linked. The close interdependence of industries made it difficult to reserve and expand the domestic market for industrial goods in a technologically backward country like India. The initial progress of mass-consumer industries—with which industrialization necessarily had to commence—depended on imports of good economical machinery from abroad. Any attempt to initiate consumer and capital goods industries simultaneously could only entail high costs for the consumer goods industries and thus constrain the market for the capital goods industries. On the other hand, dependence on imports of capital goods from abroad to expand consumer goods industries at home involved a heavy and continuous leakage of gains resulting from that expansion. Till almost the very end of the period under review, the machinery and chemicals for the cotton-textile industry, the soda ash for glass manufacture, the paper and chemicals for the match industry, and the machinery for the jute, sugar and paper manufactures had to be imported from abroad. Not surprisingly the progress of the various engineering and chemical industries was slow.

The new demand generated within the economy by the expansion of the mass-consumer industries was not perhaps on a scale large enough until the very end of the inter-war period to support economic units in new capital goods industries. It was therefore all the easier for the engineering and chemical industries of the advanced countries which had effected economies of scale to an extent impossible in India by supplying international markets to mop up the new demand generated within the Indian economy during the inter-war period. In these conditions, the Indian Industrial Commission's report at the end of the First World War, that new industries such as the metallurgical and chemical ones offered doubtful and in many cases apparently smaller profits than the established industries, continued to be true during the next two decades. For instance, in 1927–8, when capital was in unusually plentiful supply, the *Investor's India Year Book* reported: 'Once again a great deal of money has been available for investment, but it has not been an easy matter to find a suitable outlet for such funds when a better return than is available on Government and Trustee Stocks, coupled with reasonable security, has been looked for.'[15] Again in 1934–5 the *Investor's India Year Book* reported that the rise in security prices and the reduced yield to be derived from industry had driven investors to the good companies, so that the yield on ordinary shares of this nature had been driven down in turn. All this was a result of the accumulation of savings which the absence of fresh flotations of good character and the nervousness of capital bred by the world slump was driving into the bottleneck of existing channels. The *Investor's India Year Book* commented that this tendency would be aggravated until capital could be tempted into fresh avenues of exploitation.[16] However, unless the structure of demand altered sufficiently to permit entry into 'fresh avenues of exploitation', it was vain to expect capital to behave otherwise than it did. The inter-war period saw no fundamental changes in the demand structure of the economy. Such changes had to await the extraordinary levies and diversion of resources of the Second World War.

It will not do, however, to attribute the low and uncertain return on investment in fresh avenues entirely to the pattern of demand within the country before the Second World War. From the studies of selected industries already undertaken, it is possible to cite several instances in which investment was delayed in spite of the existence of a suitable market on account of the difficulties of assembling the factors of production at a sufficiently low cost to make it a business proposition. There is also another facet of the problem to be taken into consideration. Given the large natural advantages which India was somewhat uncritically supposed to enjoy, surely it should have been possible for a wide range of industries to outgrow their constrained domestic markets by engaging in exports. In the late thirties, when the depression lifted and foreign

[15] *Investor's India Year Book 1927–28.*
[16] Ibid., 1934–35.

trade began to expand, a cost reduction and export drive was one strategy which might have ensured the continued growth of the mass-consumer industries which were approaching the ceiling of the domestic market in the import-substitution process. Yet in sugar manufacture, the industry which did hit the ceiling, Indian industrialists were far from enthusiastic about the prospects of successful competition in foreign markets. With caustic humour B. M. Birla, representative of a leading sugar manufacturing house, pronounced in his presidential address at the Indian Chamber of Commerce:

We have already arrived at a stage where India is able to produce all her requirements of sugar and the time is not far off when we would need an export market. Our position in this respect is practically the same as that of Lancashire. Lancashire is unable to compete with other countries in the sale of her piece-goods in the Indian market, just as India is unable at present to supply England with a[s] cheap sugar as she may be getting from other countries. What is required therefore is sufficient preference for Indian sugar in [the] U.K. market as against the preference sought by Lancashire in the Indian market.[17]

In addition to limitations of demand, it is necessary to examine the supply constraints in the economy in order to understand two problems. In the first place, why was substitution of imports delayed in several mass-consumer industries, which enjoyed protection during the inter-war period? Secondly, when several of these industries approached the limits of the domestic market, why was there no confidence in an export drive?

2. *Supply Constraints*

A. *Natural Resources*

Social scientists are apt to point out the extent to which a given geographical setting can be transformed in spite of severe natural limitations by the human element working on it. Economic miracles like that achieved by Japan, a country poorly equipped in minerals, have encouraged this tendency. It ought to be borne in mind, however, that such miracles have occurred historically only at a certain level of development of the existing resources, a point which is underlined by the economic level attained by Japan during the Tokugawa period preceding the take-off that occurred with the Meiji Restora-

[17] *Indian Chamber of Commerce, Calcutta: Annual Report for the Year 1934*, Presidential address of B. M. Birla, 19 February 1937.

tion.[18] In a poor and underdeveloped country like India, where the gap between potential resources and economic utilization of them is immense, caution must be exercised in estimating the possibilities of an economic miracle. Economic historians would do well to consider the warning uttered by a leading geographer of India, O. H. K. Spate, in his careful study of the resources of the country: 'Apart from the great industrial foci of N. America, N.W. Europe and the U.S.S.R., it does indeed seem possible, or even likely, that India has greater industrial potentialities than any other industrial country except Brazil. Nevertheless it may be questioned whether India, though certainly not poor, is in fact so *rich in relation to size and population* as her more cheerful publicists assume....'[19] It is necessary to survey the actual resources and their state of development at the beginning of our period, a task admirably performed by the Indian Industrial Commission during the First World War.

1. *Agricultural products.* The Indian Industrial Commission rightly pointed out that the output and quality of Indian crops had to be improved very considerably for the required advance of industry in several directions.[20] India's decisive advantage lay in her practical monopoly of the jute crop, but other fibre crops, such as sisal, hemp, flax or rhea, though suitable for India, were either not grown at all or only to a limited extent. There had been no intensive agricultural research for the improvement of oil-seeds, a principal crop which contributed largely to India's exports. Long-staple cotton spread slowly and in consequence cotton mills did little in the way of fine weaving until the technique of mixing imported long-staple cotton with the indigenous short-staple variety was adopted. Sugar-canes were of poor type in the principal crop areas of north India and per acre productivity remained so far below Java, Mauritius and Queensland that Indian sugar could not attain a competitive position in the world market after monopolizing the domestic market with the aid of protection.

2. *Minerals.* Mineral deposits in India were sufficient to maintain most of the key industries except in a few important respects. Locational factors were not uniformly favourable for the development of

[18] C. D. Shelton, *The Rise of the Merchant Class in Tokugawa Japan*, New York, 1958; T. C. Smith, *The Agrarian Origins of Modern Japan*, Stanford, 1959.
[19] O. H. K. Spate, *India and Pakistan: A General and Regional Geography*, London, 1963, p. 257.
[20] *Industrial Commission Report*, pp. 34–6.

mineral-based heavy industries and in several fields the initial break-through depended on the investment of a very considerable sum.[21] The steel industry was located at the excellent site of Sakchi only after a long and patient search in which large sums were spent by Jamsetji Tata without any expectations of profit in the immediately foreseeable future. India enjoyed important advantages in respect of mica, manganese and bauxite. But the exploitation of India's bauxite ores was delayed considerably due to the absence of cheap power. There were locational problems for the aluminium industry arising from the fact that the sources of cheap hydroelectricity in the south (when developed in the 1930s) lay far from the bauxite deposits in the north. The salt and limestone supplies in India were too expensive and too inferior in nature, according to the I.C.I., to make her a natural chemicals producer. Locational problems arising from costly transport of coal and limestone marred the efficiency of the pioneering Tata and Govan alkali concerns.

3. *Power.* Coal was distributed unevenly in India and was not available in southern and western India at all. Large deposits of good coking coal were available only in Raniganj and Jharia but their high ash content and the consequent low calorific value reduced their radius of economic use. Large-scale export of coal which would have alleviated the problems arising from the low and uncertain consumption of coal at home, could not be developed on account of these defects. Forests being situated mainly in the hills, the cost of wood fuel was prohibitive. India was not well endowed in oil resources. As for water power, it was difficult to develop on account of the seasonal character of rainfall which made storage a necessity. The outlay necessary for the construction of storage facilities, unless the water could be used for irrigation afterwards, tended to raise the cost of water power in relation to other sources of power. The Indian Industrial Commission recommended, on the ground that only the government could afford the long period necessary for the hydro-electric works to be profitable, that the construction of hydroelectric plants be made a national enterprise.[22] But government initiative in this direction was slow and halting and it was not until the late thirties and the forties that water power became available for the new industries—such as aluminium and alkalis—whose development depended on cheap hydroelectricity.

4. *Forests.* India's large forest resources were concentrated mainly

[21] Ibid., pp. 38–9.   [22] Ibid., pp. 64–70.

in Assam, the Himalayas and the hilly tracts of the west coast, remote from commercial centres and incapable of proper exploitation for lack of transport facilities. Since there were no railways and rivers in the hills were not suitable means of transport, valuable timbers could not be transported from these areas. The Indian Industrial Commission also commented upon the lack of proper forest research and the absence of information of commercial value about forest resources.[23] The Indian forests contained no aspen wood—the best wood for the match industry—and suitable timbers for the development of the match industry were difficult to come by. Wood pulp could not be produced sufficiently cheaply in India to promote the paper industry because of the limitations of her forest resources. It took a long time to develop bamboo as a material for manufacturing paper on a commercial basis.

The slow spread of improved varieties of key cash crops like cotton and sugar, the decimation of forest reserves of India's plains, the underdeveloped state of hydroelectric power, the limited radius of the economic use of Raniganj and Jharia coal, and the mineral deficiencies with regard to heavy chemicals created organizational and locational problems for the initiation of industries which could not be solved all at once. Locational problems were complicated by transport deficiencies. Road transport was undeveloped in India. The only considerable inland river navigation system was confined to eastern Bengal and Assam. India had a well-developed railway network at the beginning of the period, but railway transport costs were heavier than the costs of river traffic, which seemed to be declining because of the decaying upcountry inland navigation system along the Ganga. The cost of long haul of coal on the railways was sometimes prohibitive for centres of manufacture in south and west India, and the coal industry itself suffered acutely from shortage of wagons, which in turn created considerable problems for large-scale industrial consumers. The railway network had developed during the nineteenth century in such a way as to promote exports (mainly in raw materials) and imports (mainly in manufactures) through the ports and there were complaints that the fare structure discouraged domestic manufacture for the domestic market.

B. *Technology*

Technological innovation was by no means absent from Indian

[23] Ibid., pp. 40–5.

industrial performance during the inter-war period. Very considerable technological achievements were represented by the manufacture of specialized steels by TISCO during the Second World War, the reduction of high grade ferro-tungsten from the Jodhpur wolfram ore by the Research and Control Laboratory at Jamshedpur, and the manufacture of commercial bamboo pulp for paper manufacture by Andrew Yule during the early thirties. However, these innovations took a long time to mature and the breakthrough in the manufacture of paper and specialized steels had to wait in consequence until the thirties and forties.

The metallurgical, chemical and engineering industries represented extremely complex technological problems. It was these technological problems which, paradoxically, compelled the big nationalist houses which were driven into these fields by the inner logic of their socio-political ethic, to seek collaboration with foreign interests. For automobile manufacture within the country with a view to replacing foreign cars and developing road transport, the houses of Birla and Walchand had perforce to enter into tie-up agreements with Morris and Fiat. Avoidance of foreign collaboration tended to land the Indian houses in immediate technological difficulties, and this in turn was an invitation to the multinationals located outside India to enter the field in a big way. The unbalanced plant of the J.K. group for aluminium manufacture was an instance of Indian shortcomings of this kind which placed the Canadian–British venture in aluminium manufacture in India in a more favourable position initially. The Tata and Govan ventures in alkalis ran into difficulties immediately which arose from complex technological problems of location which the ICI plants were apparently able to avoid. Progress in chemicals was necessarily slow and halting, as by-products had to be produced commercially in order that the cost of manufacture of the main products might leave a margin of profit.

The big Indian houses lacked the experience and specialization that were necessary for the solution of such technological problems. Yet smaller specialized firms lacked the organizational and financial resources that the big houses engaged in many fields possessed in such ample measure for the initiation of new industries. The problem was prominently illustrated by the take-over of Cooper Engineering Works, a machine tools concern which had run into financial difficulties, by the Walchand group. There were too many specialized lines in machine tools production and groups like Walchand which possessed the resources to initiate them were by definition barred from specialization.

Until, moreover, the basic industries, steel and heavy chemicals, developed to a considerable extent, there was no question of initiating specialized engineering and chemical industries. The steel industry did not develop properly until the Greater Extensions of TISCO in the twenties and there was no question before then of the development of industries like automobiles, machine tools and textile machinery. Complex industries like textile machinery and automobile manufactures, moreover, depended on the easy and cheap availability of innumerable manufactured component parts. In advanced countries such components were produced by specialized firms on a mass scale, which reduced the cost of the manufacturers of the finished products. In India hundreds of components had to be manufactured by the parent automobile and textile machinery concerns, since these were not manufactured in the country at all. Many component industries developed only in response to the growth of the principal industries, so that the financial costs and technological problems of initiating the latter were extremely formidable. The narrow technological base of the industrial sector in India was a very serious hindrance to the initiation of new industries. The gestation period for such industries was accordingly long, the length of the period being determined in each instance by the progress in basic manufactures like specialized steels and heavy chemicals, many of which in turn developed only during the Second World War.

C. *Labour*

Closely connected with the availability of technology was the supply of labour. There was apparently no great difficulty in obtaining supplies of unskilled labour, but the training of labour for the adoption of the proper type of technology required considerable initial investment. Not that the time required for training labour for new industries was always long. The glass industry, which was initiated before the First World War, relied initially on skilled Japanese and Austrian workers, but due to the excellent training and research facilities offered by the non-commercial and patriotic Paisa Fund Glass Works, the foreign personnel had entirely disappeared by 1932, being replaced by native workers on low wages. However, the advantage of the lower rate of wages in India should not be exag-

15

gerated with regard to new industries during the initial decade or two, when the costs of training labour and the low *per capita* productivity tended to cancel the advantage of cheap labour *vis-à-vis* the advanced countries. The initial cost of training labour in the TISCO works pushed up the cost per unit of steel to a point where protection became necessary for the survival of the steel industry. However, the huge initial investment by TISCO in constructing the township of Jamshedpur as a suitable place for their labourers to live in and in setting up excellent technical training facilities for steadily replacing foreign with indigenous skilled personnel ultimately resulted in raising per man productivity from 5.52 tons in 1918–23 to 36.32 tons in 1935–9. This reduction in labour cost enabled TISCO to dispense with protection, but the achievement took a gestation period of more than two decades.

Apart from the striking success in solving the labour problems of the steel industry, there is no evidence in the case of the more important of the organized industries of India that there was any great rise in per man productivity and drastic fall in cost of labour per unit of production during the inter-war period. This must be considered along with the known fact that during the inter-war period labour costs in competing countries like Japan fell steeply on account of a rapid rise in the efficiency of labour. Until 1921 per man productivity in the coal industry, for instance, did not compare unfavourably with the competing countries, but after 1921 per man output in India progressively fell behind those countries. This failure to improve the efficiency of labour kept the technological level of mining very low in India. Even so wages were so low that the cost of labour per unit of coal at pit-head prices remained lower in India than in any country except South Africa. In the case of the cotton-mill industry, however, the low productivity of labour encouraged more serious competition from abroad. The cost of labour per unit of cloth in India was lower than that in Britain and most other cotton manufacturing countries, but between 1927 and 1932 India lost this advantage in relation to Japan, whose cheap cotton goods flooded the Indian markets in the thirties. Labour costs were so drastically reduced in Japan by raising per man output that the cotton-mill industry of India weathered the crisis only with the help of timely protection. The adoption of automatic looms which raised *per capita* productivity in Japan was made possible by the rising efficiency of labour in that country. In India the lower efficiency of labour and the consequent higher cost of the use of automatic looms prevented the widespread adoption of these looms.

The rising efficiency of labour in Japan was the result of group spirit, higher literacy and facilities for technical and physical training. In India primary education had hardly spread among the masses, and nutrition and training of labour left much to be desired except in the township of Jamshedpur. That Jamshedpur stood out as a shining example to the rest of India was the result of considerably heavier inputs of social overhead capital. Without a rise in the standard of living, health and literacy of the masses, the productivity of Indian labour could not be raised. But this improvement of the human material again presupposed a higher level of the economy and a greater input of social overhead capital. Only massive government initiative could provide a solution to the problem. Private capitalist initiative did work isolated miracles in new industries like iron and steel, but there is enough evidence to show that it made good sense for capitalists in established large-scale industries like coal, tea and jute to rely simply on ill-paid, uneducated, exploitable labour. While the low wages of Indian labour, arising from lack of education and organization, gave the existing Indian industries a definite advantage in relation to advanced countries, this very combination of illiteracy, exploitation and low productivity hindered rapid progress on the lines of Japan during the inter-war period.

D. *Capital*

There being only two organized stock exchanges in India (i.e. the ones in Bombay and Calcutta) and banking facilities being still somewhat rudimentary, the task of mobilizing capital resources for industrialization fell mainly on big business houses and merchant communities. The smaller entrepreneurs encountered formidable difficulties in raising capital for their enterprises. Those industries which were mainly run by small entrepreneurs, such as glass, sulphuric acid and matches (before the entry of Wimco), prominently illustrated the problems of short capital supply. The key industries, which required huge initial investment, could be run only by big houses able to command large resources. The dominance of managing agencies in the process of industrialization was a natural consequence of this situation. It was also a device which largely succeeded in providing a solution to the problems of capital supply for the initiation of new industries. It must not be thought that the big houses invariably succeeded in finding the necessary financial resources at a sufficiently low cost. The Tatas nearly ran into the red in raising the formidable sums required for the Greater Extensions of TISCO, while at the same time the Bird group and Martin Burn flatly told the government that they would be unable to raise the capital for their projected steel works without a guarantee of protection for ten years. Walchand had to give up the project of an overseas line (the Hind Lines) requiring a large initial investment when the Government of India refused a loan in 1937 and later during the Second World War his attempt to launch a shipbuilding yard with costly loans nearly drove the Scindias to the rocks. Birlas were more fortunate in getting Hind Motors (paid-up capital Rs 5 crores) and Texmaco (paid-up capital Rs 1 crore) going during the Second World War without the financial difficulties encountered by the Tatas at Jamshedpur and by Walchand at Visakhapatnam.

It must be emphasized that in the overall context there was no absolute shortage of capital for the rate at which industrialization was going on up to 1947. There were in fact large accumulations from trade and banking which did not find sufficiently attractive outlets in the industrial sector during the period under review. The most striking example of this was perhaps the Nattukottai Chettiars, the chief banking and money-lending community of the Madras Presidency. By 1930 they had invested enormous sums in Burma, estimated by Furnivall at about Rs 75 crores.[24] But this enterprising and adventurous merchant community, which had spread its operations so far afield as South-East Asia, had not invested anything in manufactures in their native province until then. Their capital, originally acquired in trade and agriculture in the mid-nineteenth century, had been practically all transferred since the seventies and eighties to Burma, Ceylon, the Malayan Straits, etc. This immense export of capital obviously took place because the domestic economy offered lower rates of return. When the Nattukottai Chettiars finally started experiments with industrial investment in the Madras Presidency in the thirties, the results were not particularly encouraging.

However, this must not be interpreted as indicating no lack of capital for rapid industrialization in India from 1914 to 1947. The difficulties experienced by Tata and Walchand in raising the money for their large new ventures in steel and shipbuilding give some indication of the tightness of the money market which would certainly

[24] Bagchi, op. cit., p. 207.

have been encountered if several such new works had been launched to achieve a much faster rate of industrialization. The rapid structural transformation of the Indian economy required very large surpluses for investment which that economy was certainly not generating in the inter-war period. It was only in terms of the slower pace of industrial activity during the period that there was, as A. K. Bagchi has pointed out, a slack in the resources for industrial development. The declining profitability of trade and money-lending in the thirties probably assisted the inflow of sufficiently large sums for the going rate of industrialization. In terms of the prevailing rate of industrialization, the capital market did not show any tightness after 1933, since money was plentiful because of the lower cost of financing trade in commodities whose prices had gone down.[25]

However, this brings us to another fundamental aspect of the problem of capital supply. If there were large accumulations which were not attracted to industry until the returns from and the costs of financing trade went down in the thirties, what could have been done at the beginning of the inter-war period to transform the structure of returns from investment in the various sectors of the economy in such a way as to encourage a greater inflow of industrial investment for a much faster expansion of manufactures? The answer obviously was massive social overhead investment in education, health, communications, power and water supply, irrigation and drainage systems, etc. The slack in capital resources for the prevailing rate of industrialization was not unconnected with the fact that social overhead investment in India in the inter-war period was so low and so unbalanced.[26] Most of the public investment went into railways. The problems of hydroelectric power supply, which could be made into a commercial proposition only in conjunction with large-scale irrigation works, were not taken in hand by the Government of India in earnest. *Per capita* government expenditure on primary education and health services remained ridiculously low.

For the rate of industrialization which was needed for the transformation of the Indian economy, there was an absolute lack of capital within the country. There was no means of supplying this deficiency except a massive and formidable government programme

[25] *Investor's India Year Books*, vols. 17 (1929–30) and 21 (1933–4).
[26] See T. M. Healey, *The Development of Social Overhead Capital in India 1950–1960*, Bombay, 1965, pp. 7–9.

of intervention in the economy. Minor reforms like easier bank credit facilities would not have solved the problem.

For the sake of convenience of argument, the limitations on industrial growth imposed by demand and supply constraints have been analysed separately. However, these constraints were inter-related and represented aspects of the same problem—that is to say, the low level of the Indian economy. It was this underdeveloped character of the economy—the low *per capita* income, productivity and consumption—that bred the constraints on both sides.

We have seen that the growth of manufacturing output in India during the inter-war period was significant, but not as great as that of Japan or Russia. At the rate that output was growing, there was scope for expansion within the limits of the domestic market and even though there were difficulties, the required resources of capital, technology and skilled labour were mobilized for sustaining the prevailing rate of expansion. But the considerable expansion of manufacturing output brought about no breakthrough in the economy, since agriculture and unorganized industries did not fare as well as organized industries and the growth of population occurred at a faster rate. Offsetting these disadvantages would have required a much greater rate of expansion of manufacturing output and such a rate could not have been sustained either by the size of the available market or by the supply of the existing resources.

The instance of the coal industry may be cited here to illustrate the close interdependence of demand and supply constraints on the expansion of output at a faster rate, and the common origin of these constraints in the underdeveloped character of the economy. This was one industry which offered considerable scope for cost reduction by expansion of output, since economies of scale could be substantial in an industry with so many small and inefficient units which co-existed with some big concerns often running at far below their full capacity. Since *per capita* consumption was so low and so inexpensive, any cost reduction drive immediately tended to land the industry in a crisis of overproduction. Such an unhopeful market condition was scarcely an inducement to rationalization of the industry which, besides suffering from the high ash content of Indian coal that restricted exports, was also crippled by transport shortages, inefficient labour and low mining technology. On the other hand, unless these deficiencies could be removed by a massive programme of rationalization, tackling the problems of transport, technology, labour and organization at the same time, the low *per capita* consumption of coal could not be expected to rise rapidly of its own volition.

The low level of the Indian economy (whatever its historical roots) made it no easy matter to create a market for its budding industries. With a narrow and imperfect technology, it was futile to rely on an export drive for its manufactures. For a long time to come, industrial advance could take place only within the walls of a reserved domestic market. Since the technological capacity for producing basic capital goods was so narrow in an unbalanced economy, the industrial expansion within the walls of the domestic market necessarily involved heavy and continuous leakage of gains through imports of machinery and chemicals necessary for various manufactures. This meant that there was no guarantee that the domestic market for industrial goods of an increasing range would expand sufficiently to give a push to basic capital goods industries, so that the leakages would diminish within a short time. On the other hand an attempt to force the pace by simply delinking the Indian economy from the rest of the world would certainly drive up the prices of capital goods within the country, leading through a slowing down of industrial production to the contraction of the walls of the domestic market. A policy of protection provided no panacea for the market problems of Indian industries. Nor was such a policy calculated to promote technological efficiency and export breakthrough, unless discrimination was exercised in giving protection. A broad, integrated and discriminating approach to the whole problem was necessary, especially because of the interrelated difficulties on the supply side.

These supply constraints—as M. D. Morris has emphasized recently—should not be underrated;[27] nor should they—one might add—be seen in isolation from demand limitations. To break these constraints it was necessary to promote massive social overhead investment in irrigation, power supply, transport, education and other infrastructural facilities—and these were precisely the facilities which would also promote effective demand.

Given sufficient time, no doubt the factors of production could

[27] Morris David Morris, 'Private Investment on the Indian Subcontinent 1900–1939: Some Methodological Considerations', review article in *Modern Asian Studies*, vol. 8, pt 4, October 1974.

(and did) respond to expanded demand. In course of time the situation improved. Areas under improved varieties of sugar-cane and long-staple cotton spread. Bamboo pulp technology was made commercially feasible for paper manufacture. Skilled Indian labour replaced foreign technical personnel in the steel and glass industries. Hydroelectricity became available for exploiting India's excellent bauxite deposits for aluminium manufacture. The expanding needs of the glass industry for soda ash were supplied from within the country. Specialized steels and steel components began to be manufactured for the production of automobiles, textile machinery, bicycles, machine tools, sewing-machines, etc. But there were special difficulties which had to be overcome. All this took time—and the delay caused in this way was a tangible indication of the long period during which supply constraints inhibited progress in spite of the existence of demand.

These difficulties—arising from the underdeveloped technical and organizational structure of a backward economy—were bound to affect the private businessman's calculations about the costs of production. And the resulting uncertainties in the investment decision-making process were, as Professor Morris has noted,

truly formidable . . . There were difficulties of selecting appropriate technology from what existed in the developed countries. This technology inevitably had to be adapted to different relative factor prices, to the fact of more costly capital and cheaper labour. At the same time the indigenous capacity for redesign was limited and very costly. The lack of skilled labour meant that the entrepreneur had to train his own. The costs of training were hard to predict and the rate of turnover was difficult to estimate. . . . Lack of complementary facilities means that the entrepreneur typically had to provide his own power and his own repair and replacement facilities and inventories. Thus, he needed not only more fixed capital but more working capital than the same enterprise would require in a developed system. Yet the businessman faced a situation where capital was typically more costly than in developed regions. Because local credit systems were badly underdeveloped, capital would flow only in fitful fashion. . . . All this suggests that the entrepreneur encountered higher real costs that needed the promise of higher rates of return if a gamble was to be taken. . . . The great areas of uncertainty combined with the obvious objective obstacles to inhibit rapid expansion of modern industry.[28]

One need only add to the above that so far as Indian entrepreneurs

[28] Ibid.

were concerned, one additional and very big uncertainty was the possibility of official bias, racial discrimination and cut-throat foreign competition. If, as the case studies of the selected industries have already suggested, Indian entrepreneurs (at any rate some of them) were willing to face higher risks than the established European houses, then this additional uncertainty which affected only Indians and not Europeans was a very important factor indeed. The nature of government policy and the behaviour of foreign and indigenous enterprise must now be examined in an overall context.

CHAPTER 5

Government Initiative and Private Enterprise in Indian Industrialization 1914–47

Given the magnitude of the problems facing Indian industrialization as sketched in the previous chapter, there could be no soft approach, no line of least resistance, that might hold out a remote promise of achievement of the goal. Let there be no lack of clarity about this: only savage, single-minded determination and will-power, that brooked no obstacle or resistance, that did not quail at any sight of privation and suffering, could have carried the Indian economy forward at a pace comparable to that of Japan or Russia during the inter-war period. Such a procedure needed, above all, a national will, an aggressive appetite for transformation, that had characterized Japanese and Russian society from the late nineteenth century.

To what extent did the constituent elements of Indian society possess such a national will for transformation? The urban intelligentsia, which had largely led the nationalist struggle since the late nineteenth century, had exhibited a yearning for economic transformation that had found expression in the writings of Dadabhai Naoroji, Romesh Dutt and a host of other writers. What was more important, during the inter-war period important business groups in India were seized by the aggressive nationalistic desire for achieving an economic miracle and eradicating the ills of backwardness. Significant elements of Indian society were influenced by the keen desire for transformation that hardly touched many of the smaller underdeveloped regions of the world at this time. These elements inevitably pressed for a more dynamic role of the government in the economy; and in so far as constitutional reforms led to increasing transfers of influence and power to Indians, some important changes in the tariff and stores purchase policy of the government were brought about during the inter-war period. There were modifications in the negative attitude of the Government of India towards the industrial transformation of the country. Nevertheless, that government was almost exclusively preoccupied with problems of political control and strategic security in an era when the future of the British in India itself became increasingly uncertain. The sprawling apparatus of government, stretched to its limits in dealing with the problems of political unrest, devolution of power and external threats from Europe and the Far East, was hardly a suitable instrument for promoting development. Its profound nineteenth century bias against an industrial solution for India's problems was eroded only to the limited extent that Indians gained positions of power within the political and economic system. And as more and more elements of a diverse society were drawn into the competitive political process leading to independence and partition, it did not appear as if the ramshackle political coalitions generated by the process would be the monolithic instruments of transformation able and willing to take the total measures required for development, to inflict the necessary sufferings on the population, and to face the social costs of economic engineering.

However, that problem lay in the future, well beyond the scope of this study. During the period under review a better rate of growth —it has been alleged by S. K. Sen—could have been attained if the Indian bourgeoisie had seized all the opportunities available to them. A. K. Bagchi, pursuing an altogether different line of argument, has stressed that there was a potential for faster growth that could have been tapped by a more adequate tariff policy on the part of the Government of India. What were the missed opportunities, within the limitations of the setting, that can be laid at the door of either public policy or private enterprise during the inter-war period? To this question, it is possible to find some concrete answers (rather than vague speculations) from the case studies of selected industries already undertaken.

So far as private enterprise is concerned, it seems that cotton mill owners missed some opportunities of production with finer counts of yarn and manufacture of bleached, dyed and printed piece-goods during the twenties. They rapidly covered the lost ground in the thirties, assisted by the protection given by the Government of India. However, it was not until the Second World War period that textile enterprise in India succeeded in eliminating imports; given Japan's advantages of labour and technology, this delay was inevitable, and tariff policy was certainly not the factor which delayed full import-substitution in the thirties.

In the case of the steel industry, official patronage and Tata enterprise ensured that output of steel should expand as far as possible within the confines of the domestic market up to 1935. After that year some opportunities for expansion of steel production by opening new units on a big scale were missed by Tata, Bird, and Martin Burn, though the point must be emphasized that the expansion of demand from 1935 to 1939 was not all that encouraging. After the outbreak of war demand expanded much more rapidly, but the overall structure of government policy (not just its tariff aspects) prevented the opening of new units.

The progress of Indian shipping after the First World War was an impressive feat of aggressive nationalist enterprise against discriminatory official policies. If the Government of India had accepted the Mercantile Marine Committee's recommendations of coastal reservation and aid to shipbuilding, then the shipping and shipbuilding industry might have attained in 1939 the state of progress it was to attain a decade later in 1949.

So far as coal was concerned, it has been noted that there was no discriminatory political factor that impeded the expansion of output. Indeed, the expansion of coal output was faster than strict market considerations should have encouraged colliery owners to undertake, leading to frequent overproduction.

The paper industry had enjoyed protection since 1925. The big European houses which dominated the industry then, and the new Indian houses which entered it after 1935, came out with striking innovative responses to the technological challenges of paper manufacture in India. The breakthrough in the paper industry was delayed by a decade after 1925 due to the gestation time necessary for solving the complex problems of bamboo pulp technology.

Protection was offered to the sugar industry only in 1932 and new entrepreneurs were drawn into the field as a result. Progress was so rapid that within half a decade full import-substitution had been attained. This positive response to protection was made possible by the spread of improved varieties of cane in the previous years. If the sugar industry had come to enjoy protection in the early twenties, there would still have been formidable problems with regard to sugar-cane supply, which would have taken some time to solve. In any case the lost ground was regained extremely rapidly in the thirties.

The glass industry was one of the clear instances in which inadequate government policy inhibited progress in the inter-war period. If protection had not been refused to this industry, then it would have expanded considerably in the favourable market conditions of the twenties and the late thirties. As it was, the industry attained some degree of maturity only during the Second World War.

The match industry, on the other hand, came to enjoy a high revenue tariff as early as 1922, and the response of small-scale Indian enterprise to this stimulus was splendid. The Swedish multinational, Wimco, was compelled to manufacture in India to preserve its market, and this ensured a fairly high production technology. Within a few years import-substitution was complete.

The chemicals industry had complex technological problems which could be solved only in course of time, but more effective government protection (which was extended and quickly withdrawn in the thirties) might have helped to some extent. The big houses entered the industry only in the late thirties and until then the organization and management of the industry left much to be desired. This is one industry in which the factors are somewhat incalculable on account of its technological complexities, and it is no easy matter to surmise what could have been achieved with greater help and private initiative.

The automobile industry was taken up by aggressive nationalist enterprise on a scale and at a time which were not justified in a strictly business sense. Birla and Walchand took enormous risks, and their courage and foresight undoubtedly placed them in the rank of the Japanese Zaibatsu and the Chinese comprador bourgeoisie, with whom Indian entrepreneurs have been compared unfavourably by S. K. Sen. The houses of Birla and Walchand, backed by no national government, indeed faced a much more unfavourable situation than Chinese or Japanese combines. The industry enjoyed no protection; however, the cost of this should not be exaggerated. Before 1935 the limitations of the technological base of Indian industry had in any case ruled out automobile manufacture.

Similarly in aluminium, Indian and foreign enterprise started units in the late thirties without expectation of protection, in spite of complex technological problems. This initiative could not have been reasonably expected until that time, in view of the state of exploitation of power resources in India. Government stepped in with aid as soon as the Second World War broke out, so that in this case no opportunities were missed (as in the case of automobile manufacture) due to lack of official patronage.

In the case of textile machinery manufacture, it has been calculated that the basic commercial and technological preconditions of manufacture were provided by the middle of the twenties. Due to lack of government help, private entrepreneurs did not venture to take up the challenge until the late thirties. They were subsequently obstructed by official measures.

Neither commercial nor technological considerations permitted production of machine tools on a substantial scale before the Second World War. Since there was simply no adequate market in India, protection—which was not extended—would have been no help, nor can private enterprise be blamed for pusillanimity in this instance.

To sum up then, there were a few cases of missed opportunities which can be laid at the door of private enterprise, but not many. The ground lost by cotton mill owners in the twenties was rapidly recovered in the thirties and there were instances, such as automobile manufacture, in which Indian entrepreneurs committed large sums when there were apparently no opportunities. As for tariff policies (considered apart from the larger aspects of government policy which will be taken up in an overall context below), a few industries, such as glass, shipping and alkalis, were denied protection outright though they exhibited features which promised success under protective tariff.[1] There was of course no question of offering protection to machine tools, automobiles, aluminium, etc. in the twenties, when the basic supply conditions were non-existent. Sugar manufacture got protection somewhat late in 1932, but here as in cotton manufacture the ground lost was covered very fast in the thirties.

It seems reasonable to say that up to the outbreak of the Second World War, the industries in India missed some available opportunities, but not many. This is far from saying that a different kind of government could not have created big new opportunities in the inter-war period. Again, during the Second World War very broad opportunities of industrialization could not be utilized on account of the nature of wartime planning by the Government of India. It is

[1] In the case of shipping, read coastal reservation instead of protective tariff.

in its overall structural aspect that government policy must be viewed. This overall view must also embrace those positive changes in government policy which contributed to the significant rate of expansion of manufacturing output during the period under review.

1. Government Policy

Official policies towards Indian industrialization were by no means unilinear. It has been established by A. K. Bagchi with massive documentation that imperial interests, often contradictory to the development of the Indian economy, profoundly influenced the overall structure as well as the operational details of the economic policies of the government at all levels. It needs to be added here that these imperial interests were at all times somewhat diverse, and increasingly in course of the decline of the British Raj the wide range of imperial interests began to produce pulls and pressures in different directions. The somewhat unusual consistency of direction in the policies of the Raj in the heyday of nineteenth century *laissez-faire* no longer survived the crisis of imperialism after the outbreak of the First World War. The subtle but increasing shift from the commercial to the financial (and strategic) aspects of British imperial interests in India in the inter-war period produced a profound uncertainty on the part of policy-makers with regard to the role of the government in the economy. That uncertainty was enchanced by the fact that an increasingly substantial part of government came to be Indianized during the period.

The consequences of financial and strategic considerations for policy-making need emphasis. Increasingly they eroded the *laissez-faire* ethic of nineteenth century British imperialism, which had operated in India with important modifications in those areas of policy-making in which British economic interests had needed large-scale official intervention (e.g. supply of labour to tea plantations). The financial and strategic considerations increasingly compelled British policy-makers to pay consideration to the development of the resources of India in a manner that no longer contributed to the strengthening of the import–export relationship between India and Britain, which had been promoted both by free trade and by government investment in the nineteenth century.

Even in the high noon of imperialism in India, before the First World War cast a long shadow, the implicit tension between commercial and strategic considerations had produced a perceptible shift in policy at the turn of the century. As the Raj reached its apogee under the imperious and autocratic Viceroyalty of Lord Curzon, it assumed increasingly the aggressive pursuit of British (and British Indian) strategic interests in the Persian Gulf, in Central Asia, in Tibet. In this pursuit of imperial glory, Lord Curzon envisaged the building up of India as a source of manpower and munitions, as a second centre of British power that would take on increasingly the strategic burden east of Suez. His invaluable support of the Tata steel works at Jamshedpur, which he extended without consulting the interests of Birmingham, was due to the strategic vision of India as a second base of British power east of Suez. The importance of India in the overall war effort and not merely in defence east of Suez was brought home to British statesmen during the First World War. As an important source of manpower and munitions during wartime, India had to be built up as an industrial power, albeit to a limited extent. As military expenditure mounted in the inter-war period, there was greater tapping of the industrial potential of India in response.

This brings us to the financial considerations which became increasingly important in the inter-war period. The mounting expenditure of the government necessitated a search for fresh sources of revenue as well as for possible economies. Gradually customs duties replaced land revenue as the most important source of income for the British government in India. Even the levy of increasing duties on imports, however, could not solve the financial crisis. In the thirties there was an attempt to reduce the burden of the Home Charges of the Government of India, which were eating into its revenues. Stores which were purchased by the Government of India in Britain now began to be purchased within India. Thus important changes were wrought in tariff and stores purchase policies by the strategic and financial considerations of the Raj.

Fiscal Policy

The first major breach in the settled British policy of keeping the Indian market open to British manufactures occurred in 1917 under the pressure of war needs. In order to make a contribution of £100 million to the Imperial Treasury, the Government of India imposed duties on cotton goods. Meanwhile the general rate on imports of all kinds, fixed at 5 per cent *ad valorem* since 1896, was raised to

7.5 per cent *ad valorem* in 1916. After the war, faced with an enormous budgetary deficit of Rs 19 crores, the Government of India raised the general rate to 11 per cent *ad valorem*. In spite of increased taxation, the budgetary position continued to deteriorate and in 1922 the general rate was enhanced to 15 per cent *ad valorem*. The result was a substantial change in India's position, compared to other countries, regarding the amount of revenue tariff against British goods (see Table 38). Her position in this regard was equalized with that of other Empire countries.

TABLE 38

INDEX NUMBER EXPRESSING THE ESTIMATED *ad valorem* INCIDENCE OF
TARIFF APPLIED TO BRITISH GOODS

		1914	1924
Empire	India	2.75	10.50
	Australia	6.25	9.75
	Canada	15.25	13.25
	South Africa	7.50	9.00
	New Zealand	8.25	8.50
Foreign Countries	USA	19.50	32.00
	Germany	17.25	10.00
	Argentina	24.00	20.50
	France	21.75	12.50
	Japan	19.25	10.25
	China	5.00	5.00
	Netherlands	2.75	2.75
	Brazil	88.00	41.00
	Belgium	10.00	8.50
	Italy	18.25	15.75
	Spain	42.00	37.25
	Sweden	23.00	12.25

SOURCE. C. N. Vakil, *Memorandum on the Need for Revision of the Indian Customs Tariff*, Bombay, 1928, p. 9.

However, the tariff wall was still low and it was a purely revenue tariff. Discriminating protection was adopted for the first time with the grant of protective tariff to the steel industry in 1924. Subsequently a wide range of industries obtained protective tariffs, especially in the thirties. The only instances in which the Government of India turned down the recommendation of protection by the

16

Tariff Board were the cases of the glass industry in 1931 and the woollen industry in 1934. However, being aware of the stringent conditions for the grant of protective tariff under the policy of discriminating protection, many industries did not apply for protection to the Tariff Board at all. These conditions laid down that for an industry to qualify for protection, it must have an assured supply of raw materials at home, a sufficiently large domestic market and a promise of being able to dispense with protection eventually. These were not conditions that all infant industries were able to fulfil, and thus there was no question of their applying for or obtaining protection.

Although protection remained fairly discriminating, the revenue tariff continued to rise in the thirties under sheer budgetary pressures. In 1930 the Government of India, faced with a Rs 5.5 crore deficit, raised duties on cotton goods, sugar and kerosene. The following year the deficit mounted to a crushing Rs 17.24 crores, and in a drastic attempt to balance the budget the Government of India raised the level of the general revenue tariff from 15 per cent *ad valorem* to 25 per cent *ad valorem*.[2] This was sufficiently high to afford some degree of uncertain protection to many industries that did not qualify for discriminating protection.

Meanwhile the rules of government purchase of stores were being gradually modified. In 1922 the Indian Stores Department accepted the principle of preference to Indian manufactures, following which government purchase of industrial goods in India went up substantially. Nevertheless sterling payments for stores still amounted annually to £4 million on an average in the twenties. An agitation was set up in the Indian Legislative Assembly for rupee tenders in India in 1924, but the government accepted the Assembly's resolutions only in 1929, when new rules of purchase were drawn up. However, under exceptions specifically stated in the new rules, ordnance stores, railway materials, locomotives and a wide range of other stores continued to be imported.[3]

The value of stores purchased in India by the government had mounted to Rs 4.29 crores in 1929–30 from the low level of Rs 1.64 crores in 1922–3. As a result of the Great Depression, it went down to Rs 3.30 crores in 1932–3, but rose quickly to Rs 4.76 crores in

---

[2] For a detailed account of tariffs, *see* B. N. Adarkar, *The History of the Indian Tariff 1924–39*, Office of the Economic Adviser, Delhi, 1940.

[3] S. K. Sen, *House of Tata*, pp. 181–9.

1934–5. As railway expenditure recovered, engineering firms such as Jessop, Martin Burn, Balmer Lawrie and Braithwaite made considerable progress in the manufacture of wagons, bridge materials, cranes, etc.[4]

It will be noted that the engineering firms which benefited most from government and railway expenditure were European firms. Owing to official bias against Indian competitors, orders placed by the government and railway authorities tended to be monopolized by big British houses. Instances of discrimination can be multiplied. The coal purchased by the railways—the biggest consumer—was mostly supplied by European managing agencies, which also enjoyed a lion's share of wagons for dispatch of coal. Again, the British shipping companies—B.I. and P & O—enjoyed a practical monopoly of the postal subsidies of the Government of India, and no part of the very lucrative mail contract was conceded to Scindia Steam Navigation Company.

What were the consequences of discrimination for the level of investment? Obviously it kept down the share of Indian investment in the total capital employed in India. But if Europeans were willing to set up enterprises in India provided the returns were attractive, this need not necessarily keep down the overall level of investment. The only consequence would be that the European share in investment would be greater than it would otherwise have been. As M. D. Morris has pointed out, 'Discrimination would have affected the level of private investment only if equal access to capital at the same interest rates would have led Indians to invest more—i.e. take more risks—than Europeans would'.[5]

As a matter of fact several European concerns in India during the period under review showed a dynamic response to opportunities of investment in India. Profitability being the guiding motive, capital was not withheld by them when the returns promised to be favourable. No social ethic, political motivation or tie-up with concerns at Home was strong enough to counteract the pull of profitable investment in the colony, however harmful that might be to the firms in Britain supplying India. The European engineering firm of Burn & Co., for instance, went in for manufacturing inland river steam vessels when it was found that substantial economies would be made if the vessels were manufactured in Calcutta instead of being imported from Britain. There was no hesitation to risk the opposi-

[4] Ibid.   [5] Morris, 'Private Investment 1900–1939'.

tion of vested interests at Home, and in time Burn even began to export vessels to Burma, so long supplied only by firms in Britain.[6]

The expansion of Burn in this and other directions was no doubt generally assisted by the patronage of government to which European firms in Calcutta had a monopoly of access. Again, the big European managing agencies in the coal business were able to maintain a fairly high technological level on account of their lucrative supply contracts with the railways. As far as possible, the European managing agencies in Calcutta and elsewhere sought to take advantage of the domestic market in the inter-war period,[7] and the favouritism shown to them by the authorities, while restricting the field for Indian entrepreneurs, sometimes ensured the inflow of better technology.

However, there are less obvious factors peculiar to the inter-war period which must be taken into account in judging the impact of racial discrimination on the overall level of investment. In the first place, in so far as Indian capital gained strength in the private sector, the pressure for a more active role of government in the economy mounted. To be sure, European managing agencies agitated for protection against imported manufactures when it lay in their interest to do so. Bird and Martin Burn insisted in the twenties that government must extend protection to steel for ten years in order to enable them to set up new steel enterprises. But the general climate of opinion in the European business community in India was against protection. The Bengal Chamber of Commerce, their most important organization, vehemently opposed the grant of discriminating protection to steel. In so far as racial exclusiveness enabled the European element in business and industry to remain strong, it also enabled the Government of India to resist the pressure for adoption of more radical policies for development.

Secondly, there is enough evidence to show that during this period there emerged big Indian houses, such as Birla and Walchand, which were impelled by the driving force of economic nationalism to go beyond normal business considerations in the initiation of new

---

[6] *Report of the Indian Tariff Board regarding the Grant of Protection to the Ship-Building Industry*, Calcutta, 1926.

[7] The only prominent exception was in the case of coastal shipping, in which B.I. utilized its monopoly to maintain high rates and thus to restrict carriage by sea. The entry of Scindias resulted in substantial expansion of the coastal carriage trade.

industries. A rational calculation of the rates of profit, the amount of risk and the length of time involved would not have permitted the headlong plunge into automobile manufacture and shipbuilding which they took during the Second World War. No European house would have taken these risks. The European managing agencies in Calcutta were conservative, insistent on sound finance and much less prone to romanticism. If there had been active support of the big Indian houses by the government instead of indifference and obstruction, then the level of investment might have been raised significantly.

Finally, during the period under review European investment decisions in India came to be closely affected by considerations of repatriation. Increasingly the balance to be struck between reinvestment and repatriation of profits turned in favour of the latter. Indian houses had no repatriation of profits to make and naturally the rate of reinvestment of profits under Indian ownership tended to be higher. This change in European investment behaviour was partly a result of the monetary policies of the Government of India, though there were other complex political and economic factors also.

Monetary Policy

If financial considerations compelled the Government of India to change its fiscal policies in such a way as to favour Indian industries, the effect of these financial considerations on its monetary policies worked in an opposite direction. The dominant principle of finance, to which the Government of India adhered persistently, was to balance the budget. In order to achieve this, it had raised customs duties and had sought to curtail sterling expenditure in Britain. With the same purpose in view, it also proved determined to maintain a high parity of the rupee with the pound. Devaluation of the rupee would have at once raised its sterling expenditure at Home. Balancing the budget required keeping the Home Charges down, and the Government of India was therefore resolved at any cost to appreciate the value of the rupee in relation to the pound. The rising value of the rupee in relation to the pound after the First World War entailed deflation and curtailment of the purchasing power of the people, as well as massive repatriation of profits to Britain. Thus the monetary policies of the Government of India had powerful inhibitive effects on the demand as well as the supply factors in the growth of industrial production.

During the last stages of the First World War the sterling value of the rupee began to soar upwards from its pre-war level of 1s. 4d. In 1920 the Babington-Smith Committee fixed the value of the rupee at the very high level of 2s. This high sterling parity of the rupee after the war proved to be the signal for a vigorous demand, mostly speculative, for remittances to London on account of European businessmen waiting to repatriate their accumulated wartime profits.[8] For every rupee sent from India, it was now possible to obtain more sterling in London.

The rupee–sterling parity fixed by the Babington-Smith Committee, however, was artificially high, and it soon proved extremely difficult to maintain. Now the traditional method of the government to maintain the exchange value of the rupee, whenever it showed signs of falling, was to sell what was known as Reverse Councils, i.e. sterling drafts sold by the government in Bombay and Calcutta in exchange for rupees and encashable in sterling in London. Soon after fixing the rupee at 2s. the Indian trade balance became unfavourable as imports rose and exports fell, and as a result the rupee became unstable. The combined result of all this was a persistent demand for sterling drafts which the government continued to sell at a little over 2s. The government was unwilling to devalue the rupee as its Home Charges would then increase at a time of budget deficit.[9]

By sale of Reverse Councils to counteract inflation, India's gold reserves in London, increased by her huge favourable balance of trade, were whittled away. Charges and counter-charges began to fly. On 17 February 1920, S. R. Bomanji wrote in the *Times of India*: 'An enormous wrong and legalized plunder of India's resources are taking place at the present moment. It is nothing more nor less than an organized loot of our sterling resources which it has taken us so many years to accumulate.' It was further alleged that this was an organized attempt on the part of the Indian bureaucracy surreptitiously to multiply its salaries and pensions, and also that the enhanced rupee helped Manchester and Dundee exporters by imposing a burden equivalent to 100 per cent excise on their competitors in

---

[8] Federation of Indian Chambers of Commerce and Industry, *Indian Currency and Exchange 1914–30—How Government Have Managed It*, no place, 1931, pp. 20–1; Radhakamal Mukherjee and H. L. Dey, *Economic Problems of Modern India*, London, 1941, p. 226.

[9] Ibid.

India.[10] B. F. Madon, a spokesman of critical Indian business opinion, claimed that the £23 million Reverse Councils sold in the process of shoring up the rupee had gone mainly into the pockets of bankers and merchant princes.[11] European business opinion, on the contrary, was quick in coming to the support of the Government of India. M. de. P. Webb of the Karachi Chamber of Commerce gave strong support to the government's currency policy.[12] It is curious to note that European businessmen wanted a higher exchange rate of the rupee even though this would produce an adverse impact on exports of jute, tea and other export products controlled mainly by European interests in India. Nothing more clearly underlined the fact of their preference for remittance as against reinvestment of their war profits.

Indian businessmen continued to agitate against the high parity of the rupee, especially through the Indian Merchants' Chamber in Bombay which made the currency question particularly its own.[13] Ultimately the government appointed the Royal Commission on Currency and Finance, which finally recommended the exchange value of the rupee to be 1s. 6d. This was much too high for Indian business opinion, but it was nevertheless given effect to in 1927.

The discontent of Indian businessmen found expression in subsequent years in the charge that the Great Depression in India was not a result of the Wall Street crash, but a consequence of the government's currency policy. In 1931, the organ of nationalist business opinion, the Federation of Indian Chambers of Commerce and Industry, published a booklet in which it argued that the prevailing depression originated in India long before the Wall Street crash. Its cause was alleged to be the appreciation of the value of the rupee by the government, which had resulted in the reduction of the purchasing power of the people.[14] Similar arguments were heard at the Bombay Mill-owners' Association, where the Chairman of the annual general meeting on 25 February 1930 expressed the opinion that the Wall Street crash could not wholly explain the depression in India, where it was much more severe than in Britain, Germany or Japan. He also pointed out the massive export of capital which had begun

[10] *A Chapter in India's Currency History*, no date, no place, p. 54.
[11] Ibid., pp. 105–6.   [12] Ibid., p. 112.
[13] *Annual Report of the Indian Merchants' Chamber for the Year 1925*, speech of Phiroze C. Sethna at the annual general meeting, 23 January 1926.
[14] *Indian Currency and Exchange 1914–30*, pp. 52–4.

with the depression. This meant that less was available for investment in India, and he blamed this entirely on the high rate of exchange.[15]

'There was a time', wrote G. D. Birla to Walter Layton on 20 May 1932, 'when the British investors would not remit the return of their investments to England but would reinvest the same in India. For the last eight or ten years this habit is partially changed. The investor is trying nowadays to send his earnings as much as he can across the boundaries of India.'[16] A week later Sir Purshotamdas Thakurdas repeated the same argument in a letter to John Maynard Keynes, pointing out that the considerable flight of capital from India, on which Keynes had recently commented, was not peculiar to 1931, as revealed by the figures of the past few years. 'In fact this phenomenon is very strikingly noticed since the conclusion of the War. The explanation may be that the investment of English investors in India at the conclusion of the War had so immensely grown up that he no longer thought it desirable to reinvest his Indian profits within India and increase his stake further. The tendency of the British merchant in India before the war was to reinvest his profit in India, a habit which he changed in the latter period.'[17]

This flight of capital, which so worried G. D. Birla and Purshotamdas Thakurdas, was not simply a product of changes in the parity of the rupee. But Indian business opinion had a tendency to blame everything on the government's currency policy. The charge that the depression in India was a result of deflationary policies pursued by the Government of India was an instance of this. Nevertheless, it will not do to ignore the aspects of the problem which contemporary Indian business opinion stressed so often in the course of the controversy over the currency question. Until adequate research is done on the origins and the extent of the Great Depression in India, nothing can be pronounced definitely on the subject. All the same, it seems probable that the problems of international depression were further complicated in India by the currency policy of the government. It is indeed somewhat curious that there were signs of depression in India before the Wall Street crash. The *Investor's India Year Book* commented that the year 1928 was remarkable 'chiefly for the dull-

---

[15] *Report of the Bombay Millowners' Association for the Year 1929*, chairman's speech at the annual general meeting, 25 February 1930.

[16] Purshotamdas Thakurdas Papers, file no. 107, pt I, 1931, Birla to Walter Layton, 20 May 1932.

[17] Ibid., pt II, Thakurdas to J. M. Keynes, 28 May 1932.

ness that pervaded most markets and for the tightness of money that prevailed in the prolonged busy season'.[18]

During the years of the depression, difficulties were enhanced by the doses of deflation administered by the Government of India for balancing its budget. From 1931 to 1932 the bank rates of the Imperial Bank of India were extraordinarily high and the Government of India issued loans at high rates of interest, giving rise to complaints among businessmen that all the investors' money was being drawn away into government securities. The tightness of the money market which the handling of the currency question caused at the height of the Depression was relieved from 1933 onwards, partly as a result of the lowered costs of financing trade in commodities, which released some capital for industrial investment. On balance, it seems probable that the effects of the government's fiscal and monetary policies, which were both profoundly modified by financial considerations, tended to cancel each other out in the early thirties. A. K. Bagchi crisply points this out: 'One could argue that the stimulating effects of the measures of tariff protection adopted in 1930 and 1931 were largely smothered by the deflationary fiscal and monetary policy of the government.'[19]

Over a more extended period, the balance of effects flowing from the fiscal and monetary policies of the Government of India was more favourable for industrial growth. From 1933–4, the rate of the increase of capital quickened considerably, partly because industrial prices recovered more quickly than agricultural prices. The recovery of industry, assisted by high revenue and protective tariffs, at a time when depression continued in agriculture, partly due to the continuing effects of deflationary policies, probably meant that a substantial surplus was squeezed out of the villages into the towns. Increased consumption of a more diverse range of industrial goods in the towns would explain why the market was so remarkably firm in the thirties and why it became possible to initiate so many new industries in the latter half of the decade. Of course throughout this time the flight of foreign capital continued. It was estimated by the *Indian Finance* that between 1920 and 1935, £250 million of foreign capital was withdrawn from India. But even this cloud had its silver lining for Indian capitalists, whose strength in the private corporate sector steadily increased. The tough negotiations over the Ottawa

[18] *Investor's India Year Book*, vol. 16, 1928–9.
[19] Bagchi, *Private Investment*, p. 66.

agreements and the Modi-Lees Pact indicated their improved bargaining position.

Wartime Planning of the Economy, 1939–45

The quickening pulse of industry in the late thirties was succeeded by an accelerated spurt of growth after the outbreak of the Second World War. The war effort under government direction profoundly altered the structure of India's industrial economy. Important changes took place not merely in the *pace*, but also in the *range*, of industrial production in the large-scale organized sector under private enterprise. The industrial war effort was directed by the War Resources Committee (earlier War Supply Board) through its executive agency, the Supply Department. Competitive tendering used in the early stages of the war was replaced by contracts placed with the private sector on ascertained costs and profit margins.

The value of the contracts placed by the Supply Department from 1939–40 to 1942–3 was £408 millions, as stated earlier. Supply Department purchases from 1 September 1939 to 31 December 1941 fell under the following main groups: engineering, hardware and miscellaneous, £73 millions; cotton textiles, woollens and other textiles, £72.8 millions; foodstuffs, £12.1 millions; leather and leather goods, £7.6 millions; timber and wood, £6.8 millions; total purchases, £172.3 millions.[20] The engineering and textile industries absorbed more than 80 per cent of the contracts placed by the Supply Department. At the beginning of the war there were only 600 workshops capable of producing engineering components. At the end of the war 1,500 engineering workshops were supplying the government. The output of machine tools had risen from less than 100 a year to 350–400 monthly.[21] A rapid beginning was made with many types of goods not previously manufactured in India, especially in the engineering and metallurgical industries. Output of chemicals and dyes for war purposes also expanded enormously. As for the more established industries, the Supply Department took about 3,900 million yards of cloth out of the total production of 26,000 million yards during the war, as well as 5,200 cwt of paper and wasteboard, amounting to 43 per cent of the total output from 1939 to 1945.[22]

The growth of India's industrial output in some key sectors during the war is set out in Table 39. This does not include muni-

[20] Prest, *War Economics*, p. 34, table 5.   [21] Ibid., p. 32.   [22] Ibid., p. 33.

TABLE 39

INDUSTRIAL PRODUCTION IN INDIA 1939-44

Commodity	1938	1939	1940	1941	1942	1943	1944
Coal (m. tons)	28.3	—	29	29.2	28.9	25.5	26.5
Paper (000's cwt)	1,184	1,416	1,753	1,871	1,821	1,752	2,001
Pig Iron (000's tons)	1,576	—	1,959	2,015	1,804	1,687	1,303
Steel ingots (000's tons)	977	—	1,285	1,363	1,299	1,366	1,264
Cement (000's tons)	1,512	—	1,727	—	2,183	2,112	2,044
Sugar (000's tons)	650	1,241	1,095	778	1,070	1,216	985
Jute fabrics (000's tons)	1,221	1,277	1,108	1,259	1,052	947	975
Cotton piece-goods (m. yds)	4,269	4,012	4,269	4,493	4,109	4,870	4,695
Cotton yarn (m. lbs)	1,303	1,243	1,349	1,577	1,533	1,680	1,620
Footwear (m. pairs)	—	—	—	7.6	16.2	13.2	6
Sulphuric acid (000's cwt)	512	—	778	—	813	848	778

SOURCE. A. R. Prest, op. cit., p. 37, Table 7.

tions output in government and other workshops, which grew considerably, nor does it include the output of small-scale industries, some of which apparently decreased, especially cotton goods. A somewhat pessimistic estimate of the growth of India's industrial output up to 1944 gave figures of 50 per cent increases for organized industries and 25 per cent for unorganized industries.[23] The estimate of output increase for the organized industries seems to be not too pessimistic in the light of the figures given in Table 39, but it must be pointed out that this table does not give figures for many new industries in which real breakthroughs occurred for the first time. A more optimistic estimate of the increase of the combined industrial output of the organized and unorganized sectors was made by V. K. R. V. Rao at the beginning of 1944, in which the overall expansion was stated to be 60 per cent in real terms.[24]

Although there was a significant breakthrough in industrial production during the years of the Second World War in relation to the pre-war years, the progress did not fulfil the great expectations aroused among India's businessmen and economists. Nationalist business opinion was in consequence disposed to be severely critical of the war organization of the industrial sector. G. D. Birla alleged in *India's War Prosperity: The Myth Exploded* that Britain was not allowing India to purchase machinery out of the latter's accumulating sterling assets due to fear of Indian industrialization. India should be allowed, Birla demanded, to import machinery instead of gold when repatriating her sterling assets to London. 'There is no planning for production', he fretted, even in wartime.

There is no facility for the disposal of the exportable surplus. The prices, therefore, have in many cases failed to respond to the newly created demand. In many cases they have depreciated. And our sale proceeds have been utilized not with a view to the expansion of our industries. Our gold reserves are frittered away when they could have been used for buying plant from America which would have been to England's advantage.[25]

A more professional critique of the organization of India's war economy stated:

On the whole, it must be admitted that there has been progress both in the pace and range of production since the outbreak of war, but

[23] *Eastern Economist*, 11 August 1944, cited in ibid., footnote 2, p. 38.
[24] *Commerce*, 26 February 1944.
[25] G. D. Birla, *India's War Prosperity*.

it has been more a matter of necessary production by placing orders with pre-selected producers rather than a serious and scientific attempt at mobilization of the industrial resources of the whole country. The Supply Department has been anxious to have these necessary orders executed on a system of priorities, and has been dominated by the desire not to harness the entire resources of the civil industry as rapidly as possible, but to interfere as little as possible.[26]

Comparisons with the wartime organization of the economy in the advanced Western countries made the disappointment of Indian businessmen and economists keener. It was pointed out that in Britain all economic activities were well planned from the beginning, whereas in India the Government sought to tackle each problem of economic control separately with little reference to allied problems.[27] Statements of U.S. war production by Donald Nelson, U.S. War Production Board Chief, were wistfully quoted: 'The largest armament programme the world has seen has been geared up to fast action here and now. It dwarfs everything done by America in the past. By mid-summer [of 1942], military aeroplane and engine production will be so vast that the problem will be where to find rail and transport to handle the load.'[28] Above all, comparisons with war production in Australia lent bitterness to the disappointment of nationalist business opinion in India. It was noted that in 1932 Australia did not produce one ounce of steel, whereas in 1942 she was producing 1.5 million tons of steel, more than the annual production of India, a country equipped with a steel industry before the First World War. Australia's aircraft factories had begun to produce the most up-to-date fighter and bomber planes at the rate of a thousand a year, her shipyards were now building destroyers, cruisers and merchant ships of 10,000 tons, her automobile factories were producing 50,000 automobiles, her engineering industries were turning out rifles and Bren guns in huge numbers. All this industrial war effort, it was noted bitterly, had been mounted in a country of 7 million people who a decade before had been producing raw materials and agricultural products for export to Britain, U.S.A. and Japan.[29] The frustrated nationalist businessmen of India did not pause to consider that India had a very narrow technological base, from

---

[26] L. C. Jain, *Indian Economy during the War*, London, 1944, p. 52.
[27] Ibid., p. 121.   [28] Quoted in ibid., p. 53.
[29] Ibid., p. 53.

which it was not possible to mount, with the best intentions in the world, an armaments programme on the scale of even Australia (until then a predominantly agricultural country), not to speak of Britain or the United States. Nevertheless, more dynamic handling of the war economy by the government could have improved India's industrial war effort in two directions, as pointed out by Birla and others. In the first place, the acute shortages of coal and transport which impeded industrial production in many lines could only have been dealt with properly by total control and mobilization of the economy. In the absence of proper war planning, manufacturers in India could not take advantage of the new demand which sprang up with the war. Secondly, even with the current level of war production, India succeeded in acquiring through her stepped-up exports very substantial foreign assets, which were not utilized with a view to long-term expansion of heavy industries by buying American plant and technology, as recommended by the American Technical (Grady) Mission. Government control of the economy, largely designed to meet immediate military needs, took no account of post-war aims of development, a deficiency which, the American Technical Mission stressed, ought to be made good at an early stage. The response of the Government of India to these American criticisms of the Indian war effort was simply to withhold the report of the Grady Mission,[30] which showed a distressing tendency to side with Indian businessmen on all points of controversy with the Government of India.

The ambitions of Indian business groups like Birla and Walchand to commence production of ships, aeroplanes, automobiles, etc. were frustrated by the obstructive attitude of civilian as well as military officials. Moreover, plants for production of textile machinery, sewing-machines and other sophisticated engineering products, which had been installed on the eve of the war by aggressive entrepreneurs like Shri Ram and G. D. Birla, were taken over by the government during the war for production of munitions. As a result, manufacture of these new products could not commence properly during the war, when there was a very large unsatisfied demand for them due to the fall in imports.

Planners of the war effort argued that heavy armaments like ships,

[30] Bishweswar Prased (ed.), *Official History of the Indian Armed Forces in the Second World War: General Administration and Organization,* 111, *Indian War Economy,* p. 44.

aircraft and motor-vehicles, which Walchand and others were so keen to produce as part of the war production programme, could not be turned out in appreciable quantities in India soon enough to produce an impact on the world-wide war production of the Allies. In this they were right, but they hardly paused to consider that war-time effort would bear fruit in the post-war period. Post-war reconstruction was not an important element in the war planning of the Indian economy anyway.

A typical instance of the slow response of officials to proposals of heavy armaments production from private businessmen was the affair of Walchand's aircraft factory. At the outbreak of war in 1939, Walchand presented a plan for manufacturing aircraft in India to the government, which reacted with customary dilatoriness. Only after the fall of France and the Japanese threat to South-East Asia did the Government of India approve his scheme in 1940 (the fate of Britain itself being uncertain at the time). The British ministry of aircraft production under Lord Beaverbrook at first opposed the proposal. It gave way under political pressure, but with the proviso that the aircraft factory proposed to be set up in India must not import the necessary component parts, machines, tools and raw materials from America or England, but must arrange to obtain these from other countries. The objection to India buying materials in the United States was based on the ground that all that America could produce was needed for Britain's own defence.[31] It was not the Government of India, but the Indian state of Mysore, that came to Walchand's aid in raising the capital for the company. The Government of India placed a small order for 200 planes in two years with the Hindustan Aircraft Company. It neither placed giant orders as did the Canadian or Australian governments, nor did it give aid for building a factory equipped for such large-scale production. The small orders were reluctantly placed under the pressure of opinion of British officials and businessmen in India.[32] In 1942, under the threat of Japanese attack, the Government of India took over the company from Walchand.

As for ship and car manufacture, the Government of India not only refused to extend any assistance at all, but positively sought to obstruct Walchand's strenuous efforts in these directions, on the ground that the new plants would divert resources from urgently needed munitions production.

[31] *Walchand Hirachand*, pp. 353–63.   [32] Ibid., pp. 365–70.

Birla and Walchand professed to see behind this obstructive attitude a Machiavellian British design to keep India underdeveloped and to prevent exploitation of her industrial potential. This was not, however, the real motivation of British statesmen. For them, the urgent need was to ensure the maximum efficiency of war production on a world-wide basis through proper international division of labour. This could be ensured only if the United States, Britain and other advanced Commonwealth countries concentrated on production of heavy armaments, while the technologically backward members of the Commonwealth stepped up the supply of essential raw materials and munitions. The wartime exports of India were raw jute and cotton, jute and cotton goods, tea, oil-seeds, manganese ore, mica, rubber, lac, etc.[33] It was in the increased export production of these goods that India could make the biggest contribution in world strategic terms. To set her to the task of manufacture of heavy armaments on her narrow technological base was to divert industrial resources from the advanced countries in order to enable her to manufacture them, when it could be done so much better and faster in the UK, USA and other white Commonwealth countries.

Up to the outbreak of the Second World War, as we have seen, the missed opportunities of industrialization within the limitations of the inter-war setting were not many and great. But during the Second World War India really missed splendid opportunities of initiating heavy industries on a large scale. A nationalist government would have seized these opportunities with a view to long-term development of India's industries after the war. The imperial government concentrated on the war and on nothing else, for the future of India after the war was quite uncertain. The future industrial development of India, which was such a major issue to Indian businessmen, was a minor consideration in the global strategic calculations of British statesmen fighting a world war. India's industrial potential was tapped, not in terms of her own future growth, but in terms of the most efficient international organization of war production and distribution in order to defeat the Axis. The international division of labour idealized by nineteenth century *laissez-faire* economics was propagated in a modified form by the penetrating controls of twentieth century warfare.

The changes in British economic policies during the 1914–47 period

[33] Prest, op. cit., p. 35, table 6.

were on balance favourable to industrial growth and must constitute a crucial part of the explanation for the substantial increase of manufacturing output during the period. That these policies continued to be guided by imperial and not nationalist considerations of course affected the whole context of economic growth, but there is no way of computing the economic costs of this fact, except during the Second World War when tangible opportunities slipped by simply because war production was organized from a global and not a national point of view.

During the inter-war period tariff policies made it profitable to invest in a broad range of industries. But no integrated programme of action was launched for breaking the overall constraints of demand and supply that had so far prevented a breakthrough in *per capita* production and income. In comparison with the massive public investment during the Five Year Plans, the public investment during this period appears to be very low indeed (see Table 40). The level of public investment was not such as to solve the interrelated difficulties in the way of assemblage of factors of production and the growth of new demand.

TABLE 40

TRENDS IN PUBLIC INVESTMENT BEFORE AND AFTER THE SECOND WORLD WAR

(million rupees)

Pre-war Years	Gross Public Investment	Post-war Years	Gross Public Investment
1925–6	644	1948–9	2,100
1926–7	735	1949–50	2,570
1927–8	827	1950–1	2,620
1928–9	750	1951–2	2,860
1929–30	814	1952–3	3,035
1930–1	670	1953–4	3,375
1931–2	488	1954–5	4,300
1932–3	338	1955–6	5,700
1933–4	334	1956–7	6,900
1934–5	350	1957–8	8,300
1935–6	436	1958–9	8,600
1936–7	359	1959–60	7,800
1937–8	358	1960–1	9,600

SOURCE. J. M. Healey, *The Development of Social Overhead Capital in India 1950–60*, p. 8, Table 1.

It is only fair to point out that the massive public investment of the later period of the Five Year Plans could not have been reasonably expected of any non-communist government in the inter-war period. The social welfare state lay yet in the future. The figures for pre-war and post-war public investment in Table 40 are not therefore in any sense comparable. However, in terms of the possibilities of the inter-war period, a much more dynamic approach to industrialization was open to a nationalist government. The nation undergoing the most rapid economic development during this period, Japan, benefited greatly from a *national* military policy. The drive to build Japan up as a great military power involved rapid industrialization under active patronage of the government. In so far as India had to be built up as a base of British power east of Suez, Indian industries also got government patronage during the period. But the defence programme for India as an integral part of an imperial system was bound to be substantially different from that of an independent nationalist India which had to provide for her own defence. India was not being built up by the British as a power in her own right, but only as an appendage to Britain's global imperial power. Necessarily this strategic fact involved a different kind of military–industrial effort in India, a part of a global distribution of power rather than a defence programme complete in itself. The consequences of this were most clearly felt by Indian businessmen during the Second World War, but even before that a government bent on independent defence of India would surely have adopted a more integrated approach to the problems of industrial growth than the piecemeal approach to these problems that was demonstrated by the policy of discriminating protection.

2. *Private Enterprise*

From the First World War to the advent of independence, the growth of organized industries took place very largely under the control of big business, both European and Indian. This was the period when many of the big houses which dominate the industrial scene in India today were founded. They played a pioneering role in the initiation of new industries. For this reason, we shall concentrate mainly on the role of big business in this section. Small firms had played a pioneering role in the previous *swadeshi* period, especially in Bengal where professional Bengalis opened new units of industry in the days of patriotic fervour following the partition of Bengal. A majority of these ventures perished within a few years. The main reasons for their failure were lack of capital and lack of business experience.[34] In the inter-war period, small firms continued to play an important role in those industries which could be run without large capital, such as glass, matches and chemicals of the sulphuric acid group. The owners of such small firms were drawn from rather more diverse backgrounds than the owners of big business. The majority of the small firms were concerns run by traders, but quite a few were directed by professional men, often inspired by patriotic fervour, or by progressive landlords, who were willing to risk a part of their income from land for patronizing industrial development. While some of these concerns were successful and grew into medium-sized firms (especially in the glass and match industries), others languished, or perished altogether. The main difficulty was lack of adequate capital reserves to tide over difficult periods. The initiative passed largely to big houses which had large assets and long (often hereditary) experience in commerce. This growth of big business was a response to the difficulties of production in an underdeveloped economy. The supply constraints described earlier profoundly influenced the structure of business which emerged after the First World War.

The most striking changes in the field of big business was the rapid expansion of big Indian family businesses, the slower growth of European managing agencies, and the entry of multinational groups in India from abroad. Table 41 shows the paid-up rupee capital of the companies under the management of some European as well as Indian groups, as reported in the *Investor's India Year Books* for 1914, 1922, 1937 and 1947. The coverage is by no means adequate for Indian houses, whether in Calcutta or elsewhere. Nor is it adequate for European groups located outside Calcutta. Full details are recorded only for European groups in Calcutta. It is, therefore, necessary to exercise caution in interpreting the trends shown by the figures in this table. The advance of big Indian houses, such as Thapar, Dalmia, Walchand and Juggilal Kamlapat, is certainly understated in the table. Even so, it is apparent from these figures that the balance was changing in favour of Indian groups. There was a tendency towards stagnation in the case of

[34] J. A. L. Swan, *Report on the Industrial Development of Bengal*, Calcutta, 1915.

TABLE 41

GROWTH OF BUSINESS HOUSES IN INDIA 1914–47

(paid-up rupee capital in Rs '000)

	1914	1922	1937	1947
CALCUTTA				
A. *European*				
1. McLeod	9,275	26,500	20,348	22,498
2. Martin[1]	16,865	29,984	31,298	32,215
3. Burn	4,900	35,626	35,887	35,467
4. Gillanders Arbuthnot	10,740	60,854	39,731	22,100
5. Hoare Miller	3,824	5,965	3,690	3,690
6. Andrew Yule	24,105	53,082	64,763	59,203
7. Shaw Wallace	8,034	8,598	10,559	10,369
8. Bird	28,524	43,334	38,881	40,121
9. Heilgers	10,595	14,435	13,603	17,606
10. Macneill	5,949	14,799	19,467	19,462
11. Balmer Lawrie	3,370	7,501	6,937	5,707
12. Octavius Steel	3,512	5,110	14,609	14,513
13. Jardine Skinner	11,074	15,218	23,458	11,650
14. George Henderson	800	4,000	4,200	4,600
15. Jardine Henderson	—	—	—	8,900
16. Mackinnon Mackenzie	N.A.	14,851	11,180	11,996
17. Duncan	13,058	14,408	18,218	20,488
18. Begg Dunlop	4,809	22,005	12,835	11,697
B. *Indian*				
19. Karamchand Thapar	—	—	N.A.	7,418
20. Juggilal Kamlapat (Kanpur)	—	—	N.A.	8,900
21. Bangur	—	—	—	4,500
22. Birla	—	6,523	17,897	218,504
23. Surajmull Nagarmull	—	—	—	3,250
24. N. C. Sircar	3,133	3,418	—	—
25. Janoki Nath Roy	—	—	3,316	8,000
26. Ramkumar Agarwala	—	—	—	10,000
27. Adamjee Hajee Dawood	—	—	4,500	4,500
BOMBAY				
A. *European*				
28. Killick Nixon	37,808	68,900	3,025	7,424
29. Turner Morrison (Bombay)	2,175	1,600	863	1,671

(Continued)

TABLE 41 (*Contd.*)

	1914	1922	1937	1947
30. Turner Morrison (Calcutta)	—	1,500	—	2,000
31. James Finlay (Bombay)	3,000	1,000	N.A.	N.A.
32. James Finlay (Calcutta)	100	6,525	7,166	10,065
33. David J. Sassoon	4,550	8,250	—	—
34. E. D. Sassoon	2,700	61,700	—	—
35. Greaves Cotton	5,031	—	—	—

B. Indian

36. Tata Hydro-Electric	—	N.A.	N.A.	96,697
37. Tata Sons	37,089	266,013	104,594	140,748
38. Morarjee Goculdas	1,950	1,950	N.A.	N.A.
39. Walchand	—	3,888[2]	4,881	60,006
40. Scindia Steam Navigation	—	45,000	N.A.	60,000

C. Mixed

41. Associated Cement Companies	—	—	70,542	79,279

MADRAS

A. European

42. Binny	2,400	11,018	11,051	11,054
43. Parry	N.A.	N.A.	1,530	2,692

NORTH INDIA

A. European

Begg Sutherland	N.A.	9,350	14,335	14,370

B. Indian

45. Narang	—	—	2,400	2,700
46. Govan	—	—	3,300	12,850
47. Dalmia	—	—	16,000	8,500[3]

SOURCE. *Investor's India Year Books*, relevant years.

NOTES. 1. Martin & Co. was a partnership between a European and a Bengali, but in its tendencies the firm certainly fell within the European group.
2. Includes Tata Construction Company.
3. The decline in paid-up capital is due to inadequate coverage in *Investor's India Year Books*.

European managing agencies in Calcutta after 1922. In Bombay the repatriation of the Sassoon interests and the collapse of Greaves Cotton decreased the weightage of European capital in the cotton-mill industry. This overall tendency towards stagnation of European rupee capital set in after the collapse of the post-war boom of 1921–2. The aftermath of the First World War saw a substantial expansion of many big European managing agencies, though the expansion is probably somewhat exaggerated due to inadequate coverage in the *Investor's India Year Book* of 1914 compared with that of 1922. In short, from 1914 to 1922 the established European houses expanded quite fast, and some Indian houses broke through in the field of industry. After 1922, the European houses expanded slowly or not at all, while more and more Indian houses entered the arena and rapidly built up their assets. By the end of the period, there was no European managing agency in India that could compare in size with the giant combines of Tata and Birla. However, by that time a number of multinationals had entered the scene and there were signs of increasing linkages between the national combines and the multinationals. These new developments occurred against the background of the decline of the old-style European managing agencies after the Second World War and the take-overs of companies under their control by speculative Indian interests.

The Stagnation of European Managing Agencies

The managing agency in its classic form in India was the European import–export house based on Calcutta which took up the initiation and management of tea, jute and coal companies and later on branched out into some other industries as well. Andrew Yule, Shaw Wallace, Jardine Skinner and many other Calcutta-based European houses conformed to this classical model. Some of these import–export houses never took up the management of industrial concerns on a substantial scale. Hoare Miller, for instance, continued to be mainly large importers of cotton piece-goods and merchandise sustaining the infinite variety of general bazar trade, as well as exporters of jute and tea, and agents for shipping and insurance companies.[35] In 1914 they were managing a few railway, coal, tea and miscellaneous companies whose total paid-up capital was Rs 38 lakhs; by 1947 this sum had declined to Rs 36 lakhs. Other houses exhibited a more dynamic approach and grew very big by pioneering tea, jute

[35] Allister Macmillan, *Seaports of India and Ceylon*, London, 1928, p. 70.

and coal companies as well as new concerns. But import–export trade continued to be a very crucial element in their business.

Concentration of tea, jute, coal, navigation and insurance interests was the most striking feature of the managing agency system as it developed in Calcutta. A number of progressive managing agencies in Calcutta also took up the management of railway, engineering and other manufacturing companies. Only a few European firms developed outside the orbit of the managing agency system as specialized engineering concerns, such as Jessop, Braithwaite and Marshall. Outside Calcutta, European managing agencies concentrated on other products, such as cotton (Sassoons in Bombay, Binny in Madras, etc.) and sugar (Parry in Madras, Begg Sutherland in Kanpur, etc.). Two big houses, James Finlay and Turner Morrison, straddled both Calcutta and Bombay, being based on London rather than Calcutta, unlike the majority of the European managing agencies in India. James Finlay managed cotton mills in Bombay, as well as tea companies and jute mills in Calcutta; and at the same time they were large importers of cotton piece-goods, large exporters of raw jute and gunnies, and big insurance and shipping brokers and general commission agents.[36] Turner Morrison, basically a shipping agency controlled from London by Asiatic Steam Navigation Co., managed ship-repairing, engineering, coal, paint and tar companies in Calcutta and engineering (Alcock Ashdown), shipping (Mogul Line) and other manufacturing companies in Bombay. A contemporary description of the comprehensive nature of their business noted that

if a steamer meets with an accident and arrives in a damaged condition at Calcutta the firm can discharge her, repair her, paint her inside and out, engage the requisite cargo for her return voyage, load her, insure her hull and cargo if necessary, supply her with bunker coal and stores, and despatch her without having to go outside the concerns which they control, being, it may be added, the only firm in Calcutta who can do so.[37]

This description is a good clue to why Indian competitors found it so difficult in breaching the European monopolies in business and industry. The vertical integration of all industries related to each other in the ongoing process of production under the managing agency system gave decisive advantages to the European monopoly houses. It ensured the supply of necessary factors of production and at the

[36] Ibid., p. 61.   [37] Ibid., pp. 66–7.

same time provided an assured market to the industries involved. At the same time, this very strength in their bargaining position enabled them to monopolize the patronage of the government and the railways, though racial affinity was also an important factor. A big managing agency like Andrew Yule which controlled jute, coal and inland navigation companies at the same time derived multiple advantages from this vertical integration. Its collieries had assured customers in its jute mills and navigation company; as big industrial consumers these navigation and jute companies were in a position to ensure the supply of scarce railway wagons to the coal companies; transport of raw jute and supply of power was assured to the jute mills by the navigation company and the collieries respectively; the navigation company flourished on the custom of tea and jute companies, and received monopolistic privileges of through-booking with the railways on account of the important interests it was serving. It is easy to see how deeply rooted the managing agency system was in the underdeveloped industrial situation in India. It enabled entrepreneurs to overcome the formidable constraints of demand and supply; at the same time it so bolstered the position of the established entrepreneurs that it deterred the entry of new indigenous competitors who had additional problems of official bias to contend with. However, as already stated, these monopoly and discriminatory features might not have lowered the overall level of investment, if the European managing agencies could have been relied on to exploit all possibilities of growth and take full advantage of the existing market. Were they willing to diversify their manufactures when opportunity beckoned? What was their attitude to the industrialization of India and the role of the government in the economy? To what extent was their attitude affected by their general involvement in import–export trade and their connections with firms at home, which sometimes but not frequently amounted to overall control of the managing agencies in India by big business empires located in London? On all these topics we have touched in general terms. To deal with these questions in more concrete terms, we now turn to an examination of the entrepreneurial behaviour of three of the most progressive European managing agencies, Binny, Andrew Yule and Bird Heilgers during the period under review.

1. *Binny*. Binny, an old trading and cotton manufacturing firm of Madras which came to the brink of financial ruin in 1906, was helped out by B.I. interests and became part of the growing Inchcape

(at that time James Mackay) empire in India, a huge shipping and industrial complex that embraced two managing agencies in Calcutta, Mackinnon Mackenzie and Macneill. Formerly a medium-sized firm with a limited capital base, Binny acquired new resources with the expansion of the Inchcape empire, which reached its zenith with the fusion of P. & O. and B.I. in 1914 and the later amalgamation of other associated shipping lines, for all of which Mackinnon Mackenzie in Calcutta served as managing agents, besides managing a few jute, coal and other industrial companies.[38] Macneill, which was also a part of the Inchcape complex, controlled one jute mill, one rope company, one river navigation company, 23 tea companies, six coal companies, one printing company and two trading and transport companies. The Inchcape connection thus brought Binny extensive contacts and large resources.[39]

At the turn of the century, export–import trade, labour contracting, and cotton manufacture were the main businesses of Binny. Binny's main imports were piece-goods and yarn from Britain, timber from Burma, tobacco from Sumatra and a wide range of products from Europe (including Britain)—paper, sheet iron, bars and nails, window glass, yellow metal, eau-de-cologne, aniline dyes, typewriters, cycles, candles, and wines and spirits. For handling these imports, Binny charged commission from foreign companies. They were exporting hides and skins to Japan and the United States. They held several shipping and insurance agencies, including the important agency for B.I. in the south. They were suppliers of emigrant Indian labour to the rubber plantations in Malaya. They extensively financed coffee planters and in consequence (through failure of the mortgagees) were in coffee planting as well. They also made some unsuccessful mining ventures before the First World War. But by the end of the First World War they had turned away from new ventures to concentrate on their staples, banking and insurance as well as trading agencies and services.[40] Their innovative role was confined to their main branch of manufacture, i.e. cotton spinning and weaving. In this field they made several experiments in fine weaving with improved cottons and automatic looms and the success of their large-scale khaki manufactures for the infantry ultimately persuaded Binny to pioneer the sodium bichromate industry for khaki dye during the Second World War.

[38] Ibid., p. 74.   [39] Ibid., p. 78.
[40] The House of Binny, p. 197.

Binny built up a splendid domestic market organization for their cloth manufactures in the thirties and forties. The Binny mills' sales organization, perfected by the gifted Chief Salesman K. M. Subramanian during 1942–5, was a solid pyramidal structure that stretched all over India and was arranged in five tiers—the two mill units at the top, then their native guarantors who guaranteed the good behaviour of wholesalers and retailers in their respective territorial zones, below them approximately 400 wholesalers and at the bottom 6,000 retailers.[41] No other mill in India, whether European or Indian, had such a comprehensive domestic marketing organization.

What was the attitude of Binny to the broader aspects of government policy and industrialization in India? As a supplier of woollen goods to the army, we find Binny vigorously protesting against the stores purchase policy of the government in 1904 for favouritism shown to British wool interests. They put forward a memorial to the government through the Madras Chamber of Commerce which complained that

the policy—not Government's own but forced upon it by the Secretary of State for India—has been to purchase as much as possible in England and as little as possible in India. The explanation of this policy, so contrary to the interests of any other State and so hostile to Indian interests, is without doubt to be found in the existence, within the India Office, of the powerful vested interests of the Stores Department.[42]

In the early thirties we find Binny's agents rushing to Gandhi's *ashram* during the boycott of European manufactures in course of the civil disobedience movement in order to persuade the nationalists not to put Binny on the black list of '*videshi*' concerns and successfully obtaining a clean chit from the Congress nationalists. Yet Binny, which was financed by Mackinnon Mackenzie and other Inchcape concerns, voted to retain the deferred rebate system during the debate over Indianization of coastal shipping in the early twenties. In the thirties, as agents for B.I., Binny successfully forced Scindia out of the Madras–Singapore run by a fierce rate war.[43]

2. *Andrew Yule.* This large managing agency of Calcutta, which had its original interests in agencies for Horrocks' long cloth and three insurance companies,[44] were by 1902 managing four jute mills,

---

[41] Ibid., pp. 230–1.   [42] Ibid., p. 138.   [43] Ibid.
[44] *Andrew Yule and Co. Ltd., 1863–1963*, p. 5.

one cotton mill, fifteen tea companies, two flour mills, one oil mill, a small railway company, a jute press, and a zamindari company.[45] Its position at the beginning of the First World War, and its subsequent growth and final decay, are shown in Table 42.

During the First World War Andrew Yule diversified mainly into industries subservient to its existing enterprises. In 1917 they opened Port Engineering Works Ltd. to meet the requirements of their jute mills and shipping company. In 1919 they set up Dishergarh Power Supply Co. Ltd. and Associated Power Co. Ltd. for supply of power to their big collieries in Raniganj. In the same year, however, they floated a pioneering concern, India Paper Pulp Co., which they sustained at great loss until it became sufficiently established to be converted into a public company in 1933 and its shares to be thrown open to the public. In 1931 Andrew Yule initiated Tobacco Industries (India) Ltd., but this proved unsuccessful and was wound up.[46] During the First World War and the decade after it Andrew Yule also became managing agents for a sugar company, a firebrick and pottery company, a printing company, an aerated gas factory, a tide water oil company and Magadi Soda Co. Ltd. After this fresh investment virtually stopped, except for the failed tobacco company and an insurance company in 1931 and the flotation of an investment company in 1946. Andrew Yule's biggest innovation, the commercialization of bamboo pulp for paper manufacture, was a means of sustaining the existing European production of ordinary varieties of paper in India. They never seriously considered, like Martin Burn or Bird Heilgers, of going into heavy metallurgical and engineering industries, though their resources were very large indeed. The group suffered take-overs and corners after the Second World War from Dalmia, Bangur, Thapar, etc.

3. *Bird Heilgers*. Bird was an old European managing agency in Calcutta which had originated as a firm of contractors supplying labour to the railways. The firm expanded rapidly, so that by the beginning of the First World War it controlled the largest block of investment in jute and coal in India. F. W. Heilgers, a group with smaller interests in jute and coal but with large funds sunk in the biggest paper manufacturing complex in India (the Titagarh mills), merged with Bird in 1917. The combined organizations and their associated concerns had a capital of £20 million, a revenue of £3

[45] Ibid.
[46] Ibid., pp. 17–18.

TABLE 42

ANDREW YULE—COMPOSITION OF CAPITAL 1914–47

(thousand rupees)

Year	Rail	Coal	Cotton	Jute	Tea	Miscellaneous	Sugar	Total
1914	0	7,959	0	9,198	3,398	3,554	0	24,105
%	0.00	33.01	0.00	38.15	14.08	14.74	0.00	100.00
1922	0	8,622	0	24,245	3,010	17,205	0	53,082
%	0.00	16.24	0.00	45.67	5.67	32.41	0.00	100.00
1937	0	8,427	0	28,136	3,670	23,430	1,100	64,763
%	0.00	13.01	0.00	43.44	5.66	36.17	1.69	100.00
1947	0	7,449	0	24,236	4,424	21,994	1,100	59,203
%	0.00	12.58	0.00	40.93	7.47	37.15	1.85	100.00

SOURCE and NOTES. *Investor's India Year Books*, relevant years. The headings of the *Investor's India Year Book* fall into two categories: the established industries in rail, coal, cotton, jute and tea, and the newer industries grouped under miscellaneous and sugar. The coverage is incomplete, as will be evident from the omission of the railway and cotton mill companies under Andrew Yule, perhaps due to the fact that Place, Siddons & Gough, the stockbrokers publishing the *Investor's India Year Book*, did not consider them good investments. It will be noted that investment in coal and tea stagnated throughout the period; in jute it shot up during 1914–22, but stagnated thereafter; in sugar and miscellaneous industries there was steady expansion up to 1937, when it rose to 37.86 per cent from only 14.74 per cent in 1914. By 1947 Andrew Yule was evidently on the decline, investment having come down in all categories.

million and employees numbering over a hundred thousand.[47] As we shall see, concentration proved to be a more prominent feature than genuine expansion in the case of this giant industrial and trading combine. The real increase in assets and diversification in manufactures took place up to 1919; thereafter the complex no longer grew to any significant extent.

During the war, stimulated by the growing needs of TISCO, Bird floated in 1915 Kumardhubi Fireclay and Silica Works for supplying silica bricks to TISCO, Loyobad Coke Manufacturing Co. for supplying coke to TISCO, and also Kumardhubi Engineering Works for supplying structural steel works as well as repairs. In 1916 Bird set up Sijua Electric Supply Co. to supply the growing power needs of the coal mines of Jharia. TISCO's demands for limestone also led to the expansion of another Bird company, Bisra Stone Lime Co., from 1917.[48] The search for coal, iron ore and limestone during the war and the problems of manufacturing processes at Kumardhubi convinced Bird of the value of science to industry. Bird opened a research department in 1918 with geologists, chemists and a mining engineer for examining new prospects and giving advice to Bird concerns and others on their possibilities and resources.[49] Bird displayed in this respect the enlightened approach so characteristic of Tata. After the end of the war, Bird planned the largest steel works in Asia, TUSCAL, conceived as a plant with a very broad capital base using the latest technology and able to draw most essential supplies—coal, coke, iron ore, limestone, dolomite, electricity and refractory bricks—from within the Bird complex of companies. But this was one Bird 'war baby' which was never born. With the changes in the post-war situation, there came a subtle change in Bird's attitude which we must now examine.

Bird's 'war babies' were all born in 1918 or 1919 influenced by the prevailing optimism at the end of the war. India Tanneries Ltd. was floated in 1918 and India Leather Manufacturing Co. for producing boots and shoes shortly afterwards. Both perished in the collapse of the world market in leather in 1920. Indian Graphite Co., formed to work quarries in Orissa, ceased to function after 1925. Surma Valley Saw Mills Ltd., floated in 1917 for producing tea-boxes, collapsed owing to selection of unsuitable woods which ruined the tea. Assam Saw Mills and Timber Co., producing ply boxes, was floated in

---

[47] *Bird and Company*, pp. 115–18.
[48] Ibid., pp. 108–9.   [49] Ibid., pp. 113–14.

1918, and though it ran at a loss for several years, it survived unlike other war babies.[50]

The collapse of the war babies induced a growing feeling that rash things had been done. A swing back took place under the cautious management of Lord Cable. His successor, Edward Benthall, recalled later:

The firm had bitten off more than it could chew and we were soon to learn that any fool can form a company in boom times, but that it takes good men to make it pay. We had not the men with experience to manage so many ventures beyond the firm's normal experience, and within a few years most of the new ventures were wound up. Large losses on our shares were incurred by the public, and the firm itself had to write off Rs 90 lakhs in 1921 accounts alone.[51]

Lord Cable decided that the war babies which seemed to require endless finance without assurance of final success must be ruthlessly liquidated. Benthall commented on this change in Lord Cable's policy:

It was not that they [war babies] were all badly conceived, and given time and good management some of those which had to be put to sleep might have been pulled through, but the cumulative effect of these ventures was most serious and some should never have been started. On the other hand the core of the business was sound, its earning power very great, and taxation, although increased, was still at a level which allowed very substantial capital formation to replace that lost. Once the badly conceived ventures were cut adrift and the drain on finance stopped, and provided the sound business was properly managed, the recuperative powers of the firms were immense. The work of the next few years was to consolidate the business and to repair the damage caused by becoming involved in the war and post-war boom.[52]

The total cost of Bird's clean-up operations was £1.25 million, a loss that fundamentally shook the firm without destroying it. In the twenties, Bird's coal and jute interests were expanded by new flotations in coal and take-overs in jute, while the Kumardhubi Works struggled through the crisis and Loyobad Coke and Sijua Power flourished. But nothing was done about TUSCAL.[53] By 1928, as figures for gross annual sales for different departments showed, Bird Heilgers had been reorganized on a sound conservative basis, jute manufactures and trading overshadowing everything else, next

[50] Ibid., pp. 110–13.   [51] Ibid., p. 134.
[52] Ibid., pp. 135–6.   [53] Ibid., pp. 139–57.

the coal companies, and Titagarh paper coming not far behind the entire coal group; other manufactures fell far behind.[54] During the thirties, due to depression and political turmoil, a 'really forward policy was out of reach. The main aims, perforce, were to keep things going, avoid serious mistakes, and increase protective holdings.'[55] The lesser concerns, such as the Kumardhubis, just kept going, and TUSCAL remained on the shelf under the management of Edward Benthall. Pursuing a conservative policy even during the Second World War, Bird Heilgers floated no new ventures. After the war Bird Heilgers concentrated on renovation, reconstruction and expansion of existing enterprises, cautiously putting into cold storage some projects that had been planned.[56] Due to strong protective holdings, Bird Heilgers suffered no take-overs like Andrew Yule in the rampant speculation of the post-war and independence years, but they fell far behind Birla, Dalmia, J. K., Walchand and others.

The phrases used by Edward Benthall, such as 'sound business' and 'ventures beyond the firm's normal experience', are significant clues to the entrepreneurial behaviour of European managing agencies in Calcutta. It was not that they were averse to innovations, but the emphasis was on 'sound business'; innovations were subservient to the firms' existing interests and were disapproved of when they fell outside their 'normal experience'. As a result the task of pioneering new ventures in unexplored fields fell mainly to multinationals with specialized technical knowledge of the problems involved, or Indian houses with a marked speculative (e.g. Dalmia) or adventurous (e.g. Walchand) bent of mind. As for the specialized European engineering firms in India, such as Jessop, Marshall and Britannia, they originated mainly as importers of iron, steel and machinery, and repairers of imported machines and manufacturers of spare parts which were costly to import. Their main task was to service the European-dominated railway and manufacturing complex that had grown up around Calcutta; their business expanded and diversified in response to this growing complex, but never broke out of its confines to transform it structurally.[57]

The Entry of the Multinationals

If the conservative European managing agencies fell behind in the

---

[54] Ibid., p. 161.   [55] Ibid., p. 168.   [56] Ibid., p. 231.
[57] See the description of the business of Britannia, Marshall and Jessop in Allister Macmillan, op. cit., pp. 77, 81–2, 130. See also Bagchi, op. cit., ch. 10.

race after the First World War *vis-à-vis* their Indian competitors, there was at the same time a renewed invasion of foreign interests in the private sector in the shape of multinational firms mostly based in Britain. This was the time when Imperial Tobacco, Lever Brothers (Unilever), Imperial Chemicals (ICI), Dunlop, etc. began to spread their networks in India. The Swedish multinational, Swedish Match Company (Wimco), forcefully captured more than half of the domestic market for safety matches in India during this period by setting up a chain of factories in the country. Canadian–British interests in aluminium manufacture also started competing with national aluminium enterprise by starting manufacture in India.

The multinationals which entered the industrial scene in India during the inter-war period almost invariably enjoyed strong trading connections with the country dating back to the pre-war period. Lever Brothers (India) were formed to combine the India, Burma and Ceylon (Sri Lanka) interests of Lever Brothers (incorporated in U.K.), Joseph Crosfield & Sons Ltd., and William Gossage & Sons with those of Premier Soap Co. of India.[58] ICI's trading subsidiary in India, Brunner, Mond & Co. (India) Ltd., was originally formed in 1923 in order to take over the business of Brunner, Mond & Co. (incorporated in U.K.) in India, Burma and Ceylon, where the latter company had traded for many years through branches established in Calcutta and elsewhere. Upon the formation of the giant chemical combine of Imperial Chemical Industries in Britain by the fusion of Brunner, Mond & Co., Nobel Industries Ltd., British Dye-Stuffs Corporation and United Alkali Co., the subsidiary company Brunner, Mond & Co. (India) Ltd. became the sole distributors of the products of Imperial Chemicals in India, Burma and Ceylon. ICI's main exports to India were soda ash and other alkalis, sulphate of ammonia and other fertilizers and an extensive range of dyes.[59] Manufactures were not commenced in India until at the very end of the inter-war period; in 1937 Imperial Chemicals floated the Alkali and Chemical Corporation of India to commence production of soda ash. Nor did Lever Brothers commence large-scale manufactures in India until the thirties; in 1933 they floated a new Lever Brothers (India) Ltd. for the purpose. Similarly Dunlop Rubber also commenced manufactures in the thirties after a prolonged period of trading from Britain since the end of the nineteenth century. From

[58] Arun Kumar Banerjee, *India's Balance of Payments*, App. B.
[59] Allister Macmillan, op. cit., pp. 70–1.

1898 to 1926 the Dunlop Rubber Company in Britain supplied a considerable proportion of motor tyres in India. To handle its growing business, a trading subsidiary—Dunlop Rubber Co. (India) Ltd.—was formed in 1926. From a humble beginning in the latter stages of the nineteenth century with only a depot in Bombay, the parent British company had extended its activities, embracing Calcutta, Delhi, Rangoon, Madras, Colombo and Karachi. The new trading subsidiary achieved further extensions with a new depot at Lahore and sub-branches at Nagpur, Gauhati, Mandalay, Lucknow, Bangalore and Rawalpindi. Messrs Peirce, Leslie & Co. of Calicut and Messrs John Fleming & Co. of Karachi were also recruited as distributors on the western coast of India in the twenties. During this decade, the parent company already had factories located in France, Germany, Canada, USA, Australia and Japan, but no factory was set up in India.[60] Only in the mid-thirties did Dunlop enter the manufacturing field in India and they dominated tyre manufactures since that time.

What were the reasons behind the switch-over from trade to manufacture by the multinationals? One obvious answer was the steady increase of revenue tariff on imported goods in the inter-war period. We have seen that Wimco entered the manufacturing scene in India after the imposition of a revenue duty of Rs 1–8 per gross of boxes in 1922 threatened it with the loss of its vast market in the country to native competitors. Similarly, the fact that the revenue duty on cigars and cigarettes had climbed to 75 per cent *ad valorem* and on manufactured tobacco to Rs 2–4 per lb by 1922 was no doubt a strong inducement to Imperial Tobacco to climb over the heightened tariff wall by commencing manufacture in India.[61] The increasing revenue tariffs in the thirties also coincided with changes in the differential locational advantages of manufacture in favour of India—a big market in its own right—in a world of contracting trade. To take the example of the rubber industry, the International Rubber Restriction Scheme, which restricted rubber exports from the main rubber producing countries during the Great Depression, succeeded in shoring up the world prices of rubber. By contrast the price of rubber in India continued to be low, affording considerable advantages to local rubber manufacturers. There was also the advantage of comparatively cheap labour in India. The response to these changed conditions was decentralization of production by large

---

[60] Ibid., pp. 240–1.   [61] Adarkar, *History of Indian Tariff.*

overseas manufacturers and establishment of subsidiary factories in India. Bata Shoe Co. commenced operations in 1933; Dunlop started their tyre factory in Bengal in 1935–6; Firestone Tyre & Rubber Co. started another rubber factory in Bombay in 1939–40.[62]

The initial Indian business reaction to the entry of the multinationals on the industrial scene in India was extremely hostile. Nationalist businessmen agreed with Gandhi that this was dumping of foreign industries instead of foreign goods on India. M. A. Master, the great executive of Scindia, said in 1945 at the annual meeting of the Indian Merchants' Chamber in Bombay:

> It is well known that the India Limiteds, which have, taking advantage of the present half-hearted policy of protection, firmly established themselves in this country, are in fact the subsidiaries of foreign companies registered in this land. They have practically monopolized for themselves such industries as Chemicals, Automobiles, Rubber, Matches, Soaps, Cigarettes, Boots, Shoes, etc. They have thus been able, particularly in view of their superior financial resources, to stifle the endeavours of Indian enterprise in the same field, whether it was on a large scale or on a small scale.[63]

How far was this criticism of the role of multinational enterprise as a destructive force justified? We have examined the question in some detail in the case of Wimco and the match industry. In the match industry, the entry of the multinationals did not crush indigenous enterprise. Healthy competition ensured a higher level of technology and cheaper prices, which benefited the consumer. However, there were certainly considerable leakages of gains, not only through repatriation of profits but through imports of foreign raw materials for manufacture in India. Production under Indian control, while it might have resulted in lower technical efficiency, might also have led to a higher rate of investment and expansion of the market for subsidiary industries within India. As a matter of fact the entry of the multinationals did not bring any appreciable addition to the level of investment. Imperial Tobacco's capital in India in 1921 was Rs 4 crores; in 1938 it had risen to Rs 4.16 crores. Wimco's capital remained stationary at Rs 1 crore during this entire period.[64] Many Indian businessmen, such as M. A. Master in his

[62] Government of India, Department of Commerce, *Report of the Indian Tariff Board on the Rubber Manufacturing Industry*, Bombay, 1947.

[63] *Annual Report of the Indian Merchants' Chamber for the Year 1944*, Proceedings of the annual general meeting, 31 January 1945, speech of M. A. Master.

[64] A. K. Banerjee, op. cit., App. B.

capacity as President of the Indian Merchants' Chamber, passionately denied that foreign capital would be needed for the development of India. Resources, they insisted, would be found in India.

But at the end of the Second World War they were fighting a losing battle. The strength of the multinationals was not so much in capital as in technology. The Indian national houses had by now grown so big that there was no question of free or unimpeded entry for the multinationals. But the multinationals could offer important technical collaboration in new industries to big Indian business, which was poor in experience and expertise in technical matters. At the same time the multinationals could reduce the burden of their own initial outlay by using the vast resources and connections of the big national houses. In these circumstances, a tie-up of the multinationals with precisely those nationalist business houses which had fought foreign interests tooth and nail became inevitable. Sorrowfully Mahomed Husain Hasham Premji, M. A. Master's successor as President of the Indian Merchants' Chamber, told the house at the beginning of 1947:

We have now and then been hearing of references both in the Press and elsewhere, relating to the propositions for the establishment of new industries on the basis of tie-up agreements or other arrangements with foreign industrialists. The general feature of all such agreements, it is understood, is that foreign interests are allowed a share in varying form and proportion in ownership, control and management of such industrial undertakings. This development is a matter of serious concern to all those who have the permanent interests of the country at heart. The main object of increasing the industrial activities in the country is that the profits, perquisites and fruits resulting from such industrialization should go to the sons of the soil. If foreign capital is allowed to acquire interests in such industries, it is quite obvious that the above objective will not be served and the profits relating to the extent of such foreign ownership will, as in the past, go out of the country. We had the bitter experience of the menace presented by the India Limiteds in the past. These foreign offshoots which were Indian subsidiaries of parent companies located elsewhere were probably designed with a view to take advantage of the protection afforded by the Tariff wall in the country intended as a measure of encouragement and assistance to Indian undertakings. We do not want to have this mischief perpetrated on a permanent basis.[65]

[65] *Annual Report of the Indian Merchants' Chamber for the Year 1946*, Proceedings of the annual general meeting, January 1947.

What happened at the time of independence was a two-fold process: take-overs of the European managing agencies by big Indian houses and their tie-up with multinationals at the same time. Dalmia took over Bennet Coleman; Thapar, Greaves Cotton; Tata, Macneill Barry and Kilburn; Birla, Cotton Agents; Goenka, Octavius Steel and Duncan Bros.[66] At the same time Tata was connected by joint deals with Daimler Benz in automobiles, Harnischfeger Corporation in engineering, American Power Company in electronics, James Finlay in tea packing, ICI in chemicals. Birla became associated with Studebaker and the Nuffield combine in automobiles, Babcock and Wilcox in manufacture of smoke-tube boilers, Howa Machinery Ltd. (Japan) in manufacture of full range textile machinery and Mitsubishi Electric Manufacturing Co. in manufacture of house service materials. The national houses which had grown by competition with foreign enterprise now began to expand in association with it. However, that lay in the future. We turn now to their growth and entrepreneurial behaviour during the period under review.

The Growth of the Indian Houses

If nationalist-minded professional and service groups had exhibited the keenest interest in industrialization among all classes of Indians in the *swadeshi* period preceding the First World War, after the war the task of promoting new industries was taken up mainly by traditional merchant communities who accumulated immense assets by wartime speculation and branched out from trade, contracting and speculation to modern industrial and manufacturing activities in the boom following the war. Especially prominent in this process of transformation of traditional merchant communities into modern entrepreneurial groups were the Gujarati Banias, whether Jain or Hindu, from whose ranks came Walchand Hirachand, Ambalal Sarabhai and Kasturbhai Lalbhai; the Punjabi Hindu Khatris, Aroras and Banias, among whom figured Lala Shri Ram, Karamchand Thapar and Gokulchand Narang; and most dramatically of all, the Rajasthani (including parts of the Punjab) Maheshwaris, Agarwals and Oswals, both Hindu and Jain, grouped together under the generic name Marwaris, whose migrations throughout India threw up such large groups as Birla, Dalmia, Juggilal Kamlapat, Sarupchand Hukumchand, Surajmull Nagarmull, Jaipuria, Bangur,

[66] M. L. Kothari, *Industrial Combinations: A Study of Managerial Integration in Indian Industries*, Allahabad, 1967, p. 35.

Goenka, etc. The Parsi houses, those early industrializers, fell behind in the race, except the giant house of Tata, of whom it was reported in 1928: 'In magnitude and variety of interests there is perhaps no other concern in the British Empire that embraces activities so widespread as this house.'[67] Bengali, Marathi and Tamil entrepreneurs, who built up some medium-sized concerns (N. C. Sircar, the Bhagyakul brothers, Kirloskar, Sheshashayi, etc.), never succeeded in operating on a really large scale. The characteristics of the big houses thrown up by the merchant communities were extreme diversification and rapid growth. Both processes accelerated during the Second World War. As a result there was no question of specialization by the bigger Indian houses of merchant caste. A few concerns of rather smaller size did exhibit a tendency towards specialization, but the pioneers of such firms, e.g. Mafatlal, Kirloskar and Sheshashayi, had a non-Bania, professional (or agricultural) background. Some details of the origins and investment patterns of some growing Indian houses during this period are recorded below.[68]

1. *Tata.* Tatas emerged in the industrial field in the late nineteenth century as one of the three biggest Parsi houses in early cotton manufacturing enterprise, the other two being Wadias and Petits, who fell behind in importance after the First World War. The capital base for J. N. Tata's entry into cotton manufacture was acquired in trade with the Far East, as in the case of the British (Jewish) textile house of the Sassoons of Bombay. Like the Sassoons, Tatas continued their import–export business with China, Japan and elsewhere on an extensive scale after their entry into manufactures. The import–export business was handed over to a new concern, R. D. Tata & Sons, with branches in Osaka, Shanghai, Rangoon, Liverpool and New York, and trading in cotton yarns, rice, metals, sugar, etc. with a capital of Rs 15 million.[69] Unlike the Sassoons, who commanded equally large resources, the Tatas considerably diversified their industrial interests beyond cotton manufacture and even tried unsuccessfully to break the British monopoly of shipping between India and the Far East. By 1914 Tata interests embraced trade, hotels, cotton manufacture, iron and steel and hydroelectricity. Industrial

[67] Allister Macmillan, *Seaports of India.*, p. 192.

[68] Except when otherwise stated, the details are drawn from R. K. Hazari, *The Structure of the Corporate Private Sector: A Study of Concentration, Ownership and Control*, Bombay, 1966, and from the preceding text.

[69] Allister Macmillan, op. cit., p. 192.

banking, insurance, construction, soap and cement were taken up after the First World War. Tata's wartime enterprises, like Bird's 'war babies', were hard hit by the slump which succeeded the post-war boom. The group had to give up Tata Industrial Bank to the Central Bank of India, Tata Construction (floated in association with Walchand) to Walchand, the three hydroelectric companies to American managerial control. Unlike Bird, Tata's investing propensities, though temporarily checked, were not destroyed by the disaster in the long run. When the crisis had passed, the group still enjoyed a combined capital of £50,000,000 and was providing maintenance for about a quarter of a million people.[70] The thirties saw the flotation of Tata Airlines, the forerunner of Air India. The Investment Corporation of India (1937) marked the return to investment business. Compared to other Indian houses, Tata was rather cautious during this decade, which was no doubt due to the chastening experience of the post-war years. They let slip an opportunity to set up a new steel mill in 1937 when the steel market revived. The Second World War and its aftermath brought about another giant stride by Tata, as reflected in the flotation of Tata Chemicals (1940), Tata Tube (1940), Investa Machine Tools and Tata Locomotive (TELCO).

2. *Birla*. Birla Bros., Maheshwaris from Pilani (Rajasthan), reputedly grew into a firm with a capital of Rs 80 lakhs from a base of Rs 20 lakhs by trading operations during the First World War.[71] They established several industries between 1918 and 1922, breaking into that close preserve of European enterprise in eastern India—jute. After a fierce battle against racial exclusiveness, G. D. Birla established direct connections with the London jute market during and after the war, becoming a leading raw jute exporter of Calcutta.[72] From this position of strength, he set up a jute mill in Calcutta. In addition he set up two cotton-textile mills in Delhi and Gwalior, and later on acquired one in Calcutta. In the thirties the firm became the second biggest national house, branching out into sugar, paper, newspaper publishing and insurance. From this base followed expansion at a breakneck pace during and after the Second World War: further expansion of cotton and jute interests; manufacture of

[70] Ibid.

[71] Thomas Arnold Timberg, 'The Rise of Marwari Merchants as Industrial Entrepreneurs to 1930', Harvard Ph.D. Thesis, 1972, p. 89.

[72] Of this, more will be said later on.

textile machinery, automobiles, bicycles, ball-bearings, fans, non-ferrous metals, rayon, plastics, plywood and vegetable oil; take-overs of tea and coal interests; entry into aviation; expansion of insurance, assumption of banking and flotation of investment and trading companies on a large scale.

3. *Dalmia.* Ramkrishna Dalmia, a Maheshwari of the Jain faith from Rohtak in the Panjab, strikingly illustrated the migratory and speculative aspects of the history of the Marwari commercial community. A big trader in Bihar, he originally made his fortune in 1917 by speculating on the rise of silver prices in London from his base in Calcutta during wartime. From speculation in bullion, he moved into trade at Dinapore (Bihar) in the twenties, from which sphere he largely financed the Salt Satyagraha and the Civil Disobedience Movement in his own area in the early thirties.[73] It was at that point that he moved into industry. He set up a sugar mill in Bihar, which he later diversified as Rohtas Industries. This initiative was followed up by manufacture of cement on his own; deliberately he kept away from the giant cement combine, ACC, offering it strong competition in the late thirties. He also set up the Universal Bank of India at Dalmianagar in 1938. Although Dalmia emerged as an important group in the industrial complex of India in the thirties, it was really in the next decade that very rapid expansion through acquisition of large existing companies, setting up of new companies and expansion of existing companies brought Dalmia up to the position of probably the third largest group among the Indian business houses. This expansion, it must be admitted, was achieved more by specula-tion, take-overs and cornering of shares in the stock market than by real investment in increased productive capacity, though the latter was also a factor in the development of Dalmia. Between 1948 and 1952 Ramkrishna Dalmia acquired control over the Punjab National Bank, Bharat Insurance, Lahore Electric, Bennet-Coleman (*Times of India*), Govan group (Dhrangadhra Chemicals, Raza Sugar, Buland Sugar, Indian National Airways), Shapoorji Broacha and Madhowji Dharamsi Cotton Mills (Bombay), Keventer Dairy (Delhi), and three large Andrew Yule jute mills through stock ex-change manipulations. At the same time he took care to build up Rohtas Industries Ltd. as a diversified concern producing sugar,

[73] Seth Ramkrishna Dalmia, *A Short Sketch of the Beginning of My Life and and a Guide to Bliss*, Delhi, 1962, pp. 15–17; *Dalmia Cement Silver Jubilee Souvenir 1939–64.*

cement, paper, vanaspati, chemicals, spun pipe, etc. He also expanded the group's cement interests and airways. Together with all these multifarious activities, he continued large-scale financial, trading and speculative activities. His malpractices led to the winding up of the two Bombay cotton mills he had acquired, as well as of Lahore Electric, Dalmia Airways, Bharat Bank and Bharat Insurance. It would appear that he acquired control over several established and reputable companies with the premeditated objective of diverting large sums from them to his own purposes. Unlike many other industrialists of merchant caste, he never gave up speculative business. He ran into the red after independence as a result of speculation, and his business malpractices, which had resulted in the liquidation of so many good existing concerns, finally landed him in jail.[74] For a far cleaner record, with an emphasis on genuine industrial expansion, we turn to Walchand, J. K. and Shri Ram.

4. *Walchand.* Walchand Hirachand, a Gujarati Jain Bania settled in Sholapur in Maharashtra, was the most inspired and adventurous entrepreneur of his age in India, and in its own way his achievement was no less impressive than that of Jamsetji Nusserwanji Tata. He accumulated his capital as a contractor in buildings, railway works and other construction during the First World War, in which he soon built up such a solid reputation that after the war he was invited to float in association with the Tata group the giant Tata Construction Co. for large-scale municipal construction in Bombay. One receives the impression that his own capital base was too small for his impatient eagerness to get on with the initiation of more and more new industries. He never cared to touch established enterprises like cotton mills and did not participate in trading activities. G. D. Birla, who proceeded more patiently and built up huge reserves by well-established activities like trading and manufacture of jute and cotton, was never afflicted with any acute shortage of funds like Walchand. Due to his comparatively narrow capital base and keen patriotic ambition to move on as fast as possible with the industrialization of India, Walchand did not display the familiar concern of India's merchant-industrialists to undertake industrial expansion only at a rate that was consistent with the maintenance of tight family control over the new enterprises. His greatest achievement, Scindia Steam Navigation Co. (1919), was floated in association with the house of Morarji Goculdas and others. As a result, it

[74] Ibid.

never was within the Walchand group of industries as such. In construction also, he proceeded in partnership with the Tatas in the early twenties, though by the beginning of the following decade he had annexed Tata Construction to the Walchand group as Premier Construction. In the thirties he set up the Ravalgaon Sugar Farm Ltd. (1933) and another cane farm–sugar mill complex under a defunct construction company named Marshland, Price & Co. which he took over. Meanwhile Premier Construction grew into a giant complex by acquiring control over three other construction companies besides Marshland Price: Hindusthan, All-India and Building Construction Companies. In the same decade Walchand went into reinforced concrete hume pipe manufacture by acquiring the Indian Hume Pipe Co. He also acquired control over two languishing engineering works, Cooper Engineering and Acme Manufacturing, pressing them into manufacture of more sophisticated machinery and engineering goods manufacture. In the forties much of Walchand's strenuous efforts went outside the Walchand group into steamship-building under Scindia. He was also responsible in 1940-1 for the establishment, outside the Walchand group, of the Hindusthan Aircraft Ltd. which he floated in co-operation with the Mysore Government, Tulsidas Kilachand and Dharamsi M. Khatau. With the latter two partners he also floated Premier Automobiles in 1944 within the Walchand group. Minus the giant Hindusthan Aircraft and Scindia Steam which developed outside family control, the Walchand group had grown by the time of independence into a concern of over Rs 6 crores, distributed in the following manner:[75]

	Paid-up capital (Rs)
1. Construction Companies	
(a) Premier Construction Co. Ltd.	10,506,250
(b) Hindusthan Construction Co. Ltd.	6,100,000
(c) All India Construction	200,000
2. Sugar Manufacturing Companies	
(a) Walchandnagar Industries Ltd.	10,450,000
(b) Ravalgaon Sugar Farm Ltd.	4,400,000
3. Engineering Companies	
(a) Cooper Engineering Ltd.	2,520,000
(b) Acme Manufacturing Co. Ltd.	1,240,000

(Continued)

[75] Walchand Hirachand Papers, file No. 333, 'Walchand Group of Industries: Brief History (1955)'.

4. Automobile Industry
   (a) Premier Automobiles Ltd.   22,500,000
   (b) Bombay Cycle & Motor Agency   1,140,000

5. Pipe Industry
   (a) Indian Hume Pipe Co. Ltd   8,000,000
                                                  _____
                                                    67,056,250

As a group Walchand had not grown as vast as Birla, but the magnitude of Walchand Hirachand's achievement may be gauged from the fact that he played a pioneering role in sugar manufacture on modern scientific lines, shipping, shipbuilding, aircraft manufacture, automobile manufacture, engineering and machine tools, and building and bridge construction.

5. *Shri Ram.*[76] More patient and with a longer industrial background than Walchand, the Shri Ram group, a Panjabi Agarwal Bania family settled in Delhi, started their industrial activities at a leisurely pace in cotton manufacture in the late nineteenth century. Lala Shri Ram's family made its fortune in the service of the commissariat during the Mutiny and the profits of office and army supply business were invested in Panjab land. The family promoted with other Delhi businessmen the Delhi Cloth Mills (1888), where Lala Shri Ram's uncle became a Secretary. Delhi Cloth Mills grew into a big concern during the First World War by supplying tents to the army under Lala Shri Ram's direction. A second and a third mill were set up under the Delhi Cloth Mills in 1918 and 1929 respectively. In the thirties Delhi Cloth Mills decided to spread risk by diversification on the same principle as Dalmia's Rohtas Industries Ltd., and sugar protection in 1932 induced Shri Ram to venture into sugar manufacture in UP. In 1934 he set up a new cotton mill in Panjab. In the same year Shri Ram acquired the Maharaja of Kasimbazar's languishing Bengal Pottery Works in Calcutta and turned it into a profitable concern. In 1938 he acquired the Jay Engineering Works, a small concern in Calcutta turning out a few sewing machines, and a larger plant was set up under his managing agency with Karamchand Thapar and Padampat Singhania as the directors of this renovated and prestigious concern. During the Second World War Shri Ram further diversified his activities by opening a power alcohol plant

[76] Following details are from Khushwant Singh and Arun Joshi, *Sriram: A Biography*, Bombay, 1968.

and distillery in association with his sugar mill at Daurala. At the same time DCM opened its own chemical works for supplying its own needs of sulphuric acid for cloth manufacture and in 1945 Shri Ram added to this a superphosphate plant for artificial manures. DCM Chemical Works also went into manufacture of *vanaspati* oil in 1945, and took up alkali manufacture in 1947 by buying a caustic soda plant from the United States. Starting as a small cotton yarn spinning mill in 1889, DCM had taken up the manufacture of more than a thousand varieties of cloth, developed a chemical industry producing heavy chemicals such as sulphuric acid, hydrochloric acid and caustic soda, and successfully initiated the manufacture of sugar, confectionery, alcohol and *vanaspati*. The other large concern in the Shri Ram group, Jay Engineering Works, also commenced production of Usha sewing machines in the later stages of the Second World War.

6. *Juggilal Kamlapat*. An Agarwal family from Bikaner (Rajasthan), the Singhanias were settled in the industrial centre of Kanpur from the nineteenth century, and like the Shri Ram family commenced their industrial activities in a small way before the First World War. By 1905 they had a sugar factory and distillery, oil and flour mills, and cotton gins. Juggilal Singhania and his son Kamlapat set up four textile mills in Kanpur after the First World War and in addition had heavy investment in the European-controlled mills there. In the thirties J. K. set up a jute mill in Calcutta and branched out in engineering and insurance. But their great period of expansion was the forties, which saw their entry into manufacture of aluminium, paper and chemicals, flotation of investment and trading and banking companies, acquisition of insurance companies in Calcutta and expansion of textile interests.

7. *Thapar*. Khatris from Ludhiana (Panjab), the Thapars were wholesale merchants and coal agents in Calcutta at the beginning of the twentieth century. Karamchand Thapar & Bros. Ltd. was incorporated by Lala Karamchand Thapar in 1919, with the head office in Calcutta and branches in Lahore, Ludhiana and Jharia. From this base in coal trade and other trades, the company acquired six collieries in the thirties in the Jharia region and also a paper mill in the Panjab which it renovated and expanded. Thapar also set up during this decade two sugar manufacturing companies, an insurance company, two trading and agency companies, and an electric supply company; and commenced manufacture of starch (Bharat

Starch and Chemicals Ltd.) and dry ice (Dry Ice and Refrigeration Ltd.).[77] From this diversified beginning in the thirties, Thapar further progressed during the Second World War by acquiring Greaves Cotton and setting up another insurance company.

8. *Bangur*. The Bangurs were Maheshwaris from Didwana (Rajasthan) who came to Calcutta as traders and speculators and they rose to industrial prominence only after the Second World War. The Bangur group strongly resembled Dalmia, another Maheshwari family, in its somewhat uncreative speculative activities. In the thirties and the forties they made a fortune in land speculation and buying and selling of jute and shares. They registered a small bank and some finance and investment companies, acquired a cotton mill in Bombay (1934), set up a cotton mill in Rajasthan (1944) and opened a cement factory in Saurashtra (1944). Soon after the war they acquired a large number of jute mills from European managing agencies in Calcutta, and thus became a big industrial house overnight without employing much real assets.

9. *Mafatlal, Sheshashayi and Kirloskar*. Unlike the above, these three groups were not drawn from trading castes, nor did they diversify on the scale of the rest. The Mafatlal family were Patels from Ahmedabad; Sheshashayi, Tamil Brahmans from Tiruchirapalli; Kirloskar, Marathi Brahmans from Belgaum. Mafatlal Gaglbhai started as a small cloth trader at the beginning of the twentieth century and made a fortune in trade during the First World War. In the twenties and the thirties, he took over eight established mills in financial difficulty, a jute mill in Calcutta and a real estate in Bombay. Mafatlal soon earned a reputation as a prosperous and well-managed textile group in Bombay. Mafatlal Gaglbhai also floated Rutnagar Steam Navigation Co. but handed it over to Scindia in the battle against British shipping interests. The Sheshashayis started as road transport operators around their town during the First World War and took up business as electrical contractors in the twenties. They pioneered power generation and distribution in rural areas of Madras. Their three power companies were merged in 1940 as South Madras Electric Co. Immediately before the Second World War they took over Mettur Chemicals, which had developed with hydroelectricity in the south. After the war they also managed state companies in Travancore connected with electro-chemicals.

[77] *Silver Jubilee Souvenir of the United Provinces Chamber of Commerce 1914–1939*, pp. 90–1.

They also tried their hand at minerals and cotton mills but lack of success induced them to concentrate on the interrelated complex of power and chemicals. The Kirloskars started in the bicycle business. They pioneered manufacture of agricultural machinery after the First World War. Later on they specialized in machine tools, electric motors and allied machinery.

However, the tendency towards specialization did not really develop on account of the preponderance of the merchant communities in the industrialization process after the First World War. They had no technological experience, which they regarded as merely a commodity to buy, like any other factor of production. Their extraordinary success, compared to progressive-minded professional groups who had tried their hand at industry unsuccessfully earlier, was due to the fact that when large opportunities for industrial investment opened up after the First World War, it was the merchant communities who commanded the necessary liquid assets and marketing networks to avail themselves of these opportunities. These were not advantages that encouraged specialization. On the contrary, they encouraged the characteristic fusion of the merchant caste–family control–managing agency complex that so dominated postwar industrialization.

The process may be better understood with reference to the contrasted industrial performance of the Bengalis and the Marwaris in Calcutta. The Bengalis, both traders and professional men, had set up a few firms of small or medium size in coal, cotton and chemicals before the First World War. After the war, during the twenties, the Banga Laksmi Cotton Mills—the pride of patriotic professional Bengalis—languished and had to write down its capital. The Bengal Chemical and Pharmaceutical Works, another piece of professional Bengali entrepreneurship, lacked the funds and contacts that would enable it to start production on a broad expanded basis, though it had a long record of technical experience going back to the last years of the nineteenth century. N. C. Sircar & Sons, the leading Bengali group in the coal-mining enterprise, collapsed in the depression of the thirties due to the lack of staying power. The common problem for all these concerns was lack of sufficient reserves and liquid assets.

The Marwaris, on the other hand, did not try their hand at industry at all until the end of the First World War. But during the war they steadily built up a position for assaulting British monopolies by acquiring large liquid assets in trading, speculating and financial operations, and by improving their market networks. They had long dominated the cotton import trade and had channels throughout India for marketing piece-goods. More significantly they broke into the raw jute export market during the war, acquired direct connections with overseas markets and at the same time came to control the stock exchange in Calcutta. These changes in the economic world of Calcutta broadened their capital-accumulating base and expanded their marketing network, and they were thus able after the war to start several jute mills (Sarupchand Hukumchand, G. D. Birla, Surajmull Nagarmull) and cotton mills (Birla, Hukumchand, Juggilal Kamlapat).

What was it that enabled the Marwaris, in contrast with the Bengalis, to acquire this strong position in commerce? A detailed study of the Marwari community has suggested that it was due to their superior 'resource group'. The merchant communities in India had traditionally enjoyed much larger resource groups—i.e. pools of experience, networks and finance in which smaller groups and budding entrepreneurs could benefit from larger groups and established entrepreneurs within the caste—than the rest of the population. Of the Marwaris—the most outstandingly successful of such merchant communities—it has been observed by a specialist:

They attained and retained their capital-accumulating position in the social structure for several reasons. They did not sink too much of their capital in land—but preferred more risky and perhaps more profitable pursuits (a psychological and ideological explanation). They had relatively easy access to credit, information, and manpower because of their organization as a commercial community (an institutional–structural explanation). Their circumstances and connections enabled them to migrate throughout India and enter several profitable commercial lines opened up by the British (an historical circumstantial explanation). If any of the above statements had not been true, their success would have been foreclosed. The integrating element is that the psychological and ideological attitudes were developed by an institutional–structural specialization in trade and the presence of historical opportunities which traders from a declining area could search out.[78]

Although more orthodox in their outlook on life than the highly politicized professional and service classes, the merchant commun-

---

[78] Timberg, op. cit., pp. 235–6.

ities in their own way were quite as deeply imbued with the spirit of nationalism, and this was an important influence on their entrepreneurial behaviour. Their aggressive willingness to sustain losses for the sake of national enterprise was exhibited in the refusal of Scindia directors to accept the tempting Inchcape offer of 1922, as also in their refusal to participate in the rate war against smaller Indian shipping lines on the west coast by B.I. and other British lines. Again, in the matter of the flotation of Hind Motors and Premier Automobiles, Birla and Walchand were not motivated by profit incentives, but by much larger considerations, since neither technological nor market factors encouraged any visions of profitable car manufacture in India in the foreseeable future. To take another instance to illustrate this point, Lala Shri Ram at one stage during the Second World War refused to entertain a suggestion from an executive in Calcutta that Jay Engineering Works should make profits by wartime speculation in buying and selling scrap. The ethic behind the Jay Engineering Works was clearly spelt out in Shri Ram's letter to his manager in Calcutta:

The [scrap] proposal must definitely mean the diversion of the energies of all of you. No doubt, in whatever we do, the money motive is there, but there is a better motive and that is to serve the country by producing things which have not yet been produced. If I had cared in my life to get rich quick, I might perhaps have taken to speculation and the Stock Exchange and either become a multi-millionaire or a beggar . . . If I had cared for money perhaps I would have considered the proposal for the sale of J.E.W. But I have not cared for money and I want the J.E.W. to occupy a position in its own way, equal to that of the TATA Iron and Steel Works although their lines are entirely different to our own.[79]

There was, of course, the strikingly different approach of Ramkrishna Dalmia on this issue, but then even he was not immune to the call of satyagraha and civil disobedience in the early thirties.

A morbid preoccupation with the development of the industrial resources of India in order to remove the poverty and social misery on the subcontinent was quite as characteristic of the deeply religious, pietistic and conservative merchant entrepreneurs as the highly-educated intellectuals from the professional classes who began to respond to socialist doctrines in the inter-war period. Consider, for instance, the following speech by Walchand Hirachand at the Dena Bank in his native Sholapur in August 1943:

[79] *Sriram*, p. 105.

I long for the day when we shall have India-made motor-cars, locomotives, railway coaches, tramways, buses, aeroplanes, ships, electrical goods, machinery, and the thousand and one things for which
we have to depend on imports. When that consummation is realized,
I assure you, Gentlemen, there will not be anyone in our country
who will go to bed hungry, there will not be a beggar asking for alms,
the standard of living of our countrymen would have risen tremen-
dously and to the level obtainable in prosperous countries such
as the U.S.A., poverty would have been a thing of the past, and
everywhere there would be plenty and prosperity.[80]

There was scope for disagreement with the emphasis on heavy
industry as a means of removing underdevelopment that was so
characteristic of the Indian businessmen's nationalist ethic. All the
things desired by Walchand came to be manufactured in some
quantity or other after independence, but underdevelopment was
not to be removed by mere reduction of imports. One favourite
attitude among contemporary British officials was that the fascina-
tion with heavy industry was a wrong strategy for India and that
the available investment should go into agriculture. Here, it needs
to be noted in passing that agricultural investment did not go by
default on account of the indifference of Indian entrepreneurs. Both
Birla and Walchand were driven into agricultural experiments by
that same driving force of nationalism that had bred their preoccupation with heavy industry. Curiously enough, G. D. Birla's
agricultural experiments won the cordial approval of both Mahatma
Gandhi and Lord Linlithgow in a measure that was not extended to
his heavy industries. None the less, the investment in agriculture
proved fruitless. He set up a dairy at Pilani, his native village,
importing good bulls from abroad. From the financial point of view
this venture in pastoral farming was not a success; and in the agricultural farm he lost money in 1935 and so gave up the experiment.
Besides agriculture and pastoral farming, handicrafts were also tried
at Pilani, on lines suggested by Gandhi, apparently with indifferent
success.[81] Walchand, in contrast, approached the problem in the
spirit of a pure capitalist and purchased the Ravalgaon farm in 1923
with the object of realizing his vision of industrializing agriculture.
On this farm he produced jaggery, cotton, sugar-cane, tobacco,
jowar, bajra, wheat, maize, groundnuts and turmeric. He prepared
an orchard producing grapes, papayas, pomegranates, guavas,

[80] *Walchand Hirachand*, preface, pp. xxxvii–xxxviii.
[81] G. D. Birla, *India's War Prosperity*, p. 154.

mangoes, etc. and also planted betel-leaves. Thousands of rupees were spent on improving agriculture in Ravalgaon, but these activities did not produce adequate monetary returns. The government's shifting monetary policies in the twenties and the collapse of agricultural prices in the thirties played havoc with Walchand's experiment in capitalist farming.[82] Walchand was therefore forced to turn to sugar-cane cultivation by forming the Ravalgaon Sugar Farm Ltd. in 1933 when protection was granted to sugar.[83] Sugar manufacture was certainly not the original purpose of the Ravalgaon experiment. Cane cultivation and sugar manufacture, to which purpose he turned the farm after the failure of the agricultural experiment, proved by contrast so profitable that he turned a construction company within his group into a sugar company in the same year. The plain fact of the situation was that industrial investment was a lot more profitable than capitalist farming, especially in the thirties. There was no point, given the structure of returns from different sectors of the economy, in blaming capitalists for neglecting agriculture for industry.

Another criticism which has been recently directed against Indian business groups in this period by A. K. Bagchi is that in respect of industrialization their economic thinking really did not go far ahead of British attitudes towards the role of the government in the Indian economy. They were afraid to leave the safe nineteenth century moorings of free enterprise, their economic thinking being bound within a basically capitalist structure. Admittedly they wanted a more vigorous policy of protection and a lower sterling parity of the rupee.

But their views did not advance beyond such mercantilist platitudes. The removal of the basic obstacles to industrial development in India in the 1920s would have required the adoption of a framework of socialist planning: the Government of India would certainly not have encouraged any such revolutionary development, nor would the Indian capitalists have risked stirring up the whole social order in this fashion. Hence they contented themselves by demanding tariff protection, which would be profitable to them in the short run and which would be granted by the then Government of India— under pressure. The pattern that was thus initiated at the beginning of the 1920s became set in the thirties: industrial development was limited almost entirely by what would be permitted in a framework of tariff protection excluding all other kinds of government action.[84]

[82] *Walchand Hirachand*, p. 140.   [83] Ibid., pp. 142–3.
[84] Bagchi, op. cit., pp. 426–7.

This statement raises important issues, which may be briefly explored here. As we shall see in the next chapter, Indian businessmen in the inter-war period were spasmodically disturbed by the 'Red Scare' and were acutely concerned with any manifestations of liaison between Congress and socialism. They were divided over the appropriate strategy for dealing with the problem. Some were naive, but others—as we shall see later on—approached it in a remarkably sophisticated manner. If as capitalists they opposed socialist politics, this should come as no surprise. What comes more as a surprise is the growing *rapprochement* at the level of economic thinking between the big businessmen of India and those leftist politicians to whom they were so vehemently opposed. The subtle shifts in the economic thinking of the Indian business world in the inter-war period have yet to be chronicled and analysed, but if one is to give some weightage to European exclusiveness as a barrier to investment—as A. K. Bagchi does—these shifts have to be taken into account. For if Indian business opinion was not far in advance of official thinking and foreign business opinion on government economic policy, then one cannot expect any big change in the behaviour of the private sector upon the removal of racial discrimination.

The nature of economic and political thinking within nationalist India—both commercial and professional—was, as Professor Bagchi has rightly pointed out, central to the issue of Indian industrialization. In exploring the closely interrelated demand and supply constraints on the economy, we have reached the conclusion that adoption of protective measures, provision of banking facilities, stores purchase within India and other such steps would not have been sufficient to break those constraints.[85] Of course these had been prominent features of the state patronage of industries in Russia, Prussia and Japan in the late nineteenth century. Had these measures been adopted in India in the late nineteenth century, when Britain was the only industrialized country in the world, they might have been far more productive of the desired results than proved to be the case for India in the inter-war period. But by 1914 the world economic situation had radically altered due to the spread of the industrial revolution in many other countries, and the underdeveloped and advanced countries had been more closely fitted into the pattern of a dynamic international economy in which technological

[85] This is a point on which A. K. Bagchi and M. D. Morris, in spite of their divergence of outlook, are in agreement.

innovation was setting the pace of change and widening the gulf between the two. What had sufficed in nineteenth century Japan would no longer suffice in twentieth century India. A much broader array of interrelated facilities had to be provided by government planning of the entire economy and by public investment on a massive scale. Capitalist thinking, not merely in India but anywhere in the world, moved to favouring such a strategy slowly. The strategy was adopted, ineffectively as it turned out, at the level of implementation in independent India during the Five Year Plans, but by then the subcontinent was already experiencing an unprecedented population explosion. Yet the fact that the strategy was adopted so soon after independence with a sort of national consensus was not without its pre-independence history. Imperceptibly in the late thirties and more dramatically during the Second World War, Indian business opinion was groping forward to precisely the kind of strategy that won national consensus in independent India. As the Indian economy began to swing into a quickened pace of activity in 1936–7, a number of Indian business groups initiated several proposals for setting up entirely new industries that were to bear fruit only during and after the Second World War. Jay Engineering Works, Texmaco, Premier Automobiles, etc. were all proposed at this time outside the framework of protection (since none could be given to entirely new industries under the policy of discriminating protection). Indian entrepreneurial behaviour was beginning to grow out of the restricted sphere defined by 'mercantilist platitudes'. The gulf between their economic thinking and the policy of a government increasingly marking time widened during the Second World War. Complex interrelationships were at the same time woven between the Congress and big business, and the drift towards planning was common to both from 1937 onwards. The political attitudes, alignments and conflicts that gave shape to the changing modes of economic thinking will be explored in the next chapter.

CHAPTER 6

Business and Politics in India
1914–47

A strong sense of nationalism and *swadeshi* spirit increasingly came to mould the political behaviour and economic thinking of big Indian business from the outbreak of the First World War to the advent of independence. The relationship between capitalist development and nationalist struggle was a subtle and complex one which will not lend itself to any blunt formula or clear-cut generalization. The dynamic process of interaction between the British Raj and big business in India combined elements of conflict and co-operation in varying proportions at all times. Moreover, the reasons that dictated the increasing hostility of big Indian business to the Raj and their informal alignment with the Indian National Congress were not just material interests and economic antagonisms, but embraced social, cultural and religious elements as well.

In the very nature of things there could be no head-on collision between the Raj and big business. For big business to carry on physically, co-operation with the administrative authority was at all times necessary and unavoidable. Many Indian businessmen were playing a complex and ambiguous game with the authorities, co-operating and opposing at the same time. P. Thyagaraja Chetty, a leading spokesman of the South Indian business community, played an important role both in the South Indian Chamber of Commerce, a nationalist business organization close to Mrs Besant's Home Rule League, and in the South Indian Liberal Federation, a non-Brahman collaborationist group which foreshadowed the Justice Party. From 1917 to 1920 he played a double role—accepting the Montagu–Chelmsford reforms in the South Indian Liberal Federation and pressing for more sweeping reforms (including the creation and transfer of a ministry of trade) in the South Indian Chamber of Commerce. He lost in his contest for election to the Madras Legislative Council in 1916 because of an adverse vote from the European business community which was very hostile to the South Indian Chamber of Commerce; subsequently he became a member of the first Indian ministry of Madras in 1920 with European support, which was solidly behind the South Indian Liberal Federation.[1]

Such instances can be multiplied. They may easily create the misleading impression that Indian business and politics were conducted within a competitively collaborationist framework and that nationalist criticism was the frustrated response of those seeking to claim the attention of their rulers when they had been passed over for a more favoured collaborationist group. So far as Indian businessmen were concerned, they co-operated as far as possible with the administrative authorities in order to preserve and expand their existing business. Political favours are a recognized means of building up profitable business and no sensible businessman can be expected to spurn such favours. Nevertheless pressures were being steadily generated from within the existing framework of Indian businesses for the British to quit.

There was no real contradiction in the behaviour of those businessmen who were prepared to work the reforms granted by their rulers and at the same time to finance agitations against such inadequate reforms. It was a strategy of one piece, conceived with a masterly grasp of the overall pattern, by Gandhi's disciple, Ghanashyamdas Birla, who like his master was one of the most clear-sighted men among his contemporaries. The strategy which he pursued unwaveringly as the leading spokesman of Indian capitalism was a combination of pressure and compromise designed to achieve the substance of economic and political power in the minimum possible time. Not all Indian businessmen were as clear-sighted as this disciple of Gandhi, but the cumulative results of their varied actions constantly renewed the conscious or unconscious pursuit of the overall strategy: to grab what was within reach in order to acquire a position of strength for the next round and, from a position of enhanced strength within the existing system, to press for more fundamental changes, until the enemy gave way over the substance in his stage-by-stage retreat.

This was a contest primarily over material issues. Yet the alignments were cemented, and the antagonisms deepened, by social sentiments and religious traditions as well. Merchants were the

[1] D. A. Washbrook, 'Political Change in the Madras Presidency 1880–1921', unpublished fellowship dissertation, Trinity College, Cambridge, 1972.

group in Indian society who most constantly encountered in their daily business racial discrimination and social humiliation, which sharpened in their minds a keen perception of racial aggression and racial abasement. Indelibly impressed on the sensitive mind of young Ghanashyamdas and of others like him doing business with European firms was the memory of having to climb the stairs while the white man took the lift.

Some well-established Indian business groups, such as the family of J. N. Tata in Bombay and Sir Rajendranath Mukherjee in Calcutta, successfully achieved integration with European social life and cultural values. This is far from saying that they were comprador groups in the strict sense of the term. If anything, the combined contribution of the Tata and Mukherjee families in iron and steel, power, heavy engineering and construction work was decisive for the growth of a domestic industrial production system no longer entirely subordinated to the colonial import–export sector which had so far been dominated by the European managing agencies. Perhaps the very fact that much of their investment went into fields beyond the established sphere of European manufacturing enterprise in India enabled them to avoid competition and discrimination, making possible their excellent record of co-operation (in the case of the Mukherjee family full business partnership) with European businessmen and officials in India. The structure of Indian business and industry, as determined by its subservience to the colonial import–export sector, had made industrial investment in the fresh fields sought out by Tata and Mukherjee relatively less profitable in the beginning. But this was an effect of *structure*, not a result of conscious design on the part of the European managing agencies. There was no difficulty on their part in extending co-operation and cordiality to native business groups operating outside their traditional sphere. In fact they often stood to benefit from the expansion of the industrial complex beyond its traditional boundaries. Many Bird companies sprang up directly in response to the growth of TISCO.

It was otherwise with the more tradition-bound Indian business groups which arrived later. The Marwari business groups in Calcutta, including Birla, started out as subordinate trading groups servicing the European import–export sector, importing and distributing piece-goods and collecting and pressing raw jute. Their economically subordinate or comprador (in the strict sense of the term) role exposed them to a pervasive set of racially humiliating social relationships which only served to enhance their dislike of white rule and culture. When they broke into industry after the First World War they chose those spheres of European manufacturing enterprise in which they had consolidated their position as compradors. Naturally they encountered fierce economic competition which assumed the form of racial antagonism. Paradoxically the most bitter racial antagonism and fierce nationalism were generated in that sphere of business which most completely expressed India's economic subordination to Britain. On the western side of India, the Gujarati mill-owners of Ahmedabad did not encounter racial discrimination in their immediate social environment, but the feeling of racial antipathy was fed from a distance by the machinations of Manchester.

Under the stimulus of racial animosity, the deep attachment of the merchant communities to their traditional religion and culture turned into a defensive nationalist reaction. It expressed itself in their attachment to the *swadeshi* ideal as defined by Mahatma Gandhi, to *khadi* and the spinning wheel, to the protection of cows and the uplift of the depressed castes within the traditional framework of the *varna* system. None of this would have been possible if the *swadeshi* ideal as defined by Gandhi had not answered to a very deep social and cultural need in their consciousness. There was certainly something paradoxical in the sight of big Marwari and Gujarati mill-owners (who were so efficiently pushing the frontiers of large-scale textile enterprise) religiously wearing *khadi* and performing their daily prayer of *swadeshi* on the spinning wheel.

It was no 'protestant ethic', shaped by Western social and cultural values, that influenced the behaviour of the new entrepreneurial groups that rose to prominence after the First World War. Their values were expressed in a traditional social and religious idiom. The deep religious faith of the new entrepreneurs was the most striking element in the ideology and culture of the emerging Indian capitalist class. Extremely religious as a child, Ramkrishna Dalmia, for instance, pursued his studies in the Advaita philosophy even in the midst of his growing business commitments. His *Guide to Bliss*, written in jail under sentence of imprisonment for his business malpractices, shows an intensely conservative commitment to all the traditional ideas and virtues of Jain–Hindu society and religion. This type of orthodox attachment to native religion proved a strong

bond in binding the traditional merchant communities to the nationalist movement under Gandhi. The process may been seen in the
characteristic saint–follower relationships that bound the families of
Ambalal Sarabhai and Ghanashyamdas Birla to Mahatma Gandhi.
In one interesting passage in his memoir on his guru, G. D. Birla
comments:

There was not much in common between us so far as our mode of
life went. Gandhiji was a saintly person who had renounced all the
comforts and luxuries of life. Religion was his main absorption and
this interest of his drew me irresistibly towards him. His outlook on
economics, however, was different. He believed in small-scale industries—*charkha*, *ghani* and all that. I, on the other hand, led a
fairly comfortable life and believed in the industrialization of the
country through large-scale industries. How then did we come to
have such a close association?[2]

The puzzling question raised by G. D. Birla will certainly repay
examination. Gandhi's philosophy, particularly his economics,
certainly cannot be regarded as the ready-made answer to the economic needs of the Indian capitalist class. His conception of Hind
Swaraj, properly realized, left no room for capitalists. Yet Hindu
and Jain capitalists from all over India flocked in large numbers to
the *ashram* at Sabarmati; they even (or their wives and female
relatives) spun the *charkha* daily, and G. D. Birla, for all his
somewhat contemptuous reference to '*charkha*, *ghani* and all that',
spent large sums on precisely those objects. The answer may partly
lie in the fact that Gandhi's philosophy provided the merchant
capitalists with a rationale for their existing role before the attainment of full Hind Swaraj. His concept of trusteeship of wealth by
capitalists on behalf of the people had considerable appeal for them.
The validity of the trusteeship concept at the level of reality was
proved in their own eyes by the very large sums which they spent on
charitable works, especially in the constructive programmes of
Gandhi. Large charities were characteristic of the traditions of all
merchant communities in north India, and the concept of trusteeship lent a larger rationale and ideological under-pinning to an
established behaviour pattern. Thus one element in Gandhi's philosophy, trusteeship, overshadowed another element, the break-up of
capitalist concentrations of business and industry into self-sufficient
units of agriculture and cottage industries. Ideology, as Max Weber

[2] G. D. Birla, op. cit., introduction, p. xv.

once stated, is seldom an outright reflection of material interests; but a body of doctrines is bound to be complex, and some part of it may be magnetic to felt social needs while other parts of it may recede on account of being out of line with the developing logic of a social situation. Something of this sort certainly happened to Gandhi's philosophy. It was a negation of capitalism; nevertheless the features attractive to capitalists in Gandhi's philosophy lent it a good deal of currency as a merchant ideology. Gandhian ideology was not a reflection of capitalist interests, but capitalist interests were attracted to some of its concepts.

Yet there was certainly more to it than that. Gandhi did not merely provide the merchant communities with a rationale for their material wealth in their own eyes. The aura of his saintliness appealed to much deeper spiritual and religious needs of salvation in their consciousness. To repeat G. D. Birla's words, 'Religion was his main absorption and this interest of his drew me irresistibly towards him.' It was not the relationship of a nascent capitalist class to a bourgeois ideologue that bound the rising merchant communities to Mahatma Gandhi. A much more traditional and historical behaviour pattern was at work here. India's merchant communities, since time immemorial, had exhibited deep devotion and attachment to her saints. Often this expressed itself through individual preacher–disciple relationships. Such individualized preacher–disciple relationships certainly prevailed between Mahatma Gandhi and the Birla and Sarabhai families. More generally, the Gujarati and Marwari merchant communities were attracted to the charismatic role of Gandhi as saint and saviour, and as such their large financial contributions to the Congress constructive programmes are to be seen, not as insurance policies, but as charities. Gandhi in their eyes stood in the long succession of India's saints, seers and saviours; and they responded to him as generation upon generation of their forefathers had responded to such persons. Only his appeal to them was now much wider and more heavily politicized than that of any of his saintly predecessors.

Formation of Assocham

The growing politicization and conflict within the private corporate sector in India during the twenties was reflected in the emergence of rival all-India unions of British and Indian commercial interests.

These came to be known respectively as Assocham (Associated Chambers of Commerce) and FICCI (Federation of Indian Chambers of Commerce and Industry). The Assocham was a coalition of all the European Chambers of Commerce in India, Ceylon (Sri Lanka) and Burma that had been formed in the nineteenth century. These chambers felt the need of coming together under a common umbrella at the end of the First World War. The Indian business community replied to the Assocham by forming the FICCI.

The European Chambers of Commerce in the three major ports of Calcutta, Bombay and Madras were of long standing. They were formed soon after trade was thrown open to private traders by the Charter Act of 1833. To protect and promote the interests of the European agency houses, the Bengal Chamber of Commerce, the Bombay Chamber of Commerce and the Madras Chamber of Commerce were formed in the next three years, 1834–6. The Karachi Chamber of Commerce was established in 1860 and the Upper India Chamber of Commerce in 1888. In the beginning most of these European Chambers of Commerce had some native participation. But slowly the native element was weeded out and by the outbreak of the First World War all these Chambers of Commerce, except that in Bombay, were frankly racialist associations that virtually denied membership to native merchants. They were, as A. K. Bagchi has stressed, efficient means of promoting European unity and of eliminating native competition.[3] They were extremely influential and had lines into the administration, being helped by 'the mystic bond of racial affinity with the rulers of the land'.[4] G. D. Birla has recorded from his long personal experience of business and politics in Calcutta how strongly the British ICS officers were influenced by

the die-hard views freely expressed amongst the businessmen, with whom they closely associated socially. Indeed it could be remarked that, whereas some of the businessmen of humble origin were anxious that their sons should enter the I.C.S. or the Indian Army because they regarded this as a rise in the social ladder that they wished to climb, officials, on the contrary, besought their business-friends to take their sons into firms in order that they should have more prosperous financial careers than fell to the average official.[5]

[3] A. K. Bagchi, *Private Investment in India*, p. 170.
[4] Ibid., p. 166.   [5] G. D. Birla, *India's War Prosperity*, p. 183.

In Calcutta the critical nationalist press often referred to the Bengal Chamber of Commerce, by far the biggest and most influential in India, as the power that really ruled the land. The Bombay Chamber of Commerce, which had to share the business and commerce of Bombay with a strong native business community, was more liberal in its attitude. It had on its register the names of some of the oldest and best known Indian firms.[6]

It was the Bengal Chamber of Commerce that took the lead in forming Assocham in 1921 and in giving that body its reactionary character. Since the Montagu Declaration of 1917 promising increasing devolution of power to Indians, the European business community in Calcutta had been galvanized into political activity by the threat to their interests posed by the promised Indianization of government. They fought at every step leading to the grant of the Montagu–Chelmsford reforms and by their strenuous resistance succeeded in securing substantial representation for the European commercial community in the Indian and Bengal (where most European business was concentrated) legislatures. Before the First World War, European businessmen in Calcutta had not played any active role in politics, being content to utilize their informal links with the administration as well as their more formal channels of communication through the Bengal Chamber of Commerce for the protection of their business interests. In the changed political situation after the First World War, they resolved to play an active political role in the legislatures in order to defend those interests.[7] At a special meeting of the Bengal Chamber of Commerce in 1920 to discuss the Montagu–Chelmsford reforms, one member stated:

It is in the ante-room and not in the council chamber itself that the real work of the councils is done . . . In the future unless men are not only permitted but encouraged to serve on the Reformed Councils, European commerce will not only suffer, but its continuance may prove quite impossible. It is very difficult for men who have been out of India for more than one or two years to realize how completely the conditions have changed and how absolutely the future depends on the personality of their representatives, and on the

[6] Raymond J. Sullivan, *One Hundred Years of Bombay: History of the Bombay Chamber of Commerce, 1836–1936*, Bombay, n.d., p. 209.

[7] Proceedings of the Calcutta Branch of the European Association commencing from 23 April 1918: 8th meeting of the Calcutta Branch, EA, speech of A. J. Pugh.

enlistment of friendly Indians against the onslaught of rabid and self-seeking politicians.[8]

The emphasis on the personality of European business representatives and on the enlistment of friendly Indians clearly indicated a two-pronged strategy. One part of this strategy was to pool together the political resources and talents of European business communities in the different centres all over India, so as to enable them to play an effective role in the Indian Legislative Assembly. The other part of the strategy was to foment communal and other divisions amongst the native majority in the Assembly by using the European block vote as a bargaining counter. Such a political strategy could only be co-ordinated by an all-India organization through which the existing European Chambers of Commerce could co-operate with each other. It was felt that such co-operation was essential in the sharper spirit of trade rivalry that had followed the First World War. These considerations led to the formation of the Associated Chambers of Commerce in 1921. The Bengal Chamber of Commerce was its executive organ; and it imposed on the new association a reactionary policy that thoroughly antagonized Indian business opinion. Assocham was a comprehensive European business federation that included the Bengal, Bombay, Burma, Ceylon, Calicut, Chittagong, Coconada, Cochin, Karachi, Madras, Narayanganj, Panjab, Tellicherry, Tuticorin and Upper India Chambers of Commerce. Import–export trade was clearly the dominant interest in this assembly; the manufacturing interest within India came a long way behind.

Soon after the formation of Assocham, the Bengal Chamber of Commerce was spurred to further political activity by the development of fresh threats to European interests. In the Indian Legislative Assembly, newly set up under the Montagu–Chelmsford reforms, Indian members brought forward a bill for removing racial discrimination in legal matters; outside the Assembly there were widespread *hartals*, strikes and riots in Bombay, Calcutta and other towns in connection with the non-cooperation movement. Provoked by these occurrences, the President of the Bengal Chamber of Commerce, Robert Watson-Smyth, delivered a notoriously racist speech at the beginning of 1922 that provoked a sharp Indian business reaction and

---

[8] *Report of the Bengal Chamber of Commerce*, 1920, vol. II, proceedings of a special general meeting on 12 October 1920, speech of Mr Pitchford.

left a lasting memory of bitterness. Opening his theme, Watson-Smyth said:

Reform and agitation, side by side, have affected the Government of this country to such an extent that the whole fabric not only of Government, but of society also, is shaken and threatened, and it, therefore, behoves every man to take a hand in the game, so that he may be prepared to resist aggression and defend his rights.

With the recent disturbances which had paralysed life in Calcutta in mind, he told the meeting:

The business community in Calcutta is being attacked, and they will be attacked still more in the future, and it requires the very best men to put up an adequate defence... There still exists a prejudice amongst some of the great firms against allowing their seniors to do anything but their own business, but I solemnly warn the members of this Chamber that this cannot continue, and that all must take their share of the burden. It is a selfish and a wicked act for any one firm to be willing enough to take advantage of all this Chamber does for it, but unwilling to allow the attention of their Senior to be distracted for a moment by any thoughts outside making money for the home partners.

Robert Watson-Smyth then brought up the matter of the bill against racial discrimination in the Assembly. Legislative Councils, he said, had realized their power and were looking about to see how by legislation they could work off some of their racial jealousies. They had raised the Ilbert Bill controversy again, and had shown that the threat to the European business community was very real. European businessmen would have to stick together, as it might be a fight for their very existence. There was, Watson-Smyth felt sure,

a certain amount of bluff on the part of many Indians over this matter. It is a question of twisting the Lion's tail, as has been done so often by the continental powers, and the usual process is to go on twisting, keeping a sharp eye on the other end of the lion to see how far it is safe to go before he begins to bite.

Robert Watson-Smyth's advice to the Chamber was, therefore,

to show your teeth as soon as possible. I have been asked what we can do, or what we are going to do. My answer is that we are going to do everything that lies in our power. I am not of course going to give away our plans prematurely, nor am I going to indulge in threats, but I can assure the Legislative Assembly that if they pursue this course they are taking on a good deal more than what they probably bargain for.

The President of the Bengal Chamber of Commerce proposed 'to raise a storm that will sweep any proposed legislation before it, even if the Reforms have to go too'. He then went on to say 'unhesitatingly that no matter what may happen at Delhi, the Europeans of India will not stand any encroachments on the legal rights that we have found necessary in the years past and which we are convinced will be still more necessary in the future'. 'Let but this safeguard be taken from us,' Watson-Smyth assured the Chamber, 'and not one of us will be safe from a charge of any foul crime up to murder, with the certainty of a conviction.' He then went on to express the opinion that the constitutional as well as the unconstitutional activities of many Indians were

aiming at one thing, and one thing only, which is to make matters so impossible for us Britishers in India, that we will get out. But let them be well assured that we will not get out. Are we [asked Watson-Smyth rhetorically] going to be juggled out of our birthright by a parcel of lawyer politicians? Are we going to relinquish the heritage which our fathers won with the blood of some of the best men that ever came out of Britain? Are we going to sit quietly and submissively by to accept from any Legislative Assembly or from any organization of Mr Gandhi, what is vulgarly known as the order of the boot?[9]

There was widespread condemnation of this irresponsible speech in the Indian press, and Indian business organizations and chambers of commerce reacted fiercely to the threats uttered by the President of the Bengal Chamber of Commerce. The matter of the discrimination bill was in the end amicably settled. But the spirit of open racial antagonism that had been generated continued to persist on account of fresh conflicts.

Hard upon the heels of this outburst of racial animosity came a controversy over more material issues, i.e. protection for Indian industries and reservation of the coastal trade for Indian shipping. Under pressure of Indian political and business opinion at the end of the First World War, the Government of India had appointed two committees, the Indian Fiscal Commission and the Indian Mercantile Marine Committee, for examining these issues. The appointment of these committees provided Indian businessmen and politicians with a suitable forum in which to press their demands. In order to force the pace, a Madras politician, T. V. Sheshagiri Ayyer,

[9] *Report of the Bengal Chamber of Commerce*, 1921, vol. I, proceedings of the annual general meeting, 28 February 1922.

had introduced two bills in the Assembly for banning the practices of rate-cutting and deferred rebate resorted to by foreign shipping interests in order to preserve their monopoly. These bills were successfully blocked by stalling tactics. But in the matter of protection the Government of India was now prepared to extend discriminating protection to steel, a measure which the European business community saw as the thin end of the wedge for autarchic economic policies.

Once again the Bengal Chamber of Commerce took up the task of moving through Assocham in 1923 a resolution against the grant of protection to the steel industry. In protest, all leading Indian members of the Bombay business community who had been invited to the meeting—Purshotamdas Thakurdas, Walchand Hirachand, R. D. Tata, Fazalbhoy Currimbhoy, Cowasji Jahangir, Pheroze Sethna and Lalubhai Samaldas—absented themselves in a body from the meeting. No Indian businessman attended the fifth session of Assocham in Bombay except a colliery proprietor from the Panjab Chamber of Commerce, who turned up at the meeting after consulting other Indian businessmen in order to oppose the resolution.[10] The solidarity of Indian business opinion on this issue was also demonstrated by cables received from native chambers of commerce protesting against the attendance of the Finance, Commerce and Industries Members of the Government of India at the Bombay session of Assocham, on the ground that their attendance would imply official countenance of anti-national resolutions. The three members attended the session, ignoring these protests.[11] The Bombay Chamber of Commerce, which had friendly relations with the Indian business community in Bombay, sought to move an amendment watering down the strongly-worded resolution of the Bengal Chamber of Commerce against protective tariff for steel and expressing sympathy for legitimate Indian aspirations.[12] But the amendment was lost as most of the European Chambers represented in Assocham were involved mainly in import–export trade and contained no substantial manufacturing interests in their composition. With strong support from the Karachi, Burma and other chambers, the resolution of the Bengal Chamber of Commerce was carried through Assocham.

[10] Purshotamdas Thakurdas Papers, file no. 42, FICCI 1923–34, pt IV.
[11] *Report of the Marwari Association for the Year 1923*.
[12] *One Hundred Years of Bombay*, p. 161.

The Assocham resolution against protection to the steel industry had no practical effect on government tariff policies. In spite of European protests, discriminating protection was taken up by the Government of India as a matter of policy. But the Assocham resolution produced an immediate impact on Indian business organization in its political aspects. The resolution galvanized Indian businessmen into a new effort to build up an all-India organization of their own. Native merchants, brokers and industrialists in different towns and cities, excluded on racial considerations from the powerful European Chambers of Commerce, had long ago set up their own local chambers of commerce. The need for an umbrella organization under which all these native chambers of commerce at different centres could come together was now strongly felt. On 7 December 1923, G. D. Birla wrote from Calcutta to the Bombay Cotton King, Purshotamdas Thakurdas:

I have been watching very closely the activities of the Associated Chambers for the past few years, and I feel that their strong organization will be very detrimental to Indian interests if steps are not taken immediately to organize a similar institution of the Indians ... You will, perhaps, agree with me that if we do not check their activities in time, their influence with the Government will increase to an extent which Government will find it most difficult to resist ... If you take up the lead, I am sure, you will have whole-hearted support from Calcutta, and it would be a great glory to see merchants from all parts of India standing on one platform and putting their well considered and combined views before the Government with a force which will carry greater weight than those of the combined European institutions.[13]

P. Thakurdas, in reply, was pessimistic about the immediate prospects of a federation.[14] He blamed this on the destructive effects of the non-cooperation movement, which he had been strongly opposing in Bombay. That movement had drawn very substantial financial support from the hard-pressed native traders, brokers, speculators and merchants of Bombay, though industrialists as such had been far less evident as financial backers of the Congress. In Calcutta one industrialist, G. D. Birla, and two merchants and speculators, Sukhlal Karnani and Kesoram Poddar, had been the principal contributors to the Tilak Swaraj Fund opened by Mahatma Gandhi.

[13] Purshotamdas Thakurdas Papers, file no. 42, pt IV, G. D. Birla to Thakurdas, 7 December 1923.
[14] Ibid., 7 January 1927.

With these large merchant donations, the Congress had rapidly grown in 1920–1 as a well-organized party capable of waging a non-cooperation movement through the length and breadth of the country.[15] P. Thakurdas, who disagreed completely with this strategy, argued that a more constructive approach might be worked out through the Legislative Assembly for the advancement of Indian business and industry. Three years elapsed before G. D. Birla's proposal for a federation bore fruit. In the meanwhile, non-cooperation died down and Thakurdas' line of working the reforms was tried out in the Indian Legislative Assembly. The demands of Indian capitalism in several directions were vigorously pressed by politicians and businessmen in the Legislative Assembly. Through this parliamentary work, a greater appreciation of the value of a representative body for Indian merchants and industrialists emerged.

Formation of FICCI

The demands of Indian capitalism, voiced with increasing insistence in the Legislative Assembly, were not radically new and had been formulated long ago by Dadabhai Naoroji, M. G. Ranade and R. C. Dutt. In that sense, Indian business thinking had as yet made no departure from its moorings in nineteenth century economic thought. All Indian political parties showed themselves in complete agreement about the necessity of protection. Under Jinnah's leadership the Assembly passed resolutions calling for government purchase of stores by rupee tenders in India. A tug-of-war went on over the coastal reservation recommended by the Indian Mercantile Marine Committee, which the Government of India refused to implement. Bitter denunciations of the high parity of the rupee were periodically heard from Indian members of the Assembly, while European businessmen and industrialists continued to approve it quietly. Indian businessmen also voiced complaints about the lack of adequate banking facilities and argued that the government should take the lead in pressing banks to finance industrial development as in Germany and Japan.

It may be doubted if the concession of all these demands together would have been sufficient to ensure a rate of growth fast enough for

[15] For details of Congress organization and merchant donations, *see* Gopal Krishna, 'The Indian National Congress, 1918–23', unpublished Oxford Ph.D. thesis, 1961.

20

the take-off of the Indian economy. Nevertheless the expressed opinions of Indian businessmen, economists and politicians during the 1920s need not be dismissed as 'mercantilist platitudes'. The stage of production where planning would be needed for the further growth of Indian capitalism had not yet been reached. The domestic market had yet to be captured by Indian manufacturers from foreign competitors. There was considerable room for growth by import-substitution, and for this purpose Indian businessmen and politicians were pressing the appropriate demands in the Assembly. There was, moreover, no certainty that these demands would be granted. Certainly the gulf between Indian and European thinking was wide on the issues relevant to the speeding up of import-substitution. Demands for socialist measures were not practical politics until more power was handed over to the Congress, nor was there as yet an urgent economic need for such measures within the Indian capitalist system. As soon as the pace of import-substitution picked up and the manufacturing sector began to approach the ceiling of the domestic market, rational thinking on the part of businessmen would dictate planning, but not as yet.

To safeguard Indian business interests against any reactionary measures and to promote these current demands for liberalization of government policies, G. D. Birla and his Marwari connections in Calcutta launched a fresh initiative for a federation of Indian commercial interests at the end of 1926. During that year important developments had taken place in the commercial world of Calcutta due to the setting up of the Indian Chamber of Commerce. Originally proposed at Birla Park in October 1925, this body was organized the following year with G. D. Birla as President and with Anandji Haridas & Co., A. C. Banerjee & Co., Scindia Steam Navigation Co., Soorajmull Nagarmull, D. P. Khaitan of Kesoram Cotton Mills, the Central Bank of India and important Marwari firms on the Committee. The Chamber had on its roll the members of the only considerable *swadeshi* shipping company, leading Indian shippers of jute, hessian, gunny, rice and other country produce and importers of piece-goods, hardware and other merchandise. The export and import interests represented on the Indian Chamber of Commerce were stated to be in the aggregate not less than those of all other Indian commercial bodies put together.[16] From the outset

[16] *Indian Chamber of Commerce, Calcutta: Annual Report of the Committee for the Year 1926.*

the Indian Chamber of Commerce, controlled by Birla and his friends, overshadowed the older, Bengali-dominated Bengal National Chamber of Commerce. It also began to step up the increasing Marwari opposition to European interests in the sphere of Calcutta trade and industry. The battle for the control of the import–export sector in Calcutta led to a revival of interest in an all-India federation against European business interests, overwhelmingly concentrated in that city.

A liaison was established between the Indian business interests which had taken the offensive in Calcutta and Sir Purshotamdas Thakurdas and others in the Bombay area. Initially the FICCI was organized in Calcutta, where a fund was established for beginning the activities of the federation. P. Thakurdas, Dinshaw Petit, G. D. Birla and Lala Harkishen Lal paid Rs 1,000 each into the fund, and B. F. Madon, D. P. Khaitan and A. C. Banerjee contributed Rs 500 each.[17] Subsequently P. Thakurdas was elected first President of FICCI. Its executive committee consisted of G. D. Birla (Indian Chamber of Commerce, Calcutta), Dinshaw Petit (Indian Merchants' Chamber, Bombay), M. Jamal Mohamed Saib (Southern India Skin and Hide Merchants' Association, Madras), Sir M. C. T. Muthia Chettiar (Southern India Chamber of Commerce, Madras), S. A. S. Tyabji (Burma Indian Chamber of Commerce), Fahirjee Cowasjee (Buyers' and Shippers' Chamber, Karachi), Rai Bahadur Vikramjit Singh (U.P. Chamber of Commerce, Kanpur), F. M. Abdul Quddus (Mysore Chamber of Commerce, Bangalore), B. F. Madon (Indian Merchants' Chamber, Bombay) and Kasturbhai Lalbhai (Ahmedabad Millowners' Association, Ahmedabad). It was decided to locate the secretariat in Bombay and to have it shifted to Delhi or Simla during the sessions of the Indian Legislative Assembly. For this purpose, large donations were made by P. Thakurdas, G. D. Birla, Walchand Hirachand, Fahirjee Cowasjee and Lala Shri Ram.[18]

The formation of the FICCI was a rude shock to European business interests. By the middle of 1927 overtures for an understanding were made from European quarters to the rising Marwari groups in Calcutta, but the gulf was too wide to be bridged. D. P. Khaitan,

[17] Purshotamdas Thakurdas Papers, file no. 42, pt IV, Thakurdas to Kasturbhai Lalbhai, 7 January 1927.

[18] Ibid., pt III, Report of the Executive Committee of the Federation of Indian Chambers of Commerce.

reporting such an overture from the Europeans, wrote to a member of the Birla family:

Colonel Crawford came and saw me in connection with forming an alliance with Europeans regarding the political question now before the country. I definitely told him that that was not to be, as the political convictions of Indians and Britishers (in their present mentality) are quite wide apart. He conveyed to me, however, that they were convinced that it was a sad day for Europeans, when fifteen or twenty years back they insisted upon keeping Indians out of their (European) Chamber of Commerce. I said that I was quite sure that in trying to keep everything to themselves, the Europeans had done us a service and made us more active, and generally speaking, better able to look after ourselves . . . The Europeans are genuinely nervous about our Federation, and would like to see a stop put to this activity of ours. I write this, therefore, to ask you and other friends to build up the Federation.[19]

It was not without reason that the European business community in Calcutta felt nervous about the activities of Indian business organizations. A sustained assault on their monopoly position had been mounted by G. D. Birla through the Indian Chamber of Commerce, which was, as Birla wrote with satisfaction to P. Thakurdas, 'getting very powerful day by day'. Under its aegis the East India Jute Association had been organized to offer a challenge to the powerful European jute interests. All this added to the bitterness of race relations in the business world of Calcutta. There were cases of European non-cooperation with the Marwaris in the field of daily business. Pressure was exerted by the Europeans through the Imperial Bank of India which—Birla reported in the same letter—was not behaving properly in some cases. 'I should not like to fight them unnecessarily, but if I have to I must.'[20] This attitude of aggressive self-assertion was typical of the Birla group and it was strikingly demonstrated through the methods by which G. D. Birla established direct contacts with the jute market in Europe, overcoming the barriers of racial exclusiveness. He was in fact the only Indian member of the London Jute Association. He was admitted because he threatened to start business directly with the continent under continental arbitration. This threat had its desired effect and the London Jute Association was compelled to take him. But he still got no admission to the Sale Rooms in London where the actual

    [19] Ibid., D. P. Khaitan to Deviprosadji, 9 September 1927.
    [20] Ibid., G. D. Birla to Thakurdas, 2 May 1928.

sale and purchase business was conducted. Prominent among these were the Commercial Sale Rooms and the Baltic Exchange. He negotiated with the Baltic Exchange for membership, but to no effect. Although he was a member of the London Jute Association which was affiliated with the Commercial Sale Rooms, he had no admission there, and had to employ an English clerk, 'any Tom, Jack or Ragstraw', to attend and conduct business on his behalf. 'This', complained Birla to Thakurdas in the autumn of 1928, 'is the most humiliating situation—because although they take all nationalities including the Americans and Japanese they have kept the doors closed for Indians.'[21] This glaring case of racial discrimination was taken up by the FICCI and as a result of pressure from Indian business quarters the ban against Indians was lifted at the end of 1928 by the Baltic Exchange and other commercial bodies.[22]

Divisions within the Indian Business Community

It must not be thought that Indian businessmen of the inter-war period formed a monolithic community united against foreign business and administrative interests. They became an identifiable and self-conscious capitalist class during this time, a fact clearly reflected in the formation of the FICCI. But divisions persisted within the class and the relationship of the different sections to foreign business and administration ranged from bitterness to cordiality, though there were ambiguities even in the most cordial or the most bitter relationships. Consequently it will not do to present the divisions within the Indian capitalist class in terms of a simple dichotomy between comprador and national bourgeoisie. In basic economic terms, the most readily recognizable distinction was between the traders, merchants, speculators, brokers and marketeers of different sorts on the one hand and the industrialists on the other. To some extent this distinction was blurred by the fact that even the most advanced Indian industrialists (e.g. Tata and Birla) were heavily engaged in import–export business, while the Indian businessmen engaged primarily in servicing the import–export sector were sometimes recruited as directors of industrial companies (e.g. P. Thakurdas, primarily a cotton merchant, was also a director of several industrial companies). Nevertheless the distinction between 'mar-

[21] Ibid., G. D. Birla to Thakurdas, 19 November 1928.
[22] Ibid., pt V, P. Thakurdas to Stephen Demetriadi, 11 December 1929.

keteers' and 'industrialists', recently advanced by A. D. D. Gordon,[23] is a useful one. It is not, however, a distinction that can be squared with the comprador–national bourgeoisie dichotomy. By far the largest share in the financial contributions to the non-cooperation and civil disobedience movements came from the 'marketeers'. In Bombay the heaviest subscribers to the Tilak Swaraj Fund were grain merchants, cotton brokers and shroffs.[24] Industrialists, though some of them participated in the Congress movements, were on the whole more cautious. This caution was due to their unavoidable dependence on the government of the country, which was a major purchaser of industrial materials. Traders and speculators had greater scope for expressing political dissent and their subservient, 'comprador' position in the import–export sector constantly brought them into friction with the dominant foreign business interests and with administrative policies geared to the latter's needs. The twenties and thirties were decades of exceptional trading difficulties, which tended to radicalize the political outlook of the 'marketeers' as a body. Thus distinctions in political behaviour did not necessarily follow cleavages along economic roles. The most readily identifiable comprador elements in economic terms often appeared as the most nationalist in political terms. The divisions within Indian business were complex and ambiguous.

Nowhere was the ambiguity of the relationship between economic role and political behaviour more pronounced than in the case of the groupings within the business world of Bombay in the twenties and the thirties. The Bombay mill-owning class—both European and Indian—mixed freely amongst themselves at the social level. The Indian mill-owners, who had by then adopted the English style of living in many respects, were regarded with scorn by conservative merchants and businessmen as 'aliens'. The government sought to maintain good relations with the Bombay industrialists as it was feared that their resources would otherwise go to the Congress.[25]

On the other hand, the 'marketeers' came under increasing pressure from the government during this period. They were as a class less endowed with Western education and Western manners than the Bombay mill-owners. They were heavily dependent on the mill

[23] A. D. D. Gordon, *Businessmen and Politics: Rising Nationalism and Modernising Economy in Bombay, 1918–1933* (Australian National Universit Monographs on South Asia 3), Manohar Book Service, Delhi, 1968.
[24] Ibid.   [25] Ibid.

owning class and their relationship with the mill-owners was fraught
with friction on account of this subservience. The main markets—
the share market, the native piece-goods market, the mill-stores
market, the raw cotton market, the bullion market, the money
market—had all arisen with the mills and were dependent on their
patronage. The informal liaison between the government and the
mill-owning class regarding various business practices increasingly
pushed the marketeers into an attitude of political opposition during
the inter-war period.[26] The plans for rationalization of the cotton
trade and industry which the government sought to implement in
alliance with the mill-owners involved squeezing out the inter-
mediary and speculative levels of business by administrative measures. The measures adversely affected the smaller marketeers
reared on traditional methods of business, though cotton kings of
the modern type, such as Sir Purshotamdas Thakurdas, were not
similarly threatened by these plans of rationalization. In consequence the traditional marketeers, especially the shroffs, were
extremely nationalistic. Some shroffs in fact served as Congress
'dictators' during the civil disobedience movement in Bombay.[27]

As far as the top section of Indian business and industry was
concerned, which included a few big merchants and speculators of
the modern type as well as a number of rising industrial entrepreneurs, one can identify groupings in political terms which remained
fairly stable throughout the period. Quite close to the administration
stood the Tata group and its vast connections in Bombay business
and industry, as well as the Bombay mill-owning class generally and
the prominent allies of foreign interests. More nationalist in composition was the top leadership of the FICCI—P. Thakurdas, G. D.
Birla and Lala Shri Ram. Significantly the Tata group played no
direct role in the FICCI. Walchand Hirachand, who was connected
with the Tata group but was an extreme nationalist in economics
and a close friend of Vallabhbhai Patel, was a member of the outer
core of FICCI leadership. At the other end of the scale, the disciples
of Gandhi, the Birla and Sarabhai families, were openly opposed to
the administration. Purshotamdas Thakurdas was a consistent
middle-of-the-road politician between the Tatas on the one hand
and the Birlas on the other. Lala Shri Ram tended at first to lean
towards G. D. Birla's policy of opposition, but later moderated
his attitude considerably. The top section of the Indian capitalist

[26] Ibid.   [27] Ibid.

class was thus divided by its attitude into loyalists (e.g. Tatas and their connections), moderate nationalists (e.g. P. Thakurdas and, later, Lala Shri Ram) and aggressive nationalists (e.g. Birla, Sarabhai and quite a few 'marketeers', such as Jamnalal Bajaj).

The political divisions and tensions within the top Indian capitalist class were brought into sharp focus in the late twenties and the early thirties by two events. One was the 'Red Scare' of 1929, which brought the Tata group into open conflict with the FICCI leadership. The other was the Civil Disobedience Movement and the Round Table Conference of 1930–1, which brought out the differences of approach within the FICCI leadership between moderate and aggressive nationalists.

The 'Red Scare' of 1929

Because of their pre-eminent position in power and iron and steel, Tatas were looked up to by all groups of Indian industrialists as the leaders of the *swadeshi* movement in business and industry. In the political sphere, however, the Tatas held aloof from *swadeshi* enthusiasts, and their strong connections with foreign business and administration were a disappointment to those nationalist business elements who looked to them for leadership. Considering the fact that the government (including the railways department) was the largest purchaser of steel and that it relied in wartime on TISCO for munitions, the connections between the Tata group and the administration were bound to be strong. What came as a shock to nationalist business opinion was the growing liaison between the Tata group and foreign interests. In the beginning of August 1929 rumours spread that Sir Dorabji Tata was negotiating with an American syndicate to sell all his interests in India. G. D. Birla, perturbed by these rumours, wrote to Sir Purshotamdas Thakurdas, a director of several Tata companies, 'That the Indian industry which the Tatas have built with so much Indian money and cooperation should pass into the hands of Americans is a thing which should upset all of us'.[28] P. Thakurdas wrote back, correcting the wrong impression that all Tata interests were being sold out, but revealing the disquieting news that Sir Dorabji had in fact sold half his interests in the hydro-group agency for Rs 37.5 lakhs. He agreed

[28] Purshotamdas Thakurdas Papers, file no. 68, G. D. Birla to Thakurdas, 12 August 1929.

with Birla that the consequences of this sale of Tata electrical interests to the American syndicate would be grave.[29] At a meeting of
the Board of Directors of Tata Power Co., P. Thakurdas 'could not
help remarking that both the press and the country will not look
upon the introduction of Americans in the Agency with favour and
that it would militate a lot against the House of Tatas which was so
far considered to be a national house'. He also objected to the
increase of the commission taken by the managing agency from the
company. Protests were raised at a shareholders' meeting against
the increase of commission, but to no effect.[30]

   The rift between the Tata house and the FICCI leadership had in
the meanwhile widened due to an ill-advised attempt by the Tata
group to start a capitalist party in the Indian Legislative Assembly in
alliance with foreign business. In the spring of 1929 the FICCI
leadership was planning to spend nearly half a lakh of rupees on
elections throughout India to win strong representation in the
Indian Legislative Assembly to counter the European group's plan
to finance the Central Muslim group in the Assembly. They did not
intend to form a separate party, but to work through the existing
nationalist groups, keeping out of the Swarajist Congress, but maintaining an understanding with it. To avoid any contest with the
Congress, a committee was to be formed consisting of P. Thakurdas,
a moderate independent, G. D. Birla, a member of the Nationalist
party, and two Congressmen, Motilal Nehru and M. M. Malaviya.
The money was to be spent through consultation among the four.[31]

   In the midst of these plans for fighting foreign business interests
came a bombshell.[32] Provoked beyond endurance by the Bombay
textile strike and the activities of the left-wing Girni Kamgar Union
under the alleged instigation of the communists, two loyalist textile
magnates, Sir Ibrahim Rahimtoola and Sir Cowasji Jahangir, made
a move to organize a party of Bombay 'capitalists' of both races,
supported by Sir Dorabji Tata, who had in quick succession experienced costly strikes in the steel works in Jamshedpur and the textile
mills in Bombay. This party was to act in the Legislative Assembly
in competition with other political parties which had not supported

[29] Ibid., Thakurdas to Birla, 16 August 1929.
[30] Ibid., file no. 65.
[31] Ibid., file no. 42, pt II, Birla to Thakurdas, 26 April 1929.
[32] The following account is based on various correspondence in file no. 42
above. *See especially* nos. 59, 61, 66 and 67 in pt II.

the mill-owners in the textile strike (above all the Congress) and to co-operate with the Europeans for guarding against the 'Red Spectre' and Moscow infiltration. Naturally, Motilal Nehru and M. M. Malaviya reacted very sharply to the move for an anti-Congress political association of capitalists. G. D. Birla and P. Thakurdas both urged Sir Dorabji very strongly against the move as it would lose the Indian capitalist class the sympathy of all nationalist parties.

Pointing out that a capitalist party would never command the necessary following in the Indian Legislative Assembly, Sir Purshotamdas wrote to the Tatas: 'They have not more than four people in the Assembly, and even these have one or the other of the various political labels of political parties in the Assembly, viz. Birla, a nationalist, myself an independent, Jamna-das Mehta, a Congress-man, and so on.' Under these circumstances, he felt that a political association of the capitalists would be 'the surest method of alienating the sympathies of the various political parties in the Assembly, who, whilst all agree as to the protection and relief to be given to Indian commerce and industry, would feel somewhat exasperated at an additional rival to them in elections etc.' He pointed out that Indian commerce and industry had so far been above party politics, as amply borne out by the common attitude of all parties in the Assembly on the following questions: cotton excise duty, steel protection, protective duties on imported piece-goods, Kalyan Power House and the rupee–sterling ratio. He asked how far the Europeans would support Indian aspirations on issues like cotton cloth protection, Coastal Reservation Bill, Indianization of the services and preferential treatment to Indians regarding industrial enterprises.

As you know the country as a whole has strong views about these questions. The Europeans are wholeheartedly and unanimously opposed to progress in any of these directions. How are the European members of this new Association likely to regard legislation in any of these questions and what mandate does Sir Dorabji think the new Association would be able to give to their representatives in the Legislature on any of these questions? I am convinced that the Europeans will never give way in such vital matters as mentioned by me above, and it will not be long before the new Association has split.

Sir Purshotamdas Thakurdas then went on to make the very illuminating comment:

I believe that there is great scope for co-operation between Indian and European merchants and industrialists, but that can only be successful when the Europeans reconcile themselves to what I said in my speech at Calcutta before the Viceroy last December, viz. that Indian commerce and industry are only an integral phase of Indian nationalism, and that deprived of its inspiration in Indian nationalism Indian commerce and Indian industry stand reduced to mere exploitation.[33]

G. D. Birla expressed complete agreement with these sentiments: 'I can very clearly see the insincerity of Labour Leaders who are vilifying Gandhiji and Nehru but I find it difficult to understand the stupid mentality of the Mill-Owners who in their interests are losing the sympathy of all right-thinking men.'[34] A few days afterwards he wrote again to Sir Purshotamdas: 'The salvation of the capitalist does not lie in joining hands with the reactionary element. Why is it that Sir Ibrahim could not influence Mr Subhas Bose when the latter threatened a strike in the Tatas? The reason is obvious. Men of his type do not command confidence. The politicians feel that our capitalists are out for exploitation hand in hand with the foreign capitalists, and this new association can only confirm the suspicion.'[35]

Sir Dorabji Tata's project for a United Capitalist Party was still-born. The reasons were obvious. The gulf between European and Indian businessmen was too wide to be bridged by a multi-racial party. As Birla pointed out, the members of the projected party carried weight neither with the masses, nor with the middle classes. Although the plan did not succeed, its very failure was a significant event. The controversy highlighted two alternative strategies for Indian capitalists and pointed out which strategy was the politically feasible one in the prevailing situation. It was proved beyond question that a united front of European and Indian capitalists, allied with the administration against national aspirations, was not a feasible strategy. It was also substantially proved that the logical strategy for big business in India was to work through the existing nationalist parties for the attainment of those national objectives which were also their own. Mark once again the very significant words of Sir Purshotamdas Thakurdas: Indian commerce and industry were only an integral phase of Indian nationalism, and deprived of its inspiration in Indian nationalism, Indian industry

[33] Ibid., P. Thakurdas to N. M. Mazumdar, 7 June 1929.
[34] Ibid., Birla to Thakurdas, 19 June 1929.
[35] Ibid., pt V, Birla to Thakurdas, 30 July 1929.

and Indian commerce stood reduced to mere exploitation of labour. The *raison d'être* of Indian capitalism was its identification with national progress, on both political and economic fronts. The Indian capitalist class, a weak and repressed element in the colonialized structure of India's underdeveloped economy, was not strong enough to stand on its own, and could not do without the support of the Indian National Congress. That body was a coalition of many interests and aspirations beyond the control of capitalists, but henceforth there was a steady interpenetration of Congress and big business.

Civil Disobedience and the Indian Capitalist Class

The process of Congress–big-business interpenetration started in right earnest with the civil disobedience movement and the Round Table Conference, though it must be pointed out at the outset that Congress never became an instrument of big business as such, being a national coalition of many politicized elements with which big business ultimately had to come to a compromise. The Congress Raj which emerged after 1947 amidst the tensions of this dynamic adjustment has been controversially depicted as an intermediate regime, standing midway between a fully socialist regime and a capitalist regime under big business hegemony.[36] The ambiguities of policy which flowed from this stalemate of social forces and produced such important consequences for the subsequent development of the Indian economy fall outside the scope of this work. But it is clearly important to trace the beginnings of the Congress–big-business interpenetration in view of its long-term impact on subsequent economic and political history.

There were important divisions within the Indian capitalist class and the Indian National Congress, and the interpenetration naturally took place at the periphery of each, along the points of contact between those elements on each side which were closest to each other. The complexities of this interpenetration, so pregnant with explosive tensions, must not be underrated. The differences of approach to the Congress and its policies within the top FICCI leadership contributed to these complexities.

The initiation of the Civil Disobedience Movement by the Congress

[36] See K. N. Raj, 'The Politics and Economics of Intermediate Regimes', in *Economic and Political Weekly*, 7 July 1973.

brought out these differences of approach within the FICCI leadership. Sir Purshotamdas had always favoured the following policy: 'Cooperate with your elected members in the Councils, by means of Indian tax-payers' money, for the solid, sure and substantial advancement of India.'[37] This was no counsel of collaboration. At the beginning of 1930 we find Sir Purshotamdas, in association with Motilal Nehru and M. M. Malaviya, getting a resolution passed through the Legislative Assembly for further transference of powers to Indians in conformity with Congress demands.[38] But he was certainly against non-cooperation with constitutional reforms, the reason why he had played a prominent role in the Anti-Non-Cooperation Committee in Bombay. In his view, working the reforms and pushing for further doses of reforms was the quickest and surest approach to power. With this strategy G. D. Birla was in agreement, but his attitude to non-cooperation and civil disobedience was much more ambiguous. Explaining his political position, he told the Governor of Bengal in 1932 (as recorded in his diary): 'I told him that I was one of the worst critics of the Government in political and economic spheres. Though I did not take any active part in the Civil Disobedience Movement I had done everything else to embarrass the Government and had liberally subscribed to Gandhiji's constructive programmes.'[39] Apparently Birla was quite sincere about not being a participant in civil disobedience and took mortal offence when in 1940 Viceroy Linlithgow, with whom he had friendly relations, refused to see him on the ground that he was financing it. 'My devotion was to Bapu, to whom I could refuse nothing and who was accustomed to turn to me in all his plans. But Bapu was well aware that I was not a Congressman and he did not either ask me to subscribe to the Civil Disobedience Movement funds or divert any of the sums received through me for such a purpose.'[40] Linlithgow, however, was objectively right when he refused to make the fine distinctions about the purpose of Birla's financial contributions, about which the latter was so serious. His large donations to the constructive programme strengthened the Congress organization considerably as an instrument capable of mobilizing people; and it was the khadi and other constructive

---

[37] Purshotamdas Thakurdas Papers, file no. 24, address by P. Thakurdas at Surat.

[38] Ibid., file no. 40, cutting from *The Times*, 20 February 1930.

[39] Birla, op. cit., p. 55.   [40] Ibid., p. 276.

workers who turned out in large numbers as Congress volunteers in civil disobedience, so that no direct diversion of funds received from Birla by Gandhi for the constructive programmes to civil disobedience was necessary. Birla may have been serious about his refusal to subscribe to the Congress creed, but Lord Linlithgow was more concerned about his penetrating informal contacts with the Congress leadership than with his fine ideological distinctions.

Immediately on the outbreak of civil disobedience, tensions within the FICCI leadership became apparent with regard to the FICCI policy towards the Round Table Conference and the Civil Disobedience Movement. In a confidential letter late in the year 1930 to Sir Purshotamdas Thakurdas, Ambalal Sarabhai, Ahmedabad mill-owner and a disciple of Gandhi, took the stance that the Civil Disobedience Movement was not unconstitutional and so the Federation should take up the boycott of foreign goods and push it vigorously. He felt that the Round Table Conference, shunned by both Congress and FICCI, would not be able to come to any settlement on the communal question and so the possibility of obtaining Dominion Status was very remote.[41] P. Thakurdas, who had been opposed to the movement since its inception in spring, replied that civil disobedience might not be unconstitutional, but it could certainly prove a very dangerous weapon in the hands of a largely illiterate population.[42] This attitude had already provoked local Congress hostility in Bombay. Throughout the year bulletins published by the Bombay Congress under the control of extremist left wing elements stridently condemned the 'plutocrats', especially P. Thakurdas, for opposing boycott and picketing. But P. Thakurdas, who would otherwise have liked to attend the first Round Table Conference along with the moderates, had to bow to the FICCI mandate against it. He refused to go to London even in his personal capacity when the FICCI instructed its members not to attend the Conference on an official or personal basis. Younger members had gained ascendancy in the Indian Merchants' Chamber in Bombay and they were very hostile to participation in RTC committee work.[43] The ordinarily cordial relations between the European and Indian business communities in Bombay had reached

[41] Purshotamdas Thakurdas Papers, file no. 42, pt VII, Sarabhai to Thakurdas, 17 November 1930.

[42] Ibid., Thakurdas to Sarabhai, 18 November 1930.

[43] Ibid., file no. 104.

their nadir. The Bombay Native Piece-goods Merchants' Association was threatening to repudiate contractual obligations with British businessmen if the political demands of the Congress were not met and had passed a resolution condemning police measures against *satyagrahis*. Exchange of letters for establishing peace between the Indian Merchants' Chamber and the Bombay Chamber of Commerce did nothing to resolve the growing business conflict between the two races.[44]

Meanwhile lines of communication had been opened up between the Marwari piece-goods merchants in Calcutta and the Gujarati mill-owners in Ahmedabad for eliminating imports from Manchester. Instrumental in setting up this Ahmedabad–Calcutta axis was G. D. Birla, who on behalf of the big Marwari importers of cloth approached Ambalal Sarabhai as the representative of the Ahmedabad mill-owners.[45] Naturally the political views of these two disciples of Gandhi were closer to each other than to those of Sir Purshotamdas Thakurdas, who cultivated good relations with the European business community in Bombay. However, Birla's approach to the whole political problem was much more sophisticated than that of Sarabhai, who was primarily concerned with *swadeshi* and boycott. From the inception of civil disobedience Birla looked forward to the ultimate settlement between the Raj and the Congress, and while taking care not to participate in the movement, he gave it quiet approval as a means of bringing pressure on the British to come to the desired settlement. At the beginning of 1931 he wrote to P. Thakurdas:

Regarding the present agitation and the results of the Round Table Conference, I agreed that we should try our best to get the country out of the present political turmoil. But I do not see my way clear so far. There could be no doubt that what we are being offered at present is entirely due to Gandhiji. Even the papers in America and the Continent have confessed this and cartoons are being published depicting Mahatmaji moving like a ghost around Westminster. This leads one to the conclusion that if we are to achieve what we desire the present movement should not be allowed to slacken. We should, therefore, have two objects in view: one is that we should jump in at the most opportune time for a reconciliation and the other is that we should

[44] *One Hundred Years of Bombay*, p. 153.

[45] Purshotamdas Thakurdas Papers, file no. 100, Birla to Sarabhai, 30 April 1930; also, Sumit Sarkar, 'The Logic of Gandhian Nationalism: Civil Disobedience and the Gandhi–Irwin Pact 1930–1', *Indian Historical Review*, July 1976.

not do anything which might weaken the hands of those through whose efforts we have arrived at this stage.[46]

Birla's letter neatly summed up what amounted to a long-term strategy of applying steady, mounting and relentless pressure, seizing every point conceded by the opponent, and working each successive parcel of reforms for all they were worth in order to gather strength for demanding the next act in the transfer of power. Lala Shri Ram, elected President of the FICCI in 1930, guided the Federation along the lines chalked out by G. D. Birla rather than P. Thakurdas during the troubled times of civil disobedience. Under him FICCI declared its adherence to the minimum eleven-point programme of reforms insisted upon by Gandhi. 'No constitution', read its resolution, 'will be acceptable to the country including the Indian mercantile community which does not give sufficient and effective power to a responsible Indian Government to carry out the administrative and economic reforms indicated by Mahatma Gandhi in his eleven points and which does not vest full economic control in the legislature of India.'[47] The Federation resolved that unless Gandhi attended the Round Table Conference, it would not send any representative of Indian business and would not allow any member to attend even in his personal capacity. It also recorded its protest against police atrocities on passive resisters. When, upon the conclusion of the Gandhi–Irwin Pact, Gandhi decided to go to the RTC, the Federation also sent its nominee. As soon as the second RTC failed and civil disobedience was resumed, the Federation announced its refusal to participate in the RTC in protest against the incarceration of Gandhi and police repression.[48] Lala Shri Ram, as President of the FICCI, then organized the Swadeshi Prachar Association which drew up a list of mills which did not use foreign yarn and stamped their product as genuine *swadeshi*. Shri Ram, himself a big mill-owner of the DCM textile complex, insisted that there was to be no profiteering under the conditions of boycott of foreign cloth and that mill-owners must undertake not to make more than 8 per cent profit.[49]

[46] Ibid., file no. 42, pt VII, Birla to Thakurdas, 16 January 1930.

[47] *Indian Chamber of Commerce Report 1930*, Presidential address of D. P. Khaitan, 11 February 1931.

[48] Purshotamdas Thakurdas Papers, file no. 42, pt VII, FICCI press communiqué dated 24 January 1924.

[49] *Shri Ram*, pp. 200–1.

By the spring of 1931 FICCI was claiming a return on its heavy political investment in the Congress, insisting that in all economic matters Congress should consult FICCI before formulating any policy. Shri Ram persuaded Gandhi to open the annual meeting of FICCI on 7 April 1931. At this meeting he voiced the complaint,

It has happened time and again that the Congress had committed itself to certain economic ideas of far-reaching effect without consulting the business community. Economics is our field and we could be of real service to the country and the Congress. . . . We should therefore suggest to you, Sir [Mahatma Gandhi], a sort of convention for the future that in all matters pertaining to the realm of economics, the Congress before making up its mind will allow us to offer it our suggestions and if necessary have discussions with our members.[50]

Gandhi, graciously accepting Shri Ram's suggestion, replied: 'I want you to make the Congress your own and we will willingly surrender the reins to you. The work can be better done by you.' Gandhi also imposed the condition that the Federation must regard themselves as 'trustees and servants of the poor'.

Your commerce [he added] must be regulated for the benefit of the toiling millions and you must be satisfied with earning an honest penny. I do not for a moment believe that commercial prosperity is incompatible with strict honesty. I know businessmen who are absolutely honest and scrupulous in their dealings. It is thus easily open to you to take charge of the Congress.[51]

In these mutual exchanges of Shri Ram and Gandhi, the formation of a fairly close liaison between the Federation and the Congress was clearly in evidence. Indian big business, in its rationale and self-image, was consciously rooted in nationalism, without which, as Sir Purshotamdas Thakurdas had explicitly stated, it stood reduced to mere exploitation of the masses. On the other hand, the National Congress, in the person of Gandhi, was clearly offering big businessmen an ideology of trusteeship that carried conviction in their own minds, resolved their inner doubts about their proper role, and lent substance to their self-image.

But the Congress, which contained leftist elements, was not a monolithic block; and within big business the tensions in respect of the approach towards civil disobedience continued. On the eve of his resignation from the FICCI Presidentship, Lala Shri Ram, who

[50] Ibid., p. 201.   [51] Ibid., p. 202.

had been instrumental in lining up the Federation behind the Congress, split with Birla as he wanted to modify the non-cooperation resolution taken after the break-up of the second RTC and the resumption of civil disobedience. At his insistence the Federation adopted a compromise resolution condemning government repression but also recording the FICCI's 'duty to take part in the framing of a suitable constitution for India'.[52] Relations between Birla and Shri Ram remained cool to the end of Shri Ram's life. After the outbreak of the Second World War, Shri Ram insisted that the Congress must not bargain with the British government and squeeze out promises until the war was over.[53] In spite of these disagreements, under the triumvirate of P. Thakurdas, G. D. Birla and Lala Shri Ram, the relations of the Federation with the Congress continued to grow closer. The very tensions within the Congress and the Federation with regard to their mutual relationship, in so far as temporary solutions and compromises were achieved for containing these tensions, assisted the growing interpenetration of the Congress and big business during the next period of intensive bargaining over constitutional reforms leading to the Congress assumption of office in 1937.

The Reforms of 1935

In the long and tortuous process of negotiations, resulting in the Act of 1935, G. D. Birla apparently played a crucial role. He, more than any one else, shaped the long-term political strategy of the Indian capitalist class during the thirties. In the first place, this strategy involved a closer liaison between big business and the Congress centre in order to counteract the increasing activities of leftist politicians within the Congress. Secondly, the crux of the national demand was seen to lie in full national control over economic policy, and in order to achieve this end Birla was prepared to let the British have their way on other issues for the moment. Thirdly, his tactics for achieving the goal of full economic control was to promote informal contacts between the Viceroy and his officials on the one hand and Gandhi and his centrist lieutenants on the other in order to break the deadlock arising out of the Civil Disobedience

[52] Ibid., p. 205.
[53] Purshotamdas Thakurdas Papers, file no. 239, pt I, Shri Ram to Amritlal Ojha, May 1940.

Movement. These aspects of the consciously laid-out strategy were closely interrelated, for it was the impatient and immature left wing within the Congress which was seen to constitute the main threat to a necessary and useful compromise between the Government and the Congress, and thereby to endanger the attainment of economic control in the immediate future.

At the beginning of the Civil Disobedience Movement, G. D. Birla had suggested to Motilal Nehru a settlement with the British on the basis of reservation of the army by the British government. Motilal insisted that the grant of the right of secession was the test of Great Britain's sincerity, no compromise being possible without this concession. 'I was not convinced on this point', wrote Birla to Thakurdas,

but he said although we didn't want to secede, so long as Great Britain was afraid of secession that merely showed that they wanted to continue their present exploitation. He agreed with me that full economic control was the crux of the full demand and he also told me that Jawaharlalji entirely agreed with me. But he said so long as the army of occupation remained in India we could not have full economic control. There is much in what he said but it appeared to me that when proper time came for a settlement he would not insist on impossible terms.[54]

Birla, in a pragmatic approach to self-government, wanted full control of finance and felt that the 'safeguards' included by the British in the financial clauses of the proposed constitution took away ninety-nine per cent of the control after granting full control to Indians in a formal sense. He identified these safeguards as the Reserve Bank, the Statutory Railway Board, the Consolidated Fund Charge for debt service, salaries and pensions, the army and the power of the Governor-General to intervene.[55] Regarding the army, he told the Governor of Bengal, Sir John Anderson,

we realized we could not get immediate control but Gandhiji would suggest certain formulae which may be acceptable to all. About finance we were prepared to put ourselves in the position of a factory proprietor who had to deal with debenture holders. The debenture holder should not poke his nose into our day to day affairs so long as we paid him his dues.[56]

Birla realized that the only hope of securing 'the crux of the full

[54] Ibid., file no. 42, pt VII, Birla to Thakurdas, 28 November 1930.
[55] G. D. Birla, op. cit., pp. 42–5.   [56] Ibid., p. 56.

demand' was to bring the Congress leaders to a compromise with the British. To promote personal contacts between the two parties with a view to breaking the deadlock, he went to London in 1935 and campaigned actively to get the reforms going.[57] He wanted the reforms to be set in motion although for the moment eighty per cent of the revenue was engaged to the services and the debt.[58] This willingness to moderate the demand for full financial control was induced by the repeated assurances of the British leaders that they were earnest about responsible government in India. He wrote to Gandhi from London that in his estimate the British would not use the constitutional safeguards for meddling with the affairs of ministers. Mere sweet words, he wrote, had never impressed him in his business dealings and he believed that all this talk did not merely represent hollow sentiments.[59]

The increasing activity of socialist radicals within the Congress, however, filled him with anxiety, for their influence was directed precisely against the kind of compromise that he was trying so strenuously to bring about. His strategy for counteracting the pressure of socialists was to forge a close alliance between the Congress centre and big business.

You know [he wrote to Thakurdas on 3 August 1934] the mischief which is being done by the so-called Socialist party. In U.P. a lot of irresponsible writing is being spread. Gandhiji has taken up a very hostile attitude to this. He has said many things publicly but many more privately to the socialists which when [they] come in cold print are likely to give the greatest provocation to the socialists. Vallabhbhai, Rajaji and Rajendra Babu are all fighting communism and socialism. It is therefore necessary that we who represent healthy capitalism should help Gandhiji as far as possible and work with a common object.'[59]

Many loyalist businessmen, especially the pro-government sections of the Bombay mill-owning class, were incapable of appreciating the subtle methods of G. D. Birla. What Birla was seeking to achieve was a closer rapport between the national movement and big business, an object with which they did not sympathize. They were moreover frightened by the growth of socialism within the Congress. There was a fresh Communist scare in 1936, a year after the reforms were passed, which seemed to endanger Birla's moves to persuade the Congress to accept office under the reforms.

[57] Ibid., p. 156.   [58] Ibid., pp. 165–6.   [59] Ibid., p. 164.

Acceptance of office by the Congress was central to his scheme for obtaining financial control. The socialist radicals in the Congress were opposed to the acceptance of office. While Birla was trying to counter them from within the Congress by strengthening the hands of Gandhi, certain sections of the Bombay capitalists gave way to hysteria against the newly elected socialist President of the Congress, Jawaharlal Nehru.

The occasion for this new fear of Communism was young Nehru's socialist speeches as Congress President, at a time when a tussle was going on within the Congress over acceptance of office. Birla, who was not unduly disturbed by the young man's socialist talk, saw clearly that acceptance or rejection of office by the Congress was the central issue. Other businessmen, who lacked his clarity of vision, were frightened by Nehru's expression of socialist sentiments. Twenty-one 'Mercantile Leaders' of Bombay issued a manifesto denouncing Nehru's socialist tendencies. The incident was an unpleasant surprise for Nehru, but no less so for Birla, who saw in such open denunciation a loss of leverage within the Congress.[60]

The twenty-one signatories to the manifesto against Nehru's socialism included only two members of the FICCI leadership, P. Thakurdas and Walchand Hirachand, who were quickly brought back into line by the admonitions of G. D. Birla. Otherwise, as bio-data about the signatories collected by Nehru showed, they were opposed to Congress policies.[61] The principal business interests represented by them were the Tata group, the Bombay mill-owning class and foreign insurance, match, cotton and textile interests. Sir Naoroji Saklatwala was the head of the house of Tatas. P. Thakurdas and A. D. Shroff were both represented on the boards of Tata concerns. H. P. Mody was the sponsor of the politically unpopular Modi–Lees Pact between Lancashire and Bombay. Sir V. N. Chandavarkar, nominated Vice-Chancellor of the Bombay University by the Government, was the President of the Bombay Mill-Owners' Association. Sir Cowasjee Jahangir, a prominent figure in the previous 'red scare' of 1928, was a textile magnate and a champion of the British connection. Seth Iswardas Laxmidas, an aspirant for knighthood and an ex-sheriff of Bombay, was connected with the Sassoons, the biggest foreign textile group in Bombay. Seth Mathura-

[60] Purshotamdas Thakurdas Papers, file no. 42, pt VII.
[61] For a more detailed account, *see* Bipan Chandra, 'Jawaharlal Nehru and the Indian Capitalist Class', Indian History Congress, 1974.

das Vissonji, who was connected with certain foreign houses and was interested in Australian wheat, had been instrumental in breaking the boycott of foreign cotton firms in Bombay during civil disobedience. Sir Pheroze Sethna, a representative of foreign insurance companies and chairman of Swedish match manufacturing interests in India, was a liberal leader who had always opposed the Congress. Among other signatories to the Bombay manifesto against the President of the Congress were nonentities like Sir Shapurji Bilimoria, 'a colourless gentleman' who audited the companies of big groups, and Rahimtoola Chinoy, who had been pushed into positions of advantage because he was a Muslim. Both were protégés of the government. One prominent signatory, a liberal leader who had served as a member of the Executive Council of the Government of Bombay, was Sir Chimanlal Setalvad, a leading lawyer of the local High Court who had never been a merchant at all.

Reacting sharply and swiftly against the Bombay manifesto, G. D. Birla pulled up his colleagues in FICCI who had openly sided with anti-Congress business interests against the formally elected President of the Congress. To Walchand Hirachand he wrote severely:

Do you think you were right in signing that manifesto against Jawaharlal? If its merits are to be judged by the results then I must say that you have been instrumental in creating further opposition to capitalism. You have rendered no service to your castemen. It is curious how we businessmen are so short-sighted. We all are against socialism and yet nothing is being done to carry on argumentative propaganda and even people like Vallabhbhai and Bhulabhai who are fighting against socialism are not being helped. It looks very crude for a man with property to say that he is opposed to expropriation in the wider interest of the country. It goes without saying that anyone holding property will oppose expropriation. I do not mean that expropriation is not against higher interests but the question is, 'Are you or myself a fit person to talk?' Let those who have given up property say what you want to say. If we can only strengthen their hands, we can help everyone. Apart from this, our duty does not end in simply opposing socialism. Businessmen have to do something positive to ameliorate the condition of the masses. I feel that your manifesto, far from helping, has done positive harm to the capitalistic system.[62]

To P. Thakurdas, his elder, Birla wrote in a milder tone of complaint:

[62] Purshotamdas Thakurdas Papers, file no. 177, G. D. Birla to Walchand Hirachand, 26 May 1936.

About your signature on the manifesto, need I tell you that I was painfully surprised to see your name in the crowd? Of course, on principle we are all opposed to socialism or communism, but in my opinion the way in which the manifesto was worded did not do full justice to Jawaharlal. Have you heard it commented in the press that the manifesto has virtually demanded Jawaharlal's arrest? This is the last thing you intended. . . . The manifesto has given impetus to the forces working against capitalism—another result which you did not intend. I have not come across one paper putting a favourable comment on the manifesto.[63]

Within a few days of the publication of the Bombay manifesto, it became clear that not merely the advanced and far-sighted sections of the leadership of FICCI, but also the nationalistic mass of 'marketeers' in western India, had disowned the petulant outburst of the Tata group, the Bombay mill-owning class and foreign business interests.[64] On the very day the manifesto was published, the marketeers of the Bombay Bullion Exchange, presenting Nehru with a purse of Rs 1,500, expressed their satisfaction at his devoted work for 'the uplift of the peasants and workers of India'. Next day, other marketeers in Bombay—especially brokers in cotton, seeds and grains as well as Marwari and other native merchants in miscellaneous branches of trade—rushed to present Nehru with another address. On the day after that Nehru received further eulogistic addresses from grain merchants, sugar merchants, seed merchants, grain dealers and country-made fancy and grey cotton piece-goods merchants, in one of which his ceaseless work for the betterment of the conditions of the teeming millions of workers, labourers and peasants of India was warmly praised. Finally fifteen leading members of the aggressively nationalistic Indian Merchants' Chamber of Bombay met Jawaharlal Nahru, affirming their continued support of the Congress and assuring him that the Bombay manifesto did not reflect the sentiments of the mercantile community as a whole. Nehru was requested 'to explain what he meant by socialism, when it would be achieved and whether the merchants with their limitations could give their quota in the movement of socialism'.

The Bombay manifesto thus succeeded merely in provoking a reaction that revealed the extent to which the political sentiments of the merchant communities of India had been radicalized by the mid-thirties. The 'red' spectre was capable of frightening the pro-

---

[63] Ibid., Birla to Thakurdas, 1 June 1936.
[64] For details, see Bipan Chandra, op. cit.

British sections of the topmost business and manufacturing class of
Bombay. But in the country as a whole the mercantile community—especially the intermediaries in various markets who had
come under the pressure of trade depression—had come to realize
that the conditions of the masses and their purchasing capacity had
a very close bearing on the conditions of trade and industry. The
President of the Country-Made Fancy and Grey Cotton Piece-goods
Merchants Associations specifically said in his speech of welcome to
Nehru that 'we are of the opinion that our advancement is inter-
dependent upon the advancement of the masses'.[65] A substantial
range of Indian business interests had thus begun to see in mild
socialist measures a means of expansion of the domestic market and
consequent recovery of trade and industry.

There was to be no more frontal attack by 'capitalists' on socialism. In subsequent years the Indian capitalist class as a whole including the Tata group and the Bombay mill-owners, moved in favour
of socialist control and planning of the economy. The growing
solidarity of that class—its consciousness of itself as a distinct element in Indian society—had been underlined by G. D. Birla's ad-
monition to Walchand: 'You have rendered no service to your
castemen'. There was, moreover, greater appreciation by businessmen of the political strategy of Birla, who had consistently opposed
the formation of a distinct capitalist group adopting an independent capitalist role in politics, and had preferred to work indirectly through the Congress centre. As the Congress slowly moved
towards accepting office, all kinds of businessmen gathered around it.

Refusing to be perturbed by Nehru's socialist utterances, G. D.
Birla had insisted throughout the crisis that a realistic understanding
with Jawaharlal was both possible and desirable. He pointed out
to Sir Purshotamdas that Nehru's speech as Congress President was
in a way thrown into the waste-paper basket since all the resolutions
passed by the Congress were against the spirit of that speech. Only a
small minority of 100 had voted for Nehru at the Congress session,
as against 600 opposed to his programme. Nehru, to his credit, had
fully realized his position and had not abused his powers as Congress
President. Most important of all, the Working Committee of the
Congress which he had selected contained an overwhelming majority
of the 'Mahatmaji group'. He could have caused a split by resigning,
but he did not. From his conduct at the Congress, Birla concluded:

[65] Ibid.

'Jawaharlalji seems to be like a typical English democrat who takes defeat in a sporting spirit. He seems to be out for giving expression to his ideology, but he realizes that action is impossible and so does not press for it. He confessed in his speech that tall talk was a bad habit in India and that there was no chance of any direct action in the near future.'[66] Birla felt confident that things were moving 'in the right direction', and events proved him right. Sir Purshotamdas Thakurdas agreed with him: 'I never had any doubt about the bona fides of J; in fact, I put them very high indeed', but he also felt that 'a good deal of nursing will have to be done to keep J on the right rails all through'.[67] Nehru was, indeed, carefully nursed back to the main Congress line of approach by his mentor, whom he called Bapu. The Indian National Congress accepted office in 1937, and the decision caused no split in the Congress, no break-away of the socialist wing.

Indian Capitalism on the Offensive

Indian businessmen generally, including those who had been consistently loyalist, came to have a greater appreciation of the commercial and industrial benefits of national rule from their experience of the Congress tenure in office from 1937 to 1939. Congress rule in the provinces coincided with the passing of the Great Depression. Together these two factors induced investment in several new fields and the initiation of new industrial enterprises. The tightness of the money market had now disappeared and both export and import trade showed signs of revival. There was, as the President of the Indian Chamber of Commerce noted in his Presidential address, smooth progress in the political sphere due to the successful working of Congress ministries in seven provinces. Conditions were stable and encouraging for the growth of Indian capitalism.[68] These developments disarmed the opposition of many hitherto loyalist businessmen to the Congress.

Far from proving a signal for expropriation, Congress rule was seen by businessmen of all sorts to provide the kind of patronage

[66] Purshotamdas Thakurdas Papers, file no. 177, Birla to Thakurdas, 20 April 1936.
[67] Ibid., Thakurdas to Birla, 23 April 1936.
[68] *Indian Chamber of Commerce Report 1937*, Presidential address of M. L. Shah, 25 February 1938.

necessary for the flotation of new ventures (such as Walchand's Premier Automobiles) which had so long been impracticable on account of official indifference. Then came the outbreak of the Second World War and the Congress resignation from office. The government patronage which had been extended to several new flotations during Congress rule was suddenly withdrawn under the bureaucratic administration. Government adopted a generally obstructive attitude to such ventures as automobile and aircraft manufacture, shipbuilding and manufacture of textile machinery and sewing machines. Splendid opportunities of war production in new technological directions were lost on account of the Government of India's insistence on supply of necessary raw materials for the conduct of war. Had the Congress ministries been in power, they could have offered valuable help to ambitious industrialists like Walchand, Shri Ram and Birla in numerous ways. New demand had been created for several products, of which no advantage could be taken on account of the unimaginative war production policy of bureaucrats and military officers. The contrast between imperial and national administration could not have been sharper. The absence of the Congress from office was clearly seen by Indian businessmen to be a hindrance to industrial growth.

In consequence a new truculent note crept into the political attitudes of the Indian business world. Once again the 'marketeers' were in the lead in offering political opposition to the administration. Upon the arrest of Congress leaders in August 1942, business activities in the country were outwardly suspended by merchants. Of course private dealings took place very freely, so that business did not go down far below the normal level. In course of time merchants realized this and the commodity and stock exchanges were reopened. However, it was not until December that normal trading was resumed in the Bombay area.[69] The prolonged outward suspension of business activity from August to December was an indication of the extent of alienation of the Indian mercantile community in western India.

This form of protest by businessmen petered out, as it was bound to do. But there was plenty of evidence that the Bombay merchant community had lost all patience with foreign rule. They were eagerly expecting and looking forward to home rule at the end of the war. They expressed their expectations repeatedly in strident and violent

[69] *Report of the Bombay Mill-owners' Association 1942.*

terms.[70] Indian capitalism, which had reached a certain degree of maturity after 1937, was now ready to burst the bonds of the imperial economic framework that had nurtured and constricted it.

Congress rule from 1937 to 1939, which was an important factor in this development of Indian capitalism, initiated a counter-offensive against foreign business interests. The *Harijan*, Gandhi's paper, announced on 26 March 1938:

It has become a fashion nowadays to bamboozle the unwary public by adding '(India) Limited' to full-blooded British concerns. Lever Brothers '(India) Limited' have their factories here now. They claim to produce *swadeshi* soap and have already ruined several large and small soap factories in Bengal. Then there is the Imperial Chemical (India) Ltd. which has received valuable concessions. This is dumping foreign *industries* instead of foreign *goods* on us.[71]

The *Harijan* went on to say that in addition to the '(India) Limiteds' there were companies with Indian directors but in fact managed by non-Indians. Gandhi pronounced that he had no objection to foreign capital as such, but he insisted that management must be in Indian hands for an industrial undertaking to be truly *swadeshi*.

The occasion for this pronouncement was the dispute between the Killick Nixon-controlled Bombay Steam Navigation Ltd. and Walchand's Scindia Steam Navigation Ltd. The dispute was important not so much for the volume of shipping involved as the solidarity which Indian business interests achieved on this issue with the aid of Congress leaders. From 1936 the Scindia Steam Navigation Co., which had taken over two small Indian lines plying on the Konkan Coast, had introduced three steamers in the Goa trade, hitherto a close preserve of Bombay Steam Navigation Ltd., and had reduced rates by 50 per cent. Scindias also threatened the Bombay Steam Navigation Company's Karachi–Mangalore–Aleppey trade and spared no effort to acquire control of that company. In retaliation Killick Nixon proposed to enter the Burma rice trade, in which Scindias enjoyed a privileged position. The dispute placed Sir Purshotamdas Thakurdas in a delicate position. He was a director of Bombay Steam Navigation Ltd., and was called upon by the company's managing agents, Killick Nixon, to render all

[70] *See especially* the *Annual Reports of the Indian Merchants' Chamber* during the Second World War.

[71] Purshotamdas Thakurdas Papers, file no. 205, cutting of *Harijan*, 26 March 1938.

possible aid. At the same time he was asked by Vallabhbhai Patel and G. D. Birla to resign from the company and to help Scindias obtain two seats on its board. P. Thakurdas refused at first to entertain this request. But a press campaign was mounted, the Congress gave important political aid to Walchand, and Thakurdas came under irresistible pressure from his colleagues, especially G. D. Birla. A misunderstanding had arisen between Thakurdas and Walchand over the leadership of the Indian Merchants' Chamber in Bombay and this might have initially influenced Sir Purshotamdas to take an adverse attitude to the demands of the Scindia Steam Navigation Co. But in the face of pressure from the FICCI leadership he could not long maintain this attitude. Under the joint arbitration of P. Thakurdas and G. D. Birla, the managing agency of Bombay Steam Navigation Ltd. was ultimately transferred from Killick Nixon to Scindias.

This was a remarkable demonstration of the closing of ranks by nationalist businessmen against foreign interests in spite of the connections which necessarily existed between Indian and European business interests. The affair also showed the importance of Congress rule to Indian capitalism, for Walchand's triumph was in no small measure due to the valuable aid which he had received from Vallabhbhai Patel.[72]

Planning and Capitalism

Nothing demonstrated the radicalization of the Indian business world more clearly than the attitude of important business groups to the planning of the entire economy by the government. The Congress economic programme, largely inspired by Jawaharlal Nehru, had come to embrace socialist planning. Upon coming into power in seven provinces, the Congress initiated measures for planning. A conference of ministers of industries from provinces amenable to the Congress programme met in Delhi in October 1938 under the Congress President, Subhas Bose. The conference appointed a National Planning Committee, including well-known leaders of the business world, such as Purshotamdas Thakurdas, A. D. Shroff, Ambalal Sarabhai and Walchand Hirachand.[73] Two prominent

[72] Ibid., file on Bombay Steam Navigation Ltd., 1937–40.
[73] K. T. Shah, *Handbook of the National Planning Committee*, Bombay, 1946, pp. 7–8.

signatories to the Bombay manifesto of 1936 against Nehru's socialism, Sir Purshotamdas and Walchand, were now important members of the Planning Committee.

The swing of Indian business opinion in favour of a planned economy on the lines proposed by the Congress was reflected in the speech of the President of the Indian Chamber of Commerce at the beginning of 1939. Reviewing the developments of 1938, A. R. Dalal, the President of the Chamber, pronounced on 27 February 1939:

The step taken during the course of the year by the Indian National Congress in collaboration with the various Provincial Governments in establishing a Planning Committee to survey and prepare the ground for the formulation of an all-India scheme for India's economic regeneration should be welcomed by us as a move in the right direction.[74]

Since the Birla group dominated the Indian Chamber of Commerce, the speech of A. R. Dalal obviously reflected the expectations of growth of Indian capitalism. At the beginning of 1939 leading Indian industrialists were hoping that the new economic policy of the Congress in power would enable them to break out of the constraints imposed by the imperial framework of the economy.

In marked contrast with Indian business opinion, European business opinion was hostile to the activities of the National Planning Committee. The National Planning Committee circulated a questionnaire in 1939 that aroused the lively apprehensions of the European business community in India. The Bengal Chamber of Commerce consulted the Upper India and Bombay Chambers of Commerce, the Assocham and the European party in the Bengal legislature, and decided to make no reply to the questionnaire as neither the Government of India nor the anti-Congress Government of Bengal intended to take action on it. But the Bengal Chamber explored 'the dangers to British commercial and industrial interests in certain of the questions framed by the National Planning Committee'.[75] It was decided not to act in haste as that would create an atmosphere of panic. But it was resolved to refer the proposals antagonistic to British interests to the associations of the particular industries concerned to prepare them against any attack and to

[74] *Indian Chamber of Commerce Report 1938*, Presidential address of A. R. Dalal, 27 February 1939.
[75] BCC Committee meeting, 4 April 1939.

collate necessary information from the various affected trade associations.

With the outbreak of war in September 1939 this threatened advance towards national planning was suddenly interrupted. The Congress resigned from office to the great relief of European business interests, and no more was heard of a restructuring of the economy through planned allocation of resources. Certainly there was war planning. But that was with a view to mobilizing the resources for war, not for the peace-time growth of India's industry at the end of the war. Had the Congress remained in office, wartime controls and the enhanced powers of government might have enabled the Congress leaders to achieve a swift transition towards a constructive allocation of resources with long-term ends in view. As it was, planning was not adopted until the early fifties, at a point when India was poised for a drastic acceleration of the growth of her population. This increased rate of population growth from the fifties largely neutralized the benefits of industrial expansion under the Five Year Plans. In retrospect, it is impossible not to regard the Congress decision to resign from office as a serious blow to the prospects of India's economic progress.

That the Indian business class had not favoured planning in 1938–9 simply in order to propitiate the party in power was soon to be proved. That class *as a whole* was seriously committed to planning, and this became clear after the Congress had resigned from office. The dissatisfaction of Indian industrialists with the war planning of the Government of India contributed to this crystallization of opinion. In 1944 the leading men of Indian business and industry came together to publish what is known as the Bombay Plan for the development of India.[76]

The eight signatories to the Bombay Plan were representative of a wide cross-section of India's business world. In proper order of succession these signatories were Sir Purshotamdas Thakurdas, 'King Cotton' of Bombay; J. R. D. Tata, of the house of Jamsetji Tata; G. D. Birla, representing the second biggest business house in India; Sir Ardeshir Dalal, a Parsi stockbroker of the modern type; Sir Shri Ram, of the DCM complex of north India; Kasturbhai Lalbhai, the leading mill-owner of Ahmedabad; A. D. Shroff, a stockbroker of Bombay; and John Matthai, an economist and

[76] Sir Purshotamdas Thakurdas *et al.*, *A Brief Memorandum Outlining a Plan of Economic Development for India*, Bombay, 1944.

a Tata director. The significant feature of the Bombay Plan was that it was signed not merely by pro-Congress businessmen like Birla, but also by representatives of the most moderate and consistently loyalist house of Tata, which had so long been out of step with the FICCI leadership. The Bombay Plan was a demonstration of the solidarity of the Indian business class in favour of a structural transformation of India's colonialized economy.

Even more surprising was the content of the Bombay Plan. It was in no sense a 'moderate' plan, lip service to progressive economic ideals by cautious businessmen hedging their bets. It was as radical as any Congress socialist with sound practical sense would have proposed, and there was in it a ring of conviction that the signatories meant what they wrote. The Bombay Plan rested squarely on a political assumption:

Underlying our whole scheme is the assumption that on termination of the war or shortly thereafter, a national government will come into existence at the centre which will be vested with full freedom in economic matters. . . . we think that no development of the kind we have proposed will be feasible except on the basis of a central directing authority which enjoys sufficient popular support and possesses the requisite powers and jurisdiction.[77]

This sounded like a warning of the Indian capitalist class to the imperial Government of India, and it was being uttered by them as a class.

The signatories first defined their goal: the doubling of the present *per capita* income in India within fifteen years. They estimated the increase of population at the existing rate of five million per annum according to the census of 1941. At this rate, the doubling of *per capita* income would necessitate a trebling of the aggregate national income in fifteen years. The net output of agriculture would have to be doubled, and of industry, large and small, to be expanded five times. In the initial stages effort was to be directed to production of power and capital goods, for nothing had more seriously hindered the development of India's industrial resources than the absence of these basic industries. Progress in this direction would reduce India's dependence on foreign countries for plant and machinery.[78] Priority would have to be given to power (electrical), mining, metallurgy, engineering, machinery of all kinds, chemicals, armaments, transport, railway engines, shipbuilding, automobiles, aircraft, etc.

[77] Ibid., p. 2.   [78] Ibid., pp. 3–5.

The planners claimed that they had placed a plan before the country which, given favourable conditions (i.e. a strong and independent government), could be realized within the prescribed time. But they could not take into account, at that point in time, the accelerated growth of Indian population in the fifties and the great leap in technological sophistication in the advanced countries after the war.

The attainment of the above goals depended, of course, on the mobilization of a previously unthinkable amount of capital resources. Conscious of this apparent improbability, the planners stated: 'The estimates of capital expenditure contained in the memorandum are of such colossal dimensions that the whole scheme may appear impracticable to people whose minds are still dominated by orthodox financial concepts. In matters of this kind, the war has been a great education.'[79] Fortified by the experience of wartime finance, the Bombay Plan signatories proposed an expenditure of Rs 10,000 crores, spread over a period of fifteen years (see Table 43). Interestingly enough, the eventual expenditure under India's first three Five Year Plans came to Rs 16,369 crores. Allowing for depreciation of currency, the real value of the Bombay Plan was probably comparable to that of the Five Year Plans over the first fifteen years. To have conceived a plan in such financial terms in the year 1944 implied considerable boldness and imagination.

Having estimated the colossal requirements of capital that was needed for a breakthrough, the signatories to the Bombay Plan did not shirk the problem of the means by which the capital could be raised. In dealing with this problem, India's leading capitalists proposed what was practically a social democracy, on practically the same pattern as of the Nehru regime of the fifties. ' . . . practically every aspect of economic life will have to be so rigorously controlled by government that individual liberty and freedom of enterprise will suffer a temporary eclipse.'[80] In facing up to this need for regimentation of the entire economy, the signatories to the Bombay Plan were very conscious of the Soviet model, to which they referred explicitly. 'Planning without tears is almost an impossibility. But we can learn some lessons from the Russian experiment and avoid the errors to which the planners in their over-enthusiasm are liable.'[81] The two main mistakes of the Soviet planners, according to the Bombay manifesto of the Indian capitalists, were indifference to consumer goods and the building of large plants which took years to come into operation.

[79] Ibid., p. 5.   [80] Ibid., p. 48.   [81] Ibid., pp. 51–2.

To avoid these mistakes, the Bombay Plan assigned, out of Rs 4,480 crores earmarked for industry, Rs 3,480 crores to basic industries and Rs 1,000 crores to consumer goods industries.[82] This ratio of 3:5 was substantially lower than that in the USSR.

TABLE 43

ESTIMATED EXPENDITURE UNDER THE BOMBAY PLAN

Sector	Amount (crore rupees)
Industry	4,480
Agriculture	1,240
Communications	940
Education	490
Health	450
Housing	2,200
Miscellaneous	200
TOTAL	10,000

In a second publication[83] soon after the announcement of the Bombay Plan, the signatories (excluding Ardeshir Dalal) made detailed proposals for the mobilization of resources within the economy, on the assumption that no foreign aid would be available. A steeply graduated income-tax was recommended. The fiscal system, it was conceded, would have to rely more on direct taxation for the removal of inequalities.[84] The industrialists also supported the abolition of zamindari and suggested that a ryotwari system, recommended recently by the Floud Commission for Bengal, should be extended to other parts of India as well.[85] They also recommended extensive controls on production, distribution, consumption, investment, foreign trade and exchange, and wages and working conditions.[86]

It will thus be seen that the social and political contours of the regime envisaged by the leading industrialists of India conformed in many essential respects to that which Nehru eventually sought to set up in independent India. India's post-independence socialist

[82] Ibid., p. 52.

[83] Purshotamdas Thakurdas et al., Plan of Economic Development for India, pt II.

[84] Ibid., pp. 20–1.   [85] Ibid., p. 16.   [86] Ibid., p. 32.

22

regime had its roots in the economic concepts which had developed in the late thirties and the early forties. These conceptions, which were tinged with radicalism, had won a national consensus. The leading industrialists of India had come to subscribe to these conceptions during the Second World War, and even before that. They did so in the conviction that unless radical measures were adopted, India's industrialization would not be sustained and in consequence the growth of their capitalist enterprises would be checked. At that point in time the Government of India, being still British in composition, remained tied to older economic ideas that had become irrelevant with the change in circumstances. The Indian economy in consequence bore a high cost of imperialism in the last stages of British rule in India.

Conclusion

I

The progress of historical research into the economic growth of India under the Raj has raised the analytical content of the subject to a higher level of sophistication. Explanations of economic backwardness are no longer sought by serious economic historians in the other-worldly values of Hindu culture, the immobilizing effects of the caste system or the conservative instincts of the trading classes. Instead attention has shifted to the scope for profitable investment within the economy, the limits of opportunity for entrepreneurship and the objective factors that constituted the economic environment, such as the size of the market, the costs of production and the availability of the essential technology and infrastructural facilities. In this work also the focus has been upon the objective factors governing the profitability of investment. For no longer is it possible to assume, *a priori*, that there existed a vast area of unexplored opportunities of profitable investment and creative entrepreneurship, which the Indians proved incapable of exploiting on account of their non-economic and non-rational standards of behaviour. This work has attempted a more precise definition of the area of opportunity for investment in the private corporate sector, based on an appreciation of the existing circumstances of specific industries.

Given these circumstances, it is difficult to see how private investment in industry could have been very much higher than it was. The structure of profit incentives, as determined by the overall structure of the economy, practically ruled out a higher rate of investment under private initiative. The dominating influence on the structure of profit incentives was the extremely low level of India's underdeveloped economy, which pre-determined a correspondingly low level of profitable investment in industry. Whatever the reasons for it, India was a backward country at the beginning of the twentieth century, and the extreme poverty of the population had a self-perpetuating tendency. No amount of private initiative, in view of the severe profit restrictions on the scope of its operations, could be expected to break the vicious circle. The only way out of the vicious circle lay in the provision of a broad range of inter-related facilities by the government, the lack of which had hitherto rendered a whole range of economic activities unprofitable. The solution to the problem was large-scale government intervention in the economy and a planned approach to economic growth. Tinkering with the fringes of the problem, such as the imposition of higher tariffs on imported goods, would not solve it.

Protection was extended to a large number of indigenous manufactures after the First World War, but such protection could only stimulate growth within the limits of the domestic market. Industrial growth was bound to hit a ceiling if the domestic market remained depressed on account of the poverty of the population. The low level of the Indian economy implied on the one hand a low level of effective demand for goods and services, and on the other hand only a small surplus for investment in the production of goods. It implied, in fact, a huge resource gap between the actual conditions and the desired objectives. The requisite surplus could not be mobilized without the infliction of necessary sufferings and exactions on the population by a determined government.

One point on which there have been disagreements among scholars is concerned with the relative importance to be given to the demand limitations and the supply constraints on Indian industrial growth. A. K. Bagchi has sought to demonstrate the inadequacies of an explanation of underdevelopment in terms of shortage of entrepreneurship, capital, labour, technical skill, raw materials and other supply factors. He points out that in macro-economic terms there was under-utilization of available resources. The available capital, labour and raw materials could have sustained a higher rate of industrial growth if there had been a greater demand for industrial products. According to this analysis, the crucial constraints on the economy were on the side of demand, not of supply. M. D. Morris, who does not deny the importance of the limitations of demand, has nevertheless indicated his disagreement with this approach. In his view the backwardness of the organizational and technological structure of the economy imposed important supply constraints on its growth. The private businessman's calculations about the costs of production were beset by formidable uncertainties on account of these organizational and technological inadequacies. It was no easy matter to select the appropriate technology from the advanced countries and to adapt it to the conditions of a backward country. These conditions also dictated that the entrepreneur must train his own skilled labour and provide his own power and other complementary facilities. Costs of production were thus pushed upwards by the absence of trained labour and complementary facilities. The private businessman was faced with greater needs for fixed and working capital in precisely a situation in which capital was more costly than in developed systems.

The differences of approach exhibited on this point appear at first sight to be more formidable than they really are. There were obviously different rates of growth at which the Indian economy would encounter demand limitations and supply constraints. At a slower pace of growth, the supply constraints might not come into play, and the slow pace itself might be fully explained by the brakes on further advance imposed by the size of the market. But if the rates of growth quickened (assuming for the sake of argument that the demand limitations had ceased to operate), then at one point supply deficiencies would obviously act as a fresh obstacle to growth. The issue may be examined in relation to the actual rate at which the Indian industrial sector grew during the period under review and the estimated rate of growth that was necessary for a take-off.

The actual rate of growth of organized industry in India from the time of the First World War onwards was by no means negligible, especially when compared with growth rates in other countries. According to the League of Nations estimate, India's large-scale manufacturing output grew during 1913–38 at the rate of 5.6 per cent per annum, a rate well above the world average of 3.3 per cent. It must be remembered, of course, that these comparative measurements rest on an extremely unsatisfactory data base. Measurements of the rate of capital formation are equally difficult. The officially recorded figures of the total paid-up capital of joint stock companies in India, though much more reliable than indices of industrial production, are no satisfactory clue to the real capital invested in business and industry. It is nevertheless interesting to note that the index of paid-up capital of joint stock companies registered in India rose from 100 in 1914–15 to 387 in 1938–9 (at an annual rate of growth of 11.9 per cent) and to 639 in 1946–7 (at an annual rate of growth of 16.8 per cent).

Two interesting features of capital formation in India since the First World War should be noted. In the first place, the figures of paid-up capital reveal changes in the pattern of investment, consisting in a perceptible shift from transport, banking, plantations and mining to manufactures. The comparatively high rate of investment in manufacturing industries was due to the extraordinary growth of certain new types of manufactures, such as chemicals, iron and steel, shipbuilding and engineering goods of various sorts. By contrast, established manufactures like jute increased at a slower pace than industry as a whole. There was a significant though not perhaps radical diversification and sophistication of industrial production. The years from 1937 to 1947 witnessed efforts at the production of basic chemical, metallurgical and engineering goods that belonged to a higher level of technological sophistication.

The second notable feature of capital formation from 1914 was the growth of Indian control in the private corporate sector. The Indianization of the private corporate sector was partial rather than complete, but at any rate the practical European monopoly of large areas of modern business and industry was brought to an end. Investment under Indian control—so far as the admittedly partial statistics indicate—grew considerably faster than European investment.

The industrial performance of the Indian economy during the period between the two world wars was thus not unimpressive. There was significant growth of manufacturing output, and that mainly in new directions under largely Indian initiative. Yet considerable as this growth was, it was not enough to bring the economy to the take-off point. Population grew much faster after 1920 than before, so that the *per capita* increase of manufacturing output was considerably less than the total increase. Moreover, unorganized small-scale and cottage industries grew at a much slower pace than modern business and industry. Finally, as Blyn has shown, agricultural trends after 1920 were not on the whole favourable to India's growth. To counter these less favourable trends, India needed a much greater rate of growth of organized industry than she in fact enjoyed for achieving an economic miracle. The League of Nations survey of the period shows that the Soviet Union achieved a rate of 32.9 per cent annual increase of manufacturing output and Japan 18 per cent. Without similar rates of industrial growth, India, which was at a much lower level of economic development than either country, could hardly be expected to break out of under-development.

At the actual rate of industrialization in India, supply difficulties did not prove insuperable obstacles. The required resources of capital, technology and skilled labour were mobilized—though not entirely without difficulties—for sustaining the prevailing rate of expansion of industrial output. Given sufficient time, as we have seen in our studies of particular industries, the factors of production could and did respond to expanded demand. This proposition is supported by the gradual spread of the area under improved varieties of sugar-cane and long-staple cotton, the perfecting of bamboo pulp technology for paper manufacture, the replacement of foreign technical personnel by skilled Indian labour in the glass and steel industries, and so on. This considerable achievement was neverthe-less far short of sustaining the required rates of growth.

It was only in terms of the existing pace of industrial activity that there was, as A. K. Bagchi has pointed out, a balance of unutilized resources. For the rate of industrialization which was needed for the transformation of the Indian economy, there was an absolute lack of the necessary capital and the requisite technology in India. The narrow technological base of the industrial sector in India practically ruled out a pace of industrial activity much faster than that which the country in fact enjoyed after the First World War. The initiation of specialized engineering and chemical industries, which came at the very end of our period, depended on the produc-tion of specialized steels and heavy chemicals. These basic materials were not produced in India until the 1930s. The supply constraints which inhibited a higher rate of industrial growth in India could not have been broken except by massive social overhead investment in education, public health, communications, power and water supply, irrigation and drainage systems, etc. The under-utilization of re-sources at the prevailing rate of industrialization was not uncon-nected with the fact that social overhead investment in India was so low and so unbalanced. For if no scope could be found for the full application of the available resources, it was because the infrastruc-ture was lacking. Such infrastructure could be created only by the government and without that there was no prospect of full employ-ment of resources.

If huge doses of public investment in infrastructural facilities were necessary for breaking the supply constraints, these were precisely the facilities which would also promote effective demand. The supply constraints should not be seen in isolation from the demand limitations. These obstacles were interrelated and arose from the same problem, the low level of the Indian economy. It was this underdeveloped character of the economy that bred the constraints on both sides.

After all, the costs of production could be reduced only by production on an economic scale for a sufficiently large market. Conversely, the raising of consumption, essential for creating such a market, depended on cost reduction by application of the most modern technical innovations. The interdependence of market expansion and technical advance was very close indeed. Each factor acted as a drag on the other and determined the specific character of industrial growth in India. The pattern of industrial growth in India was dominated by technologically imperfect production for a protected domestic market, a pattern which inhibited innovative technological responses to the challenge of competition in world markets.

The Indian economy was thus at too low a level to generate either an adequate demand or a sufficient surplus for its transformation, unless indeed the government undertook to solve the problem by overall control of production and distribution. In the absence of such a policy, the confines of the economy remained so narrow, and in consequence the returns from investment so unpromising, that it was a matter of surprise that the rate of capital formation in India remained at so high a level. It would not in fact have been possible without the imperial crisis produced by the new thirty years' war in Europe.

One large question remains. If the level of the Indian economy was so low at the beginning of the First World War, and if this explains its unsatisfactory performance subsequently, what was it that had produced the underdevelopment in the first place? The explanation obviously lies in historical trends of the preceding age, which must necessarily form a separate subject of study. Yet notice must be taken of the importance of the question. An approach to the problem may perhaps be evolved along two interrelated lines: the inter-sectoral relations within the pre-modern economy of the subcontinent and the impact of colonialism on the structure of the economy subsequently. Certain tendencies within the pre-British economy of India, which were inimical to a structural breakthrough in production, were accentuated by the penetration and ascendancy of imperial interests.

The terms of the above hypothesis may be briefly spelt out here. The towns in pre-colonial India, it is now known, had a developed system of artisan industries as well as an advanced complex of banking and merchant capital. Nevertheless they had remained, in relation to rural India, essentially parasitic entities, for there was virtually no relationship of exchange of industrial products for agricultural goods between the towns and the villages. The flow of goods, both agricultural and non-agricultural, was practically one way, from the villages to the towns. The villages had from time immemorial a highly ritualized system of exchange of goods between artisan and peasant, which made it possible for them at a stretch to rely on their own resources except in some important respects. The surplus of agriculture and crafts was sent to the towns for consumption or export. In return the villages received cash; and the cash went back to the towns in the form of land revenue. The towns thus remained in essence concentration points of village produce; and although the towns had their own industries oriented to export or aristocratic consumption, this industrial sector had no connection with the vast rural market, the only market which in fact could sustain an industrial revolution in view of the relatively smaller size of the urban sector. The rural population at large did not have sufficient purchasing capacity to stimulate the growth of organized factory-type industry in the towns of Mughal India. The cash which the majority of peasants received by marketing their crops went into the payment of the heavy land revenue demand, which thus checked the growth of rural consumption and the formation of a large domestic market for mass-produced industrial goods.

The unceasing exaction of produce from the village without any equivalent return had a perpetually impoverishing effect, most dramatically revealed in the degradation of the lowest rural elements —the under-tenants, the farm labourers and the menial servants. There was not merely the direct tribute exacted in the form of the land revenue but also its indirect consequence, the growth of rural usury, which tended to produce debt bondage and agrestic servitude. Since loans were contracted mainly in order to pay taxes and other dues, usurious capital really fed on the demands of the state. The Mughal state was essentially a system of military domination based on the exaction of land revenue in the form of cash. Its demands upon the rural sector set in motion an artificially inflated outflow of goods. These enforced exports from the villages induced a high degree of commercialization and monetization of the rural economy —a process that was by no means spontaneous or healthy. The apparently 'advanced' characteristics of the Mughal economy were not in real terms very conducive to economic growth. For in so far as monetization and commercialization progressed, they did so in direct response to the increased surplus extracted from the rural sector by the Mughal state. That surplus was utilized mainly in two ways: conspicuous consumption by the nobility and commodity export by the merchants. The export of merchandise had no stimulating impact on economic activities, for the gold and other precious metals imported in return on a very large scale merely constituted hoarded, unproductive wealth.

Beneath the fabled 'wealth of Ind' lurked the massive poverty of the rural population of Mughal India. Compared to much of Western Europe, India's economic level in the mid-eighteenth century was too low to justify any facile assumption of radical transformation of the economy in the near future, especially in view of the 'Asiatic' (which is really a polemical name for the 'oppressive') features of that economy. The extractive role of the organized, parasitic state was the decisive feature of the Mughal economy, for it perpetuated the disjunction between the urban industrial sector and the rural market. The merchant capitalist class remained pitifully dependent, for the size of their commercial operations, on the amount extracted from the villages by the Mughal state. Unlike the medieval European burghers, the entrepreneurs of Mughal India had no independent base in the production system and were in no position to exert the kind of political pressure that would enable them to forge industrial links with the villages. By enforcing the essentially parasitic relationship of the towns with the villages, the land revenue mechanism of the town-based Mughal government produced an obvious mal-integration in the structure of the entire economy. This sectoral mal-integration of the pre-colonial economy of India was a severe check to the potentialities of capitalist growth.

The ascendancy of colonial interests brought about a fresh structural distortion of the economy, accentuating its oppressive features. The British connection enhanced the importance of the export–import sector within the economy. For perhaps the first time, India's villages began to receive large quantities of manufactured goods in return for their exports of primary produce. However, these manufactured goods were produced not in India but in Britain, so that it was the British rather than the Indian industrial economy that was initially stimulated by the growth of a rural market for urban manufactures. Furthermore, the total volume of the merchandise extracted from the villages greatly increased, and so did the proportion of this total that was exported abroad. The manner in which the rural surplus was extracted was much more sophisticated, there no longer being an exclusive reliance on the land revenue mechanism. In Bengal, where the land revenue was permanently limited by the settlement of 1793, it was the price mechanism which came to play a crucial role. The East India Company, and later on the private British houses, acquired the monopsony power of pricing the produce of peasants and artisans at an abnormally low level. The artificially depressed prices at which the export corporations obtained indigo and jute from the peasantry, represented an invisible extraction of surplus. But however new and sophisticated the methods of collecting tribute from the villages, the essentially parasitic nature of the relationship was intensified. In a magnified form the relationship between Britain (the metropolis) and India (the hinterland) came to exhibit the same features that had characterized the relations of town and country in Mughal India.

The most characteristic feature of India's foreign trade was a consistent and large export surplus in merchandise, which was equally consistently wiped out by the induced (if not enforced) import of 'services'. The great and growing volume of colonial India's exports, artificially inflated in order to meet obligations to metropolitan Britain, was not the spontaneous sign of a buoyant and prosperous economy. Rather, it was a consequence of India's political subordination to Britain, which found concrete expression in the form of Home Charges, for 'services' (together with stores) rendered by Britain to India. The British Home Charges contributed to the establishment of the same type of commercial relationship between Britain and India which the Mughal land revenue had induced between town and country inside India, that is to say, an abnormal excess of merchandise exports over merchandise imports, which was wiped off by imports of 'services' about which the importing party had no choice. The Indian peasant had as little choice about paying for the services rendered by the Mughal *mansabdars* as he had about paying for those rendered by the British civilians.

We need not enter here into the vexed and disputed question of the extent to which India's merchandise exports represented a 'drain'. But it is necessary to consider the overall impact of India's foreign trade on her industrial economy, a subject hitherto somewhat neglected in the debate between proponents and opponents of the drain.

In mercantilist circles of eighteenth and nineteenth century Europe an export surplus was considered to be favourable to a country's national interests. It was only in a colonial context, among early political economists of India like Dadabhai Naoroji, that an excess of exports over imports came to be identified as a source of impoverishment. After independence there was again an emphasis on the need to produce a sufficiently large volume of exports, so that essential machinery and capital goods could be imported from abroad to force the pace of industrialization even at the cost of the current consumption of the population.

This evolution of economic opinion emphasizes one point. Whether an export surplus is beneficial or harmful to a country's development depends on the use that is made of it. Furthermore, it is also clear that the use that is made of the export surplus depends to a large extent on the nature of the political regime of the country concerned. By active intervention, governments can produce a pattern of international trade very different from that which would be produced by the free play of inter-continental economic factors. Conversely the decision not to intervene in this context is itself one form of 'action', none the less effective on account of its passive character.

The crucial question, therefore, relates to the nature of the imports that a country decides to obtain in return for its exports. What were the specific items of India's imports? The main items of imported goods and services that more than counterbalanced her exports in merchandise were five in number: (1) the services and stores given by the Government of Britain to the Government of India, (2) various manufactured goods imported on private account, (3) precious metals and specie, (4) invisible business services, (5) services rendered by European residents in India, who may be regarded as India's 'human' imports. How far did the itemized imports assist the industrial development of India?

1. The Home Charges were on account of the services and stores obtained by the Government of India from the Home Government.

These consisted of civil and military charges, stores purchased in Britain, and interest on the so-called 'productive' and 'unproductive' debt of India to Britain. Among all the features of India's commercial and financial relationship with Britain, the Home Charges were the most sharply criticized element from the nineteenth century onwards. India obtained for these charges a well-organized framework of defence and law and order, but it was undoubtedly a very expensive system and many of the charges were for military operations outside India in defence of British imperial (not Indian national) interests. Much more productive in a visible manner was the railway and irrigation network financed by British loans—loans of a size which could not have been raised in India in the nineteenth century. Nevertheless these were 'guaranteed' loans, which ensured private profit at public risk. What was perhaps more significant, the secondary multiplier effects of the railway and irrigation projects 'leaked' out of India to Britain. The stores purchased in Britain for the construction projects of the public works department—rolling stock, locomotives, various engineering materials—represented, of course, a definite value to India, but the growth of the engineering industries in India was inhibited by the systematic purchase of these stores in Britain. Thus, the indirect benefits of railway and canal construction, i.e. the stimulus to heavy industry, took place more in Britain than in India. The direct benefits, i.e. the stimulus to Indian trade and agriculture, were somewhat reduced by the manner of construction of the railways and canals, which often damaged the food-producing peasant subsistence economy of India and twisted her entire economy in the direction of an export trade dominated by the colonial pattern. Finally there was the unproductive debt, which tended to swell in time, together with the interest on it. The total Home Charges were undoubtedly a severe strain on India's finances. The increasing volume of India's exports in indigo, jute, tea, raw cotton, seeds, foodgrains and hides and skins, far from reflecting the spontaneous expansion of a burgeoning economy, exhibited the compulsions of financial obligations that tended to increase with time.

2. India also began to receive in course of the nineteenth century considerable quantities of merchandise. These represented a definite consumer's value, unlike the non-usable precious metals imported by Mughal India. The imported merchandise consisted mostly of manufactured consumer goods, and later on, of some machinery,

mill-work and tools and implements. Before the First World War, India's main imports of merchandise were cotton goods, processed metals, sugar, oils, wool and silk goods, hardware and machinery and mill-work. The use value of India's imports thus rose considerably, and what was more, much of this useful factory-produced merchandise began to find its way into the villages. Thus for the first time a rural market for town-based industries was created and the villagers were able to get some useful goods for the primary produce sent to the towns. However, initially the newly-forged links with the vast rural market in the colony were practically monopolized by the urban industrial sector of the metropolitan country, and the monopoly established in this way inhibited for a long time to come the growth of large-scale organized industry in India. Before organized town-based industry in India succeeded in establishing a secure hold on the domestic market, some appreciable destruction of artisan industries had been wrought by imported British goods. The repair of the damage done in this way was delayed by the pattern of imports produced by a policy of free trade. A more active policy on Japanese and Russian lines, by restricting the import of consumer goods, would have stimulated the light consumer goods industries. It would have saved precious foreign exchange for the import of more capital goods, which in turn would have expanded the production capacity of large-scale industries. Under free trade, the bulk of India's merchandise imports continued to be consumer goods, not machinery and equipment.

3. India also continued to import, as earlier under the Mughals, large quantities of bullion and specie. Enormous quantities of silver, and to a lesser extent gold, were imported throughout the nineteenth century. The impact of these two imported metals on the commerce and industry of India must be treated separately, for while the silver circulated within the economy as currency, the gold was hoarded. As far as silver was concerned, its import was largely a result of the monetary policy adopted by the Government of India. Until 1893 the currency of India was maintained on the basis of freely minted silver, to the exclusion of any paper currency. Silver poured unrestricted into India in return for consistently heavy exports of merchandise. The increased stock of silver currency stimulated the growth of an exchange economy, but this was no unmixed blessing. As the gold value of silver was declining during this time, the value of Indian silver currency, fluctuating with the gold value of silver,

was much depreciated. The depreciation of currency had the effect of lowering the prices of export products, the total quantity of which increased due to the stimulus of devaluation. The free import of bullion and specie, and the consequent devaluation, was welcome to European exporters in India as an 'export bonus'. However, the increased profits of the exporters, resulting from the increase in exports, was largely at the cost of other sections of the population. Since imported silver was a commodity for which India exported agricultural produce and since the imported metal was subject to continuous depreciation, India as a country incurred heavy losses from this exchange. As the gold value of the increasing stock of silver currency in India remained the same, depreciating silver was used to extract an increasing quantity of primary produce from India. In consequence domestic consumption per head remained low. Gold, on the other hand, was imported for more traditional purposes of hoarding and ornaments. In the coffers of the princely and landed classes, who lacked the habits and the opportunities of investment, this imported gold was concentrated as hoarded, unused bullion and specie which was almost entirely withdrawn from circulation, a dead loss to the economy. However, not all of it was a dead loss. Much of the imported gold was thinly distributed over a large part of the urban and rural population. It gave to the population at large a mobile purchasing power in times of crisis. In an underdeveloped agricultural country like India, subject to seasonal fluctuations of harvests and food prices, the imported gold (or rather one part of it) kept the economy functioning at its low level.

4. Among the 'invisibles' imported by India in return for exports were banking, insurance and shipping services. Britain practically monopolized these services, excluding other foreign competitors from this sphere through political influence. Indian enterprise in this sphere was also throttled by deliberately monopolistic practices. No Indian shipping line was allowed to operate, either on the coast or across the ocean. The import of the invisibles therefore could not be viewed as a natural consequence of conditions determined by perfect competition. Had free competition prevailed, India might have been able to receive the benefits of cheaper Japanese, American and Continental services. More optimistically, she might herself have built up a business complex around the provision of these invisible services. The enforced import of the invisibles inhibited Indian enterprise and facilitated the leakage of India's gains from

foreign trade. In historical terms, this peculiarly colonial relationship was based on the destruction of a large indigenous business complex of banking, insurance, shipbuilding and shipping, which had flourished in Gujarat at one time.

5. Finally, India imported white businessmen, professionals and administrators, a fact reflected in 'remittances' on private account, which wiped off much of her export surplus in merchandise. India's gains from the inflow of this white 'skilled labour' was a modern business and industrial complex, and unified framework of law and administration. But here again these gains require careful calculation, for there is no doubt that this imported labour was very expensive to India, being one of the most highly priced in the world. Nor was this labour 'freely' imported, independently of political factors, for there is also no doubt that official measures and private practices had combined to exclude Indians from the higher walks of business and administration.

The colonial pattern of India's foreign trade increased the sectoral mal-integration of the underdeveloped economy of the country. There was a virtual absence of any linkage effects between the growth of modern business and industry, and the state of the rural economy. The increasing exports of tea and jute, for instance, swelled the profits of the European managing agencies based on Calcutta, but did not lead to similar real increases in the incomes of tea garden labourers and jute cultivators in the interior. Instead of stimulating capital formation in agriculture, the rural income from the rapid growth of export production in tea and jute went into increasing import of Manchester cloth, Liverpool salt and Empire sugar by villagers, which in turn held back the development of local industry. The import–export sector, which had been artificially carved out of the peasant economy by foreign corporations, never became an organic part of the internal structure of the country. This socio-economic disintegration and sectoral distortion of the economy of India, induced by its integration into an international colonial framework of division of labour, inhibited indigenous capitalist development during the nineteenth century.

The considerations set out above—the state of the Indian economy on the eve of the colonial penetration and the pattern of development under imperial rule—should in some measure explain why at the beginning of the First World War India's economic level was so low. This low level of development, as we have seen, explains that peculiar interaction of various economic factors that precluded a higher rate of growth after the war. During the period of the two world wars, the foreign trade of India underwent important changes. The impact of these changes, as shown earlier, was not uniform. The reduced import of manufactures laid down the basic conditions for the substantial measure of import-substitution and industrial development after the war. On the other hand, the greatly increased burden of the Home Charges, especially on account of the swelling unproductive debt, produced a financial crisis as during the thirties India's exports to non-sterling areas declined. The increased Home Charges and increased remittances on private account, brought about for the first time a massive outflow of bullion and specie from India in settlement of her obligations. The payment of increased interest on debt and partial repatriation of investments placed an enormous burden on the population. In the last stages of imperial rule, British assets in India, built up largely out of the profits of business and employment in India itself, were ceasing to provide any stimulus to the economy and were turning increasingly parasitic. Amidst the inter-war crisis of imperialism, the Indian capitalist class had been afforded an opportunity to forge a new link between indigenous organized industry and the rural market for industrial products. This had produced some measure of integration of the Indian economy. But this new integration within the economy was not accompanied by a corresponding expansion of its total size, because of the pressure of increased financial obligations to Britain.

II

Thus far we have been concerned with trends in production and factors governing its increase. But mere increase of production was not all there was to balanced development. Almost equally important, in the overall social context, was the question of Indian control of the processes of production. Indeed, as we have seen, one decisive factor in the growth of industrial production after the First World War was the rise of an Indian capitalist class. The emergence of this class had been impeded, before the war, by the integration of the Indian economy into a colonial pattern of international division of labour and exchange of goods and services. It was only when that pattern itself was very severely strained by the two world wars that

23

the Indian economy could assume a shape that offered greater scope for indigenous capitalist development.

One important factor assisting this development after the First World War was the slow erosion of the far-reaching arrangements which favoured European businessmen against native entrepreneurs. As the apparatus of government began to pass gradually into the hands of Indians with each successive dose of constitutional reforms, it was no longer possible to maintain these arrangements as systematically as before. The question of discrimination against Indians needs careful investigation, as it is closely connected with the question of contrasting patterns of entrepreneurial behaviour among foreign and indigenous business groups. If it can be shown that foreign and native businessmen were equally willing to invest in any profitable enterprise, then the economic importance of racial discrimination can be questioned. M. D. Morris has drawn attention to the point that discrimination in favour of Europeans would lower the level of private investment only if they invested less than Indians when given the same opportunities.

On the surface of it this point seems to have considerable relevance to the analysis of the factors determining the level of investment. The supposition that there was a conspiracy on the part of European business interests to keep India underdeveloped and subordinated to British industrial capitalism through deliberate under-investment will not bear scrutiny. British capitalist interests did not form one homogeneous force. To take an instance, Manchester textile interests did everything in their power to inhibit the cotton-mill industry of Bombay, but nevertheless that industry was built up largely with the technical assistance and credit facilities readily extended by British textile machinery manufacturers to the Bombay mill-owners. Nor is it clear that a prevailing 'social ethos' systematically inhibited British businessmen in India from investing in those enterprises whose development would damage British national interests. A. K. Sen, who has advanced this hypothesis as a substitute for the 'conspiracy' thesis, has argued his case largely with reference to the Bombay cotton-mill industry, in which British enterprise seemed to be much less active than Indian enterprise. But even in this case, a fact which is not generally appreciated is the very large role played by British interests in the development of the Bombay cotton-mill industry. In 1925 British interests were in control of 31 per cent of the spindles, 30 per cent of the looms and 48 per cent of the paid-up capital of cotton mills of Bombay. Other instances are not lacking to show that capital was not withheld when the returns promised to be favourable. The European engineering firm of Burn & Co., for instance, went in for manufacturing inland river steam vessels when it was found that substantial economies would be made if the vessels were manufactured in India instead of being imported from Britain. There was no hesitation in risking the opposition of vested interests at Home, and in time Burn even began to export vessels to Burma, so long supplied only by firms in Britain.[1] This seems to underline that no social ethic, political motivation or tie-up with concerns at Home was strong enough to counteract the pull of profitable investment in the colony, however harmful that might be to firms in Britain supplying India.

Basically, then, businessmen in India, whatever their racial stock, were guided mainly by economic incentives. It is nonetheless clear that the entrepreneurial behaviour of European and Indian business-men in India differed markedly. The record of company flotations after the First World War makes it evident that the rate of Indian investment was substantially higher than the rate of European investment. If both European and Indian business groups were responsive to economic incentives and if Europeans had equally free access to opportunities as Indians, why did Europeans invest less than Indians? The evidence of this work suggests a two-fold answer to this question: (a) the economic incentives in the case of European businessmen were not determined by pure profit considerations, but embraced other restrictive economic considerations as well; (b) Indian businessmen, on the other hand, were guided in their invest-ment by long-term economic and political considerations that went beyond immediate profit calculations, though of course profit cal-culations remained important in their case. To put it briefly, both groups were strongly influenced by profit calculations, but while the Europeans did not reach the full limit of profit calculations Indians sometimes went beyond them in the inter-war period.

To appreciate these considerations fully, it is necessary to keep in mind some factual data regarding the investment patterns of European and Indian businessmen. European investment tended to concentrate on the staples—tea, jute, coal, etc.—which were no longer growing fast. Indian investment, by contrast, had sought

---

[1] *Report of the Indian Tariff Board regarding the Grant of Protection to the Ship-Building Industry*, Calcutta, 1926.

out new manufacturing enterprises—steel, sugar, chemicals, etc.—
which developed much more rapidly. It is this differential behaviour
of European and Indian investors—their respective concentration on
the 'old' and 'new' sectors—that requires explanation.

It will not do to suggest that Europeans, due to their concentration on the export-oriented industries, left the field open to Indians
in the industries producing for the domestic market, which became
more important as a result of the difficulties of international trade
during the doldrums of the twenties and the depression of the
thirties. There are several indications that European investors were
aware of the growing importance of the domestic market and that
they made energetic attempts to claim a share in it. Nor could they
be supposed to be suffering from a handicap in respect of production
for the domestic market. In so far as racial discrimination existed,
surely it would help European industrialists in obtaining the supplies
and capturing the markets on a preferential basis within the
country. The upcountry manufacturing centre of Kanpur, where
Europeans long remained dominant, had developed in response to
the massive patronage of the army and the bureaucracy to the
European manufacturers. In the south again, the leading European
textile house of Binny came to build up in the thirties and the
forties the most splendid domestic marketing organization for the
distribution of piece-goods throughout India—an organization that
no other firm in India could match.

It would appear, therefore, that as new industries concentrating
on the domestic market developed after the First World War, the
major portion of the new rupee investment came from Indians—not
because Europeans suffered any special disadvantage in this field,
but for other reasons. This work has suggested two such reasons:
the growing tendency of European investors to remit their profits
after the First World War and the more adventurous disposition of
the new Indian business houses which entered the field in the inter-
war period.

The grant of discriminating protection to industries opened up a
whole range of new fields for profitable investment—investment that
went into manufacturing for the domestic market. Yet it was precisely during this time that European investment decisions came to
be more closely affected by considerations of repatriation than ever
before. During the Great Depression of the thirties there was a
massive repatriation of capital from India. In the main this outflow

took place from the public debt of India to Britain, but European private investment was also affected. In so far as European investors remitted their profits instead of reinvesting them in the newly opened up industries, the rate of Indian investment was higher.

The decision for reinvestment of profits is taken by foreign firms on a somewhat different basis from that of native investors. In the case of the foreign investor the periodic need for remittance dictates an attempt at striking an optimum balance between remittance and reinvestment, so that there is no question, as in the case of native investors, of a systematic and consistent attempt at maximization of profits. This is the main element in the restrictive economic considerations behind European investment that we have mentioned before. In the period before the First World War, this did not perhaps matter as much as after the war, since there was no scope for profitable ploughing back of all the profits, given the constraints on the economy. After the war there was undoubtedly vastly greater scope for ploughing back of profits, so that at this stage the loss constituted by capital outflow began to be more keenly felt.

The foreign investor in India before the war, then, reinvested profits whenever such investment was profitable, and repatriated those surplus profits that could not be profitably employed in India. He did not usually employ surplus funds to create entirely new channels of profitable investment, but tended simply to take advantage of the existing channels of investment that had been created around the middle of the nineteenth century. Indian investors employed their surplus profits either in acquiring local prestige and influence—by creating social and religious networks of patronage in their own localities[2]—or in the creation of new fields of profitable investment—of which the classic instance was J. N. Tata's venture into steel manufacture. These were the normal differences in the behaviour of foreign and native investors. After 1914 the differences were enhanced by the fact that foreign investors no longer followed the established pre-war pattern of behaviour but quite often transferred funds even when they could be profitably invested within India.

This shift in the pattern of European investment has to be understood in the light of the possibility of changes in the profitability ratio of remittance and reinvestment. This meant that in particular

[2] C. A. Bayly, *The Local Roots of Indian Politics: Allahabad 1880–1920* (Oxford, 1975), gives a good account of this phenomenon.

circumstances remittance might become economically more profitable in relation to reinvestment. Such, indeed, was the case in India after the First World War. There was the possibility of earning higher rates on exchange of the rupee for the pound, on account of the rise of the sterling value of the rupee from the pre-war level of 1s. 4d. to 2s. in 1920. The high sterling parity of the rupee immediately after the war had initiated a speculative flow of remittances to London by European businessmen waiting to repatriate their accumulated wartime profits. In the thirties this outflow received further impetus. There was an autarchical, self-sufficiency boom within Britain in the sphere of investment, which made it possible to employ more profitably at Home than abroad the profits earned on exported capital. This was, moreover, precisely the time when political insecurity became a factor on account of mass unrest in India. Political insecurity combined with economic calculations to depress the level of reinvestment of profits by the big European managing agencies.

It is not surprising, in these circumstances, that Indians proved much more forthcoming than Europeans as investors. On the Indian side, the inter-war period saw the emergence of a new type of aggressive entrepreneurship that was quite distinctively the product of the social and political atmosphere generated by the national movement. The rising Indian houses, such as Birla, Walchand and Shri Ram, were impelled by the driving force of economic nationalism to go beyond normal business considerations in the initiation of new industries. A rational calculation of the rates of profit, the amount of risk and the length of gestation would not have permitted the headlong plunge into automobile and other manufactures that these three houses took during the Second World War. In the matter of the flotation of Hind Motors and Premier Automobiles, Birla and Walchand were not motivated by immediate profit incentives, but by much larger considerations, since neither technological nor market factors encouraged any visions of profitable car manufacture in India for the foreseeable future. The ancillary industries for the manufacture of car components did not exist at the time, so that costs of production were bound to be driven upwards. It was calculated at the time that it would not be worthwhile manufacturing cars without an annual domestic demand of 30,000 vehicles. The actual demand in India was considerably below this figure. Birla and Walchand nevertheless went ahead, gambling on the future. No European business house would have taken these risks.

The European managing agencies in Calcutta and elsewhere, it appears from the evidence, were conservative, insistent on sound finance and much less prone to risky adventures than the rising Indian entrepreneurs. The reorganization of the giant combine of Bird Heilgers in Calcutta after the war illustrated this mentality. For the emphasis henceforth was on 'sound business', not innovations; and what Edward Benthall, the head of the combine, called 'ventures beyond the firm's normal experience', were definitely disapproved of. In general, innovations in the case of the European business houses were subservient to the firms' existing interests and were ruled out when such innovations fell outside the firms' 'normal experience'. As a result, the task of pioneering new ventures in unexplored fields fell mainly to the rising Indian business houses, which took the lead in chemical, glass, shipbuilding, automobile, textile machinery, sewing-machine, aluminium and other new industries.

It appears, then, that if the government, instead of systematically favouring Europeans against Indians, had assisted Indian entrepreneurs in occupying a larger sphere in the private sector, then the level of private investment might have been substantially higher. But according to our analysis, private industrial investment itself constituted a relatively small element in the backward agricultural economy of India, so that an upward variation in the level of that investment would not have been sufficient to transform the economy. In view of the limited role of private investment in the economy, one might question the importance of the factor of discrimination and the relevance of the relative position of Europeans and Indians in the private sector. That, however, would be a very narrow and misleading view of the entire problem, which had much wider implications than the mere level of private industrial investment. Among these implications must be stressed the impact of the racial composition of the private sector on two crucial areas: the pattern of foreign trade and the level of public investment.

The impact of the racial composition of the private sector on the pattern of India's foreign trade can be illustrated by comparison of the patterns of exports and imports at two centres of business—Calcutta and Bombay where Europeans and Indians respectively were predominant. During the First World War very large profits were made by European businessmen in Calcutta and Indian businessmen in Bombay. At the end of the war European businessmen repatriated a large portion of these wartime profits, in contrast with Indian businessmen in Bombay who financed new ventures from the liquid assets acquired during the war. The massive repatriation of profits from Calcutta had the immediate effect of driving up the amount of exports from Calcutta and of widening the gap between exports and imports. During the inter-war period Bengal produced a consistently large export surplus in merchandise. The unusually large excess of exports over imports from Bengal during the twenties and the thirties undoubtedly reflected the extraordinary repatriation of profits by European businessmen in Calcutta. By contrast, the Bombay Presidency, after briefly producing a much smaller export surplus in the early twenties, thereafter consistently enjoyed an import surplus till the outbreak of war.[3] Business being mainly in Indian hands in this province, the profits were reinvested within the country. This process stimulated the economy, leading to a rise in consumption and imports. Bengal received no comparable benefits from foreign trade, her increased exports merely permitting increased remittances by businessmen.

Furthermore, even though the private sector was too small to transform the economy by itself, the demands of the private sector very largely shaped the economic policies of the government and the nature and level of public investment. Since government policies substantially affected the overall level of investment (public and private), the question is important whether the attitudes of the European and the Indian entrepreneurs towards the role of the government in the economy differed markedly. For, the group which dominated the private sector would be able to bring to bear a great deal of influence on government policy. Once the anti-Indian bias was removed and Indian business houses obtained controlling influence on the private sector, they would be in a position to exert pressure on the government. The question that would then arise was whether that pressure would be exerted for a substantially greater role of the government in the economy than that advocated by European businessmen.

This work has shown that there was a very sharp conflict between European and Indian business groups after the First World War and that the conflict largely arose from the advocacy of different

[3] For a detailed regional statistical analysis of exports and imports, *see* A. K. Bagchi, *Reflections on Patterns of Regional Growth in India during the Period of British Rule*, Occasional Paper No. 5, Centre for Studies in Social Sciences, Calcutta, 1976.

economic policies. Initially the differences of economic opinion largely centred round the issue of free trade versus mercantilist measures. European businessmen were usually opposed to the demands for protection, coastal reservation and lower sterling parity of the rupee voiced by Indians in the Central Legislative Assembly. In the thirties these differences widened on account of important shifts in Indian economic thinking that paved the way for the adoption of socialist planning in independent India. Equally important was the fact that different sections of Indian businessmen achieved by slow degrees a remarkable degree of unity over demands that were opposed to European thinking and interests. The growing solidarity within each camp in opposition to the other camp was reflected in the combination of European and Indian chambers of commerce in two umbrella organizations, Assocham and FICCI respectively. Initially the Tata group and its connections in the Indian business world stayed away from this hostile confrontation between imperial and national business interests. During the Second World War, the Indian capitalist class achieved an unprecedented solidarity by unitedly presenting the Bombay Plan for the economic development of India without any foreign aid.

The fact that the strategy of planning the economy as a whole and massive investment through the public sector was adopted so soon after independence with a sort of national consensus was not without its pre-independence history. Imperceptibly in the late thirties and more dramatically during the Second World War, Indian business opinion was groping forward to precisely the kind of strategy that won national consensus in independent India. The National Planning Committee appointed by the Congress included such well-known capitalists as Purshotamdas Thakurdas, A. D. Shroff, Ambalal Sarabhai and Walchand Hirachand, some of whom had strong Congress connections. These capitalists did not enter the National Planning Committee in order to frustrate its objects, but because they saw in planning a means of further expansion of India's national capitalist economy. Later in 1944 J. R. D. Tata, G. D. Birla, Lala Shri Ram and other leading Indian capitalists issued what is known as the Bombay Plan for the development of the Indian economy. This united support of planning represented a *rapprochement* between the Congress-minded FICCI leadership (Birla, Shri Ram, and others) and the hitherto loyalist Tata connection. The level of investment proposed by these big businessmen, mainly in the public sector, did not in real terms fall far short of the actual expenditure under the Five Year Plans of independent India, to which the Bombay Plan bore a remarkable resemblance in some respects. Predictably European businessmen in India remained indifferent, and in private even hostile, to these prospects of planning.

For the reasons outlined above, the continued domination of the European managing agencies in the private corporate sector proved a hindrance to India's industrial growth. In so far as there was industrial development after the First World War, it was to some extent the result of the expanding Indian share in the private sector. The racial composition of the private sector thus had implications far wider than the level of private industrial investment, which was bound to be relatively small in any case, whether the private sector was in European hands or in the hands of Indians. For the Indian industrial economy, it was in an overall context a very hopeful development that led to the newly rising Indian business houses prevailing over the older European managing agencies at the end of the Second World War. Yet underlying this hopeful development was a deeper, latent process that ruled out the possibility of any true independence for India's national economy and her indigenous business class. For while the nineteenth century European managing agencies began to fade out from the scene, new multinational corporations, with vaster networks and technological resources, effected a slow but sure entry into the Indian economy through the supply of foreign technology.

The Bombay Plan, which had conceived of India's development without foreign aid, had reflected a genuine desire for independence on the part of the big Indian business houses. Yet precisely the same reason which induced these houses to advocate socialist planning also urged them towards collaboration with foreign firms: a haunting sense of the immensity of the task of transformation, an inescapable awareness of the huge problem of technological breakthrough. Phase by phase, in forms repeatedly modified by government control, technical collaboration developed in independent India. In the initial phase, foreign-based firms and multinational corporations were able to insist on equity participation and representation on the Board of Directors in return for supplying technological assistance to new ventures in India. Later, due to official policy, they had to content themselves more and more with receiving annual royalties over a certain period for providing technological aid, the government insisting that indigenous firms prepare themselves to dispense with foreign technology within a specified time. More recently official emphasis has been on outright purchase of technology, and on purchase by a national agency rather than by particular firms in India. However tightly the government sought to control the conditions for the inflow of foreign expertise, dependence could not be abolished in the absence of a genuine transformation of the technological base of the Indian economy. Although foreign business interests had initially insisted on exploiting equity capital and directorial representation as means of control, by slow degrees, it was found possible through informal channels to have controlling influence. The imported technology was in any case so complex that formal means of control such as equity participation were not essential. Technologically the Indian business class remained pitifully dependent on foreign expertise.

This technological dependence assisted the process of substituting for formal empire, informal control and influence. For monopolizing the market for cotton goods and the production of tea, jute and other light products, political favouritism within a framework of formal empire had been especially helpful to foreign business interests. When such special official patronage began to diminish as a result of increasing constitutional transfers of power to Indians, the European managing agencies declined in importance. The multinational corporations did not need the kind of political patronage which was essential to India-based European managing agencies. The field of enterprise for the multinationals was specialized chemical and engineering products, not relatively simple manufactures for consumption. The specialized and sophisticated technology which the multinationals had succeeded in developing in Western conditions proved to be sufficient leverage in underdeveloped countries. Further industrial progress in underdeveloped countries depended on the inflow of this advanced technology, which in turn was so complex as to constitute a natural monopoly for the most advanced nations. Formal empire was not necessary to perpetuate this sort of technological dependence. Formal empire had been necessary only to preserve a market in India for British-manufactured consumer goods and to produce export goods under monopolistic European enterprise within India.

When these interests declined, the pressure for maintaining the formal structure of empire also diminished. In the thirties the market for British goods in India contracted. Even more important, the monopolistic exports of tea, jute and other products by European managing agencies declined due to the difficulties of international trade. India thus ceased to play the crucial role of being the main earner of non-sterling foreign exchange for covering Britain's trade deficits with the rest of the world. As international trade contracted, the export-oriented European business houses in India came under strain. While the import–export sector declined, new fields of manufacturing enterprise linked to the domestic market opened up under predominantly Indian entrepreneurship. The very success of the rising Indian houses in these new fields ultimately increased the need for import of sophisticated and more advanced technology. The substantial development of India's industrial economy before and during the Second World War, by increasing its needs for advanced technology, paved the way for the entry of the multi-national corporations. The transition from formal empire to informal penetration implied changing technological imperatives in the dependent country. Andrew Yule, Jardine Skinner, Bird Heilgers, etc. had been associated with formal empire. Imperial Chemicals, Dunlop, Unilever, etc. were the agents of informal penetration.

During this process of transition, the Indian capitalist class, which had acquired a new solidarity and self-consciousness, undoubtedly made very major and significant gains. In an entirely different form, however, its dependence continued. In essence, this new dependence was technological. Technological deficiency was the ultimate, long-term brake on India's industrial growth beyond a certain point. It was only at the end of the period under review that the nature of this constraint stood fully revealed. For at the end of the Second World War, the world saw a sudden and tremendous acceleration of technological sophistication that constituted nothing less than a major revolution in the economic history of the world. The gap between the advanced countries and the newly emerging nations became much wider in consequence of this tremendous technological revolution. The new technology of North-West Europe, North America and Japan was far more advanced than anything witnessed before. It required plant on a much larger scale and increasingly greater sums of capital. More important, it was in a process of continuous modification and improvement from year to year at a pace which even relatively well-equipped underdeveloped countries like India could not hope to match. India might have started too late in the race for development by an almost tangible margin of time. Had she reached the level of industrial development which she attained at the end of the Second World War one and a half decades earlier, at the beginning of the thirties, and had a determined programme of socialist planning on the lines adopted by the future independent Government of India been initiated then, India might conceivably have attained a new level by 1945 that would have equipped her to cope with the extremely competitive technological revolution of the post-war era.

Primary Sources

No bibliography is provided here as a full one has already been provided by A. K. Bagchi, *Private Investment in India*. Only important primary sources are listed in this section. Specific references to secondary books, articles and theses are to be found in the footnotes to the text.

A. UNPUBLISHED SOURCES

1. Manuscript records preserved in the Bengal Chamber of Commerce, Calcutta:

    Proceedings of the Committee of the Bengal Chamber of Commerce, Calcutta

2. Private papers preserved in the Nehru Memorial Museum & Library, New Delhi:

    Purshotamdas Thakurdas papers. Important for the politics of the private sector

B. PUBLISHED SOURCES

1. OFFICIAL PUBLICATIONS

Two important statistical series are *Finance and Revenue Accounts of the Government of India* (Calcutta, annual) and *Joint Stock Companies in British India and the Indian States* (Calcutta, annual). For individual industries the most important sources of information are the *Reports of the Indian Tariff Board*. I have used the following reports of the Government of India Tariff Board (later, Tariff Commission) (Calcutta and Bombay, relevant years):

Aluminium Industry, 1947
Automobile Industry, 1953
Bichromates Industry, 1946
Caustic Soda and Bleaching Powder Industry, 1947
Cotton Textile Industry, 1927, 1932
Cotton Textile Machinery Industry, 1939, 1947, 1951
Glass Industry, 1932, 1950
Heavy Chemical Industry, 1929
Iron and Steel Industry, 1934
Machine Tools Industry, 1947
Magnesium Chloride Industry, 1925, 1929, 1939, 1947
Match Industry, 1929
Paper and Paper Pulp Industry, 1924, 1931, 1938, 1947
Rubber Manufacturing Industry, 1947
Sewing Machine Industry, 1939, 1947, 1951
Ship-Building Industry, 1926
Sugar Industry, 1931, 1938, 1947

Two informative reports on industry are *Indian Industrial Commission 1916–18 Report* (Calcutta, 1918) and J. A. L. Swan, *Report on The Industrial Development of Bengal* (Calcutta, 1915). The Office of the Economic Adviser to the Government of India issued the following useful publications: *Recent Social and Economic Trends in India*, prepared by S. Subramanian and P. W. R. Homfray (Delhi, 1946) and *The History of the Indian Tariff 1924–29* by B. N. Adarkar (Delhi, 1940).

2. NON-OFFICIAL REPORTS

*The Investors India Year Book*s, published by Place, Siddons & Gough from Calcutta annually from 1911 onwards, are of crucial importance for statistics regarding share capital in industry. For a study of year to year conditions in business and industry, the most detailed non-official series are *Annual Reports* of the Chambers of Commerce and Trades Associations in India. I have used the *Annual Reports* of the:

Bengal Chamber of Commerce, Calcutta
Bombay Millowners' Association, Bombay
Indian Chamber of Commerce, Calcutta
Indian Merchants' Chamber, Bombay
Indian Sugar Mills' Association, Bombay
Marwari Association, Calcutta
Marwari Chamber of Commerce, Calcutta (in Hindi)

On the interrelated problems of currency and balance of payments, important nationalist statements are *Congress Select Committee on the Financial Obligations between Great Britain and India: Report* (Bombay, 1931), and Federation of Indian Chambers of Commerce and Industry, *Indian Currency and Exchange 1914–1930: How Government Have Managed It* (1931). There are useful non-official reports on individual industries, such as *Match Industry* (issued by the Commercial Museum, Corporation of Calcutta, 1938), *The Story of Matches and the Match Industry of India: A Plea for Parliamentary Enquiry into the Practices of Wimco* (confidential booklet circulated by unnamed author, n.d., n.p.), and *The Indian Chemical Industry: A Memorandum Prepared for Submission to the Government of India by Imperial Chemical Industries* (1950). On Indian businessmen's considered opinion on planning, *see* the extremely important Purshotamdas Thakurdas *et al.*, *A Brief Memorandum Outlining a Plan of Economic Development for India*, 2 pts (Bombay, 1944).

3. NEWSPAPERS, PERIODICALS, BULLETINS

Bulletins of Indian Industrial Research, Delhi, occasional
Capital. The organ of British capital.
Commerce. The organ of Indian capital.
Harijan. The Gandhian point of view.

4. FIRM HISTORIES AND BUSINESS BIOGRAPHIES

Some of these are secondary works, but contain important primary material not easily available. Among numerous official firm histories I have used the following:

Andrew Yule & Co. Ltd., 1863–1963, 1963, printed for private circulation
Dalmia Cement Silver Jubilee Souvenir, n.d., n.p.

Geoffrey Harrison, *Bird & Company of Calcutta: A History produced to mark the firm's centenary 1864–1964*, 1964

N. C. Jog, *Saga of Scindia: Golden Jubilee Souvenir: Struggle for the revival of Indian Shipping and Ship-Building*, Bombay, 1969

Tata Steel Diamond Jubilee 1907–67, 1967

The House of Binny, Madras, 1969

Verrier Elwin, *The Story of Tata Steel*, n.d., n.p.

Three good business biographies deserve mention:

F. R. Harris, *Jamsetji Nusserwanjee Tata: A Chronicle of his Life*, Bombay, 1958

Arun Joshi, *Lala Shri Ram: A Study in Entrepreneurship and Industrial Management*, New Delhi, 1973

G. D. Khanolkar, *Walchand Hirachand: Man, His Times and Achievements*, Bombay, 1969

As primary sources, autobiographies are of special importance. I have seen:

G. D. Birla, *In the Shadow of the Mahatma—A Personal Memoir*, Calcutta, 1953. Contains extremely important correspondence between Birla and Gandhi

Seth Ramkrishna Dalmia, *A Short Sketch of My Life and a Guide to Bliss*, 3rd edn., Delhi, 1962

Most Chambers of Commerce have published souvenir volumes containing important material. I have seen:

Indian Mining Federation: Golden Jubilee Souvenir 1913–1963: Fifty Years of the Indian Coal Industry and the Story of the Indian Mining Federation, Calcutta, 1963

Raymond J. Sullivan, *One Hundred Years of Bombay: A History of the Bombay Chamber of Commerce, 1836–1936*, Bombay, 1936

Silver Jubilee Souvenir of the United Provinces Chamber of Commerce 1914–1939, 1939

24

Index

Accumulation of savings and reduced investment, 219
Acme Manufacturing Co., 193, 281
Adamjee Hajee Dawood & Co., 152
Africa, 205
Agarias, 164
Agartala, 152
Ahmednagar, 140
Ahmedabad mill-owners, 68
Air India, 278
Allied military, 215
Alkali & Chemical Corporation of India, 169
Alumina, 183–4, 186, 190
Aluminium
    Company of Canada, 185
    consumption of, 190–1
    Corporation of India, 185–6, 190
    imports, 190–1
    ingots, 183, 186
    Manufacturing Co., 184
    production, 190–1
    stages of manufacture, 184
Aluminium Industry
    capital, 187–8
    enterprise, 188–90
    foreign monopoly, 188–90
    govt. policy, 191–2
    growth, 183–92
    industry, 222
    machinery, 187–8
    market, 190–1
    power of, 186–7
    raw materials, 186–7
    technology, 187–8
Ambernath, 152, 154, 158, 160, 168
America, 102, 166, 167, 179, 205
American Civil War, 24
American cotton, 61
Amrit Match Factory, 151–2
Anandji Haridas & Co., 306
Anderson, Sir John, 323

Anstey, Vera, 119
Autarchic economic policies, 303
Anti-Non-Cooperation Committee, 317
Asiatic Steam Navigation Co. Ltd., 95, 263
Assam, 152, 154
Assam Saw Mills and Timber Co., 269
ASSOCHAM (Associated Chamber of Commerce), 297–305, 361
    executive organ, 300
    formation of, 297–305
Associated Cement Corp., 279
Associated Power Co. Ltd., 267
Australia, 102, 166–7, 179, 205
Automobile Factory Committee, 176
Automobile Industry
    capital, 177–8
    components, 179
    enterprise, 180–1
    foreign collaboration, 178–9
    government policy, 181–2
    growth, 176–83
    market, 179–80
    technology, 178–9
Axis, 255
Ayyer, T. V. Sheshagiri, 302

Babington-Smith Committee, 246
Bagchi, Amiya K., 2–3, 23, 37, 82, 83, 142, 210, 211, 229, 235, 239, 249, 289–90, 298, 340, 343
Bajoria, 128, 131, 133, 135
Balmer-Lawrie, 126, 129, 132, 136, 243
Baltic Exchange, 309
Bamboo pulp, 129–31, 133–6
Bande Match Factory, 151
Banga Lakshmi Cotton Mills, 284
Bangur, 267, 276, 284
    cotton mill, 284
    cement factory, 284
Bania classes, 24, 26

24A